FOCUS
ON
GRAMMAR

AN INTEGRATED SKILLS APPROACH

THIRD EDITION

IRENE E. SCHOENBERG

PEARSON
Longman

FOCUS ON GRAMMAR 2: An Integrated Skills Approach

Pearson Education, 10 Bank Street, White Plains, NY 10606

Vice president, multimedia and skills: Sherry Preiss
Executive editor: Laura Le Dréan
Development manager: Paula H. Van Ells
Vice president, director of design and production: Rhea Banker
Executive managing editor: Linda Moser
Production supervisor: Christine Edmonds
Production editor: Laurie Neaman
Art director: Ann France
Marketing director: Oliva Fernández
Senior manufacturing buyer: Nancy Flaggman
Photo research: Aerin Csigay
Cover design: Rhea Banker
Cover images: Large shell, Alan Kearney, RM; background, Comstock Images, RF
Text design: Quorum Creative Services, Rhea Banker
Text composition: ElectraGraphics, Inc.
Text font: 11/13 Sabon, 10/13 Myriad Roman

Photo credits: see p. xii.

Illustrators: Steve Attoe pp. 280, 310; A. J. Garces pp. 148, 179, 186; Chris Gash pp. 45, 53, 76, 87, 129 (bottom), 130, 142, 145, 146, 231; Dave Klug pp. 88, 94, 265; Jock MacRae, pp. 198–199; Paul McCusker pp. 85, 256–257; Suzanne Mogensen p. 54; Tom Newsom pp. 12, 15, 122, 126, 395, 428; Chris Pappas, pp. 38, 46, 129 (top), 159, 162–163, 180, 340, 342; Dusan Petricic pp. 20, 229, 347, 350, 390; Steve Schulman pp. 400, A-5; Dave Sullivan, pp. 80, 358; Gary Torrisi, pp. 56, 164, 304, 353; Meryl Treatner pp. 77, 116.

Library of Congress Cataloging-in-Publication Data

Focus on grammar. An integrated skills approach — 3rd ed.
    p. cm.
    ISBN 0-13-147466-9 (v. 1 : student book : alk. paper) — ISBN 0-13-189971-6 (v. 2 : student book : alk. paper) — ISBN 0-13-189984-8 (v. 3 : student book : alk. paper) — ISBN 0-13-190008-0 (v. 4 : student book : alk. paper) — ISBN 0-13-191273-9 (v. 5 : student book : alk. paper)
    1. English language—Textbooks for foreign speakers. 2. English language—Grammar—Problems, exercises, etc.
PE1128.F555 2005
428.2'4—dc22

                                                                2005007655

ISBNs: 0-13-189971-6 (Student Book)
        0-13-189972-4 (Student Book with Audio CD)

LONGMAN ON THE **WEB**

Longman.com offers online resources for teachers and students. Access our Companion Websites, our online catalog, and our local offices around the world.

Visit us at **longman.com**.

Printed in the United States of America

11 12 13 14 15 16 —VO64— 15 14 13 12 11 10 (Student Book)

10 11 12 13 14 15 —VO64— 15 14 13 12 11 10 (Student Book with Audio CD)

CONTENTS

PART V   PRESENT PROGRESSIVE; IMPERATIVES; *CAN/COULD*; SUGGESTIONS: *LET'S, WHY DON'T WE*

PART **VIII** REVIEW AND CONTRAST—VERBS

PART **IX** THE FUTURE

PART **XII** COMPARISONS

APPENDICES

GLOSSARY OF GRAMMAR TERMS

REVIEW TESTS ANSWER KEY

INDEX

ABOUT THE AUTHOR

Irene E. Schoenberg has taught ESL for more than two decades at Hunter College's International English Language Institute and at Columbia University's American Language Program. She has trained ESL and EFL teachers at Columbia University's Teachers College and at the New School University. She has given workshops and academic presentations at conferences, English language schools, and universities in Brazil, Chile, Dubai, El Salvador, Guatemala, Japan, Mexico, Nicaragua, Peru, Taiwan, Thailand, and throughout the United States.

Ms. Schoenberg is the author of *Talk about Trivia*; *Talk about Values*; *Speaking of Values 1: Conversation and Listening*; *Topics from A to Z*, Books 1 and 2; and the basic level of *Focus on Grammar*. She is the co-author with Jay Maurer of the *True Colors* series and the introductory level of *Focus on Grammar 1*.

Ms. Schoenberg holds a master's degree in TESOL from Columbia University.

CREDITS

Grateful acknowledgment is given to the following for providing photographs:

p. 3 Patrick Olear/PhotoEdit; **p. 4** *(left)* Russell Boyce/Reuters/Corbis, *(right)* Reuters/Corbis; **p. 8** *(top)* Mike Powell/Getty Images, *(bottom)* Bend It Films/Film Council/ The Kobal Collection/ Parry, Christine; **p. 10** *(Matsui)* Reuters/Corbis, *(Hamm)* Darren McCollester/Getty Images, *(Lee)* Rufus F. Folkks/Corbis, *(Spielberg)* Rufus F. Folkks/Corbis, *(Rubio)* Frank Trapper/Corbis, *(Beyonce)* Reuters/Corbis, *(Rowling)* Rune Hellestad/Corbis, *(Marquez)* Jorge Uzon/AFP/Getty Images; **p. 19** Getty Images; **p. 22** Annebicque Bernard/Corbis Sygma; **p. 38** *(top)* RubberBall Productions, *(bottom left)* Reuters/Corbis, *(bottom right)* Henri Cartier-Bresson /Magnum Photos; **p. 41** Ron Chapple/Getty Images; **p. 42** Henri Cartier-Bresson /Magnum Photos; **p. 44** Henri Cartier-Bresson /Magnum Photos; **p. 48** Walter Bibikow/Index Stock Imagery; **p. 50** www.Gamirasu.com; **p. 51** Tom Bean/Corbis; **p. 59** Christie's Images/Corbis, ©C. Herscovici, Brussels; **p. 62** Bettmann/Corbis, ©Salvador Dali, Gala-Salvador Dali Foundation/Artists Rights Society (ARS), New York; **p. 70** Catherine Karnow/Corbis; **p. 75** Ryan McVay/Getty Images; **p. 90** Omni-Photo Communications, Inc.; **p. 102** *(top)* Gary Conner/PhotoEdit, *(bottom)* Stephanie Maze/Corbis, *(right)* Bob Krist/Getty Images, *(left)* Martin Barraud/Getty Images; **p. 107** Dorling Kindersley; **p. 112** Will Hart; **p. 119** Digital Vision; **p. 122** Timothy O'Keefe/Index Stock Imagery; **p. 128** Sally Brown/Index Stock Imagery; **p. 150** Peter Samuels/Getty Images, *(left)* Reuters/Corbis, *(right)* TM and ©Twentieth Century Fox Film Corp./Photofest, *(bottom)* AP/Wide World Photos; **p. 151** CBS Photo Archive/Getty Images; **p. 158** Michele Burgess/Index Stock Imagery; **p. 167** Dorling Kindersley; **p. 173** Dr. Ronald H. Cohn/ The Gorilla Foundation; **p. 174** *(left)* Nektarios Pierros/Reuters/Corbis, *(right)* Greg Epperson/Index Stock Imagery, *(bottom)* Snuba® diving in Hawaii/www.snuba.com; **p. 188** *(right)* Sally Brown/Index Stock Imagery, *(top)* Walter Bibikow/Index Stock Imagery, *(left)* Michele Westmorland/Corbis; **p. 197** Nik Wheeler/Corbis; **p. 206** Newline Cinema/ Photofest; **p. 212** Bettmann/Corbis; **p. 222** James Marshall/Corbis; **p. 239** *(left)* Gary Buss/Getty Images, *(right)* Greg Ceo/Getty Images; **p. 249** www.CartoonStock.com; **p. 256** Javier Pierini/Getty Images; **p. 266** Art Wolfe/Getty Images; **p. 274** *(right)* David Chalk/ Omni-Photo Communications, Inc., *(middle)* Will & Deni McIntyre/ Photo Researchers, Inc., *(left)* ATC Productions/ImageQuest, *(1)* Kevin Peterson/Getty Images, *(2)* RubberBall Productions, *(3)* Kevin Peterson/Getty Images, *(4)* Barbara Penoyar/Getty Images; **p. 275** *(left)* RubberBall Productions, *(right)* Barbara Penoyar/Getty Images; **p. 284** Museum of the City of New York/Corbis; **p. 286** Bettmann/Corbis; **p. 319** Jeff Greenberg/PhotoEdit; **p. 344** *(top)* Getty Images, *(bottom)* Niall Benvie/Corbis; **p. 345** *(top to bottom)* Kevin Peterson/ Getty Images, RubberBall Productions, RubberBall Productions, Kevin Peterson/Getty Images, Barbara Penoyar/Getty Images, Kevin Peterson/Getty Images; **p. 354** Royalty-Free/ Corbis; **p. 376** RubberBall Productions; **p. 385** *(top)* Stockbyte, *(bottom)* Tony Freeman/ PhotoEdit; **p. 386** *(left)* Judd Pilossof/Getty Images, *(right)* Royalty-Free/Corbis; **p. 412** *(top)* Alan Becker/Getty Images, *(bottom)* Richard Cummins/Corbis; **p. 422** Jacobs Stock Photography/Getty Images; **p. 433** *(left)* Barbara Penoyar/Getty Images, *(right)* RubberBall Productions, *(bottom)* RubberBall Productions; **p. 438** Paul A. Souders/Corbis.

INTRODUCTION

The *Focus on Grammar* series

Written by ELT professionals, *Focus on Grammar: An Integrated Skills Approach* helps students to understand and practice English grammar. The primary aim of the course is for students to gain confidence in their ability to speak and write English accurately and fluently.

The **third edition** retains this popular series' focus on English grammar through lively listening, speaking, reading, and writing activities. The new *Focus on Grammar* also maintains the same five-level progression as the second edition:

- Level 1 (Beginning, formerly Introductory)
- Level 2 (High-Beginning, formerly Basic)
- Level 3 (Intermediate)
- Level 4 (High-Intermediate)
- Level 5 (Advanced)

What is the *Focus on Grammar* methodology?

Both controlled and communicative practice

While students expect and need to learn the formal rules of a language, it is crucial that they also practice new structures in a variety of contexts in order to internalize and master them. To this end, *Focus on Grammar* provides an abundance of both controlled and communicative exercises so that students can bridge the gap between knowing grammatical structures and using them. The many communicative activities in each Student Book unit provide opportunity for critical thinking while enabling students to personalize what they have learned in order to talk to one another with ease about hundreds of everyday issues.

A unique four-step approach

The series follows a four-step approach:

Step 1: Grammar in Context shows the new structures in natural contexts, such as articles and conversations.

Step 2: Grammar Presentation presents the structures in clear and accessible grammar charts, notes, and examples.

Step 3: Focused Practice of both form and meaning of the new structures is provided in numerous and varied controlled exercises.

Step 4: Communication Practice allows students to use the new structures freely and creatively in motivating, open-ended activities.

Thorough recycling

Underpinning the scope and sequence of the *Focus on Grammar* series is the belief that students need to use target structures many times, in different contexts, and at increasing levels of difficulty. For this reason, new grammar is constantly recycled throughout the book so that students have maximum exposure to the target forms and become comfortable using them in speech and in writing.

A complete classroom text and reference guide

A major goal in the development of *Focus on Grammar* has been to provide students with books that serve not only as vehicles for classroom instruction but also as resources for reference and self-study. In each Student Book, the combination of grammar charts, grammar notes, a glossary of grammar terms, and extensive appendices provides a complete and invaluable reference guide for students.

Ongoing assessment

Review Tests at the end of each part of the Student Book allow for continual self-assessment. In addition, the tests in the new *Focus on Grammar* Assessment Package provide teachers with a valid, reliable, and practical means of determining students' appropriate levels of placement in the course and of assessing students' achievement throughout the course. At Levels 4 (High-Intermediate) and 5 (Advanced), Proficiency Tests give teachers an overview of their students' general grammar knowledge.

What are the components of each level of *Focus on Grammar*?

Student Book

The Student Book is divided into eight or more parts, depending on the level. Each part contains grammatically related units, with each unit focusing on specific grammatical structures; where appropriate, units present contrasting forms. The exercises in each unit are thematically related to one another, and all units have the same clear, easy-to-follow format.

Teacher's Manual

The Teacher's Manual contains a variety of suggestions and information to enrich the material in the Student Book. It includes general teaching suggestions for each section of a typical unit, answers to frequently asked questions, unit-by-unit teaching tips with ideas for further communicative practice, and a supplementary activity section. Answers to the Student Book exercises and audioscripts of the listening activities are found at the back of the Teacher's Manual. Also included in the Teacher's Manual is a CD-ROM of teaching tools, including PowerPoint presentations that offer alternative ways of presenting selected grammar structures.

Workbook

The Workbook accompanying each level of *Focus on Grammar* provides additional exercises appropriate for self-study of the target grammar for each Student Book unit. Tests included in each Workbook provide students with additional opportunities for self-assessment.

Audio Program

All of the listening exercises from the Student Book, as well as the Grammar in Context passages and other appropriate exercises, are included on the program's CDs. In the book, the symbol ⌒ appears next to the listening exercises. Another symbol ⌒, indicating that listening is optional, appears next to the Grammar in Context passages and some exercises. All of these scripts appear in the Teacher's Manual and may be used as an alternative way of presenting the activities.

Some Student Books are packaged with a separate Student Audio CD. This CD includes the listening exercise from each unit and any other exercises that have an essential listening component.

CD-ROM

Focus on Grammar Interactive, Version 2, provides students with individualized practice and immediate feedback. Fully contextualized and interactive, the activities broaden and extend practice of the grammatical structures in the reading, writing, listening, and speaking skills areas. This CD-ROM includes grammar review, review tests, score-based remedial practice, games, and all relevant reference material from the Student Book. It can also be used in conjunction with the *Longman Interactive American Dictionary* CD-ROM.

Assessment Package (NEW)

An extensive, comprehensive Assessment Package has been developed for each level of the third edition of *Focus on Grammar*. The components of the Assessment Package are:

1. **Placement, Diagnostic, and Achievement Tests**

   - a Placement Test to screen students and place them into the correct level
   - Diagnostic Tests for each part of the Student Book
   - Unit Achievement Tests for each unit of the Student Book
   - Part Achievement Tests for each part of the Student Book

2. **General Proficiency Tests**

   - two Proficiency Tests at Level 4 (High-Intermediate)
   - two Proficiency Tests at Level 5 (Advanced)

   These tests can be administered at any point in the course.

3. **Audio CD**

   The listening portions of the Placement, Diagnostic, and Achievement Tests are recorded on CDs. The scripts appear in the Assessment Package.

4. **Test-Generating Software**

   The test-bank software provides thousands of questions from which teachers can create class-appropriate tests. All items are labeled according to the grammar structure they are testing, so teachers can easily select relevant items; they can also design their own items to add to the tests.

Transparencies (NEW)

Transparencies of all the grammar charts in the Student Book are also available. These transparencies are a classroom visual aid that will help instructors point out important patterns and structures of grammar.

Companion Website

The companion website contains a wealth of information and activities for both teachers and students. In addition to general information about the course pedagogy, the website provides extensive practice exercises for the classroom, a language lab, or at home.

What's new in the third edition of the Student Book?

In response to users' requests, this edition has:

- a new four-color design
- easy-to-read color coding for the four steps
- new and updated reading texts for Grammar in Context
- post-reading activities (in addition to the pre-reading questions)
- more exercise items
- an editing (error analysis) exercise in each unit
- new writing activities
- an Internet activity in each unit
- a Glossary of Grammar Terms
- expanded Appendices

References

Alexander, L. G. (1988). *Longman English Grammar.* White Plains: Longman.

Biber, D., S. Conrad, E. Finegan, S. Johansson, and G. Leech (1999). *Longman Grammar of Spoken and Written English.* White Plains: Longman.

Celce-Murcia, M., and D. Freeman (1999). *The Grammar Book.* Boston: Heinle and Heinle.

Celce-Murcia, M., and S. Hilles (1988). *Techniques and Resources in Teaching Grammar.* New York: Oxford University Press.

Firsten, R. (2002). *The ELT Grammar Book.* Burlingame, CA: Alta Book Center Publishers.

Garner, B. (2003). *Garner's Modern American Usage.* New York: Oxford University Press.

Greenbaum, S. (1996). *The Oxford English Grammar.* New York: Oxford University Press.

Leech, G. (2004). *Meaning and the English Verb.* Harlow, UK: Pearson.

Lewis, M. (1997). *Implementing the Lexical Approach.* Hove East Sussex, UK: Language Teaching Publications.

Longman (2002). *Longman Dictionary of English Language and Culture.* Harlow, UK: Longman.

Willis, D. (2003). *Rules, Patterns and Words.* New York: Cambridge University Press.

TOUR OF A UNIT

Each unit in the *Focus on Grammar* series presents a specific grammar structure (or two, in case of a contrast) and develops a major theme, which is set by the opening text. All units follow the same unique **four-step approach**.

Step 1: Grammar in Context

The **reading** or **written conversation** in this section shows the grammar structure in a natural context. The high-interest text presents authentic language in a variety of real-life formats: magazine articles, web pages, questionnaires, and more. Students can listen to the text on an audio CD to get accustomed to the sound of the grammar structure in a natural context.

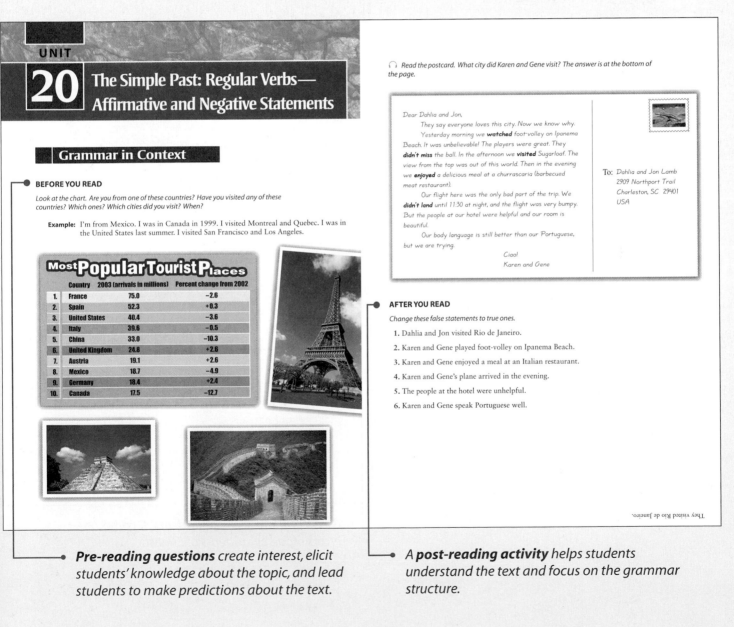

UNIT

20 The Simple Past: Regular Verbs— Affirmative and Negative Statements

Grammar in Context

BEFORE YOU READ

Look at the chart. Are you from one of these countries? Have you visited any of these countries? Which ones? Which cities did you visit? When?

Example: I'm from Mexico. I was in Canada in 1999. I visited Montreal and Quebec. I was in the United States last summer. I visited San Francisco and Los Angeles.

Most Popular Tourist Places

	Country	2003 (arrivals in millions)	Percent change from 2002
1.	France	75.0	−2.6
2.	Spain	52.3	+0.3
3.	United States	40.4	−3.6
4.	Italy	39.6	−0.5
5.	China	33.0	−10.3
6.	United Kingdom	24.8	+2.6
7.	Austria	19.1	+2.6
8.	Mexico	18.7	−4.9
9.	Germany	18.4	+2.4
10.	Canada	17.5	−12.7

🎧 *Read the postcard. What city did Karen and Gene visit? The answer is at the bottom of the page.*

Dear Dahlia and Jon,

They say everyone loves this city. Now we know why. Yesterday morning we **watched** foot-volley on Ipanema Beach. It was unbelievable! The players were great. They **didn't miss** the ball. In the afternoon we **visited** Sugarloaf. The view from the top was out of this world. Then in the evening we **enjoyed** a delicious meal at a churrascaria (barbecued meat restaurant).

Our flight here was the only bad part of the trip. We **didn't land** until 11:30 at night, and the flight was very bumpy. But the people at our hotel were helpful and our room is beautiful.

Our body language is still better than our Portuguese, but we are trying.

Ciao!
Karen and Gene

To: Dahlia and Jon Lamb
2909 Northport Trail
Charleston, SC 29401
USA

AFTER YOU READ

Change these false statements to true ones.

1. Dahlia and Jon visited Rio de Janeiro.
2. Karen and Gene played foot-volley on Ipanema Beach.
3. Karen and Gene enjoyed a meal at an Italian restaurant.
4. Karen and Gene's plane arrived in the evening.
5. The people at the hotel were unhelpful.
6. Karen and Gene speak Portuguese well.

They visited Rio de Janeiro.

Pre-reading questions *create interest, elicit students' knowledge about the topic, and lead students to make predictions about the text.*

A **post-reading activity** *helps students understand the text and focus on the grammar structure.*

Step 2: Grammar Presentation

This section is made up of grammar charts, notes, and examples. The **grammar charts** focus on the forms of the grammar structure. The **grammar notes** and **examples** focus on the meanings and uses of the structure.

Clear and easy-to-read **grammar charts** present the grammar structure in all its forms and combinations.

Each **grammar note** gives a short, simple explanation of one use of the structure. The accompanying **examples** ensure students' understanding of the point.

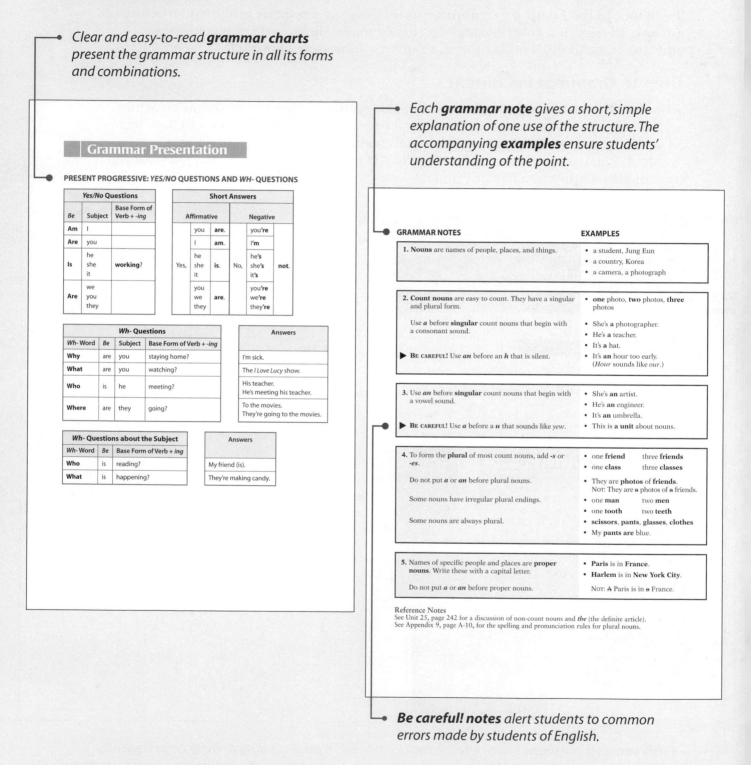

Grammar Presentation

PRESENT PROGRESSIVE: YES/NO QUESTIONS AND WH- QUESTIONS

Yes/No Questions

Be	Subject	Base Form of Verb + -ing
Am	I	
Are	you	
Is	he she it	**working**?
Are	we you they	

Short Answers

	Affirmative			Negative	
	you	are.		you're	
	I	am.		I'm	
Yes,	he she it	is.	No,	he's she's it's	not.
	you we they	are.		you're we're they're	

Wh- Questions

Wh-Word	Be	Subject	Base Form of Verb + -ing
Why	are	you	staying home?
What	are	you	watching?
Who	is	he	meeting?
Where	are	they	going?

Answers

I'm sick.
The I Love Lucy show.
His teacher. He's meeting his teacher.
To the movies. They're going to the movies.

Wh- Questions about the Subject

Wh-Word	Be	Base Form of Verb + ing
Who	is	reading?
What	is	happening?

Answers

My friend (is).
They're making candy.

GRAMMAR NOTES	EXAMPLES
1. Nouns are names of people, places, and things.	• a student, Jung Eun • a country, Korea • a camera, a photograph
2. Count nouns are easy to count. They have a singular and plural form. Use *a* before **singular** count nouns that begin with a consonant sound. ▶ **BE CAREFUL!** Use *an* before an *h* that is silent.	• **one** photo, **two** photos, **three** photos • She's **a** photographer. • He's **a** teacher. • It's **a** hat. • It's **an** hour too early. (*Hour* sounds like *our*.)
3. Use *an* before **singular** count nouns that begin with a vowel sound. ▶ **BE CAREFUL!** Use *a* before a *u* that sounds like *yew*.	• She's **an** artist. • He's **an** engineer. • It's **an** umbrella. • This is **a unit** about nouns.
4. To form the **plural** of most count nouns, add *-s* or *-es*. Do not put *a* or *an* before plural nouns. Some nouns have irregular plural endings. Some nouns are always plural.	• one **friend** three **friends** • one **class** three **classes** • They are **photos** of **friends**. NOT: They are a photos of a friends. • one **man** two **men** • one **tooth** two **teeth** • **scissors, pants, glasses, clothes** • My **pants are** blue.
5. Names of specific people and places are **proper nouns**. Write these with a capital letter. Do not put *a* or *an* before proper nouns.	• **Paris** is in **France**. • **Harlem** is in **New York City**. NOT: A Paris is in a France.

Reference Notes
See Unit 25, page 242 for a discussion of non-count nouns and *the* (the definite article).
See Appendix 9, page A-10, for the spelling and pronunciation rules for plural nouns.

Be careful! notes alert students to common errors made by students of English.

Step 3: Focused Practice

This section provides students with a variety of contextualized **controlled exercises** to practice both the forms and the uses of the grammar structure.

Focused Practice always begins with a "for recognition only" exercise called **Discover the Grammar**.

*A **variety of exercise types** guide students from recognition to accurate production of the grammar structure.*

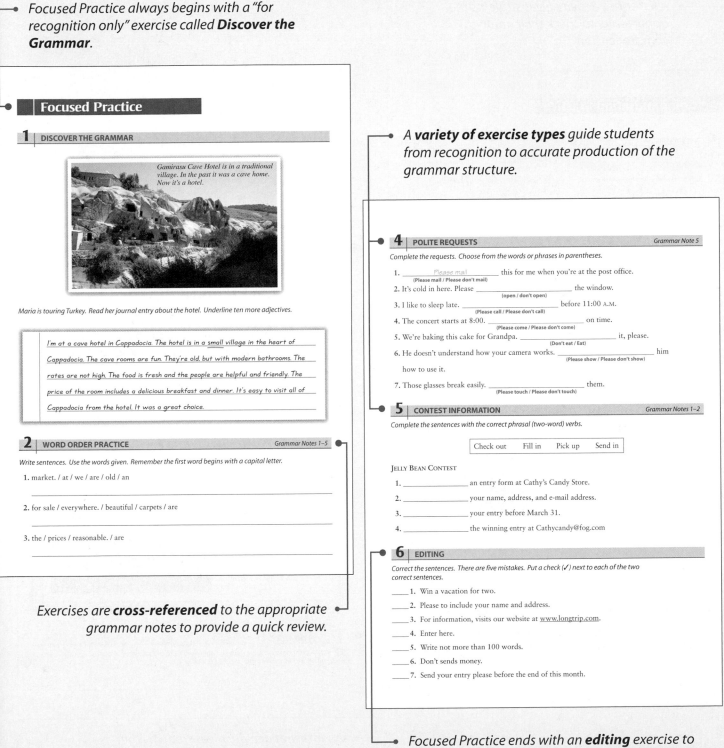

Focused Practice

1 | DISCOVER THE GRAMMAR

Gamirasu Cave Hotel is in a traditional village. In the past it was a cave home. Now it's a hotel.

Maria is touring Turkey. Read her journal entry about the hotel. Underline ten more adjectives.

> I'm at a cave hotel in Cappadocia. The hotel is in a <u>small</u> village in the heart of
> Cappadocia. The cave rooms are fun. They're old, but with modern bathrooms. The
> rates are not high. The food is fresh and the people are helpful and friendly. The
> price of the room includes a delicious breakfast and dinner. It's easy to visit all of
> Cappadocia from the hotel. It was a great choice.

2 | WORD ORDER PRACTICE   *Grammar Notes 1–5*

Write sentences. Use the words given. Remember the first word begins with a capital letter.

1. market. / at / we / are / old / an

   _____

2. for sale / everywhere. / beautiful / carpets / are

   _____

3. the / prices / reasonable. / are

   _____

4 | POLITE REQUESTS   *Grammar Note 5*

Complete the requests. Choose from the words or phrases in parentheses.

1. _____*Please mail*_____ this for me when you're at the post office.
   (Please mail / Please don't mail)

2. It's cold in here. Please _____ the window.
   (open / don't open)

3. I like to sleep late. _____ before 11:00 A.M.
   (Please call / Please don't call)

4. The concert starts at 8:00. _____ on time.
   (Please come / Please don't come)

5. We're baking this cake for Grandpa. _____ it, please.
   (Don't eat / Eat)

6. He doesn't understand how your camera works. _____ him
   (Please show / Please don't show)
   how to use it.

7. Those glasses break easily. _____ them.
   (Please touch / Please don't touch)

5 | CONTEST INFORMATION   *Grammar Notes 1–2*

Complete the sentences with the correct phrasal (two-word) verbs.

| Check out | Fill in | Pick up | Send in |

JELLY BEAN CONTEST

1. _____ an entry form at Cathy's Candy Store.

2. _____ your name, address, and e-mail address.

3. _____ your entry before March 31.

4. _____ the winning entry at Cathycandy@fog.com

6 | EDITING

Correct the sentences. There are five mistakes. Put a check (✓) next to each of the two correct sentences.

_____ 1. Win a vacation for two.

_____ 2. Please to include your name and address.

_____ 3. For information, visits our website at www.longtrip.com.

_____ 4. Enter here.

_____ 5. Write not more than 100 words.

_____ 6. Don't sends money.

_____ 7. Send your entry please before the end of this month.

*Exercises are **cross-referenced** to the appropriate grammar notes to provide a quick review.*

*Focused Practice ends with an **editing** exercise to teach students to find and correct typical mistakes.*

Step 4: Communication Practice

This section provides open-ended **communicative activities** giving students the opportunity to use the grammar structure appropriately and fluently.

• A **listening** activity gives students the opportunity to check their aural comprehension.

• A **writing** activity allows students to use the grammar structure in a variety of formats.

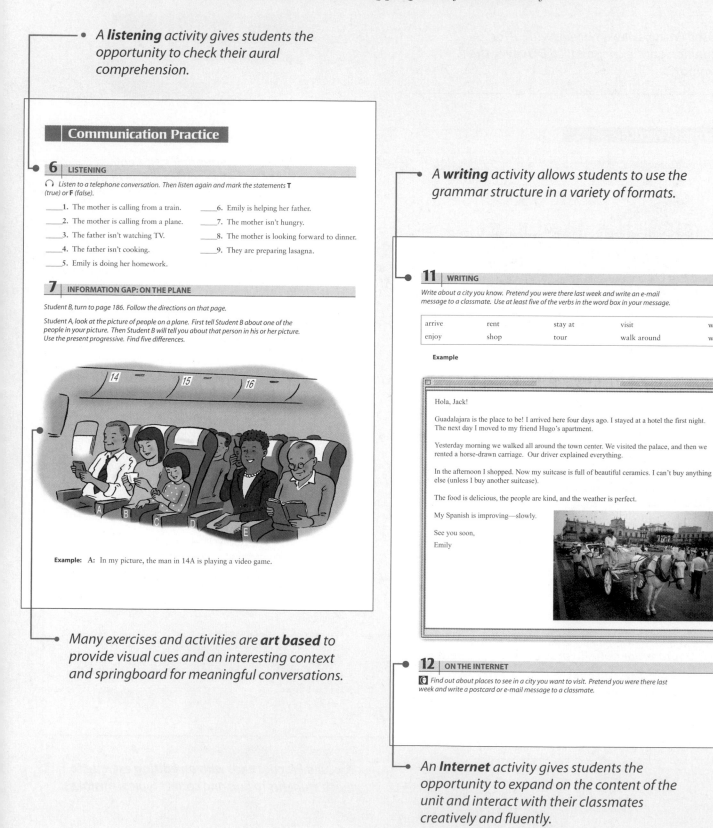

Communication Practice

6 | LISTENING

🎧 *Listen to a telephone conversation. Then listen again and mark the statements* **T** *(true) or* **F** *(false).*

_____1. The mother is calling from a train.

_____2. The mother is calling from a plane.

_____3. The father isn't watching TV.

_____4. The father isn't cooking.

_____5. Emily is doing her homework.

_____6. Emily is helping her father.

_____7. The mother isn't hungry.

_____8. The mother is looking forward to dinner.

_____9. They are preparing lasagna.

7 | INFORMATION GAP: ON THE PLANE

Student B, turn to page 186. Follow the directions on that page.

Student A, look at the picture of people on a plane. First tell Student B about one of the people in your picture. Then Student B will tell you about that person in his or her picture. Use the present progressive. Find five differences.

Example: A: In my picture, the man in 14A is playing a video game.

• Many exercises and activities are **art based** to provide visual cues and an interesting context and springboard for meaningful conversations.

11 | WRITING

Write about a city you know. Pretend you were there last week and write an e-mail message to a classmate. Use at least five of the verbs in the word box in your message.

arrive	rent	stay at	visit	want
enjoy	shop	tour	walk around	watch

Example

Hola, Jack!

Guadalajara is the place to be! I arrived here four days ago. I stayed at a hotel the first night. The next day I moved to my friend Hugo's apartment.

Yesterday morning we walked all around the town center. We visited the palace, and then we rented a horse-drawn carriage. Our driver explained everything.

In the afternoon I shopped. Now my suitcase is full of beautiful ceramics. I can't buy anything else (unless I buy another suitcase).

The food is delicious, the people are kind, and the weather is perfect.

My Spanish is improving—slowly.

See you soon,
Emily

12 | ON THE INTERNET

🅔 *Find out about places to see in a city you want to visit. Pretend you were there last week and write a postcard or e-mail message to a classmate.*

• An **Internet** activity gives students the opportunity to expand on the content of the unit and interact with their classmates creatively and fluently.

TOUR BEYOND THE UNIT

In the *Focus on Grammar* series, the grammatically related units are grouped into parts, and each part concludes with a section called **From Grammar to Writing** and a **Review Test** section.

From Grammar to Writing

This section presents a point which applies specifically to writing, for example, avoiding sentence fragments. Students are guided to practice the point in a **piece of extended writing**.

● An **introduction** relates the grammar point to the writing focus.

● **Writing formats** include business letters, personal letters, notes, instructions, paragraphs, reports, and essays.

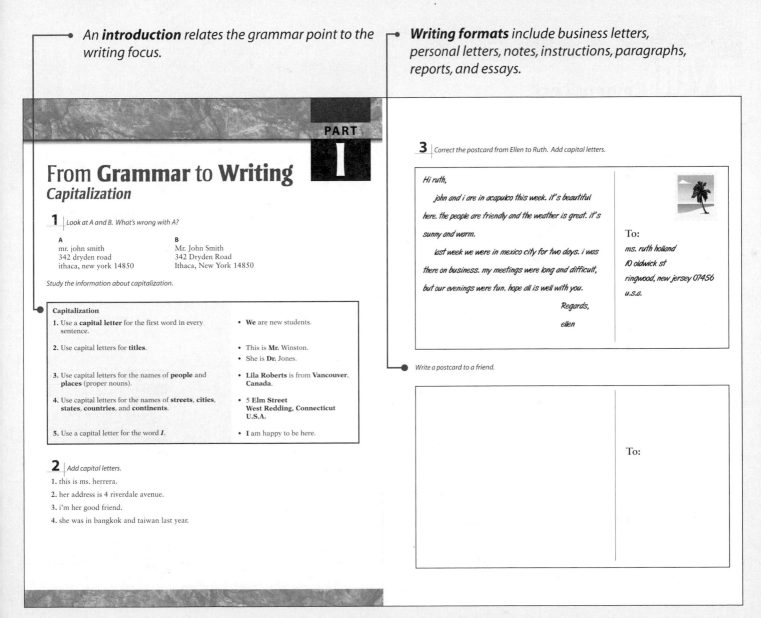

PART I

From **Grammar** to **Writing**
Capitalization

1 | Look at A and B. What's wrong with A?

A
mr. john smith
342 dryden road
ithaca, new york 14850

B
Mr. John Smith
342 Dryden Road
Ithaca, New York 14850

Study the information about capitalization.

Capitalization

1. Use a **capital letter** for the first word in every sentence.

2. Use capital letters for **titles**.

3. Use capital letters for the names of **people** and **places** (proper nouns).

4. Use capital letters for the names of **streets**, **cities**, **states**, **countries**, and **continents**.

5. Use a capital letter for the word *I*.

• **We** are new students.

• This is **Mr.** Winston.
• She is **Dr.** Jones.

• **Lila Roberts** is from **Vancouver**, **Canada**.

• **5 Elm Street**
  West Redding, Connecticut
  U.S.A.

• **I** am happy to be here.

2 | Add capital letters.

1. this is ms. herrera.
2. her address is 4 riverdale avenue.
3. i'm her good friend.
4. she was in bangkok and taiwan last year.

3 | Correct the postcard from Ellen to Ruth. Add capital letters.

Hi ruth,

    john and i are in acapulco this week. it's beautiful here. the people are friendly and the weather is great. it's sunny and warm.

    last week we were in mexico city for two days. i was there on business. my meetings were long and difficult, but our evenings were fun. hope all is well with you.

                    Regards,

                    ellen

To:

ms. ruth holland
10 oldwick st
ringwood, new jersey 07456
u.s.a.

Write a postcard to a friend.

To:

Review Test

This review section, covering all the grammar structures presented in the part, can be used as a test. An **Answer Key** is provided at the back of the book.

The Review Tests include **multiple-choice questions** in standardized test formats, giving students practice in test taking.

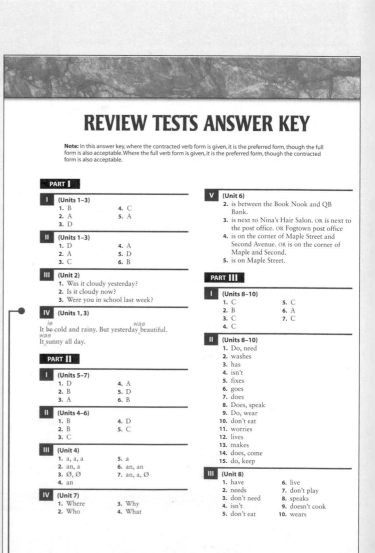

PART

VIII Review Test

I Read each conversation. Circle the letter of the underlined word or group of words that is not correct.

1. **A:** I <u>don't know</u> him very well. <u>Does he work</u> on Mondays?
           A   B
     B: I <u>don't think</u> so. He <u>works usually</u> on Tuesdays and Thursdays.
           C   D
           A B C D

2. **A:** Does she <u>like black coffee</u>?
                 A
     B: No, <u>she doesn't</u>. She <u>prefers</u> <u>drink</u> coffee with milk and sugar.
           B   C   D
           A B C D

3. **A:** <u>How often</u> <u>do you changing</u> the oil?
         A   B
     B: <u>Every three months</u>. I <u>usually check</u> my tires too.
         C   D
           A B C D

4. **A:** What <u>did he</u> <u>do</u> after the concert?
           A B
     B: <u>He met</u> some friends and <u>go to a club</u>.
         C   D
           A B C D

II Circle the letter of the correct word(s) to complete the sentences.

1. Where _____ last night?
           A B C D
   (A) you went
   (B) are you going
   (C) did you go
   (D) did you went

2. Who _____ you at the airport yesterday?
           A B C D
   (A) did meet
   (B) is meeting
   (C) met
   (D) meets

REVIEW TESTS ANSWER KEY

Note: In this answer key, where the contracted verb form is given, it is the preferred form, though the full form is also acceptable. Where the full verb form is given, it is the preferred form, though the contracted form is also acceptable.

PART I

I (Units 1–3)
1. B   4. C
2. A   5. A
3. D

II (Units 1–3)
1. D   4. A
2. A   5. D
3. C   6. B

III (Unit 2)
1. Was it cloudy yesterday?
2. Is it cloudy now?
3. Were you in school last week?

IV (Units 1, 3)
         is   *was*
It be cold and rainy. But yesterday beautiful.
was
It ˄ sunny all day.

PART II

I (Units 5–7)
1. D   4. A
2. B   5. D
3. A   6. B

II (Units 4–6)
1. B   4. D
2. B   5. C
3. C

III (Unit 4)
1. a, a, a   5. a
2. an, a   6. an, an
3. Ø, Ø   7. an, a, Ø
4. an

IV (Unit 7)
1. Where   3. Why
2. Who   4. What

V (Unit 6)
2. is between the Book Nook and QB Bank.
3. is next to Nina's Hair Salon. OR is next to the post office. OR Fogtown post office
4. is on the corner of Maple Street and Second Avenue. OR is on the corner of Maple and Second.
5. is on Maple Street.

PART III

I (Units 8–10)
1. C   5. C
2. B   6. A
3. C   7. C
4. C

II (Units 8–10)
1. Do, need
2. washes
3. has
4. isn't
5. fixes
6. goes
7. does
8. Does, speak
9. Do, wear
10. don't eat
11. worries
12. lives
13. makes
14. does, come
15. do, keep

III (Unit 8)
1. have   6. live
2. needs   7. don't play
3. don't need   8. speaks
4. isn't   9. doesn't cook
5. don't eat   10. wears

The Review Tests Answer Key provides **cross-references** to the appropriate unit(s) for easy review.

ACKNOWLEDGMENTS

A series requires the coordination of many people. Managing all aspects of a series is a daunting task. Laura Le Dréan, the series director, put her heart and soul into managing this project. I thank her for her superb handling of the series, and for her commitment to this book. Her grammar expertise and thoughtful comments were invaluable. It has been my pleasure to work with her.

I also wish to thank my development editor Paula Van Ells. Her good ear for language helped to refine many activities. In addition, I am particularly grateful for her input in developing the new Internet and writing activities.

Aerin Csigay researched and found great photos to make the pages come alive. In the production department, Laurie Neaman, Ann France, Linda Moser, and Rhea Banker put a great deal of effort into making the art and page makeup useful and appealing. To all of them, I am grateful.

I thank my colleagues at the International English Language Institute, Michelle Thomas and Gretchen Irwin, for their enthusiastic response to my changes from the second edition, as well as for their excellent suggestions.

My former student, Hye Won Paik Mohanram, who has recently become a teacher herself, gave excellent suggestions based on her knowledge of English language problems for Korean speakers.

Ellen Shaw reviewed the first few units. Her insight into what should be modified from the second edition was always on target. In addition, I thank the many reviewers of this new edition.

I am ever grateful to Joanne Dresner. The series would not have existed had it not been for her foresight.

As always, I thank my family—Dan, and Dahlia and now Jonathan—for their love and support. And I dedicate this book to Harris, whose love of language and encouragement have always been an inspiration.

I. E. S.

PART
I

The Verb *Be*:
Present and Past

Introducing Yourself

THE FIRST DAY OF CLASS

🎧 *Two students meet outside an English class.*
Read their conversation.

SHANA: Is this room 2? Basic English?

MARCY: Yes, it is.

SHANA: Great. I'm Shana McCabe.

MARCY: Hi, I'm Marceline Costa.

SHANA: Nice to meet you.

MARCY: Nice to meet you too.

SHANA: So, your first name is Marceline?

MARCY: Yes, but everyone calls me Marcy.

SHANA: OK, Marcy. Is that M-A-R-C-Y?

MARCY: Yes, it is.

THE ALPHABET

🎧 *Listen and repeat the letters of the alphabet.*

Aa Bb Cc Dd Ee Ff Gg Hh Ii Jj Kk Ll Mm Nn Oo Pp Qq Rr Ss Tt Uu Vv Ww Xx Yy Zz

CONVERSATION PRACTICE

Read this conversation. Work with a partner. Practice the conversation.
Use your own name.

A: What's your name?

B: <u>Marceline Costa</u>, but everyone calls me <u>Marcy</u>.

A: OK, <u>Marcy</u>. How do you spell that?

B: <u>M-A-R-C-Y</u>.

A: Nice to meet you.

B: Nice to meet you too.

Write the names of your classmates in a notebook.

1 The Present of *Be*: Statements

Grammar in Context

BEFORE YOU READ

Mark these statements **T** *(true) or* **F** *(false). Put a* **?** *(question mark) if you don't know.*

_____ David Beckham is a soccer player.

_____ David Beckham is from Brazil.

_____ Posh Spice is a soccer player.

_____ Posh Spice is from the United States.

_____ David and Posh are friends.

∩ *Read this article about the people in the photos.*

POP Culture News
TALENTED PEOPLE

David Beckham **is** a soccer player. He**'s** from England. David**'s** married to Posh Spice. Her real name **is** Victoria Adams. Their home **is** in England. It**'s** big. They call their home Beckingham Palace. David and Victoria **are** rich and famous. They**'re** popular all over the world.

Ramon Gomes **is** from Rio de Janeiro. He likes Beckham and he likes soccer. But Beckham **isn't** his favorite soccer player. And soccer **isn't** his favorite sport. His favorite player **is** Ronaldo. His favorite sport **is** foot-volley.

Foot-volley **is** a new game. It**'s** a combination of soccer and volleyball. Ramon plays foot-volley every day. His dream **is** to become the world foot-volley champion.

AFTER YOU READ

A *Mark these statements* **T** *(true) or* **F** *(false).*

_____ **1.** David Beckham is from Korea.

_____ **2.** Ramon Gomes is from Brazil.

_____ **3.** Ramon is a foot-volley player.

B *Complete the sentences.*

1. David and Victoria: They _____ from England.

   ('re / 're not)

2. Foot-volley: It _____ a combination of soccer and volleyball.

   ('s / isn't)

3. Ramon says: "Soccer _____ my favorite sport."

   (is / is not)

Grammar Presentation

THE PRESENT OF *BE*: STATEMENTS

AFFIRMATIVE STATEMENTS

Singular		
Subject	***Be***	
I	**am**	popular.
You	**are**	
David He	**is**	
Victoria She		
Soccer It		

Plural		
Subject	***Be***	
Masami and I We	**are**	students.
You and Josh You		
Ivona and Juan They		
Seoul and London They		cities.

Contractions			
I am	**I'm**	we are	**we're**
you are	**you're**	you are	**you're**
he is	**he's**	they are	**they're**
she is	**she's**	David is	**David's**
it is	**it's**		

(continued)

NEGATIVE STATEMENTS AND CONTRACTIONS (SHORT FORMS)

Singular	
Subject + *Be/Not*	
I **am not** I'**m not**	
You **are not** You'**re not** You **aren't**	from London.
He **is not** He'**s not** He **isn't**	
She **is not** She'**s not** She **isn't**	
It **is not** It'**s not** It **isn't**	new.

Plural	
Subject + *Be/Not*	
We **are not** We'**re not** We **aren't**	
You **are not** You'**re not** You **aren't**	in London.
They **are not** They'**re not** They **aren't**	

GRAMMAR NOTES

EXAMPLES

GRAMMAR NOTES	EXAMPLES

1. Sentences have a **subject** and a **verb**.
 	
The **subject** is a noun or a pronoun.
 	
Subject pronouns (*I, you, he, she, it, we, you, they*) replace subject nouns.
 	
▶ **BE CAREFUL!** You cannot make a sentence without a subject. You cannot make a sentence without a verb. You cannot put a subject pronoun right after a subject noun.
	subject verb
	• **Ramon Gomes is** from Brazil.
	     subject noun
	• **David Beckham is** a soccer player.
	subject
	pronoun
	• **He is** from England.
	  NOT: ~~Is from~~ England.
	  NOT: ~~He from~~ England.
	  NOT: David ~~he~~ is from England.

2. The **present of *be*** has three forms: *am*, *is*, *are*.	• I **am** a student. • He **is** from Brazil. • They **are** famous.

3. Use the verb *be* before **nouns**, **adjectives**, or **prepositional phrases**.
A noun can be **singular** (one) or **plural** (more than one). Plural nouns usually end in *-s*.

singular noun
- He is a **singer**.

plural noun
- They are **singers**.

adjective
- It is **big**.

prepositional phrase
- Emiko is **in New York**.

4. Use the correct form of *be* + *not* to make a **negative statement**.

- I **am not** from England.
- It **is not** popular.
- We **are not** famous.

5. Use **contractions** (short forms) in speaking and informal writing.

There are two negative contractions for *is not* and *are not*.

- I**'m** from Mexico.
- I**'m not** from Ecuador.
- Mr. Crane**'s** from Los Angeles.
- It**'s not** popular. OR It **isn't** popular.
- We**'re not** single. OR We **aren't** single.

Notes
For definitions and examples of **grammar terms**, see Glossary on page G-1.

Focused Practice

1 | DISCOVER THE GRAMMAR

Check (✓) the negative statements. Circle the contractions (short forms).

___✓___ **1.** David is not in England.

_____ **2.** (He's) in Spain.

_____ **3.** His eyes are blue.

_____ **4.** They're not brown.

_____ **5.** His hair is not black.

_____ **6.** It's blond.

_____ **7.** Ramon is not from England.

_____ **8.** He's not a singer.

2 | THE VERB BE

Complete the sentences with **am**, **is**, or **are**.

1. Ronaldo ___is___ a soccer player. He _____ from Brazil.

2. Soccer _____ popular in Brazil. It _____ the number one sport there.

3. I _____ not a soccer player. I _____ a soccer fan.

4. My friends and I _____ soccer fans. We love the game.

3 | BEND IT LIKE BECKHAM

Complete the sentences. Use the full form.

Parminder Nagra ___is___ an actor. She
_____ the star of the movie *Bend It Like*
2.
Beckham. It _____ a comedy. In the movie,
3.
Nagra _____ a young Indian girl in
4.
England. She _____ a good soccer player
5.
and she loves soccer. But her parents _____
6.
traditional. They _____ happy. They don't
7. (not)
want her to play soccer. They say, "Soccer _____ for girls. Marriage _____ for girls. Look
8. (not)   *9.*
at your sister." She says, "I _____ my sister."
10. (not)

🎧 *Listen and check your work.*

4 | WHAT'S TRUE?   *Grammar Notes 1–5*

Write true sentences. Use the words in parentheses. Use contractions.

1. (I / a student.) _____

2. (I / from London.) _____

3. David Beckham is a soccer player. (He / famous in this country.) _____

_____

4. Soccer is a great game. (It / popular in my country.) _____

5. Ronaldo is from Rio. (He / Brazilian.) _____

6. Ronaldo and Beckham are famous. (They / great soccer players.) _____

7. (My friend and I / big soccer fans.) _____

5 | PRONOUNS   *Grammar Note 5*

Change the underlined nouns to pronouns. Use contractions of **be**.

1. Ronaldo is from Brazil. <u>Ronaldo is</u> a great soccer player.   *He's*

2. Mr. Smith is a soccer fan. <u>Mr. Smith is</u> a baseball fan too.

3. My partner and I are new students. <u>My partner and I are</u> not in class now.

4. Soccer is a great sport. <u>Soccer is</u> popular all over the world.

5. Parminder Nagra and Halle Berry are actors. <u>Nagra and Berry are</u> talented.

6. Ms. Brown is an English teacher. <u>Ms. Brown is</u> a supervisor too.

7. Tennis and ping-pong are my favorite sports. <u>Tennis and ping-pong are</u> exciting games.

6 | EDITING

Correct this short paragraph. There are seven mistakes. The first mistake is already corrected.

My family ^is^ in Brazil. My parents they are teachers. Alessandra is my sister. She an engineer. Marco be my brother. Is a businessman. They far away, but thanks to e-mail, we close.

Communication Practice

7 | LISTENING

🎧 *Work with a partner. Look at the chart. Do you know these talented people? Try and complete the chart with words from the box. Follow the example. Then listen and check your guesses.*

Example: **A:** Who is Hideki Matsui?
B: He's a soccer player from Japan.
A: He's from Japan, but he's not a soccer player. He's a baseball player.

baseball player	Japan	singer	the United States
Colombia	Mexico	soccer player	writer
England	movie director	Taiwan	

Person	*Hideki Matsui*	*Mia Hamm*	*Ang Lee*	*Steven Spielberg*
Job	baseball player			
Country				

Person	*Paulina Rubio*	*Beyoncé*	*J.K. Rowling*	*Gabriel Garcia Marquez*
Job				
Country				

8 | GEOGRAPHY GAME

Work with a partner. Student A reads sentences 1–4. Student B reads sentences 5–8. After each sentence, your partner says, **That's right** *or* **That's wrong** *and corrects the wrong sentences. (See the map in Appendix 1, pages A-0, 1).*

Examples: A: São Paulo is in Brazil.
B: That's right.

A: France is in Paris.
B: That's wrong. France isn't in Paris. Paris is in France.

Student A	**Student B**
1. Great Britain is in Africa.	5. Mali is in Asia.
2. Mongolia is near China.	6. France is not near Spain.
3. The United States is in Argentina.	7. Taiwan is near Hong Kong.
4. Australia is near the United States.	8. Canada is in Vancouver.

Now use the map and make more statements about the world. Your partner answers **That's right** *or* **That's wrong** *and corrects the wrong statements.*

9 | WRITING

Write about a talented person.

Example: Pedro is my brother. He's 19 years old. He's in Mexico. He's a musician.
He plays the guitar. He's talented. I think his music is great.
Pedro is not famous now. But one day everyone will know him.

10 | ON THE INTERNET

Search for information about one of the people in Exercise 7. Write two new things about that person. Read your sentences to the class. Do not say the name of the person. The class guesses who it is.

Example: A: This person is the director of *Jaws, Jurassic Park, Indiana Jones and the Temple of Doom*, and *Schindler's List*. George Lucas, the director of *Star Wars*, is his friend. They made the film *Raiders of the Lost Ark* together.
B: It's Steven Spielberg.

2 | The Present of *Be*: *Yes/No* Questions

Grammar in Context

BEFORE YOU READ

Are you usually early? Are you late? Are you on time?

🎧 *It's the first day of an English class. Read this conversation.*

ARRIVING IN CLASS

CLAUDIA OLIVERA: Excuse me. **Am I** late for class?

AL BROWN: **No, you're not.**

CLAUDIA: Whew! **Is the teacher** here?

AL: **Yes, he is.**

CLAUDIA: **Are you** new here?

AL: **Yes, I am.**

CLAUDIA: Me, too.

AL: What's your name?

CLAUDIA: I'm Claudia Olivera.

AL: Nice to meet you. I'm Al Brown. **Are you** from Latin America?

CLAUDIA: **Yes, I am.** I'm from Mexico. What about you?

AL: I'm from Michigan.

CLAUDIA: Michigan? Michigan's in the United States. So you're American. Then you're not a student in this class.

AL: You're right. I'm not a student. I'm a teacher. I'm your new English teacher.

Now read the conversation with a partner.

AFTER YOU READ

Answer the questions with **Yes**, **No**, *or* **I don't know**.

1. Are the man and woman late? _____

2. Is the woman from Mexico? _____

3. Is Michigan in the United States? _____

4. Are the man and woman students? _____

5. Is the school in Michigan? _____

Grammar Presentation

THE PRESENT OF *BE*: *YES/NO* QUESTIONS AND SHORT ANSWERS

YES/NO QUESTIONS

Singular		
Be	**Subject**	
Am	I	
Are	you	
Is	he	in room 2?
	she	
	it	

SHORT ANSWERS

Singular				
Yes		**No**		
Yes,	you **are**.	**No,**	you**'re not**. / you **aren't**.	
	I **am**.		I**'m not**.	
	he **is**.		he**'s not**. / he **isn't**.	
	she **is**.		she**'s not**. / she **isn't**.	
	it **is**.		it**'s not**. / it **isn't**.	

Plural		
Be	**Subject**	
Are	we	
	you	on time?
	they	

Plural				
Yes		**No**		
Yes,	you **are**.	**No,**	you**'re not**. / you **aren't**.	
	we **are**.		we**'re not**. / we **aren't**.	
	they **are**.		they**'re not**. / they **aren't**.	

(continued)

OTHER SHORT ANSWERS

Yes.	Yes, I think so.
No.	No, I don't think so.
I don't know.	

GRAMMAR NOTES

EXAMPLES

1. In *yes/no* **questions with *be***, a form of *be* comes before the subject.

	be	subject	
•	**Are**	you	from Canada?
•	**Is**	he	late?
•	**Am**	I	on time?

---

2. We usually answer *yes/no* questions with **short answers**.

▶ **BE CAREFUL!** Don't use contractions in short answers with *yes*.

A: Are you new here?

B: Yes.   OR   **Yes, I am.**

C: No.   OR   **No, I'm not.**

NOT: YES, ~~I'm.~~

---

3. We sometimes answer *yes/no* questions with **long answers**.

You can use contractions in long answers with *yes*.

A: Are they students?

B: Yes, they are students.

OR

Yes, they're students.

---

4. When we are not sure of an answer, we say, **"I don't know."**

When we think something is true, we say, **"Yes, I think so."** or **"I think so."**

When we think something is not true, we say, **"No, I don't think so."** or **"I don't think so."**

A: Is Sydney the capital of Australia?

B: I don't know.

A: Is she a good athlete?

B: Yes, I think so.

OR

I think so.

A: Is it hot today?

B: No, I don't think so.

OR

I don't think so.

Focused Practice

1 | DISCOVER THE GRAMMAR

Look at the picture. Match the questions and answers.

  f   **1.** Is the door open?

      2. Is it ten o'clock on September 1?

      3. Is the teacher a man?

      4. Are the students hungry?

      5. Are the books open?

      6. Is the woman at the door early?

      7. Is the woman at the door unhappy?

a. Yes, he is.

b. I don't know.

c. Yes, it is.

d. Yes, I think so.

e. Yes, they are.

f. No, it's not.

g. No, she's late.

2 | ASKING *YES/NO* QUESTIONS
Grammar Note 1

Write **yes/no** *questions about the statements in parentheses.*

1. A: (It's September 2.)   *Is it September 2?*

    B: No, it's not. It's the first.

2. A: (Today is Tuesday.) _____

    B: Yes, it is.

3. A: (We are in the right room.) _____

    B: I think so.

(continued)

4. A: (You are a new student.) _____

   B: No, I'm not. This is my second year.

5. A: (She is the teacher.) _____

   B: I'm not sure. I think so.

6. A: (It's ten o'clock.) _____

   B: Yes. It's ten.

7. A: (They are in our class.) _____

   B: I don't know.

8. A: (This is your pen.) Excuse me, _____

   B: No, I don't think so.

9. A: (Kaori and Marco are here.) _____

   B: Kaori is here, but Marco is absent.

10. A: (I'm in the right room.) _____

   B: Yes, you are.

---

3 | WORD ORDER PRACTICE   *Grammar Notes 1–2*

Write **yes/no** *questions. Use the words given. Then answer the questions. Write true short answers. Use contractions (short forms) when possible.*

1. you / Are / usually early

   A: *Are you usually early?* _____

   B: *Yes, I am.*   OR   *No, I'm not.* _____

2. your watch / from Switzerland / Is

   A: _____

   B: _____

3. comfortable / Are / your shoes

   A: _____

   B: _____

4. Are / expensive / camera phones / in your country

   A: _____

   B: _____

5. your name / Is / easy to pronounce

   A: _____

   B: _____

6. Tasmania / in Australia / Is

A: _____

B: _____

7. different cities / Are / from / you and your classmates

A: _____

B: _____

8. busy / Are / your classmates / now

A: _____

B: _____

4 | LETTERS TO AND FROM A PSYCHOLOGIST   *Grammar Notes 1–2, 4*

A *Read the e-mail message. Write* **yes/no** *questions. Use the words given. Then answer the questions with short answers.*

> Dear Dr. Brown,
>
> I have two good friends. I like them a lot. They're fun and interesting. But there's one problem. They're always late. You're a psychologist. Please, tell me why. Thank you.
>
> Molly

1. Molly / always late

A: *Is Molly always late?*

B: *No, she's not.*   OR   *No, she isn't.*

2. her friends / interesting and fun

A: _____

B: _____

3. her friends / on time

A: _____

B: _____

4. Dr. Brown / a psychologist

A: _____

B: _____

B *Now read Dr. Brown's answer. Write* **yes/no** *questions. Use the words given. Then answer the questions with* **Yes, I think so., No, I don't think so.,** *or* **I don't know.**

Dear Molly,

    You're unhappy because your friends are late.

    There are different reasons why people are late. Maybe they think, "I'm late. That means I'm important." It's hard to do something about that. But maybe your friends are late, and they don't know it's a problem for you. Tell them. They may change. Or perhaps your friends are bad at planning their time. Try and help them.

    Good luck.

Sincerely,

Maria Brown, Ph.D.

---

1. Molly / unhappy

    A: *Is Molly unhappy?*

    B: *Yes, I think so.*

2. her friends / unhappy

    A: _____

    B: _____

3. her friends / important

    A: _____

    B: _____

4. her friends / good at planning their time

    A: _____

    B: _____

5. the psychologist's answer / good

    A: _____

    B: _____

5 | EDITING

Correct these conversations. There are seven mistakes. The first mistake is already corrected.

1. **A:** Are you tired?
   I am.
   B: Yes, ~~I'm.~~

2. **A:** Is late?
   B: No, it's early.

3. **A:** He Korean?
   B: No, he's isn't.

4. **A:** Am I in the right room?
   B: You are yes.

5. **A:** Is this English 3?
   B: Yes, I think.

6. **A:** Are they in room 102?
   B: I no know.

Communication Practice

6 | LISTENING

Listen to the conversation about Hugo's English class. Read the questions. Then listen again and circle the correct answer to each question.

1. Is the teacher from the United States?
   a. Yes, he is. He's from California.
   b. No, he's not. He's Canadian.
   c. No, he's not. He's Cambodian.

2. Is the teacher 40 years old?
   a. Yes, he is.
   b. No, he's not.
   c. I don't know.

3. Are all the students from the same country?
   a. Yes, they are.
   b. No, they're not.
   c. Yes, I think so.

4. Are the students good at different skills?
   a. Yes, they are.
   b. No, they're not.
   c. No, I don't think so.

5. Is Hugo good at writing?
   a. Yes, he is.
   b. Yes, I think so.
   c. No, I don't think so.

7 | OCCUPATIONS

A *Check (✓) your occupation and the occupations of people in your family.*

- ☐ a businessman
- ☐ a businesswoman
- ☐ a salesperson
- ☐ a student
- ☐ a teacher
- ☐ an actor

☐ a nurse

☐ a homemaker

☐ a doctor

☐ an athlete

☐ an electrician

☐ a detective

☐ a plumber

☐ a writer

☐ a lawyer

☐ a carpenter

B *Have a conversation with a partner. Tell about the occupations of your family and friends. Use the words from the box.*

boring	exciting	hard
dangerous	fun	interesting
easy		

Example: **A:** My cousin is a detective.
               B: Is his work <u>dangerous</u>?
               A: I think so.

8 | CARS

A *Match the cars and the countries. Then work in small groups. Check your answers with others in your group.*

_____ 1. Toyotas   **a.** Swedish

_____ 2. Ferraris   **b.** Italian

_____ 3. Hyundais   **c.** British

_____ 4. Hummers   **d.** Japanese

_____ 5. Jaguars   **e.** Korean

_____ 6. Volvos   **f.** American

> **Example:** **A:** Are Hyundais Japanese cars?
> **B:** No, they're not. They're Korean.

B *Study these words and phrases.*

big	comfortable	economical	expensive	fast	safe	small
roomy	good for a single person		good for a family		good for rough roads	

Ask **yes / no** *questions about cars.*

> **Examples:** **A:** Are Hummers very big?
> **B:** Yes, they are.

9 | ON THE INTERNET

C *Find information about a car. Your classmates ask* **yes / no** *questions about the car. Answer their questions. They then guess the car.*

> **Example:** **A:** Is it expensive?
> **B:** I think so. A new one in the U.S. is between $16,000 and $24,000.
> **A:** Is it comfortable?
> **B:** Yes. It seats five.
> **A:** Is it good for a single person?
> **B:** No, I don't think so. I think it's a good family car.
> **A:** Is it a Japanese car?
> **B:** Yes, it is.
> **A:** Is it a Honda Accord?
> **B:** Yes, it is!

UNIT

3 The Past of *Be*

Grammar in Context

BEFORE YOU READ

*Read the sentences. Check **yes** or **no**.*

	Yes	No
I have an answering machine.	☐	☐
I use e-mail.	☐	☐
I have Caller ID.	☐	☐

🎧 *Read these telephone messages.*

Message 1—Hi, Jay. This is Emily. **I'**m calling to thank you. The party **was** great. We **were** so happy to meet Gina. She's a special person. We're happy for both of you.

Message 2—Hello, Jay. This is Dave. I'm sorry I **wasn't** at the party last night. The weather in Ottawa **was** terrible. My plane **was** late. I **was** at the airport for four hours. I'm home now. Please call me at 879-0089.

AFTER YOU READ

*Read the questions. Check **yes** or **no**.*

	Yes	No
1. Was Emily at the party with someone?	☐	☐
2. Are Emily and Gina old friends?	☐	☐
3. Was Dave at the party?	☐	☐
4. Was Dave in Ottawa?	☐	☐

22

Grammar Presentation

THE PAST OF *BE*; PAST TIME MARKERS

AFFIRMATIVE STATEMENTS

Singular			
Subject	*Be*		Time Marker
I	**was**		
You	**were**	in Kyoto	**last year**.
He She It	**was**		

Plural			
Subject	*Be*		Time Marker
We You They	**were**	in Toronto	**two weeks ago**.

NEGATIVE STATEMENTS

Singular			
Subject	*Be/Not*		Time Marker
I	**was not wasn't**		
You	**were not weren't**	at the party	**last night**.
He She It	**was not wasn't**		

Plural			
Subject	*Be/Not*		Time Marker
We You They	**were not weren't**	at the party	**last night**.

YES/NO QUESTIONS

Singular			
Be	Subject		Time Marker
Was	I		
Were	you	at the party	**last night**?
Was	he she it		

Plural			
Be	Subject		Time Marker
Were	we you they	at the party	**two weeks ago**?

PAST TIME MARKERS

yesterday

the day before yesterday

last _____ (night, week, year)

(a week, two weeks, a month, two months) _____ ago

GRAMMAR NOTES

EXAMPLES

1. The past of **be** has two forms: **was** and **were**.	• She **was** at the airport. • They **were** late.
2. Use **was** or **were** + **not** to make negative statements.	• He **was not** at the party. • They **were not** in class.
3. In informal writing and speaking, use the contractions **wasn't** and **weren't** in negative statements and negative short answers.	• He **wasn't** at the party. • They **weren't** in class. • **No, he wasn't.** • **No, they weren't.**
4. To ask a **yes/no** question, put **was** or **were** before the subject.	subject • **Was she** at the airport? • **Were you** in Spain?
5. Time markers are usually at the end of statements. Time markers are sometimes at the beginning of statements. Time markers go at the end of a question.	• We were in Toronto **yesterday**. • **Yesterday** we were in Toronto. • Was he in Toronto **yesterday**?

Focused Practice

1 | DISCOVER THE GRAMMAR

*Read this thank-you note. Underline the past of **be**.*

Dear Emily and Rob,

    I was happy to meet you finally. Jay was right—you are both very special. Thanks for the CD. It was a good idea. The songs were perfect for the party.

                        Sincerely,

                        Gina

2 | CONVERSATIONS

Put the sentences in the correct order. Read the conversations.

Example
- No, it was terrible.
- Were you at the party?
- Was it any good?
- No, I wasn't. I was at a concert.

A: *Were you at the party?*

B: *No, I wasn't. I was at a concert.*

A: *Was it any good?*

B: *No, it was terrible.*

1.
   - She's not in the photos.
   - Yes, she was. Why?
   - Was Emily at the party?
   - She was the photographer.

   A: _____

   B: _____

   A: _____

   B: _____

2.
   - Yes, they were. Why?
   - Were Ali and Mo in school on Monday?
   - Their names are not on the attendance sheet.
   - I think they were late.

   A: _____

   B: _____

   A: _____

   B: _____

3.
   - It's cold. It was cold yesterday too.
   - How's the weather in Montreal?
   - Was it cold the day before?
   - I think so.

   A: _____

   B: _____

   A: _____

   B: _____

⌒ *Now listen and check your answers.*

3 | AFFIRMATIVE AND NEGATIVE OF *BE*   *Grammar Notes 1–3*

A *Look at yesterday's attendance record. Complete the sentences. Use* **was**, **wasn't**, **were**, *or* **weren't**.

Attendance Record	
	April 5
Pierre	✓
Juan	✓
Gloria	✓
Emiko	absent
Anna	✓

1. Pierre ____was____ here yesterday. He _____ absent.

2. Emiko _____ here yesterday. She _____ absent.

3. Juan and Gloria _____ here yesterday. They _____ absent.

B *Complete the sentences. Use* **was**, **wasn't**, **were**, *or* **weren't**. *Make true sentences.*

1. Our school _____ open yesterday. It _____ closed.

2. I _____ absent yesterday. I _____ in school.

3. My friend and my teacher _____ absent last week. They _____ in school.

4. Our English homework _____ easy yesterday. It _____ hard.

5. It _____ sunny yesterday. It _____ cloudy.

4 | A GREAT WEEKEND   *Grammar Notes 1–4*

Complete the conversation. Use the affirmative or negative of **was** *or* **were**.

A: How _____was_____ your weekend?
1.

B: Great. I _____ at the park on Saturday and at the art museum on Sunday.
2.

A: _____ you with Joe?
3.

B: Yes, I _____. We _____ together all day Saturday and Sunday.
4.   5.

A: Joe _____ in class this morning. _____ he at an interview?
6.   7.

B: No, he _____. He _____ at the airport. His parents
8.   9.

_____ there for a few hours. They _____ on their way to Mexico.
10.   11.

A: _____ his brothers with them?
12.

B: No, they _____. They were at home with their grandparents.
13.

5 | NOW AND THEN

Complete the sentences. Change from the present to the past.

1. They are busy now. Last month _____*they were busy*_____ too.

2. Today it's cold. Yesterday _____ too.

3. My friend is in Seoul now. _____ last year too.

4. It's not sunny today. _____ yesterday.

5. She's not in class this week. _____ last week.

6. He's at the airport this morning. _____ yesterday morning.

7. I'm in Lima this week. I _____ last week too.

8. His phone is busy. It _____ yesterday evening too.

6 | YES/NO QUESTIONS AND ANSWERS

Write questions and answers. Use the words given.

1. Dave / at the party Friday night
   No, he / in Ottawa

   A: *Was Dave at the party Friday night?*
   B: *No, he was in Ottawa.*

2. Dave / in Ottawa on business
   Yes, he / at a meeting there

   A: _____
   B: _____

3.
   the airport / closed
   No, but all the planes / late

   A: The weather was terrible in Ottawa.
   _____
   B: _____

4. Emily and Rob / at the party
   Yes, they / there for hours

   A: _____
   B: _____

5. you / at home last night
   No, I / at a party

   A: _____
   B: _____

7 | WORD ORDER PRACTICE

Write statements or questions. Use the words and punctuation given.

1. in Toronto / He / . / last week / was

    He was in Toronto last week.

2. cold / . / It / in Toronto / yesterday / was

_____

3. wasn't / It / two days ago /. / cold

_____

4. in Toronto / ? / last month / Were / you

_____

5. in Toronto / ? / Were / they / last year

_____

6. weren't / . / there / we / A week ago

_____

8 | EDITING

Correct this message. There are six mistakes. The first mistake is already corrected.

Hi Victor,

    Right now Bob and I are in a taxi on our way home from the airport.

        were

We ~~was~~ in Mexico all last week. It were great. The weather it was dry and

sunny. The people were warm and friendly. Last night we was at the Ballet

Folklorico. The dancers was terrific. There was only one problem. My Spanish no

was good. See you soon.

                                       Rina

Communication Practice

9 | LISTENING

 Listen to the telephone messages. Listen again and complete the messages.

Message #	From	Message
1	Dan	The _____ _____ great and the _____ _____ super.
2	Emiko	I _____ out of _____ all _____. I'm _____ now. Please call me. My number is _____.
3	John	I'm _____ I _____ at the _____. Please call me at _____.

10 | INFORMATION GAP: WEATHER AROUND THE WORLD

Learn these words for weather.

hot	warm	cool	cold	sunny	windy	rainy	cloudy

Work in pairs. Student B, turn to page 35. Student A, look at this page.

Student A, ask your partner questions to complete your chart.

Example: A: It's sunny in Istanbul today. Was it sunny yesterday too?

City	Yesterday	Today
Bangkok	sunny	cloudy
Beijing	cloudy	partly cloudy
Budapest	cloudy	cloudy
Guadalajara	sunny	sunny
Istanbul		sunny
Rio de Janeiro		sunny
Seoul		rainy
Vancouver		sunny

11 | WRITING

A *Work with a partner. Complete the e-mail message.*

Hi Irina,

I hope you understand my message. My homework was: Write an e-mail message in English. Well, here goes.

I ___am___ in a level two English class at Hunter College in New York City. My classmates _____ from different countries—Korea, Taiwan, Colombia, Italy, Poland, and Thailand. We _____ a class of ten women and four men! :-(My teacher _____ very good. :-) She _____ from Canada.

I _____ nervous and worried last week. It _____ my first week of classes. _____ was the only new student. But now I _____ fine.

I _____ at a party Saturday night. It _____ a classmate's 21st birthday. The party _____ fun.

It _____ warm and sunny now. _____ was cold and cloudy yesterday. That's New York weather. It _____ hard to speak English all the time. It _____ hard to be a "foreigner." But it _____ also exciting to be here.

I hope you _____ OK. Please say hi to everyone.

Best,

Ingrid

B *Write your own e-mail message to a friend. Tell your friend about your life now. Say something about last weekend. Say something about the weather. Use contractions when possible.*

12 | ON THE INTERNET

In 1876, Alexander Graham Bell invented the telephone. Find out more about him. Report to the class.

> OR

Find out about Kazuo Hashimoto. Where is he from? What did he invent? Report to the class.

From **Grammar** to **Writing**
Capitalization

1 | *Look at A and B. What's wrong with A?*

A
mr. john smith
342 dryden road
ithaca, new york 14850

B
Mr. John Smith
342 Dryden Road
Ithaca, New York 14850

Study the information about capitalization.

Capitalization

1. Use a **capital letter** for the first word in every sentence.

2. Use capital letters for **titles**.

3. Use capital letters for the names of **people** and **places** (proper nouns).

4. Use capital letters for the names of **streets**, **cities**, **states**, **countries**, and **continents**.

5. Use a capital letter for the word *I*.

• **We** are new students.

• This is **Mr.** Winston.
• She is **Dr.** Jones.

• **Lila Roberts** is from **Vancouver, Canada**.

• 5 **Elm Street**
   West Redding, Connecticut
   U.S.A.

• My brother and **I** are happy to be here.

---

2 | *Add capital letters.*

1. this is ms. herrera.

2. her address is 4 riverdale avenue.

3. i'm her good friend.

4. she was in bangkok and taipei last year.

3 | *Correct the postcard from Ellen to Ruth. Add capital letters.*

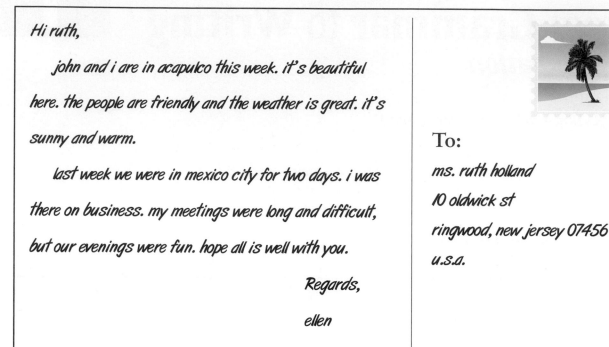

Hi ruth,

    john and i are in acapulco this week. it's beautiful here. the people are friendly and the weather is great. it's sunny and warm.

    last week we were in mexico city for two days. i was there on business. my meetings were long and difficult, but our evenings were fun. hope all is well with you.

               Regards,

               ellen

To:

ms. ruth holland

10 oldwick st

ringwood, new jersey 07456

u.s.a.

Write a postcard to a friend.

To:

Review Test

I *Read each conversation. Circle the letter of the underlined word or group of words that is not correct.*

1.   CLAUDIA: Are you <u>a</u> new student?
                        A

   ALEXANDER: Yes, <u>I'm</u>. I'm from Ecuador. Where <u>are you</u> from?
                        B   **C**

    CLAUDIA: <u>I'm</u> from Mexico.
                        D

A   Ⓑ   C   D

2.   JUAN: You're old <u>students</u>.
                        A

    YOKO: No, you're wrong. We <u>aren't</u> old students. Emiko
                        B

    and I <u>am</u> <u>new</u> students.
                        C **D**

A   B   C   D

3.   VIVIAN: <u>It's</u> hot here.
                        A

    PHIL: No, <u>it's not</u>. It's 60 degrees. <u>It's cold</u>.
                        B   **C**

   VIVIAN: Well, <u>I hot</u>.
                        D

A   B   C   D

4.   JUAN: <u>Was</u> it hot in your room <u>last night</u>?
                        A   **B**

    BILL: No, it <u>isn't</u>. <u>It</u> was cold.
                        C   **D**

A   B   C   D

5.   JAMES: <u>Was</u> Alexander and Nuray in class <u>yesterday</u>?
                        A   **B**

   STEVE: <u>I don't know</u>. I <u>was</u> absent.
                        C   **D**

A   B   C   D

II *Circle the letter of the correct word(s) to complete the sentences.*

1. Last week we _____ in Turkey.

  (A) was   **(C)** is

  (B) are   **(D)** were

A   B   C   D

2. Mike and Ivona _____ absent last week.

  (A) were   **(C)** are

  (B) was   **(D)** is

A   B   C   D

(continued)

3. _____ a photographer?   **A   B   C   D**

   (A) Is you   **(C)** Are you

   (B) You   **(D)** You are

4. Andrew _____ the United States.   **A   B   C   D**

   (A) is from   **(C)** are from

   (B) am from   **(D)** were from

5. Are you tired? Yes, _____.   **A   B   C   D**

   (A) we tired   **(C)** we be

   (B) we're   **(D)** we are

6. _____ Wendy and Mi Young home last night?   **A   B   C   D**

   (A) Was   **(C)** Are

   (B) Were   **(D)** Be

III   Write **yes/no** questions. Use the words in parentheses.

A: (cloudy / yesterday) _____
                                                    1.

B: No, it wasn't. It was sunny.

A: (cloudy / now) _____
                                                    2.

B: Yes.

A: (you / in school / last week) _____
                                                    3.

B: Yes, I was.

IV   Correct this e-mail from Jill to her father. There are three mistakes.

Hi Dad,

Thanks for the money. Books are always expensive. Today the weather is
terrible. It be cold and rainy. But yesterday beautiful. It sunny all day.

How's the weather in New York? Autumn is usually very nice.

                                        Love,

                                        Jill

▶ To check your answers, go to the Answer Key on page RT-1.

| INFORMATION GAP FOR STUDENT B | *Unit 3, Exercise 10* |

Learn these words for weather.

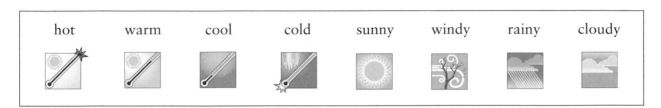

| hot | warm | cool | cold | sunny | windy | rainy | cloudy |

Student B, ask your partner questions to complete your chart.

Example: **B:** It's cloudy in Bangkok today. Was it cloudy yesterday too?

City	Yesterday	Today
Bangkok		cloudy
Beijing		partly cloudy
Budapest		cloudy
Guadalajara		sunny
Istanbul	cloudy	sunny
Rio de Janeiro	sunny	sunny
Seoul	sunny	rainy
Vancouver	cloudy	sunny

Nouns, Adjectives, Prepositions, *Wh*-Questions

Count Nouns; Proper Nouns

Grammar in Context

BEFORE YOU READ

What's in your wallet? Check (✓) true statements.

_____ **1.** I have photos of friends or family.

_____ **2.** I have a photo of myself.

_____ **3.** I don't have any photos in my wallet.

Talk about a photo in your wallet.

🎧 *Read about this photographer and this photo.*

Example: **A:** This is a photo of my sister. She's a dancer. She's 20 years old.
B: What's her name?

A PHOTOGRAPHER AND A PHOTO

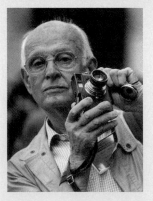

Henri Cartier-Bresson was **a photographer** and **an artist.** He was born in **France** in 1908. He died in 2004. His **photos** are famous all over the **world.**

This is a **photo** by **Henri Cartier Bresson.** It's **a photo** of **a man** and **a woman.** The **woman** is beautiful. The **man** is looking at her. They are in **Harlem,** in **New York.** It is 1947.

AFTER YOU READ

Complete the sentences. Use the words in the box.

artist	France	photographer	photos

1. Henri Cartier-Bresson was a _____.

2. He was an _____ too.

3. He was from _____.

4. His _____ are famous all over the world.

Grammar Presentation

SINGULAR AND PLURAL COUNT NOUNS; PROPER NOUNS

Singular Nouns (one)
He is **a photographer**.
He is **an artist**.

Plural Nouns (more than one)
They are **photographers**.
They are **artists**.

Irregular Plural Nouns	
Singular	**Plural**
man	men
woman	women
child	children
foot	feet
tooth	teeth
person	people

Nouns That Are Always Plural
pants   scissors   clothes   glasses 

Proper Nouns
Harlem is in **New York City**.
Maya Angelou has a home in **Harlem**.

GRAMMAR NOTES

EXAMPLES

1. Nouns are names of people, places, and things.	• a student, Jung Eun • a country, Korea • a camera, a photograph

2. Count nouns are easy to count. They have a singular and plural form. Use *a* before **singular** count nouns that begin with a consonant sound. ▶ BE CAREFUL! Use *an* before an *h* that is silent.	• **one** photo, **two** photos, **three** photos • She's **a** photographer. • He's **a** teacher. • It's **a** hat. • It's **an** hour too early. (*Hour* sounds like *our*.)

3. Use *an* before **singular** count nouns that begin with a vowel sound. ▶ BE CAREFUL! Use *a* before a *u* that sounds like *yew*.	• She's **an** artist. • He's **an** engineer. • It's **an** umbrella. • This is **a** unit about nouns.

4. To form the **plural** of most count nouns, add **-s** or **-es**. Do not put *a* or *an* before plural nouns. Some nouns have irregular plural endings. Some nouns are always plural.	• one **friend** three **friends** • one **class** three **classes** • They are **photos** of **friends**. NOT: They are a photos of a friends. • one **man** two **men** • one **tooth** two **teeth** • **scissors, pants, glasses, clothes** • My **pants are** blue.

5. Names of specific people and places are **proper nouns**. Write these with a capital letter. Do not put *a* or *an* before proper nouns.	• **Paris** is in **France**. • **Harlem** is in **New York City**. NOT: A Paris is in a France.

Reference Notes
See Unit 25, page 242 for a discussion of non-count nouns and *the* (the definite article).
See Appendix 9, page A-10 for the spelling and pronunciation rules for plural nouns.

Focused Practice

1 | DISCOVER THE GRAMMAR

Read the conversation.

MIKE: Is that you?

DOUG: Yes, it is. It's a photo of me with friends from high school.

MIKE: Where are they now?

DOUG: Well, Jasmine's in Brazil.

MIKE: Really?

DOUG: Uh-huh. She's a teacher there. And Bob's on the right. He's an accountant. He's here in New York.

MIKE: Who's she?

DOUG: That's Amy. She's a photographer. What a life! She travels all over the world. Last month she was in India. Her photos are in a show at the library this month.

MIKE: I'd love to see them.

DOUG: Them? Or her?

Find:

1. One noun that begins with a vowel: _____

2. Two nouns that begin with a consonant (no proper nouns): _____,

   _____

3. Two proper nouns: _____, _____

4. Two plural nouns: _____, _____

2 | *HARLEM, 1947*   *Grammar Notes 2–3*

A *Write **a** or **an** before each word.*

1. _____ man   6. _____ suit

2. _____ hand   7. _____ eye

3. _____ hat   8. _____ ear

4. _____ earring   9. _____ lip

5. _____ flower   10. _____ woman

B *Look at the photo,* Harlem, 1947, *below. Find the items from the list. Label the photo. Use the words from the list. Number them 1–10.*

3 | A OR AN

Grammar Notes 2–5

*Complete the sentences with **a** or **an**. Write **Ø** if you don't need **a** or **an**.*

1. Henri Cartier-Bresson was _____ photographer.

2. Henri Cartier-Bresson and Ansel Adams were _____ photographers.

3. Henri Cartier-Bresson was _____ artist, too.

4. All good photographers are _____ artists.

5. Ansel Adams was _____ pianist before he was _____ photographer.

6. Ansel Adams was born in _____ San Francisco, California.

7. For Adams, photography began with _____ trip to Yosemite National Park.

8. _____ Henri Cartier-Bresson was born in _____ Normandy.

9. _____ Normandy is in _____ France.

10. Henri Cartier-Bresson was the first photographer with _____ pictures in the Louvre Museum.

4 | PEOPLE, PLACES, AND THINGS

Grammar Note 4, Appendix 9

Look at the spelling rules for plural nouns on page 40. Complete the sentences. Use the correct form of one of the nouns in the box.

~~city~~	clothes	fish	husband	person	wife
class	country	flower	museum	watch	

1. San Francisco and Los Angeles are _____*cities*_____ in California.

2. Brazil and France are _____.

3. The Louvre and the Prado are _____.

4. Seiko and Rolex are kinds of _____.

5. The _____ of Issey Miyake and Ralph Lauren are beautiful.

6. Salmon and tuna are _____.

7. Jason is a teacher. His _____ are interesting.

8. The men are on a business trip. Their _____ are at home.

9. The women are on a business trip. Their _____ are at home.

10. There are two _____ in the photo *Harlem, 1947* by Henri Cartier-Bresson.

11. The woman in *Harlem, 1947* has a hat with _____.

5 | PROPER NOUNS

Grammar Note 5

Change small letters to capital letters where necessary.

MIKE: Hi, are you ~~amy~~ ^{*Amy*} smith?

AMY: Yes, I am.

MIKE: I'm mike cho. doug and I work together.

AMY: Nice to meet you, mike.

MIKE: It's nice to meet you.

AMY: So, mike, are you from phoenix?

MIKE: No, I'm not. I'm from san francisco.

AMY: Oh, san francisco is beautiful. I was there last year.

MIKE: Doug says you travel a lot.

AMY: Yes, I do. I was in india last year. And the year before that I was in kuwait, turkey,

jordan, and egypt.

MIKE: That's great.

6 | EDITING

Correct these sentences. There are six mistakes. The first mistake is already corrected.

1. Cartier-Bresson's photos are often of famous ~~person~~ ^{*people*}.

2. This is photo of Henri Matisse.

3. Henri Matisse was artist.

4. Matisse's paintings are in museum all over the world.

5. We see four bird in this photo.

6. In this photo Matisse was in the south of france.

Communication Practice

7 | LISTENING

🎧 *Complete the sentences with the words in the box. Then listen and check your work.*
See Appendix 9 on page A-10 for more about plural endings. Listen again and check the
sound of the endings.

| books | boxes | classes | glasses | pants | ~~photos~~ | scissors |

	/s/	/z/	/ɪz/
1. The ___*photos*___ are ready.		✓	
2. Our _____ are from 10:00 to 1:00.			
3. Be careful. The _____ are sharp.			
4. The _____ are full of old clothes.			
5. My _____ have two pockets.			
6. I don't see well without _____.			
7. Our _____ are open to page 20.			

8 | DRAW MY PICTURE

A *Choose five things. Draw a picture with the five things in it. You don't have to be an*
artist. Your picture does not have to look real!

a photo	a camera	five people	three children
an apple	an ice cream cone	flowers	earrings

B *Work with a partner. Tell your partner about your picture.*
Your partner draws your picture. Compare pictures.

Example: *My picture has three children—a boy and*
two girls. It has an apple with earrings. It
has flowers everywhere.

9 | CLASSROOM OBJECTS

A *Work with a partner. Label the pictures. Ask your partner about things you don't know.*

Example: **A:** What's this?   OR   What's this called in English?
B: It's an eraser.
A: What are these?
B: They're CDs.

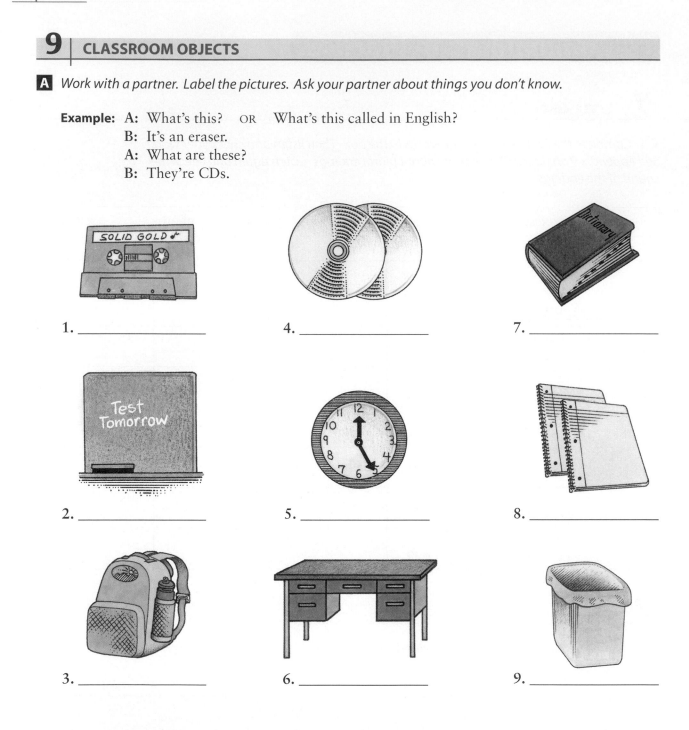

1. _____

4. _____

7. _____

2. _____

5. _____

8. _____

3. _____

6. _____

9. _____

B *Look at your classroom. Make two lists of things in your classroom.*

Our Classroom	
We have:	We have two or more:
a board	*erasers*

C *Compare your lists.*

> **Example:** A: Are erasers on your list?
> B: Yes, they are. Are windows on your list?
> A: No, they aren't.

10 | WRITING

*Work with a partner. Write sentences about people and places. Remember to use **a** or **an** with singular count nouns.*

1. *Henri Matisse was an* _____ artist.

2. _____ photographer.

3. _____ city.

4. _____ and _____ countries.

5. _____ and _____ writers.

6. _____ and _____ actors.

7. _____ and _____ students.

8. _____ teacher.

Read each sentence to a partner. Your partner asks a question. Try to answer it.

> **Example:** A: Henri Matisse was an artist.
> B: Was he from France?
> A: Yes, he was.   OR   I don't know.

11 | ON THE INTERNET

C *Look on the Internet for photos by Henri Cartier-Bresson. Print one if possible. Tell the class about the photo.*

> **Example:** This is a photo by Henri Cartier-Bresson. The place is Kashmir, India. It's 1948. The women are wearing long dresses. The photo is beautiful.

Grammar in Context

BEFORE YOU READ

Look at the photograph. What words describe this place?

> beautiful—ugly
>
> interesting—boring
>
> usual—strange

Example: It's interesting.

Were you ever in a place like this? When? Where?

🎧 *Read about Cappadocia, Turkey.*

AN UNUSUAL PLACE

Cappadocia is in the center of Turkey. It is an **unusual** place. It has underground cities and cave homes. It's a **great** place to hike. Everywhere there are **interesting** things to see. Sometimes the landscape looks like a **different** world. That's why a *Star Wars* movie was filmed in Cappadocia. In the past, people lived in the caves. Today people from all over the world visit the caves.

The climate is **mild** in Cappadocia. The days are **sunny** and **warm**, and the nights are **cool**. It is a **beautiful** place to visit.

AFTER YOU READ

Read the statements.
*Mark them **T** (true) or **F** (false).*

_____ 1. Cappadocia is in the west of Turkey.

_____ 2. It is in the center of Turkey.

_____ 3. It has underwater cities.

_____ 4. It has cave homes.

_____ 5. *Lord of the Rings* was filmed in Cappadocia.

_____ 6. The climate is tropical.

_____ 7. The days are sunny and cold.

Grammar Presentation

DESCRIPTIVE ADJECTIVES

Noun	*Be*	Adjective
The room	is	**small**.
The rooms	are	

	Adjective	Noun
It is a	**small**	room.
They are		rooms.

GRAMMAR NOTES

EXAMPLES

1. Adjectives describe nouns.	noun adjective • **Cappadocia** is **beautiful**. adjective noun • It's a **beautiful place**.

2. Adjectives can come:
  • after the verb *be*.
  • before a noun.
	• The room is **big**.
	• It's a **big** room.
	  NOT: It's a ~~room big~~.

3. Do <u>not</u> add *-s* to adjectives.	• a **sunny** day, a **cool** night • **sunny** days, **cool** nights NOT: ~~cools~~ nights

4. For **adjective + noun**: Use *a* before the adjective if the adjective begins with a consonant sound. Use *an* before the adjective if the adjective begins with a vowel sound.	• It's **a small** village. • It's **an old** village.

5. Some adjectives end in *-ing*, *-ly*, or *-ed*.	• It's **interesting**. • They're **friendly**. • We're **tired**.

Focused Practice

1 | DISCOVER THE GRAMMAR

Gamirasu Cave Hotel is in a traditional village. In the past it was a cave home. Now it's a hotel.

Maria is touring Turkey. Read her journal entry about the hotel. Underline ten more adjectives.

I'm at a cave hotel in Cappadocia. The hotel is in a <u>small</u> village in the heart of

Cappadocia. The cave rooms are fun. They're old, but with modern bathrooms. The

rates are not high. The food is fresh and the people are helpful and friendly. The

price of the room includes a delicious breakfast and dinner. It's easy to visit all of

Cappadocia from the hotel. It was a great choice.

2 | WORD ORDER PRACTICE
Grammar Notes 1–5

Write sentences. Use the words given. Remember the first word begins with a capital letter.

1. market. / at / we / are / old / an

   _____

2. for sale / everywhere. / beautiful / carpets / are

   _____

3. the / prices / reasonable. / are

   _____

4. warm. / it / and / sunny / is /

_____

5. tired / happy. / I'm / but

_____

3 | EDITING

Correct these sentences. There are five mistakes. The first mistake is already corrected.

A: Is that a ~~carpet new~~ ^{new carpet}?

B: Yes, it is. It's from Turkey.

A: The colors are beautifuls.

B: Thanks. I got it at old market in Cappadocia.

A: Were there many things interesting to buy?

B: Yes. These bowls are from Turkey too.

A: They're colors great.

B: Here. This one is for you.

Communication Practice

4 | LISTENING

🎧 *Emiko is on vacation at Mesa Verde National Park in Colorado. Listen to her telephone conversation. Then choose the word or phrase to complete the sentences.*

1. Emiko says, "Mesa Verde is _____."
   a. strange and awesome
   b. interesting and exciting

2. The cliff dwellings are very _____.
   a. cold
   b. old

3. Emiko is at a _____ hotel.
   a. clean
   b. nice

4. The weather is _____.
   a. warm
   b. cold

5. The park is _____.
   a. crowded
   b. not crowded

5 | MY CITY

A *Match the word on the left with its opposite on the right.*

_d_   **1.** usual   **a.** helpful

_____ **2.** beautiful   **b.** ugly

_____ **3.** comfortable   **c.** warm

_____ **4.** expensive   **d.** unusual

_____ **5.** traditional   **e.** friendly

_____ **6.** important   **f.** interesting

_____ **7.** boring   **g.** uncomfortable

_____ **8.** unhelpful   **h.** cheap

_____ **9.** cold   **i.** unimportant

_____ **10.** unfriendly   **j.** modern

B *Choose ten words from A. Use each word in a sentence. Write about the city you are in.*

Examples: The houses are expensive. The buses are comfortable. The people are friendly.

C *Read your sentences to a partner. Listen to your partner's sentences. Are any of your sentences the same?*

6 | OBJECTS IN OUR CLASSROOM

Work with a partner. Look around the classroom. Describe objects in your classroom. Use the adjectives in the box.

big	heavy	long	old	thick
dark	large	new	straight	

Examples: My dictionary is thick.
                 My book bag is heavy.

7 | ON THE INTERNET

Find a picture of one of these cave dwellings.

- Argentina, Cueva de las Manos
- China, Longmen Grottoes
- France, Lascaux Cave
- India, Ajanta Cave
- Spain, Altamira Cave

Read about it. Tell your class about it.

Prepositions of Place

Grammar in Context

BEFORE YOU READ

Look at these pictures. Answer the questions: What kind of doctor is Dr. Green? Where is his office?

Read the conversations of a patient and a receptionist and the patient and a doctor.

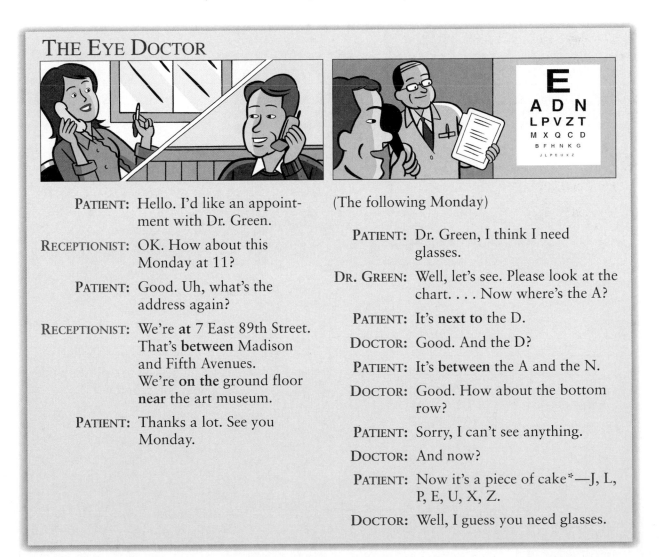

THE EYE DOCTOR

PATIENT: Hello. I'd like an appointment with Dr. Green.

RECEPTIONIST: OK. How about this Monday at 11?

PATIENT: Good. Uh, what's the address again?

RECEPTIONIST: We're **at** 7 East 89th Street. That's **between** Madison and Fifth Avenues. We're **on the** ground floor **near** the art museum.

PATIENT: Thanks a lot. See you Monday.

(The following Monday)

PATIENT: Dr. Green, I think I need glasses.

DR. GREEN: Well, let's see. Please look at the chart. . . . Now where's the A?

PATIENT: It's **next to** the D.

DOCTOR: Good. And the D?

PATIENT: It's **between** the A and the N.

DOCTOR: Good. How about the bottom row?

PATIENT: Sorry, I can't see anything.

DOCTOR: And now?

PATIENT: Now it's a piece of cake*—J, L, P, E, U, X, Z.

DOCTOR: Well, I guess you need glasses.

*a piece of cake: easy

AFTER YOU READ

Complete these sentences. Choose from the words in parentheses.

1. The D is _____ the A and the N.
(above / between)

2. The A is _____ the D.
(next to / under)

3. The doctor's office is _____ a museum.
(near / in)

4. His office is _____ the ground floor.
(on / in)

5. His office is _____ 7 East 89th Street.
(on / at)

Grammar Presentation

PREPOSITIONS OF PLACE

 The glasses are **between** the book and the watch.

 The glasses are **next to** the newspaper.

 The glasses are **behind** the box.

 The glasses are **under** the table.

 The glasses are **in** his pocket.

 The glasses are **on** the table **near** the window.

 The man is **in back of** the woman.

 The man is **in front of** the woman.

GRAMMAR NOTES	EXAMPLES
1. **Prepositions of place** tell <u>where</u> something is. Some common prepositions of place are: ***under***, ***behind***, ***on***, ***next to***, ***between***, ***near***, ***in***, ***in front of***, ***in back of***	• My bag is **under** my seat. • Your umbrella is **near** the door.
▶ **BE CAREFUL!** *Near* and *next to* are not the same. Look at the letters of the alphabet: ABCDEFGHIJKLMNOPQRSTUVWXYZ	• The letter A is **next to** the letter B. It is **near** the letter B, too. • The letter A is **near** the letter C, but it is not **next to** the letter C. • The letter J is not **next to** the letter A. It is not **near** the letter A, either.

2. We use the following prepositions in addresses:	
in before a country, a state, a province, a city, a room number	• He's **in** Canada. He's **in** British Columbia. • He's **in** Vancouver. He's **in** room 302.
on before a street, an avenue, a road	• It's **on** Main Street. It's **on** Tenth Avenue.
at before a building number	• We're **at** 78 Main Street.
on the before a floor	• We're **on the** 2nd floor.
on the corner of before a street or streets	• It's **on the corner of** Main Street.
USAGE NOTE: In informal conversation, *street* or *avenue* is dropped.	• It's on the corner of **Main Street** and **Mott Avenue**. • It's on the corner of **Main** and **Mott**.

3. Use the following prepositions before these places:	
in school OR ***at*** school	• I'm **in** school from 9 to 11. • I'm **at** school now.
at work	• She's **at** work right now.
at home OR home	• No one is **at** home. • No one is home.

Focused Practice

1 | DISCOVER THE GRAMMAR

Look at the eye chart. Read the paragraph. Find the message.

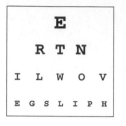

There are three words. The first word has one letter. This letter is next to an *L*. It isn't a *W* or an *S*. The second word has four letters. The first letter is between the *S* and an *I*. The second letter is under the *N*. The third letter is a *V*. A *T* is under the last letter. The third word has seven letters. A *T* is under the first letter. The second letter is an *N*. The third letter is between an *E* and the *S*. The fourth letter is an *L*. The fifth letter is an *I*. The sixth letter is between the *L* and the *G*. The last letter is an *H*.

What's the message? ___ ___ ___ ___ ___ ___ ___ ___ ___ ___ ___ ___

2 | UNDERSTANDING A MAP   *Grammar Notes 1–2*

Look at the map. Complete the sentences on the next page. Use the words in the box.

at	between	next to	~~on~~
on the	on the . . . of	under	

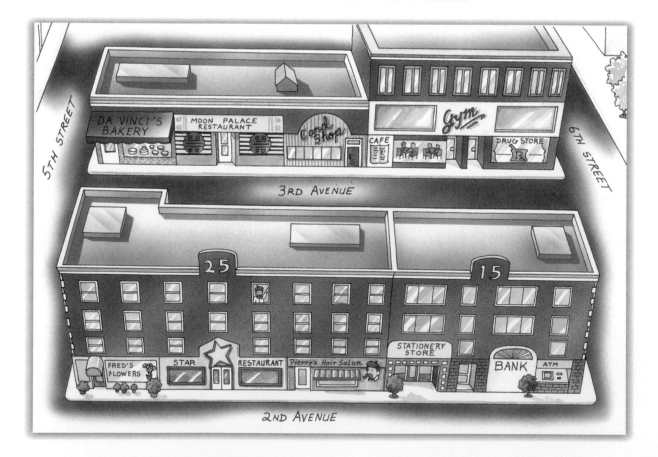

1. Fred's Flowers is _____*on*_____ 2nd Avenue.

2. Pierre's Hair Salon is _____ a stationery store and a restaurant.

3. Da Vinci's Bakery is _____ corner _____ 3rd Avenue and 5th Street.

4. The café is _____ the drugstore.

5. Pierre's apartment is _____ 25 2nd Avenue.

6. His apartment is _____ fourth floor.

7. The café and drugstore are _____ a gym.

3 | A PLACE TO MEET
Grammar Notes 1–2

🎧 *Look at the map. Listen to the conversation. Complete the sentences.*

1. They are meeting on _____ Avenue.

2. They're meeting _____ 5th and 6th _____.

3. They're meeting on 3rd Avenue _____ the restaurant.

4. The restaurant is _____ the card shop and the _____.

5. The name of the restaurant is _____.

4 | I AM IN SCHOOL
Grammar Notes 1–3

Complete the sentences. Write true sentences. Write them in class.

1. I am ___*in*___ school.

2. I am _____ room _____.

3. I am not _____ home. I'm not _____ work.

4. I am _____.
   (your country)

5. I am _____.
   (your city)

6. I am _____.
   (floor)

7. My school is _____.
   (school address)

5 | EDITING

Put a check (✓) next to the three correct sentences. Add a word or words to correct the other sentences.

_____ 1. She's next ^to^ the policeman.

_____ 2. The bookstore is on the corner Main Street.

_____ 3. He lives on first floor.

_____ 4. I'm near the museum.

_____ 5. He's not work today. He's home.

_____ 6. I'm the corner of Main and Second.

_____ 7. A man is in front the stationery store.

_____ 8. It's between the flower shop and the drugstore.

_____ 9. We're in back of the house.

_____ 10. Her office is 78 Elm Street.

_____ 11. He's Osaka now.

_____ 12. We're third floor.

Communication Practice

6 | LISTENING

A ⌢ *Look at the world map in Appendix 1, page A-1. Listen to the speaker. Write the names of the countries.*

1. __ __ __ __

2. __ __ __ __ __ __

3. __ __ __ __ __ __ __ __ __ __

4. __ __ __ __ __

B *Work with a partner. Write sentences about a country's location. Use the prepositions* **between**, **near**, **next to**, *and* **in**. *Read your sentences to your partner. Your partner guesses the country. (See the map in Appendix 1, page A-1.)*

Example: This country is in Central America. It is between Costa Rica and Colombia. What country is it?

7 | A WORD GAME

Look at Exercise 1, page 56. Write your own word puzzle. Read it to the class.

8 | ON THE INTERNET

 Look on the Internet. Find the official residence of the leader of a country.

Examples: The prime minister of Canada lives at 24 Sussex Drive in Ottawa, Canada.
The president of France lives on Champs Elysées Avenue at the Elysées Palace in Paris, France.

Wh- Questions

Grammar in Context

BEFORE YOU READ

Look at this painting. What do you see?

🎧 *A professor is speaking to his students in Art History 101. Read the questions about the painting. Then read the professor's comments and the student's test paper.*

1. **Who** is the artist?

2. **Where** is the artist from?

3. **What** is the name of the painting?

4. **Why** is this painting unusual?

PROFESSOR: Today is our first test. Look at the questions. Then look at each painting. There are 12 paintings. This is the first one. You have five minutes to answer the questions about each painting. Work fast. The test is one hour long.

Name: *Tim Smith*   Date: *November 2*

Painting #1

1. *The artist is René Magritte.*

2. *He is from Brussels, Belgium.*

3. *The name of the painting is The Son of Man.*

4. *It's unusual because an apple hides the man's face.*

AFTER YOU READ

Answer the questions. Circle **a** *or* **b.**

1. What is *The Son of Man*?
   a. a book   b. a painting

2. Who is René Magritte?
   a. a Belgian artist   b. the Son of Man

3. Where is Brussels?
   a. in France   b. in Belgium

4. Why is it important to work fast?
   a. There are many paintings.   b. There are many students.

Grammar Presentation

QUESTIONS AND ANSWERS WITH *WHO, WHAT, WHERE,* AND *WHY*

Questions		
Question Word	*Be*	
Who	**are**	René Magritte and Salvador Dali?
What	**is**	*The Son of Man*?
Where	**are**	Magritte and Dali from?
Why	**is**	the museum closed?

Answers	
Short Answers	**Long Answers**
Artists.	They're artists.
A painting.	It's a painting.
Belgium and Spain.	Magritte is from Belgium and Dali is from Spain.
It's Monday.	The museum is closed because it's Monday.

GRAMMAR NOTES	EXAMPLES
1. *Wh- questions* ask for **information**. They cannot be answered with a *yes* or *no*. Use *is* for singular subjects and *are* for plural subjects.	**Q: Where** are you from? **A:** Canada. (I'm from Canada.) NOT: ~~Yes, I am~~. • Where **is** he? • Where **are** they?
2. *Who* asks about people.	**Q: Who** is René Magritte? **A:** He's a Belgian artist.

3. *What* asks about **things**.	**Q: What** is the name of that painting? **A:** *The Son of Man.*

4. *Where* asks about **places**.	**Q: Where** is Magritte from? **A:** He's from Brussels.

5. *Why* asks for a **reason**. In long answers use *because* before the reason.	**Q: Why** is the painting strange? **A:** An apple hides the man's face. OR **A:** The painting is strange because an apple hides the man's face.

6. We often use **contractions** (short forms) for *wh*-questions with *is* in speaking and informal writing.	**Q: Who's** Salvador Dali? **Q: Where's** he from?

7. We usually give **short answers**. We can give **long answers** too.	**Q:** Where are the paintings? **A: In a museum.** **A: The paintings are in a museum.**

Focused Practice

1 | DISCOVER THE GRAMMAR

This is the information under a painting. Read the information and answer the questions.

Georgia O'Keeffe

White Rose with Larkspur

Museum of Fine Arts

Boston, Massachusetts

1. Who is the artist?_____

2. Where is the painting? In the_____

3. What is the name of her painting?_____

4. Where is the Museum of Fine Arts? It's in _____

2 | THE HERMITAGE AND RODIN
Grammar Notes 1–7

Complete the questions. Use **What's**, **Where's**, *and* **Why is**.

1. Q: _____ the Hermitage?
   A: It's a museum.

2. Q: _____ the Hermitage?
   A: It's in Saint Petersburg.

3. Q: _____ Saint Petersburg?
   A: It's in Russia.

4. Q: _____ the name of that sculpture?
   A: *Eternal Spring*.

5. Q: _____ there a special Rodin room?
   A: Because he was the most famous sculptor of the early 20th century.

3 | SURREALISM
Grammar Notes 1–7

Read about surrealism. Read the answers. Then write the questions. Use the question word in parentheses.

Surrealism is a painting style of the early 1900s. Surrealist artists use their dreams in their art. René Magritte and Salvador Dali are famous surrealist artists. Magritte is from Belgium. Dali is from Spain. Dali's most famous painting is *The Persistence of Memory*. Do you like it?

1. (What) **Q:** _____

   A: It's a painting style.

2. (Who) **Q:** _____

   A: They are surrealist artists.

3. (Where) **Q:** _____

   A: Magritte is from Belgium and Dali is from Spain.

4. (What) **Q:** _____

   A: *The Persistence of Memory*.

4 | EDITING

Read the conversation. There are four mistakes. The first mistake is already corrected.

1. A: What͎'s the name of this class?

   B: Art History 101.

2. A: Who the teacher is?

   B: Professor Good.

3. A: Where he is?

   B: He's next to the board. He's the tall man with the gray beard.

4. A: Why the students are so quiet?

   B: There's a test today.

Communication Practice

5 | LISTENING

🎧 *Listen to the conversation. Then complete the answers.*

1. Q: What is the gift?   A: It's _____

2. Q: Who is the artist?   A: John's _____

3. Q: Where is his gallery?   A: It's on _____

4. Q: Why is it closed?   A: _____

6 | WHAT DO YOU KNOW ABOUT ART AND ARTISTS?

A *Work in small groups. One student reads the answer. The others ask the question.*

Example: A: She is a famous American artist. She paints large flowers.
B: Who is Georgia O'Keeffe?

1. It is a museum. It is in Saint Petersburg, Russia.

2. He is a surrealist artist. He is from Spain.

3. He is a surrealist artist. He is from Belgium.

4. It is in Boston. It is a big museum. It has a painting by Georgia O'Keeffe.

5. He is a sculptor. He is from France. Some of his sculptures are in Russia.

B *With your group, write two sentences about artists. Your class asks the questions.*

7 | ON THE INTERNET

📀 *Download a picture of a painting. Tell your class about it. Include the following information:*

Who's the artist?

Where's he or she from?

What's the name of the painting?

Why is it a great painting?

From **Grammar** to **Writing**
Connecting with And and But

1 | *Read these sentences.*

    1. a. He's tall. He's a good basketball player.

      b. He's tall, **and** he's a good basketball player.

    2. a. He's tall. He's a terrible basketball player.

      b. He's tall, **but** he's a terrible basketball player.

And adds information. *But* shows a surprise or contrast. We usually use a comma before *and* and *but* when they connect two sentences.

    Examples: The book is good, **and** it is easy to understand.
                  The book is good, **but** it is difficult to understand.

Do not use a comma to connect two descriptive adjectives.

    Examples: I am hungry **and** tired.
                  He is tired **but** happy.

2 | *Use **and** or **but** to complete the sentences.*

    1. She's friendly _____ popular.

    2. She's friendly _____ unpopular.

    3. Her last name is long, _____ it's hard to pronounce.

    4. Her last name is long, _____ it's easy to pronounce.

3 | *Use **and** or **but** to complete the story about Henry. Then write a story about someone who made a big change in his or her life.*

        Five years ago Henry was a banker. His home was big _____ expensive. His car was fast _____ fancy. His workday was long, _____ his work was stressful. He was rich, _____ he was stressed and unhappy.

        Today Henry works in a flower shop. His home is small _____ inexpensive. His car is old _____ small. His workday is short, _____ his work is relaxing. He isn't rich, _____ he's relaxed and happy.

Review Test

I *Read each conversation. Circle the letter of the underlined word or group of words that is not correct.*

1. A: <u>Where</u> is your <u>friend</u>?
        A   B

   B: <u>She's</u> <u>on</u> Paris.
        C   D

                 A B C D

2. A: <u>Is</u> Kaori <u>in work</u> now?
      A   B

   B: No, <u>she isn't</u>. She's <u>at home</u>.
           C   D

                 A B C D

3. A: <u>Who's</u> <u>on</u> Elm Street?
       A   B

   B: <u>A post office</u> and <u>a new bank</u>.
          C   D

                 A B C D

4. A: Is the bank <u>on the corner</u> Wood Street?
                  A

   B: No, <u>it's not</u>. It's <u>between</u> Wood Street <u>and</u> Main Street.
          B   C   D

                 A B C D

5. A: <u>Is</u> the <u>new bakery</u> <u>next to</u> the <u>building tall</u>?
      A   B   C   D

   B: No, it's next to the bookstore.

                 A B C D

6. A: <u>Where</u> are the <u>olds</u> <u>newspapers</u>?
       A   B   C

   B: They're <u>on the desk</u>.
              D

                 A B C D

II *Circle the letter of the correct word(s) to complete the sentences.*

1. It is _____.

   (A) a day sunny   **(C)** sunny days

   (B) a sunny day   **(D)** sunny day

                 A B C D

2. They are _____.

   (A) child   **(C)** a child

   (B) children   **(D)** a children

                 A B C D

(continued)

3. He is _____.

    (A) artists   **(C)** an artist

    (B) a artist   **(D)** an artists

                                                            A   B   C   D

4. Is this _____?

    (A) old rug   **(C)** rugs old

    (B) old rugs   **(D)** an old rug

A   B   C   D

5. The bank is _____.

    (A) next the post office   **(C)** next to the post office

    (B) next of the post office   **(D)** next at the post office

A   B   C   D

III   *Complete the sentences. Use **a** or **an** or Ø.*

1. He isn't _____ teacher. He's _____ student. He's _____ new student in this school.

2. She isn't _____ artist. She's _____ dancer.

3. They're _____ famous. They're _____ actors.

4. Our grammar class isn't long. It's _____ hour.

5. This is _____ hospital. It's near the university.

6. He's _____ uncle. She's _____ aunt.

7. This is _____ old photograph. It's _____ photograph of my grandparents as children. It's _____ special to me.

IV   *Use the words in the box to complete the conversations.*

What   Where   Who   Why

1. **A:** _____ is your school?

   B: It's on Main Street.

2. **A:** _____ are your teachers?

   B: Ms. Thomas and Mr. James.

3. **A:** _____ is the school closed today?

   B: It's a holiday.

4. **A:** _____ is the name of your textbook?

   B: *Focus on Grammar.*

V *Look at the street. Use the word(s) in parentheses to complete the sentences.*

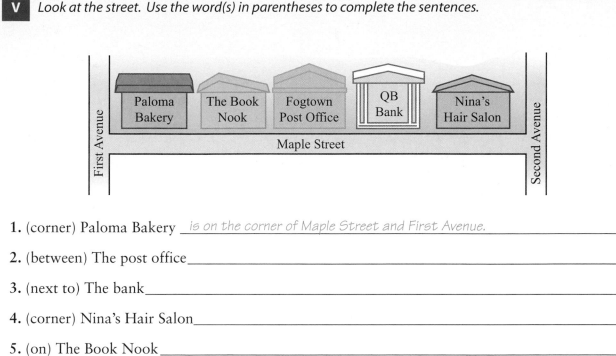

1. (corner) Paloma Bakery ___*is on the corner of Maple Street and First Avenue.*___

2. (between) The post office_____

3. (next to) The bank_____

4. (corner) Nina's Hair Salon_____

5. (on) The Book Nook_____

▶ *To check your answers, go to the Answer Key on page RT-1.*

PART III

The Simple Present

8 The Simple Present: Affirmative and Negative Statements

Grammar in Context

BEFORE YOU READ

	YES	NO
I shop for clothes often.	☐	☐
I don't shop for clothes often.	☐	☐
I look at the labels.	☐	☐
I don't look at the labels.	☐	☐

Complete the sentences.

I like to buy clothes at _____

I buy most of my clothes at _____

TEENAGE GIRLS'
FAVORITE SHOP!
STORES

UK	Topshop
France	H&M
Germany	H&M
United States	Old Navy

🎧 *Read a magazine article about teenage shoppers in Japan.*

TEEN TRENDS

Yumi **is** seventeen years old. She**'s** a senior in high school in Japan. Yumi **wears** "kawaii" boots, jeans, and sunglasses. And she **carries** a "kawaii" camera phone. "Kawaii" **is** a Japanese word. It **means** cute. Yumi **uses** the word a lot. She **doesn't buy** "non-kawaii" things.

Businesses **look** at Yumi and her friends. They **study** their clothes. Companies **know** that Yumi **is** not alone. There **are** many other teens like Yumi.

Yumi and her friends **buy** the same things. They **want** to look the same. Their clothes **don't** always **cost** a lot. But the number of teenage shoppers **is** big. And that **means** a lot of money for businesses.

In the 1990s, college girls were the trendsetters—they were the first to start a

trend. Now it**'s** high school girls. Maybe in the future it will be junior high school girls. And it**'s** not just girls. Nowadays guys **shop** and **want** a certain "look" too.

AFTER YOU READ

A *Mark these statements* **T** *(true) or* **F** *(false).*

_____ **1.** Yumi wears boots.

_____ **2.** Yumi works for a company.

_____ **3.** Yumi has friends.

_____ **4.** "Kawaii" means cute.

_____ **5.** Yumi doesn't look like her friends.

_____ **6.** Teenage boys don't like clothes.

B *In Japan girls like "kawaii" things. In the United States teens want "cool" things. Korean teens want "zahng" things. Mexican teens say, "Esta padre." In the Dominican Republic they say, "Que chulo." What do people say in your country to describe something they like? Tell your class.*

Grammar Presentation

THE SIMPLE PRESENT: AFFIRMATIVE AND NEGATIVE STATEMENTS

Affirmative Statements	
Subject	Verb
I You* We They	**work.**
He She It	**works.**

Negative Statements		
Subject	*Do not /Does not*	Base Form of Verb
I You* We They	**do not** **don't**	**work.**
He She It	**does not** **doesn't**	**work.**

* *You* is both singular and plural.

GRAMMAR NOTES

1. Use the **simple present** to tell about **things that happen again and again** (habits, regular occurrences, customs, and routines).

Now
Past — X —— X ——|—— X —— X ——▶ Future
*She **shops** every Saturday.*

EXAMPLES

- She **drinks** green tea.
- He **shops** at the mall.
- They **give** gifts on New Year's Day.
- She **goes** to bed at midnight.

(continued)

| **2.** Use the simple present to tell **facts**. | • This jacket **costs** sixty dollars.
• The word "kawaii" **means** cute. |

| **3.** Use the simple present with **non-action verbs**. | • She **is** seventeen years old.
• She **likes** that store. |

| **4.** In **affirmative statements**, use the **base form** of the verb for all persons except the third person singular.

Put **-s** or **-es** on the third person singular (*he/she/it*). | • **I want** a new sweater. **You need** a new suit. **They have** a car.
• **She wants** a camera phone.
• **He watches** TV every day. |

| **5.** PRONUNCIATION NOTE: Pronounce the third person singular ending /s/, /z/, or /ɪz/. | • /s/ He like**s** music.
• /z/ She play**s** golf.
• /ɪz/ He watch**es** TV every day. |

| **6.** In **negative statements**, use *does not* or *do not* before the base form of the verb.

Use the contractions *doesn't* and *don't* in speaking or in informal writing.

▶ **BE CAREFUL!** When *or* connects two verbs in a negative statement, we do not repeat *don't* or *doesn't* before the second verb. | • He **does not wear** ties.
• We **do not shop** there.
• He **doesn't wear** ties.
• We **don't shop** there.
• They **don't live or work** there.
• He **doesn't work or study** on weekends.
NOT: He doesn't work or ~~doesn't~~ study on weekends. |

| **7.** The **third person singular affirmative** forms of *have*, *do*, and *go* are <u>not regular</u>.

The **third person singular negative** form of *have*, *do*, and *go* are <u>regular</u>. | • She **has** a new coat.
• He **does** the laundry on Saturday.
• He **goes** to the gym at ten.
• She **doesn't have** a new hat.
• He **doesn't do** laundry on Sunday.
• He **doesn't go** to the gym at eleven. |

| **8.** The verb *be* has different forms from all other verbs. | • I **am** tired. I **look** tired.
• You **are** tall. You **look** tall.
• He **is** bored. He **looks** bored. |

Reference Notes
See Unit 27, page 267 for a fuller discussion of non-action verbs.
See Appendix 16, page A-17 for spelling and pronunciation rules for the third person singular in the simple present.
See Unit 1 for a complete presentation of the verb *be*.

Focused Practice

1 | DISCOVER THE GRAMMAR

Circle the correct word to complete the sentence.

1. My grandfather wear / (wears) a suit every day.

2. My brothers like / likes jeans and t-shirts.

3. His teacher know / knows about fashion.

4. I carry / carries my cell phone in my bag.

5. They shop / shops online.

6. The word "cool" mean / means different things.

7. You have / has a cool jacket.

2 | NEGATIVE STATEMENTS   *Grammar Notes 6, 8*

Underline the verb in the first sentence. Complete the second sentence in the negative. Use the same verb.

1. He shops at flea markets. He _____ *doesn't shop* _____ at chain stores.

2. We buy name brands. They _____ name brands.

3. I like jeans. I _____ suits.

4. I need a new jacket. I _____ a new coat.

5. She likes leather. He _____ leather.

6. It looks good. It _____ tight.

7. We are twenty years old. We _____ teenagers.

8. It is expensive. It _____ on sale.

3 | AFFIRMATIVE AND NEGATIVE STATEMENTS   *Grammar Notes 1–4, 6, 7*

Write affirmative or negative statements. Use the verb in parentheses.

1. (cost) **a.** It's expensive. It _____ *costs* _____ a lot.

    b. It's cheap. It _____ *doesn't cost* _____ a lot.

2. (need) **a.** I'm cold. I _____ a sweater.

    b. I'm hot. I _____ a sweater.

3. (want) **a.** His jacket is old. He _____ a new one.

     b. His jacket is new. He _____ a new one.

4. (like) **a.** We _____ window shopping. We often look at store windows.

     b. They _____ window shopping. They never look at store windows.

5. (have) **a.** He's rich. He _____ a lot of money.

     b. She's poor. She _____ a lot of money.

6. (go)   **a.** He loves to swim. He _____ swimming twice a week.

     b. She doesn't like to swim. She _____ swimming often.

---

4 | ADVICE COLUMN

Grammar Notes 1–4, 6–8

A *Complete the letter. Use the verbs in parentheses.*

Dear Rosa,

Our son _____*is*_____ fourteen years old. He _____ a good student, and he
      1. (be)   **2. (be)**

_____ a lot of friends. But we _____ one big problem with him. He
 3. (have)   **4. (have)**

_____ clothes. He _____ all the latest styles. And he _____
 5. (love)   **6. (want)**   **7. (prefer)**

designer clothes. We _____ poor, but I _____ it is wrong to spend a lot of
             8. (be, not)   **9. (think)**

money on clothes, especially for a growing boy.

    We _____ him spending money, but he _____ enough to buy all the
       10. (give)   **11. (have, not)**

clothes he wants. Now he _____ to get a part-time job. I _____ him to
              12. (want)   **13. (want, not)**

work, but my husband _____ it's okay. What do you think?
            14. (think)

                                           Worried Mom

B *Complete the letter to "Worried Mom." Use the words in the box.*

agree	sounds	thinks	want	works

Dear Worried Mom,

    Most teens _____ to look like their friends. It's very

normal. And I _____ with your husband. When a person

_____, that person _____ about the cost of things.

A job for your son _____ fine to me.

                                Rosa

5 | EDITING

Correct this paragraph. There are eight mistakes. The first mistake is already corrected.

     Miyuki Miyagi ~~live~~ *lives* in Japan. She work for a big advertising company. She studies teenagers. She say, "Teenagers change things. They doesn't think like the manufacturers. Manufacturers thinks of one way to use things. Teenagers find another way. For example, pagers are for emergencies. But teenagers are think they're fun and cute. They don't uses them for emergencies. They uses them for fun."

Communication Practice

6 | LISTENING

🎧 *Underline the verb in each sentence. Then listen to each sentence and check (✓) the sound of the verb ending. (See Appendix 16, page A-17 for an explanation of these endings.)*

	/s/	/z/	/ɪz/
1. He <u>shops</u> a lot.	✓		
2. She buys clothes at discount stores.			
3. She uses that word a lot.			
4. It costs a hundred dollars.			
5. He knows his business.			
6. She carries a cell phone.			
7. He misses her.			
8. She watches fashion shows on TV.			
9. He thinks about his clothes.			

7 | MY PARTNER AND I

Check (✓) the sentences that are true for you.

1. _____ I wear colorful clothes. _____ I don't wear colorful clothes.

2. _____ I like leather jackets. _____ I don't like leather jackets.

3. _____ I have more than three pairs of jeans. _____ I don't have more than three pairs of jeans.

4. _____ I buy designer clothes. _____ I don't buy designer clothes.

5. _____ I like to look at fashion magazines. _____ I don't like to look at fashion magazines.

6. _____ I like unusual clothes. _____ I don't like unusual clothes.

7. _____ I wear traditional clothes on holidays. _____ I don't wear traditional clothes on holidays.

Work with a partner. In what ways are you and your partner alike? In what ways are you different?

Example: We don't wear colorful clothes. We like dark colors like black and gray.
     I like leather jackets, but Juan doesn't.

8 | CLOTHES AND CUSTOMS FROM AROUND THE WORLD

| Argentina | China | Denmark | India | Japan | the United States |

Work with a partner. First circle the correct form of the verbs. Then guess the country.

1. People in _____ (don't wear / doesn't wear) shoes in their homes. When Sho (come / comes) home, he (remove / removes) his shoes and (put / puts) on slippers.

2. In Southern _____, the *gauchos* [cowboys] (wear / wears) baggy pants and hats with wide brims.

3. Most women (wear / wears) saris in _____. It (take / takes) six meters of cloth to make a sari.

4. On New Year's Day in _____, parents and grandparents (give / gives) children money in red envelopes.

5. In _____ people usually (don't work / doesn't work) on July 4. They (have / has) barbecues and (watch / watches) fireworks.

6. Eric Olson is from _____. On New Year's Eve he (bang / bangs) on his friends' doors and sets off fireworks.

Now check your answers below.

9 | WRITING

Think about a person you know. Write about his or her job.

Example: Jill goes to work at 4:30 in the morning. She works for a TV news channel. She does the makeup for a news anchor. Jill works only four hours a day. People say, "Jill is good at her job. She's an artist." The news anchor says, "I only want Jill. She's the best." Jill makes a good salary and she enjoys her work. But Jill has a secret. She doesn't want to be a makeup artist forever. In the afternoons Jill studies journalism. Jill really wants to be a news anchor.

10 | ON THE INTERNET

 Find information and pictures of traditional clothes from one part of the world. Tell your class about the clothes.

Example: Traditional Mexican clothes are comfortable and beautiful. Men wear cotton shirts and pants. Sombreros (hats with wide brims) protect them from the sun. In cold weather, they wear ponchos. Women wear blouses and long, full skirts. They cover their heads with shawls called rebozos. Sometimes women use their rebozos to carry their babies.

Exercise 8
1. Japan, don't wear, comes, removes, puts   2. Argentina, wear   3. wear, India, takes   4. China, give   5. the United States, don't work, have, watch   6. Denmark, bangs

UNIT

9 The Simple Present: *Yes/No* Questions and Short Answers

Grammar in Context

BEFORE YOU READ

Do you share a room? Do you live alone? Do you have a roommate? Imagine you are looking for a roommate. What questions are important to ask?

🎧 *Colleges often use questionnaires to help students find the right roommate. Read this roommate questionnaire and two students' answers.*

ROOMMATE QUESTIONNAIRE

Names:	Dan Yes	Dan No	Jon Yes	Jon No	You Yes	You No
1. **Do** you **smoke**?		✓		✓		
2. **Does** smoking **bother** you?	✓			✓		
3. **Do** you **wake up** early?		✓		✓		
4. **Do** you **stay up** late?	✓		✓			
5. **Are** you neat?	✓		✓			
6. **Does** a messy room **bother** you?	✓		✓			
7. **Are** you quiet?		✓	✓			
8. **Are** you talkative?	✓			✓		
9. **Do** you **listen** to loud music?	✓		✓			
10. **Do** you **watch** a lot of TV?	✓		✓			
11. **Do** you **study** and **listen** to music at the same time?	✓		✓			
12. **Do** you **study** with the TV on?	✓		✓			

AFTER YOU READ

A *Mark these statements* **T** *(true) or* **F** *(false).*

_____ 1. Dan and Jon both smoke.

_____ 2. Dan and Jon wake up late.

_____ 3. Dan is neat, but Jon isn't.

_____ 4. Dan and Jon are quiet.

_____ 5. Dan and Jon listen to loud music.

_____ 6. Dan and Jon don't watch TV.

_____ 7. Dan and Jon study and listen to music at the same time.

B *Discuss with a partner.*

Are Dan and Jon a good match? If so, why? If not, why not?

C *Answer the questions for yourself. Compare your answers with a partner's. Are you and your partner a good match?*

Grammar Presentation

THE SIMPLE PRESENT: *YES/NO* QUESTIONS AND SHORT ANSWERS

Yes/No Questions			Short Answers						
Do/Does	Subject	Base Form of Verb	Affirmative				Negative		
Do	I you* we they	**work**?	Yes,	you I/we you they	**do.**	No,		you I/we you they	**don't.**
Does	he she it			he she it	**does.**			he she it	**doesn't.**

* *You* is both singular and plural.

(continued)

GRAMMAR NOTES   **EXAMPLES**

1. For *yes/no* **questions in the simple present**, use *do* or *does* before the subject. Use the base form of the verb after the subject.	subject base form • **Do** you **work**? • **Does** he **have** a roommate?

2. We usually use **short answers** in conversation. Sometimes we use **long answers**.	**Q:** Do you work at the bank? **A: Yes, I do.** OR **Yes, I work** at the bank. **Q:** Does he have a roommate? **A: Yes, he does.** OR **Yes, he has a roommate.**

3. Do not use *do* or *does* for *yes/no* questions with *be*.	• **Are** you from Ecuador? • **Is** he from France? NOT: ~~Do~~ are you from Ecuador? ~~Does~~ is he from France?

Reference Note
See Unit 2, page 14 for a discussion of *yes/no* questions with *be*.

Focused Practice

1 | DISCOVER THE GRAMMAR

Read about Dan and Jon.

In many ways Dan and Jon are alike. Both Dan and Jon like music and sports, but Dan likes popular music and Jon likes jazz. Both Dan and Jon like basketball, but Jon likes tennis and Dan doesn't. Dan and Jon are both neat. They don't like a messy room. They both like to go to bed late—after midnight. They watch about two hours of TV at night, and they study with the TV on. But in one way Dan and Jon are completely different. Dan is talkative, but Jon is quiet. Dan says, "We're lucky about that. It works out nicely. I talk, he listens." Jon says, "Uh-huh."

Match the questions and answers.

___b___ 1. Do they both like music and sports?

_____ 2. Do they like to go to bed early?

_____ 3. Does Dan like popular music?

_____ 4. Dan is talkative. Jon is quiet. Does it matter?

_____ 5. Do Dan and Jon like classical music?

a. It doesn't say.

b. Yes, they do.

c. Yes, he does.

d. No, they don't.

e. No, it doesn't.

2 | YES/NO QUESTIONS AND SHORT ANSWERS   *Grammar Notes 1–2*

*Complete the questions with **Do** or **Does** and the verb in parentheses. Then complete the short answers.*

1. **Q:** (listen) _____*Do*_____ you _____*listen*_____ to music?

   A: Yes, _____*we do*_____. OR Yes, _____*I do*_____.

2. **Q:** (have) _____ your roommate _____ a TV?

   A: No, she _____.

3. **Q:** (know) _____ he _____ your brother?

   A: No, _____.

4. **Q:** (like) _____ they _____ Thai food?

   A: Yes, _____.

5. **Q:** (wear) _____ she _____ designer clothes?

   A: No, _____.

6. **Q:** (have) _____ your room _____ a big window?

   A: Yes, _____.

7. **Q:** (rain) _____ it _____ a lot in your city?

   A: No, _____.

8. **Q:** (have) _____ I _____ Internet access?

   A: Yes, _____.

9. **Q:** (go) _____ she _____ to school by train?

   A: No, _____.

3 | YES/NO QUESTIONS: THE SIMPLE PRESENT

Grammar Notes 1–3

Complete the **yes/no** questions with **Do**, **Does**, **Am**, **Is**, or **Are**. Then complete the short answers.

1. Q: ____*Am*____ I late? A: No, _____*you aren't*_____.

2. Q: _____ he come late? A: Yes, _____.

3. Q: _____ you busy? A: Yes, we _____.

4. Q: _____ they have a lot of work? A: No, _____.

5. Q: _____ they roommates? A: No, _____.

6. Q: _____ they live in a dormitory? A: Yes, _____.

7. Q: _____ she your sister? A: No, _____.

8. Q: _____ you live at home? A: Yes, I _____.

9. Q: _____ your roommate play tennis? A: No, he _____.

10. Q: _____ we in the right room? A: Yes, you _____.

11. Q: _____ you friends? A: Yes, _____.

12. Q: _____ you cook well? A: No, I _____.

4 | A ROOMMATE

Grammar Notes 1– 2

Complete the conversation. Write the questions and short answers. Use the words in parentheses. Use **do**, **don't**, **does**, or **doesn't** in every question and answer.

🎧 Then listen and check your work.

A: So tell me about your new roommate. _____*Do you like*_____ him?
                                          1. (you / like)

B: _____*Yes, I do*_____. He's a really nice guy.
          2.

A: I know he speaks English fluently, but he's not American. _____ from
                                                              3. (he / come)

England?

B: _____. He comes from Australia.
          4.

A: Oh? _____ from Sydney?
           5. (he / come)

B: _____. He comes from Melbourne.
          6.

A: What's he studying?

B: Music.

A: _____ the same kind of music?
        7. (you / like)

B: _____. We both like classical music. He has a good CD player and
        8.

hundreds of CDs.

A: _____ relatives here?
        9. (he / have)

B: _____. His uncle and aunt live here. I was at their home last night.
        10.

A: Really? _____ them often?
        11. (you / see)

B: _____. They invite the two of us for a meal at least once a month. They're
        12.

great cooks and interesting people. He's a conductor and she's an opera singer.

A: _____ them a small gift when you visit?
        13. (you / bring)

B: _____. I'm a poor student.
        14.

A: Hey, you're not that poor.

5 | EDITING

Read these conversations. There are eight mistakes. The first mistake is already corrected.

1. **A:** Does she ~~goes~~ *go* to school?

   B: Yes, she goes.

2. **A:** Does he needs help?

   B: Yes, he does.

3. **A:** Do they are like jazz?

   B: Yes, they do.

4. **A:** Do she live near the museum?

   B: Yes, she lives.

5. **A:** Does he has a roommate?

   B: Yes, he does.

6. **A:** Are you friends?

   B: Yes, we do.

Communication Practice

6 | LISTENING

🎧 *Andrea wants a roommate. She is talking to Valentina Gold. Ms. Gold helps people find roommates. Listen to Andrea's answers. Complete the chart. Then read Gloria's answers.*

	Andrea	**Gloria**
likes		parties
listens to		rock
plays	✗	basketball, soccer, tennis
studies		at night, in her room

Are they a good match? ☐ Yes ☐ No

Reason 1: _____

Reason 2: _____

7 | FIND SOMEONE WHO . . .

Find out about your classmates. Ask these questions or add your own. Take notes. Tell the class something new about three classmates.

Do you _____?

- speak more than two languages
- cook well
- know tai chi
- know sign language
- play a musical instrument
- have more than four sisters and brothers

Your question: _____

_____?

Are you _____?

- an only child
- a good dancer
- good at a sport
- clean
- messy
- easy-going

Your question: _____

_____?

8 | A TREASURE HUNT

Work in small groups. Ask questions. Check (✓) the items you have. The first group to check ten items wins.

Example: Do you have a stamp?   OR   Does anyone have a stamp?

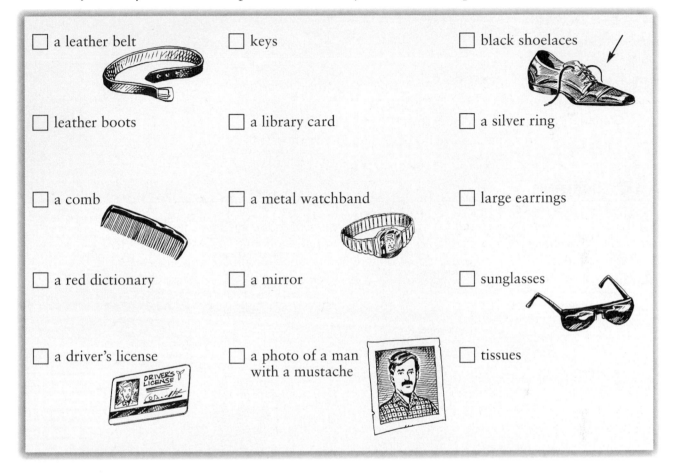

☐ a leather belt

☐ keys

☐ black shoelaces

☐ leather boots

☐ a library card

☐ a silver ring

☐ a comb

☐ a metal watchband

☐ large earrings

☐ a red dictionary

☐ a mirror

☐ sunglasses

☐ a driver's license

☐ a photo of a man with a mustache

☐ tissues

9 | PHRASES WITH *DO* AND *DOES*

A *Work in pairs. Complete the short conversations. Use the sentences in the box. Practice them with your partner.*

No, it's broken.	Yes, thanks. We need a salad.
No. I'm busy all afternoon.	Yes. It's 9:45.
Yes, it's more than two hundred dollars.	

1. **A:** Do you have time?

   B: _____

2. **A:** I have a class at 10:00. Do you have the time?

   B: _____

(continued)

3. A: Do you need any help?

   B: _____

4. A: Does it cost a lot?

   B: _____

5. A: Does it work?

   B: _____

B *Use one of the conversations above in a role play with your partner.*

Example: **A:** Do you need any help?
               B: Yes, thanks. We need a salad. Here's the lettuce.

10 | WRITING

You plan to study English at a school for international students during your vacation. The school matches you with a roommate. You receive this letter from your roommate. Answer the letter. Or write to the school. Explain why this person is or is not a good roommate for you.

> Hi,
>
> I understand you're my new roommate. I'm excited about our English language school, but I'm also a little nervous. Here's some information about me.
>
> My name is Sonia. I'm from a small town. I love English and I love to study—especially English grammar. I don't like TV or music. I'm not very neat. I usually go to bed at nine o'clock and get up at 6:00. I exercise every morning from 6:00 to 8:00.
>
> Please tell me about yourself. Do you come from a small town too? Do you like English grammar? Do you like to get up early?
>
> I hope we will be good friends. I look forward to your reply.
>
> Sincerely,
>
> Sonia

Example

> *Dear Sonia,*
>
>   *Thanks for your letter. I'm a little nervous too. Here's some information about me . . .*

11 | ON THE INTERNET

C *Some online services help people find roommates. Find out about a service like this. Report to the class.*

The Simple Present: *Wh-* Questions

Grammar in Context

BEFORE YOU READ

Do you dream? Do you remember your dreams? What do you dream about?

 Ask the Expert *is a radio talk show. Today Rob Stevens is talking to dream expert Helena Lee. Read their conversation.*

Rob Stevens: Good afternoon. I'm Rob Stevens. Welcome to *Ask the Expert*. This afternoon my guest is Helena Lee. She's the author of *Sleep and Dreams*. Thank you for coming.

Helena Lee: Thanks, Rob. It's great to be here.

Rob: Helena, we have a lot of questions about dreams. Our first question is from Carolina Gomes. She asks, **"Why do we dream?"**

Helena: That's a good question. Actually, nobody really knows why. But I think dreams help us understand our feelings.

Rob: OK. . . . Our next question is from Jonathan Lam. He asks, **"Who dreams?** Does everyone dream?"

Helena: Yes, everyone dreams. People dream in every part of the world. And what's more, scientists believe animals dream too.

Rob: Wow! That's really interesting. **How do we know?**

Helena: We have machines. They show when people or animals dream. But, of course, no one knows what animals dream about.

Rob: Our next question is from Pablo Ortiz. He writes, "People don't remember *all* their dreams. **What dreams do they remember?**"

Helena: People remember their unusual dreams. And, unfortunately, people remember their bad dreams, or nightmares.

Rob: Beata Green says, "I have the same dream again and again. **What does that mean?**"

Helena: That dream has special meaning for you. You need to think about it.

Rob: Here's a question from Samuel Diaz. **"When do people dream?"**

Helena: They dream during deep sleep. It's called REM sleep. REM means *rapid eye movement*.

Rob: I hear REM sleep is important. **Why do we need it?**

Helena: Without it, we can't remember or think clearly.

Rob: Our last question for today is from Mike Morgan. He writes, "My roommate doesn't remember his dreams. **Why do I remember my dreams?**"

Helena: Well, a University of Iowa professor says, "Creative people remember their dreams."

Rob: Thank you so much, Helena. We look forward to reading your new book.

AFTER YOU READ

Match the questions and answers.

___b___ 1. Who dreams?

_____ 2. What does *REM* mean?

_____ 3. Why are dreams good?

_____ 4. When do people dream?

_____ 5. What do animals dream about?

a. Nobody knows.

b. Everyone does.

c. They dream during REM sleep.

d. It stands for rapid eye movement.

e. They help us understand our feelings.

Grammar Presentation

THE SIMPLE PRESENT: *WH-* QUESTIONS; SHORT AND LONG ANSWERS

Wh- Questions				
Wh- Word	*Do/Does*	Subject	Base Form of Verb	
When	**do**	I	**sleep**?	
Where	**do**	you	**sleep**?	
What	**do**	we	**need**?	
Why	**does**	he	**get up**	late?
Who(m)	**does**	she	**dream**	about?
How	**does**	it	**feel**?	

Short Answers
From 10:00 P.M. to 5:00 A.M.
On the futon.
Two pillows.
He goes to bed late.
A movie star.
Good.

Long Answers
You sleep from 10:00 P.M. to 5:00 A.M.
I sleep on the futon.
We need two pillows.
He gets up late because he goes to bed late.
She dreams about a movie star.
The blanket feels good.

Wh- Questions About the Subject		
Wh- Word	Verb	
Who	**dreams**?	
What	**happens**	during REM sleep?

Answers
Everyone does.
People dream.

GRAMMAR NOTES

EXAMPLES

1. ***Wh-* questions** ask for <u>information</u>. Most questions use a ***wh-* word** + ***do*** or ***does*** + **a subject** + **the base form of the verb**.	*Wh-* word *do/does* subject base form **Q:** When do you go to bed? **Q:** What does he dream about?

(continued)

2. To ask a question about the subject, use *who* or *what* + **the third-person singular form of the verb.**

▶ **BE CAREFUL!** Do not use *do* or *does* with questions about the subject. Do not use the base form of the verb.

- **Who sleeps** on the futon?
  subject
  My brother sleeps on the futon.
- **What helps** you fall asleep?
  subject
- Milk helps me fall asleep.

  NOT: Who ~~does~~ sleeps on the futon?

  NOT: Who ~~do~~ sleeps on the futon?

  NOT: Who ~~sleep~~ on the futon?

3. *Who* asks questions about a <u>subject</u>. *Who* and *whom* ask questions about an <u>object</u>.

USAGE NOTE: *Whom* is very formal.

-              subject
  Who helps John? Mary does.
-           object
  Who does Mary help? John.
-           object
  Whom does Mary help? John.

Reference Note
For more about *who*, *what*, *where*, and *why*, see Unit 7, page 60.
For more about *when*, see Unit 11, page 104.

Focused Practice

1 | DISCOVER THE GRAMMAR

get dressed	get up	stay up	wake up

Night owls like to stay up late at night. Early birds get up early. Read about a night owl and an early bird. Then match the questions and answers.

    Doug is a night owl. He hates to get up in the morning. On weekends, he goes to bed at 1:00 A.M. and gets up at noon. Unfortunately for Doug, his first class starts at 8:15, and he needs to get up early.

    At 7:00 A.M. Doug's alarm rings. He wakes up, but he doesn't get up. He stays in bed and daydreams. At 7:20 his mom comes in. She has a big smile. She says, "Dougie, it's time to get up."

    Doug's mother is an early bird. Even on vacations she is up at 6:00 A.M. When his mom wakes him, Doug says, "Leave me alone. I'm tired."

    Finally, at about 7:30, Doug gets up. He jumps out of bed, showers, and gets dressed. At 7:50 he drinks a big glass of juice, takes a breakfast bar, and runs to the bus stop. The bus comes at 8:00.

_f_ 1. Who hates to get up in the morning?

_____ 2. How does Doug feel in the morning?

_____ 3. Why does Doug run to the bus stop?

_____ 4. What does Doug have for breakfast?

_____ 5. When does Doug sleep late?

_____ 6. What happens at 7:00?

a. On weekends.

b. Tired.

c. Doug's alarm rings.

d. A glass of juice and a breakfast bar.

e. Because he doesn't want to miss the bus.

f. Doug does.

2 | WORD ORDER OF *WH-* QUESTIONS   *Grammar Notes 1–3*

Write questions. Use the words given.

1. do / you / usually get up / When

    A: _When do you usually get up?_____

    B: At 7:00 on weekdays.

2. Where / sleep / the baby / does

    A: _____

    B: In our bedroom.

3. at night / they / How / do / feel

    A: _____

    B: They're never tired at night. They're night owls.

4. does / Who / she / dream about

    A: _____

    B: She dreams about me.

5. What / he / dream about / does

    A: _____

    B: He dreams about cars.

6. Who /daydreams

    A: _____

    B: John does.

3 | DOUG'S ROUTINE
Grammar Notes 1–3

Read the answers. Then ask questions about the underlined words.

1. Doug wakes up <u>at 7:00</u>.

   When does Doug wake up?

2. School begins <u>at 8:15</u>.

   _____

3. Doug has lunch <u>in the school cafeteria</u>.

   _____

4. Doug has <u>a hamburger and french fries</u> for lunch on Mondays.

   _____

5. Doug meets <u>Noah</u> at the soccer field after school.

   _____

6. <u>Doug and Noah</u> play soccer in West Park.

   _____

7. Doug feels <u>tired</u> after soccer practice.

   _____

8. Doug stays up late <u>because he has a lot of homework</u>.

   _____

4 | QUESTIONS ABOUT THE SUBJECT AND OBJECT
Grammar Notes 2–3

*Label the subject (**S**) and the object (**O**) in each sentence. Write one question about the subject and one question about the object. Then answer the questions. Use short answers.*

1. On Sunday mornings Sam calls his grandmother.
                   S   O

   Q: *Who calls his grandmother on Sunday mornings?*   A: *Sam does.*

   Q: *Who does Sam call on Sunday mornings?*   A: *His grandmother.*

2. My brother sees his friends after school.

   Q: _____ A: _____

   Q: _____ A: _____

3. My mother wakes me on weekdays.

   Q: _____ A: _____

   Q: _____ A: _____

4. Maria helps her neighbor.

   Q: _____   A: _____

   Q: _____   A: _____

5. Shira and Carolina meet friends at a club on weekends.

   Q: _____   A: _____

   Q: _____   A: _____

5 | EDITING

Correct these questions. There are six mistakes. The first mistake is already corrected.

1. Where do they ~~sleeps~~ *sleep*?

2. Why they need two pillows?

3. Who sleep on the sofa?

4. When does she goes to bed?

5. Who wake you?

6. Who do you dream about?

7. How he feels about that?

Communication Practice

6 | LISTENING

🎧 *Diane often has the same dream. She tells a doctor about her dream. Listen to their conversation. Complete the answers.*

1. Where is Diane in her dream? She's in _____.

2. What does the man in her dream look like? He's tall. He has a _____.

3. What does he want to do? He wants to _____.

4. What happens? First she walks fast. Then _____. She runs. Then
   _____. Then _____.

5. What does Dr. Fox tell Diane? "You're _____. You need
   _____."

7 | SLEEPING HABITS

Answer the questions. Then work with a partner. Ask your partner the questions.

	You	Your Partner
When do you go to bed?		
What days do you sleep late?		
Does anyone wake you? If so, who?		
Do you dream? If so, what do you dream about?		
Are you an early bird or a night owl?		

8 | WHO DOES WHAT?

Ask five students these questions. Take notes.

Example: YOU: Juan, do you snore?
JUAN: No, I don't, but my sister Bianca snores.

1. Who snores?
2. Who gets up before 6:00 A.M.?
3. Who goes to bed after midnight?
4. Who needs more than eight hours of sleep?
5. Who needs less than five hours of sleep?
6. Who dreams in English?
7. Who daydreams?
8. Who has insomnia? (trouble sleeping)

Tell the class interesting results.

Example: Juan's sister snores. Nobody gets up before 6:00 A.M., but sometimes Hasan goes to bed at 5:00 A.M.

9 | INFORMATION GAP: UNDERSTANDING DREAMS

Student B, turn to page 100.

A *Student A, Student B often has a dream. Find out about Student B's dream. Ask these questions.*

In your dream:

Where are you?	How do you look?
Who do you see?	What does the person say?
How does the person look?	What do you do?

Student A, you have the following dream again and again. Read about your dream. Then answer Student B's questions about it.

You are on an airplane. The pilot comes to you. He says, "I need your help." You go with the pilot. You fly the plane. You land the plane. Everyone claps. You feel good. You wake up.

B *Talk about your dreams. What do they mean?*

10 | ON THE INTERNET

Look on the Internet for "help for insomnia." Report to the class.

Questions to answer for your report:

What do people do for insomnia?	Why do they get insomnia?
What do they drink?	Where do they go for help for insomnia?
What do they eat?	

III

From **Grammar** to **Writing**
Time Word Connectors: First, Next, After that, Then, Finally

1 | *Which paragraph sounds better, **A** or **B**? Why?*

Paragraph A

I like to watch my roommate prepare tea. She boils water and pours the boiling water in a cup with a teabag in it. She removes the teabag and adds sugar. She adds lemon. She adds ice. She sips the tea and says, "Mmm. This tea is just the way I like it."

Paragraph B

I like to watch my roommate prepare tea. First, she boils some water and pours the boiling water in a cup with a teabag in it. Next, she removes the teabag and adds some sugar. After that, she adds some lemon. Then she adds some ice. Finally, she sips the tea and says, "Mmm. This tea is just the way I like it."

You can make your writing clearer by using **time word connectors**. They show the order in which things happen. Some common ones are: *first*, *next*, *after that*, *then*, and *finally*. We usually use a **comma** after these connectors.

Example: **First,** you add the water. **Next,** you add the sugar.

2 | *Use time word connectors to show the order of things in this paragraph.*

I take a shower. I have breakfast. I drive to the train station. I take a train and a bus.
I get to work.

Now write a paragraph about a routine you follow. Use time word connectors. Here are some ideas:
Every Saturday morning . . .
Every New Year's Day . . .
Every year on my birthday . . .

Review Test

I *Read each conversation. Circle the letter of the underlined word or group of words that is not correct.*

1. A: <u>Do</u> you <u>have</u> a good dictionary?   **A B C D**
         A   B

   B: Yes, I <u>have</u>. <u>It's</u> on my desk.
             C   D

2. A: <u>Where</u> does he <u>works</u>?   **A B C D**
         A   B

   B: He <u>works</u> at the bank <u>next to</u> the supermarket.
           C   D

3. A: <u>Does</u> he <u>need</u> a doctor?   **A B C D**
         A   B

   B: Yes, he <u>needs</u>. He <u>has</u> a terrible earache.
             C   D

4. A: <u>Why</u> do you <u>work</u> at night?   **A B C D**
         A   B

   B: <u>When</u> I <u>study</u> during the day.
         C   D

5. A: <u>Do</u> you <u>have</u> any sweatshirts in medium?   **A B C D**
         A   B

   B: Yes, we <u>are</u> <u>have</u> sweatshirts in all sizes.
             C   D

6. A: Irina doesn't <u>to</u> <u>live</u> in California.   **A B C D**
                  A B

   B: <u>Where</u> does she <u>live</u>?
         C   D

7. A: <u>Who</u> <u>does</u> Carol usually <u>eats</u> lunch with?   **A B C D**
         A   B   C

   B: She usually <u>eats</u> with Dan and Jon.
               D

II *Complete the sentences. Use the present tense of the verb in parentheses.*

1. _____ you _____ a suit?
                          (need)

2. He _____ the windows once a month.
        (wash)

3. Marcia _____ a sister and a brother.
             (have)

(continued)

4. Paul _____ a lawyer.
   (be, not)

5. Mrs. Smith _____ lamps.
   (fix)

6. Pete _____ to the park on Tuesdays.
   (go)

7. She _____ the dishes every morning.
   (do)

8. _____ your sister _____ English?
   (speak)

9. _____ the students _____ uniforms to school?
   (wear)

10. We _____ turkey for breakfast.
    (eat, not)

11. My uncle often _____ about his family.
    (worry)

12. Who _____ next to the Salazars?
    (live)

13. What _____ you happy?
    (make)

14. What time _____ your father _____ home from work?
    (come)

15. Where _____ they _____ their money?
    (keep)

III   *Read the first sentence. Complete the second sentence. Use the affirmative or negative of the verb in parentheses.*

1. I like blue. I _____ a lot of blue shirts.
   (have)

2. His jacket is old and worn. He _____ a new jacket.
   (need)

3. I have a lot of sweaters. I _____ to buy any more.
   (need)

4. That book is for level 8. We're in level 3. It _____ for our class.
   (be)

5. I don't like sweet things. I _____ a lot of cake or cookies.
   (eat)

6. We don't live in an apartment. We _____ in a house.
   (live)

7. I only play music in the early evening. I _____ music late at night.
   (play)

8. He knows three languages. He _____ Polish, Russian, and a little English.
   (speak)

9. She eats out almost every day. She _____ often.
   (cook)

10. He's a lawyer. He _____ a suit to work every day.
    (wear)

IV *Use the words in parentheses to complete the questions and short answers. Use the simple present tense.*

1. A: _____ your new roommate?
   a. (you/like)

   B: Yes, _____. I like him a lot.
   b.

2. A: _____ a new camera?
   a. (he/need)

   B: No, _____. His old camera still works.
   b.

3. A: _____ fluent English?
   a. (they/speak)

   B: No, _____. They're in the first level.
   b.

4. A: _____ her?
   a. (I/know)

   B: Yes, _____. She lives in our building.
   b.

5. A: _____ your dreams?
   a. (you/remember)

   B: No, _____. I always forget them.
   b.

6. A: _____ a lot in your country?
   a. (it/rain)

   B: Yes, _____. That's why everything is so green.
   b.

7. A: _____ near you?
   a. (your brother/ live)

   B: No, _____. He lives far away.
   b.

V *Write* **yes/no** *and* **wh-** *questions. Use the simple present.*

1. "Amazing" means "surprising."

   What does "amazing" mean _____? It means "surprising."

2. Sachiko always wears a hat.

   a. _____? Sachiko does.

   b. _____? A hat.

3. Jasmine gets up at nine o'clock.

   a. _____? Yes, she does.

   b. _____? At nine o'clock.

   c. _____? Jasmine does.

   (continued)

4. My friend works at a restaurant.

a. _____? Yes, she does.

b. _____? My friend does.

c. _____? At a restaurant.

d. _____? She works at a restaurant.

5. Bob usually goes to bed after midnight.

a. _____? Bob does.

b. _____? After midnight.

VI *Correct the sentences.*

1. Dan like soccer.

2. She isn't write to me often.

3. Does your friend needs an umbrella?

4. Do they wants any help?

5. My aunt is teaches Spanish.

6. Who does cooks in your family?

7. They don't work or don't live near the
   train station.

8. What means that word?

9. How you spell your name?

10. When does you get up?

11. Why they shop there?

12. How feels he?

▶ *To check your answers, go to the Answer Key on page RT-1.*

| **INFORMATION GAP FOR STUDENT B** | *Unit 10, Exercise 9* |

A *Student B, you have the following dream again and again. Read about your dream.
Then answer Student A's questions about it.*

You are in the third grade. You see your third grade teacher. Your teacher is very
big. You are small. Your teacher says, "Your schoolwork is good. You are my
favorite student." You smile. Then you laugh. Then you wake up.

Student B, Student A often has a dream. Find out about Student A's dream. Ask these questions.

In your dream:

Where are you?

Who comes to you?

What does he say?

What do you do?

How do you feel?

What happens?

B *Talk about your dreams. What do they mean?*

PART IV

When, What + Noun; Prepositions of Time; Possessives; *This / That / These / Those; One / Ones / It*

Grammar in Context

BEFORE YOU READ

What's your favorite holiday? When is it?

Read this conversation between three high school friends.

ELECTION DAY

TONY: Hey Alex.

ALEX: Hey Tony, Dino. How're you doing?

TONY: OK. And you?

ALEX: Good. By the way, what's the next school holiday?

TONY: Election Day.

ALEX: **When** is it?

TONY: It's **on** the **first** Tuesday **in** November.

DINO: Not always.

TONY: Yes, it is.

DINO: No, it's not.

ALEX: Then **what day** is Election Day?

DINO: Election Day is **on** the **first** Tuesday after the **first** Monday **in** November. This year it's not **on** the **first** Tuesday **in** November.

TONY: OK, OK. You're such a genius.

AFTER YOU READ

Answer the questions.

1. When was Election Day in the United States in 2005? Circle it on the calendar.

2. In what month is Election Day in other countries?

NOVEMBER 2005						
SUNDAY	MONDAY	TUESDAY	WEDNESDAY	THURSDAY	FRIDAY	SATURDAY
		1	2	3	4	5
6	7	8	9	10	11	12
13	14	15	16	17	18	19
20	21	22	23	24	25	26
27	28	29	30			

Grammar Presentation

QUESTIONS WITH *WHEN* AND *WHAT* + NOUN; PREPOSITIONS OF TIME; ORDINAL NUMBERS

When			Answers
When	Verb		
When	is	Independence Day in the United States?	It's on July 4th. On July 4th. July 4th.

What + Noun			Answers
What	Noun		
What	**day**	is his graduation?	It's on Monday. On Monday. Monday.
What	**time**	does it start?	It's at 2:00. At 2:00. 2:00.

(continued)

Prepositions of Time	
Her graduation is	**in** December. **in** (the) winter. **in** 2007. **in** the morning. **in** the afternoon. **in** the evening.
Is your birthday	**on** Wednesday? **on** December 25th?
The party is	**at** 7:30. **at** night.

Ordinal Numbers		
1st = first	12th = twelfth	32nd = thirty-second
2nd = second	13th = thirteenth	40th = fortieth
3rd = third	14th = fourteenth	43rd = forty-third
4th = fourth	15th = fifteenth	50th = fiftieth
5th = fifth	16th = sixteenth	60th = sixtieth
6th = sixth	17th = seventeenth	70th = seventieth
7th = seventh	18th = eighteenth	80th = eightieth
8th = eighth	19th = nineteenth	90th = ninetieth
9th = ninth	20th = twentieth	100th = hundredth
10th = tenth	21st = twenty-first	101st = one hundred and first
11th = eleventh	30th = thirtieth	

GRAMMAR NOTES

EXAMPLES

1. Use *when* or *what* + **a noun** for questions about **time**.

Q: When is your party?
A: It's on Tuesday.
Q: What day is your party?
A: It's on Tuesday.
Q: What time is your party?
A: It's at 8:00.

2. We usually use **prepositions** when we answer questions about time.

in + month, seasons, years
- It's **in January**.
- Her graduation was **in 2003**.

in + the morning, the afternoon, the evening
- My son is at camp **in the afternoon**.

on + days of the week
- It's **on Mondays** and **Wednesdays**.

on + the date
- It's **on January 4**.

at + the exact time

at + night
- It's **at ten o'clock** in the morning and at eleven o'clock **at night**.

---

3. There are two kinds of numbers:

cardinal—*one, two, three*

ordinal—*first, second, third*

Use **cardinal numbers** to tell **how many** people, places, or things.
- She has **three classes** on Thursday.

Use **ordinal numbers** to number things in a **sequence**. The spelled form is used.
- Her **first class** is English. Her **second class** is math. Her **third class** is history.

  NOT: Her 1st class is English.

Use **ordinal numbers** for streets and floors of buildings.
- Her apartment is on **Seventy-seventh Street**. It's on the **second floor**.

USAGE NOTE: For dates with the month and day, we usually use the cardinal number in writing. We always use the ordinal number in speaking.
- Writing: The conference is on **November 25**.

  Speaking: "His birthday is on **November 25th**."

Reference Notes
See Appendix 3, page A-3 for lists of cardinal and ordinal numbers, and for lists of the days, months, and seasons.
See Appendix 4, page A-4 for information about telling time.

Focused Practice

1 | DISCOVER THE GRAMMAR

Look at Karen's calendar. Then circle the correct day, date, time, and/or time of day of each event on the chart.

SEPTEMBER						
SUNDAY	MONDAY	TUESDAY	WEDNESDAY	THURSDAY	FRIDAY	SATURDAY
		1 yoga 6:00 P.M.	2	3	4 dentist 10:00 A.M.	5
6 Mary/ airport 10 P.M.	7 Labor Day	8 yoga 6:00 P.M.	9	10	11	12
13	14	15 yoga 6:00 P.M.	16	17	18	19
20	21	22 yoga 6:00 P.M.	23	24	25	26
27	28	29 yoga 6:00 P.M.	30			

Event	Day	Date	Time	Time of Day
Her yoga class is	Mondays on Tuesdays Wednesdays	✕	5:00 at 5:30 6:00	in the morning. in the afternoon. in the evening.
She has a dentist's appointment	Wednesday on Thursday Friday	2 September 3 4	9:00 at 10:00 11:00	in the morning. in the afternoon. in the evening.
Mary's plane arrives	Friday on Saturday Sunday	4 September 5 6	6:30 at 7:30 10:00	in the afternoon. in the evening. at night.
Labor Day is	Monday on Tuesday Wednesday	September _____	✕	✕

2 | CHINESE NEW YEAR

Complete the conversation. Choose from the words in parentheses.

KIM: What's your favorite holiday?

MEI: Chinese New Year. I really love the holiday.

KIM: When is it?

MEI: _____ January or February. It's on a different day every year. _____ 2004 it
     1. (In / On)   2. (In / On)

was _____ Thursday, January 22. That was the _____ day of the Year of the
    3. (in / on)   4. (one / first)

Monkey. _____ 2005, the Year of the Rooster, it was _____ February 9.
         5. (In / On)   6. (on / in)

KIM: Why does the Chinese New Year fall on different days?

MEI: It's based on a lunar calendar. There are _____ or _____ days in a lunar
                                                7. (29 / 29th)   8. (30 / 30th)

month. But 2001 was a special year.

KIM: Oh, yeah. Why?

MEI: It was a leap year.

KIM: Is that the same as a Western leap year?

MEI: No. In a Western calendar, every _____ years you add an extra day in February.
                                       9. (four / fourth)

In a Chinese leap year, you add an extra month.

KIM: So if you're born in that month, you don't get old as fast!

Year of the Monkey

Year of the Rooster

3 | DAN'S PARTY—CARDINAL AND ORDINAL NUMBERS

Grammar Note 3

Complete the conversation. Choose from the words in parentheses.

KAORI: When's Dan's Halloween party?

RUSS: _____ weeks from today—on October _____.
1. (Two / Second)   2. (thirty-one / thirty-first)

KAORI: Where does he live again?

RUSS: On _____ Street.
3. (Four / Fourth)

KAORI: Oh, yeah—the red building. What floor does he live on?

RUSS: The _____ floor.
4. (three / third)

KAORI: I love Dan's Halloween parties.

RUSS: I know. I remember his _____ party two years ago. It really was a lot of fun.
5. (one / first)

KAORI: His _____ party was great too.
6. (two / second)

4 | NATIONAL HOLIDAYS

Grammar Notes 1–3

NATIONAL HOLIDAYS

Australia—January 26th

Canada—July 1st

Korea—August 15th

Thailand—December 5th

Write questions. Then look at the flags and dates and answer the questions.

1. is / When / Australia's national holiday

Q: *When is Australia's national holiday?*

A: *It's on January 26.*

2. Thailand's / is / When / national holiday

Q: _____

A: _____

3. has / What country / on July 1 / a national holiday

Q: _____

A: _____

4. in August / has / a national holiday / What country

Q: _____

A: _____

5 | EDITING

Correct these sentences. There are six mistakes. The first mistake is already corrected.

1. Canadian Thanksgiving is on the second Monday ~~at~~ *in* October.

2. American Thanksgiving is on the four Thursday in November.

3. Many people at Japan visit the Palace on New Year's Day.

4. Labor Day is on the first Monday in September.

5. Americans celebrate Independence Day in July 4.

6. On Independence Day, many people watch fireworks in night.

7. New Year's Eve is in December 31.

Communication Practice

6 | LISTENING

Victor and Lisa are going to a party. They are confused. Listen to their conversation. Then listen again and complete the sentences.

1. John and Maria live _____ Avenue between _____ and _____ Avenue.

2. Their apartment is _____ floor.

3. John and Alice live _____ Street between _____ and _____ Avenue.

4. John and Alice's apartment is _____ floor.

7 | INFORMATION GAP: HOLIDAYS AROUND THE WORLD

Work in pairs. Student A, look at the chart on this page. Ask your partner questions to complete your chart.

Student B, look at the Information Gap on page 140 and follow the instructions there.

Examples: What country has a national holiday on _____? (date)
What month is _____'s national holiday?
What's the date of _____'s national holiday?
What country has a national holiday in _____? (month)
When is _____'s national holiday?

NATIONAL HOLIDAYS AROUND THE WORLD						
COUNTRY		MONTH	DAY	COUNTRY		MONTH	DAY
Argentina		July		Haiti		January	
Brazil		September		Italy			2
		April	16	Japan		December	22
Dominican Republic		February	27	Lebanon		November	22
Ecuador		August		Turkey		October	29
Greece			25	United States of America		July	4
Your country's national holiday:							

8 | SCHOOL HOLIDAYS

Work in small groups. Look at a school calendar. What are your school's holidays? When are they?

9 | WRITING

Write about your favorite holiday.

What is the name of the holiday? When is it? How long is it? What do you do? What do you wear? Why do you like this holiday?

Example

I'm from Changmai, Thailand. My favorite holiday is the Songkran Festival. It's the Thai New Year festival. This important Buddhist holiday usually falls in April and lasts for four days.

On the first day we clean our homes. That evening we put on our best clothes. On the second day we cook. On the third day we bring food to the temples and we begin throwing water on family and friends.

On the last day of the Songkran Festival we honor our grandparents and other older people by gently putting water on them and wishing them good luck and a happy future. Then we go outside and throw water on everyone. Water throwing is the best part of the holiday. The weather is very hot and the cold water feels great. Come to Changmai for the Songkran Festival. Bring a water gun, join the fun, and say, "Sawadee Pee Mai"—Happy New Year!

10 | ON THE INTERNET

Find out more about one of your school holidays. Tell your classmates about that day.

Example: Labor Day is on the first Monday in September. It's a holiday for workers. People celebrate it in the United States, Canada, and a few other countries. Many people celebrate the whole weekend. They have picnics and barbeques with friends and family. For many people, it marks the end of the summer. The holiday is over a hundred years old.

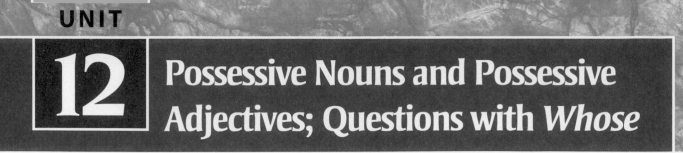

UNIT

12 Possessive Nouns and Possessive Adjectives; Questions with *Whose*

Grammar in Context

BEFORE YOU READ

Look at these sentences. Answer the questions.

My name is Michelle Young.
_____
_____

My name is Rick Mn.
_____
_____

1. Whose handwriting is neat?
   a. Michelle's   b. Rick's

2. Whose handwriting is difficult to read?
   a. Michelle's   b. Rick's

🎧 *A teacher has three papers without names. Read this conversation.*

WHOSE COMPOSITION IS THIS?

TEACHER: **Whose** composition is this?

BORIS: Is it a good paper?

TEACHER: It's excellent.

BORIS: It's **my** composition.

YOLANDA: No, that's not **your** handwriting. It's **Kim's** composition. **Her** name is right there. She's absent today.

TEACHER: Thanks, Yolanda. **Whose** paper is *this*?

BORIS: Is it a good paper?

TEACHER: It's OK.

BORIS: Then it's **my** composition.

JUAN: It's not **your** composition. It's **my** composition. See, **my** name is on the back.

TEACHER: OK, Juan. Here, Boris. *This* is **your** composition.

BORIS: Is it a good paper?

TEACHER: It needs some work.

BORIS: I don't think it's **my** composition.

TEACHER: Uh . . . I think it is. I have a grade for everyone else.

AFTER YOU READ

Write **Kim**, **Juan**, and **Boris** on their compositions.

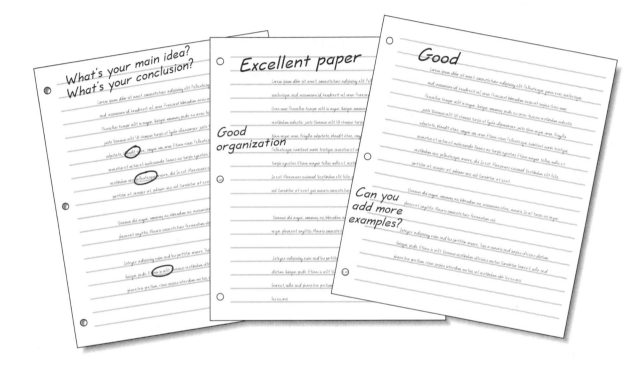

Grammar Presentation

POSSESSIVE NOUNS AND POSSESSIVE ADJECTIVES; QUESTIONS WITH *WHOSE*

Possessive Nouns	
Singular Nouns	**Plural Nouns**
John's last name is Tamez. **Russ's** last name is Stram.	The **girls'** gym is on this floor.
My **mother's** name is Rita. The **woman's** name is Carmen.	My **parents'** car is in the garage. The **women's** restroom is on the first floor.

(continued)

Possessive Adjectives		
Subject Pronouns	Possessive Adjectives	Example Sentences
I	**My**	I am a student. **My** name is Antonio.
You	**Your**	You are next to me. **Your** seat is here.
He	**His**	He is a professor. **His** subject is computers.
She	**Her**	She's my boss. **Her** name is Ms. Alvarado.
It	**Its**	It's my sister's dog. **Its** name is Lucky.
We	**Our**	We are businessmen. **Our** business is in the United States and Asia.
You	**Your**	You are students. **Your** class is in room 405.
They	**Their**	They are musicians. **Their** band is great.

Questions with *Whose*	
Questions	Answers
Whose hair is long?	Carmen**'s**. Carmen**'s** is. Carmen**'s** hair is long.
Whose eyes are green?	Svetlana**'s**. Svetlana**'s** are. Svetlana**'s** eyes are green.
Whose homework is this?	Yoko**'s**. It's Yoko**'s**. It's Yoko**'s** homework.
Whose books are these?	Ken**'s**. They're Ken**'s**. They're Ken**'s** books.

GRAMMAR NOTES

EXAMPLES

1. Possessive nouns and **possessive adjectives** show belonging.	• **Kim's car** (the car belongs to Kim) • **her car** (the car belongs to her)

2. Add an **apostrophe (')** + *s* to a **singular noun** to show possession.	• That's **Juan's** composition.
Add an **apostrophe (')** to a **plural noun** ending in *s* to show possession.	• My **grandparents'** home is next to my **parents'** home.
Add an **apostrophe (')** + *s* to an **irregular plural noun** to show possession.	• The **women's** restroom is on the first floor.

3. **Possessive adjectives** replace **possessive nouns**. Possessive adjectives agree with the possessive noun they replace.	• ~~My father's~~ ^{His} sisters are in Tokyo and Osaka. • ~~My mother's~~ ^{Her} brother is in Kyoto.

3. **Possessive adjectives** replace **possessive nouns**. Possessive adjectives agree with the possessive noun they replace.	His • ~~My father's~~ sisters are in Tokyo and Osaka. Her • ~~My mother's~~ brother is in Kyoto.

4. A **noun** always follows a possessive noun or a possessive adjective. ▶ **BE CAREFUL!** A noun + apostrophe + *s* does not always mean possession. *Anna's* sometimes means *Anna is*. Do not confuse *its* and *it's*. **its** = possessive adjective; ***it's*** = ***it is***	• Bekir's **book** is new. • His **book** is new. • **Anna's** late. (Anna **is** late.) • This is my turtle. **Its** name is Tubby. • **It's** a hot day.

5. Use *whose* for questions about possessions. ▶ **BE CAREFUL!** *Who's* is the short form of *who is*. It sounds like *whose*.	• **Whose** notebook is this? • **Who's** absent? • **Whose** name is not on the list?

Reference Note
See Appendix 10, page A-11 for more rules about **possessive nouns**.
See Appendix 9, page A-10 for more about irregular plural nouns.

Focused Practice

1 | DISCOVER THE GRAMMAR

Read about Kyoko's family.

My father is a pharmacist. My father's father is a pharmacist too.

My mother is a teacher. My father's mother is a teacher too.

My brother is an actor. My brother's wife is an actor too.

Look at Kyoko's family tree. Whose occupations do you know? Write their occupations on the line next to their photos.

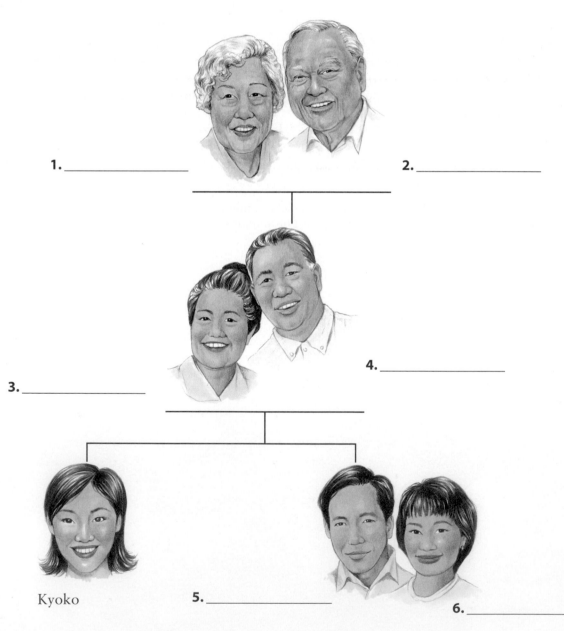

1. _____

2. _____

3. _____

4. _____

Kyoko

5. _____

6. _____

2 | FAMILY RELATIONSHIPS
Grammar Notes 1–2

Complete the sentences. Choose from the words in parentheses.

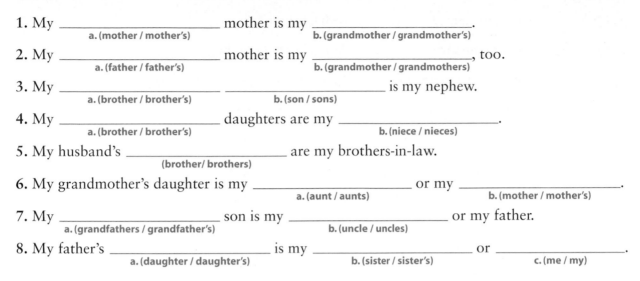

1. My _____ mother is my _____.
   a. (mother / mother's)   b. (grandmother / grandmother's)

2. My _____ mother is my _____, too.
   a. (father / father's)   b. (grandmother / grandmothers)

3. My _____ _____ is my nephew.
   a. (brother / brother's)   b. (son / sons)

4. My _____ daughters are my _____.
   a. (brother / brother's)   b. (niece / nieces)

5. My husband's _____ are my brothers-in-law.
   (brother/ brothers)

6. My grandmother's daughter is my _____ or my _____.
   a. (aunt / aunts)   b. (mother / mother's)

7. My _____ son is my _____ or my father.
   a. (grandfathers / grandfather's)   b. (uncle / uncles)

8. My father's _____ is my _____ or _____.
   a. (daughter / daughter's)   b. (sister / sister's)   c. (me / my)

3 | MY, YOUR, HIS, HER, OUR, THEIR, ITS
Grammar Notes 1, 3

Complete the sentences. Use a possessive adjective.

1. My sister studies in Toronto. ____*Her*____ school is on Victoria Street.

2. She goes to Edgewood University. She likes _____ classes.

3. Carlos's parents work at the United Nations. _____ jobs are interesting. His mother is a translator and his father is an interpreter.

4. Right now my brother is in Peru, _____ wife is in Belize, and _____ children are in the United States.

5. Does your brother like _____ job?

6. Their rabbit's name is Biddy. _____ fur is soft.

7. Do you use _____ calculator every day in math class?

8. Does your grandmother like _____ new apartment? Is she happy there?

4 | WH- QUESTIONS

Grammar Note 5

*Complete the questions. Use **where's, who's, whose, what's,** and **when's.***

1. Q: <u>What's</u> his last name?   A: It's Kwon.

2. Q: _____ the dictionary?   A: It's in my book bag.

3. Q: _____ homework is missing?   A: Sandra's.

4. Q: _____ your seat?   A: I'm next to the window.

5. Q: _____ your birthday?   A: It's next month.

6. Q: _____ last name begins with *s*?   A: My name. It's Suzuki.

7. Q: _____ his father?   A: His father is Joe Pieroni.

8. Q: _____ this book about?   A: It's about the Yucatan in Mexico.

9. Q: _____ test is this?   A: It's Jason's. I know his handwriting.

5 | USEFUL QUESTIONS AND STATEMENTS

Grammar Notes 1–5

Complete the conversations. Choose from the words in parentheses.

1. **A:** Excuse me, is this _____ seat?
   a. (you / your)

   B: No. It's _____ seat.
   b. (Leila / Leila's)

2. **A:** Excuse me. _____ dictionary was on the floor. Here.
   a. (You / Your)

   B: Thanks a lot.

3. **A:** _____ class was canceled.
   a. (They / Their)

   B: Why?

   A: _____ teacher was sick.
   b. (They / Their)

4. **A:** Is that _____ scarf?
   a. (she / her)

   B: No. It's _____ scarf.
   b. (I / my)

5. **A:** _____ book is this?
   a. (Who's / Whose)

   B: It belongs to the teacher.

6. **A:** _____ absent today?
   a. (Who's / Whose)

   B: Nobody. Everyone is here.

7. **A:** Where's the _____ locker room?
   a. (womens / women's)

   B: It's down the hall.

8. **A:** Where's the _____ room?
   a. (men's / mens')

   B: It's next to the water fountain.

9. **A:** Is that _____ seat?
   a. (he / his)

   B: No. _____ the teacher's seat.
   b. (Its / It's)

   A: Oh.

10. **A:** Is your _____ car in the garage?
    a. (fathers / father's)

    B: No. It's on the street.

---

6 | **A NEW STUDENT**   *Grammar Notes 1–4*

Read an article about a new student at the International Language Institute in Miami.
Complete the sentences with a subject pronoun or a possessive adjective.

International Language Institute Newsletter
Vol. 22

Get to Know New Students at the ILI

New Student of the Month

Sandra Gomes

__My__ name is Sandra Gomes. _____ 'm from São Paulo, Brazil. I'm happy to be studying English here at the International Language Institute. It's great to meet people from all over the world.

_____ have two brothers and a sister. My older brother and _____ sister are married. _____ older brother is an accountant. _____ lives in São Paulo with _____ wife. _____ is a travel agent. My sister and _____ husband are in Spain now. _____ 're both artists. They travel all over. _____ life is exciting. My younger brother is in college. _____ wants to be a film producer. _____ parents want him to study accounting. _____ is a difficult situation for him! _____ dream is to become a dentist, but first I need to learn English. _____ hope I succeed.

7 | EDITING

Read these conversations. There are seven mistakes. The first mistake is already corrected.

1. A: Is that ~~you~~ *your* dictionary?

   B: No. It's his dictionary.

   A: Who's?

   B: Dans.

2. A: Is Maria sister here?

   B: No, she's not.

   A: Is Maria here?

   B: No, but his brother is.

   A: Where is Maria?

   B: I think she's with his sister. Their at the movies.

Communication Practice

8 | LISTENING

🎧 *Listen to these sentences. Circle the correct word.*

1. Maria	Maria's	Marias		4. partner	partner's	partners
2. Maria	Maria's	Marias		5. partner	partner's	partners
3. Maria	Maria's	Marias		6. partner	partner's	partners

9 | GAME: WHOSE BROTHER IS THIS?

Bring in photos of family members. Write how the person is related to you on the back of the photo (for example, my sister, my mother, my aunt). The teacher collects the photos and gives each student a photo. Students ask questions about the photos.

Example: ANYA: Whose __sister__ is this?
PABLO: I think it's Juan's.
JUAN: You're right. She's my sister.

Now Juan asks a question.

10 | FIND SOMEONE WHOSE . . . / FIND SOMEONE WHO'S . . .

Complete the questions. Use **whose** *or* **who's**. *Then ask your classmates these questions.*
Write their answers.

Example: YOU: What month is your birthday?
ERIK: It's in February.

1. _Whose_ birthday is in February? _____Erik's_____.

2. _____ good in art? _____.

3. _____ name means something? _____.

4. _____ a good athlete? _____.

5. _____ eyes aren't brown? _____.

6. _____ a good cook? _____.

7. _____ first name has more than eight letters? _____.

8. _____ birthday is in the summer? _____.

9. _____ a good dancer? _____.

10. _____ handwriting is beautiful? _____.

11 | WRITING

Draw a family tree of your family like the tree on page 116. Then work in small groups. Tell
your group about different people in your family.

Example: Roberto Gomes is my mother's brother. He's my favorite uncle. He's a businessman.
He's in London now. He's an intelligent man with a good sense of humor.

Now write about yourself and your family.

Example: I'm from Recife in Brazil. I live with my parents and my younger brother. My older
brother is married. He is a pilot and his wife is a pilot too. My mother worries
about them, but she is proud of them. I want to be a pilot one day, but it's my secret
for now.

12 | ON THE INTERNET

Ⓒ *Exchange e-mail addresses with a classmate. Then send your classmate an e-mail*
message. Ask your classmate six questions about his or her family.

Examples: Where does your family live? How many people are there in your family? What are
their names? What are their favorite free time activities?

Grammar in Context

BEFORE YOU READ

Complete the sentences. Compare your answers with a partner's.

Do you like to hike or bike? I prefer to _____.

Do you like to camp or stay at a hotel? I prefer to _____.

Do you like to travel with friends or alone? I prefer to _____.

🎧 *Read this conversation about a trip to a national park.*

BRYCE CANYON NATIONAL PARK

MARIA: So how was your trip, Guillermo?

GUILLERMO: Great. I was in Bryce Canyon National Park.

MARIA: Is **that** in Utah **or** Colorado?

GUILLERMO: It's in Utah. I have over 200 pictures. **These** are my best photos.

MARIA: What are **those**?

GUILLERMO: They're called *hoodoos*. They're rock formations. **This** is me in front of a hoodoo.

MARIA: **That**'s an amazing photo.

GUILLERMO: Thanks. **This** is Fairyland Canyon. It's near the entrance to the park. **These** hoodoos come in different shapes, sizes, and colors. Some have names, like the Wall of Windows.

MARIA: Look at you! Is it really you on **that** horse?

GUILLERMO: Yes. I was on a horseback trip in the canyons. It was great. Listen, I want to send a photo to a friend in Chile. Do you like **this** picture **or that** one?

MARIA: **This** one, the picture of you on a horse.

GUILLERMO: I think you're right. I'll send it to Roberto.

MARIA: When's your next trip?

GUILLERMO: The first week in September. I'm thinking of the Canadian Rockies. Would you like to come?

MARIA: You bet!*

GUILLERMO: **That**'s great.

AFTER YOU READ

Circle the correct answer.

1. Is this national park in California or Utah?
   a. California   **b.** Utah

2. Are these rock formations called hoodoos or voodoos?
   a. hoodoos   **b.** voodoos

3. Are the rocks different colors or the same color?
   a. different colors   **b.** the same color

4. Does Bryce Canyon National Park have horseback riding or horse racing?
   a. horseback riding   **b.** horse racing

Grammar Presentation

THIS / THAT / THESE / THOSE

Singular		
This / That	Verb	
This	is	a good photo.
That	was	in Bryce.

Plural		
These / Those	Verb	
These	are	new photos.
Those	are	from my last trip.

(continued)

You bet: Sure

Singular			
This / That	**Noun**	**Verb**	
This	**photo**	is	clear.
That	**photo**	has	nice colors.

Plural			
These / Those	**Noun**	**Verb**	
These	**horses**	are	tired.
Those	**horses**	are	rested.

QUESTIONS WITH *OR* AND ANSWERS

Questions with *or*	Answers
Are you hungry **or** thirsty?	I'm thirsty.
Do you usually walk **or** drive?	I usually drive.

GRAMMAR NOTES

EXAMPLES

1. Use *this*, *that*, *these*, and *those* to <u>identify</u> persons or things.

- Trips are fun. (all trips)
- **This** trip is fun. (the trip I'm taking now)

2. Use *this* or *that* to talk about a singular noun.

This refers to a person or thing **near you**.

That refers to a person or thing **far from you**.

- singular noun
- **This** is my bag.
- singular noun
- **That**'s your bag by the door.

3. Use *these* or *those* to talk about plural nouns.

These refers to people or things **near you**.

Those refers to people or things **far away**.

- plural noun
- **These** souvenirs are expensive.
- plural noun
- **Those** t-shirts in the store window are on sale.

4. *This* and *These* can refer to events in the **present** and near future.

That and *those* can refer to events in the **past**.

- **This** vacation is very expensive.
- People travel a lot **these** days.
- **That** vacation was a lot of fun.
- In **those** times, people traveled less.

5. *This*, *that*, *these*, and *those* can be **pronouns** or **adjectives**.

When *this*, *that*, *these*, and *those* are **adjectives**, a noun always follows.

- pronoun
- **This** is my suitcase.
- adjective noun
- **This** suitcase is red.

6. In speaking we use *that's* to **respond** to something a person says.

A: I'm going to Italy.
B: That's great!

7. Questions with *or* ask for **a choice**.

▶ **BE CAREFUL!** Do not answer a choice question with *yes* or *no*.

Q: Do you like hiking **or** bike riding?

A: I like hiking.

> NOT: **Q:** Do you like hiking or bike riding?
>
> **A:** ~~Yes.~~

Pronunciation Notes

The vowel sound in *this* is short. The lips are relaxed. /ɪ/

The vowel sound in *these* is long. The lips are not relaxed. The lips are stretched. /i/

Questions with *or* use rising intonation for the first choice, and falling intonation for the second choice.

    Q: Do you like this photo or that photo?

Focused Practice

1 | DISCOVER THE GRAMMAR

*Read the conversations. Then circle **a**, **b**, or **c**.*

1.   GUILLERMO: Who's that man over there?

          HUGO: He's a park ranger.

   a. Guillermo is asking about one park ranger. The ranger is near Guillermo.

   b. Guillermo is asking about park rangers. The rangers are not near Guillermo.

   c. Guillermo is asking about one park ranger. The ranger is not near Guillermo.

2.   GUILLERMO: Are those snakes dangerous?

     PARK RANGER: No, they're not.

   a. Guillermo is asking about a snake. The snake is not near Guillermo.

   b. Guillermo is asking about snakes. The snakes are not near Guillermo.

   c. Guillermo is asking about snakes. The snakes are near Guillermo.

3.   GUILLERMO: Is this a pine tree?

     PARK RANGER: Yes, it is.

   a. Guillermo is asking about a tree. The tree is near Guillermo.

   b. Guillermo is asking about a tree. The tree is not near Guillermo.

   c. Guillermo is asking about trees. The trees are near Guillermo.

4. PARK RANGER: Is this your first trip to a national park?

      GUILLERMO: Yes, it is.

   a. The park ranger is asking about Guillermo's trip. The trip was last year.

   b. The park ranger is asking about a national park. The park is not far.

   c. The park ranger is asking about Guillermo's trip. It's the trip he's taking now.

2 | THIS ISN'T MY BACKPACK

Grammar Notes 1–4

Maria is unpacking her backpack. Complete the conversation with **this**, **that**, **these**, *and* **those**.

GUILLERMO: Is something wrong?

MARIA: Yes. _____ aren't my jeans

            1.

and _____ isn't my sweatshirt.

            2.

GUILLERMO: Is _____ your backpack?

            3.

MARIA: Uh-oh. It's the right color and shape,

but it's not my bag.

[cell phone rings]

MARIA: Hello?

SYLVIA: Is _____ Maria Hernandez?

            4.

MARIA: Yes.

SYLVIA: I'm Sylvia Green. I'm sorry. I think I

have your backpack.

MARIA: Is it green with a black pocket? Is there a pair of pink pants inside?

SYLVIA: Yes to both.

MARIA: _____ 's my bag. And _____ are my pants. Where are you?

      5.   6.

SYLVIA: I'm at the Lake Louise Tent Campgrounds.

MARIA: That's great. I am too. Let's meet in fifteen minutes at the entrance.

SYLVIA: See you in fifteen minutes. Thanks.

3 | CHOICE QUESTIONS

Grammar Note 7

Change the two questions to one question with **or**. *Then answer the question.*

1. Is Jasper in Canada? Is Jasper in the United States?

   A: *Is Jasper in Canada or the United States?* _____

   B: *It's in Canada.* _____. It's in the province of Alberta.

2. Is that a snake? Is that a stick?

   A: _____

   B: Don't worry. _____

3. Is that campground open all year round? Is that campground open only in the summer?

A: _____

B: _____ You can't reach it in the winter.

4. Is this trail easy? Is this trail difficult?

A: _____

B: _____ It's for advanced hikers.

5. Do they speak English? Do they speak French?

A: _____

B: _____ They're from Haiti.

4 | PRONUNCIATION

Listen and circle the word you hear in each sentence.

1. This	These		**4.** this	these		**6.** This	These
2. This	These		**5.** this	these		**7.** This	These
3. this	these						

5 | EDITING

Correct these conversations. There are four mistakes. The first mistake is already corrected.

1. **A:** ~~This~~ are my friends Tom and Marco.

   B: Nice to meet you.

2. **A:** Do you have a night flight or a morning flight?

   B: Yes. I leave at 9 A.M.

3. **A:** Is these your flashlight?

   B: Yes, it is. Thanks.

4. **A:** Are these men on the mountain OK?

   B: I think so. But it's hard to see them from here.

Communication Practice

6 | LISTENING

Maria is packing for a camping trip. Look at the list. Listen and check (✓) what she takes.

_____ **1.** boots   _____ **4.** a guide book   _____ **6.** batteries

_____ **2.** a sweatshirt   _____ **5.** an umbrella   _____ **7.** heavy pants

_____ **3.** guide books

7 | A NEW LANGUAGE

*Learn a few words in a new language from a classmate. Work in small groups. Your new language "teacher" points to objects in the room. He or she teaches you vocabulary in a language he or she knows. Use **this**, **that**, **these**, or **those**.*

Examples: In English, these are *keys*. In Spanish, they're *llaves*.
In English, that's *a window*. In Japanese, it's a 家 or まど" (pronounced "mado").
In English, those are *chairs*. In Russian, they're стул (pronounced "stool ya").

8 | WRITING

A *Bring in a picture of a famous tourist site. Tell the class about the site.*

Example: This is a picture of the
Great Wall. This wall is in China.

Hang the pictures up in the class. A student thinks of one of the places. The class asks choice questions. The class guesses the place.

Example: Is it in South America or Asia?
It's in Asia.
Is it in China or Thailand?
It's in China.
Is it a building or a wall?
It's a wall.
Is it the Great Wall?
Yes, it is.

B *Write about one of the places.*

Example: This is a picture of the Galapagos Islands. These islands are part of Ecuador. Giant turtles live there. These turtles have unusual bodies. They are different from turtles in other parts of the world. Their bodies help them live on the Galapagos Islands. For example, their mouths are curved. This helps them eat cactus. Their feet are not smooth. This helps them walk on rough surfaces. Tourists come to the Galapagos Islands to see different kinds of animals and plants. The first famous visitor to the Galapagos Islands was Charles Darwin.

9 | ON THE INTERNET

Download pictures and get information about one of these national parks in Canada: Banff, Jasper, Kluane, Kootenay, Nahanni, Wood Buffalo, or Yoho. Tell your class about the park.

Where is it?

What is special in this park?

One / Ones / It

Grammar in Context

BEFORE YOU READ

You get three gifts: a sweatshirt, a CD of your favorite singer's music, and a gift card. Which one do you like best? Why?

🎧 *Read these conversations of a shopper and two salespeople.*

A GIFT

SALESPERSON: Can I help you?

SHOPPER: Yes, thanks. I want a red sweatshirt.

SALESPERSON: What size?

SHOPPER: Large. It's for a friend.

SALESPERSON: Here's **one**. It's cute. It says, "Don't worry. Be happy."

SHOPPER: No. I don't think so. Not for her.

SALESPERSON: How about these sweatshirts? **This one** has pockets and **that one** has a hood. The **ones** with hoods are on sale.

SHOPPER: Hmm. I can't decide. Maybe a CD is a better idea.

(at the music store)

2ND SALESPERSON: Need any help?

SHOPPER: Thanks. I want to get a CD for a friend.

2ND SALESPERSON: What kind of music does your friend like?

SHOPPER: R & B I think.

2ND SALESPERSON: Here's **one**. **It**'s Beyoncé's latest.

SHOPPER: I think she has **it**.

2ND SALESPERSON: Well, why don't you get her a gift card? Here. This card is for $25.00. Your friend can buy any CD in the store.

SHOPPER: Will she think I'm lazy?

2ND SALESPERSON: Are you kidding? The gift card is our most popular gift this year.

SHOPPER: OK. I'll take **one**.

AFTER YOU READ

Change these false statements to true ones.

1. The salesperson shows the woman a sweatshirt. It's a ~~green~~ ^{red} sweatshirt, size large.

2. The woman wants a gift. It's for her cousin.

3. The woman looks at a sweatshirt with pockets and one with a hole.

4. Gift cards are an unusual gift this year. The woman buys one.

Grammar Presentation

ONE

	A / An	Singular Count Noun or Noun Phrase	
I don't need	a an	pen. original copy.	I have **one**.

	Adjective	Singular Count Noun	
I need a	gray	shirt.	He needs a **blue one.**

This / That	One	
This **That**	one	is my book. is Marco's.

ONES

	Adjective	Plural Count Noun				
The	**gray**	**sweatshirts**	are twenty dollars.		The **gray ones** are twenty dollars.	

IT

	The	Noun	*It*
Where's	**the**	**CD**?	**It**'s on the table.

	Possessive Adjective	Noun	*It*
Where's	**your**	**watch**?	**It**'s in the drawer.

	This/That	Noun	*It*
Where's	**that**	**book**?	**It**'s on my desk.

GRAMMAR NOTES

1. Use *one* in place of *a* or *an* plus a singular count noun.

2. Use *one* in place of a noun phrase.

3. Use *one* or *ones* after an adjective in place of a singular or plural count noun.

4. Use *one* after *this* or *that*.

▶ **BE CAREFUL!** Do not use *ones* after *these* or *those*.

EXAMPLES

A: Does he have a car?

B: Yes, he has **one**. (*one* = a car)

A: I want a red sweatshirt.

B: Here's **one**. (*one* = a red sweatshirt)

A: He wants three shirts, two red **ones** and one black **one**. (*ones* = shirts, *one* = shirt)

A: Do you like this watch?

B: No. I don't like **this one**. I like **that one**. (*one* = watch)

A: Do you want these?

B: No, I want **those**.

NOT: No, I want those ~~ones~~.

5. Use *it* in place of *the* + a noun.	**A:** Where's **the card**? **B:** **It**'s on the floor. (*it* = the card)

6. Use *it* in place of a possessive pronoun or noun (*my, your, his, her, its, our, their,* or *John's*) plus a singular count noun.	**A:** Where's **your gift**? **B:** **It**'s in my book bag. (*it* = my gift)

7. Use *it* in place of *this* or *that* plus **a** singular count noun.	**A:** Where's **that gift**? **B:** **It**'s in the closet. (*it* = that gift)

Focused Practice

1 | DISCOVER THE GRAMMAR

Rosa and Carmen are roommates. Read their conversation. Look at the underlined words. Circle what they refer to.

ROSA: What's up?

CARMEN: Maria's party is tonight. I have a blouse,

but I need a long black skirt.

ROSA: I have <u>one</u>. Here. You can borrow it.
      1.

CARMEN: Are you sure?

ROSA: Of course. And here are three belts—

a silver belt and two black <u>ones</u>.
                           2.

Choose <u>one</u>.
        3.

CARMEN: This <u>one</u> is nice. Is it OK
        4.

if I borrow <u>it</u>?
            5.

ROSA: Of course. And here's my silver

necklace. <u>It</u> matches the belt.
         6.

CARMEN: Thanks a lot.

ROSA: No problem. Have a great time.

CARMEN: Thanks.

1. a. a blouse   **(b.)** a long black skirt

2. a. a silver belt   **b.** belts

3. a. belts   **b.** a belt

4. a. belt   **b.** belts

5. a. Rosa's belt   **b.** a belt

6. a. a silver necklace   **b.** Rosa's silver necklace

2 | SHORT CONVERSATIONS

Grammar Notes 1–4

*Complete the conversations. Use **one** or **ones**.*

1. **A:** I need a birthday card for her.

   B: Here. I have an extra _____.

2. **A:** I have two new belts. This _____ is for you.

   B: Thanks.

3. **A:** How many TVs do they have?

   B: They have two old _____, and a new _____.

4. **A:** Where do the glasses go?

   B: The blue _____ go on the top shelf and the green _____ go here.

3 | HOW TO GET RID OF IT?

Grammar Notes 1–7

*Complete the sentences. Use **it** or **one**.*

A man gets a gift of a new umbrella. He decides to throw away his old _____. He puts
                                                                                            1.
the old _____ in the wastebasket. A friend recognizes _____ and returns _____. Then the
          2.   3.   4.
man leaves the old umbrella on the train. The train conductor returns _____ the next day.
                                                                        5.
The man tries hard to throw away his umbrella, but _____ always comes back. He says to
                                                      6.
his wife, "I really don't need this old umbrella. I have a beautiful new _____." She agrees.
                                                                           7.
Finally he lends _____ to a friend. He never sees _____ again.
                  8.   9.

4 | QUESTIONS

Grammar Notes 1–7

*Replace the underlined words with **one**, **ones**, or **it**.*

1. I need a gift for Tom. Do you have a *one* ~~gift~~?

2. That ring is beautiful. Where is <u>that ring</u> from?

3. I have two sweaters. Which <u>sweater</u> looks better with this skirt?

4. I like your scarf. Is <u>your scarf</u> handmade?

5. These are the old magazines. Where are the new <u>magazines</u>?

6. My dictionary is on the second shelf. I always put <u>my dictionary</u> next to my grammar book.

7. I see a lot of green apples. Do you have any red <u>apples</u>?

8. This gift is for Bill. Is that <u>gift</u> for Sam?

5 | EDITING

Correct these sentences. There are seven mistakes. The first mistake is already corrected.

1. She has two red sweaters and a blue ~~ones~~. *one*

2. These apples are delicious. Try one. But first wash one.

3. We have two gift cards. It is in your desk and one is on the counter.

4. These ones are new. Those ones are old.

5. Do you need silver earrings or gold one?

6. I don't want a new leather jacket. I have it.

Communication Practice

6 | LISTENING

🎧 *Listen to the conversation. Complete the chart. What kind of gifts does she want to get for her friends and relatives?*

1. cousins	2. friends	3. brother	4. grandmother	5. father	6. mother

7 | TALK ABOUT GIFTS

Work in pairs. Talk about gifts. Tell which ones you like to get and which ones you like to give.

handmade gifts   big gifts   small gifts   _____

expensive gifts   practical gifts   funny gifts   _____

Example: **A:** I like to get handmade gifts. I think they're the best.

8 | WRITING

Write about a special gift you gave or one you received.

9 | ON THE INTERNET

💻 *You want to buy a gift for a friend. Look at the store's online catalog. Choose two gifts (a watch, a CD player, etc.). Download pictures and descriptions. Bring the pictures and descriptions to class. Then work in small groups. Ask your group: "Which one do you like?"*

Example: **A:** Look at these watches. Which one do you like?
B: I like this one. It's beautiful, but it's very expensive.

From **Grammar** to **Writing**

Punctuation I: The Apostrophe, The Comma, The Period, The Question Mark

1 Read this e-mail. Then circle all the punctuation marks.

> **Subject:** Juan's Surprise Party
>
> Dear Hector,
>
> Are you free on the 16th? I hope so.
>
> Ray and I want to invite you to a surprise party for Juan on
> November 16th, at 9:00 P.M. It's his 21st birthday. The party is at
> Ali and Ted's apartment.
>
> Hope to see you there.
>
> Ron

Study these rules of punctuation.

The Apostrophe (')	
1. Use an apostrophe to show possession and to write contractions.	• **Carol's** book is here. • We **aren't** late.

The Comma (,)	
2. Rules for commas vary. Here are some places where commas are almost always used:	
a. in a list of more than two things	• He is wearing **a shirt, a sweater,** and **a jacket**.
b. after the name of a person you are writing to	• Dear **John,**
c. after *yes* or *no* in a sentence	• **Yes,** I am. • **No,** I'm not.
d. when you use *and* to connect two sentences.	• His house is huge, **and** his car is expensive.

The Period (.)	
3. **a.** Use a period at the end of a statement. **b.** Use a period after abbreviations.	• We are English language **students**. • The party is on **Nov.** 16th.

The Question Mark (?)	
4. Use a question mark at the end of a question.	• Are you planning a **party?** • Where are you **going?**

2 | *Add punctuation marks to this note.*

> Dear Uncle John
>
> Bob and I want to invite you to a party for my parents 25th wedding anniversary Its on Sunday Dec 11th
>
> The party is at our home at 23 Main St Its at three o'clock I hope you can make it
>
>   Emily

3 | *Invite a friend to a party. Include the following information:*

Who is the party for?

Who is giving the party?

What is the occasion?

When is the party?

Where is the party?

Review Test

I | *Read each conversation. Circle the letter of the underlined word or group of words that is not correct.*

1. A: <u>Who's</u> Mr. Vogel?   **A   B   C   D**
       A

   B: Mr. Vogel <u>is</u> <u>Ana</u> <u>teacher</u>.
            B   C   D

2. A: Do you <u>like</u> red grapes?   **A   B   C   D**
          A

   B: I <u>like</u> green grapes, but I <u>don't like</u> red <u>one</u>.
       B   C   D

3. A: <u>When</u> is your <u>first</u> class?   **A   B   C   D**
      A   B

   B: It's <u>at</u> two <u>on the afternoon</u>.
        C   D

4. A: <u>Where's</u> the library?   **A   B   C   D**
       A

   B: It's <u>near</u> the elevator <u>in the</u> <u>third floor</u>.
        B   C   D

5. A: How much are the ties?   **A   B   C   D**

   B: <u>This</u> <u>one</u> in my hand <u>costs</u> $50. <u>That</u> ties over there cost $15.
       A   B   C   D

6. A: Now <u>he's</u> <u>a</u> doctor.   **A   B   C   D**
         A B

   B: <u>This</u> <u>is</u> great.
       C   D

II | *Circle the correct word(s) to complete the sentences.*

1. My classroom is on the <u>two / second</u> floor.

2. My <u>one / first</u> class is at 9:30.

3. My grandfather is <u>seventy-five / seventy-fifth</u> years old.

4. November is the <u>eleven / eleventh</u> month of the year.

III *Circle the correct word to complete the sentences.*

1. This / These is my dictionary.

2. That / Those books are for level 6.

3. Is this / that your bag in the corner?

4. That / Those rugs are from Cairo.

5. Are this / these papers important?

IV *Use **it**, **one**, or **ones** to complete the sentences.*

1. I have a green sweater and two white _____.

2. I have a green sweater. _____ is very warm.

3. He has a blue sweater and a gray _____.

4. I like that scarf. _____ has beautiful colors.

5. I have a new computer. _____ is very fast.

6. The old tools were very good. The new _____ are terrible.

V *Read the invitation. Use the words in the box to complete the questions and answers on the next page. Use some words more than once.*

at	Nuray's	what	where
Fiore's	on	when	whose

Birthday Party
When: *November 25th*
For: *Nuray*
Place: *350 East 77th Street Apt. 2A*
Time: *9:00 P.M.*
RSVP: *Fiore at 917-980-8768*

1. Q: _____ is on November 25th? A: A birthday party for Nuray.

2. Q: _____ birthday party is on November 25th? A: _____ birthday party.

3. Q: _____ is the party? A: It's _____ 350 East 77th Street, Apt. 2A.

4. Q: _____ is the party? A: It's _____ November 25th.

5. Q: _____ time is the party? A: It's _____ 9:00 P.M.

6. Q: _____ phone number is 917-980-8768? A: _____.

VI *Write questions about the underlined word.*

1. A: _____?

   B: Uncle Mike's birthday is on <u>March 15th</u>.

2. A: _____?

   B: Scott is <u>in the park</u>.

3. A: _____?

   B: His aunt's last name is <u>Macabe</u>.

4. A: _____?

   B: <u>Ilona</u> is in the living room.

5. A: _____?

   B: <u>Rick's</u> car is in the garage.

VII *Cross out the underlined words. Use* **His**, **Her**, **Its**, *or* **Their**.

1. <u>Mary's</u> uncle is a professor.

2. <u>The Browns'</u> car is big.

3. <u>Tom's</u> sister is a history teacher.

4. This is my bird. <u>My bird's</u> name is Lucky.

5. <u>The students'</u> tests are on the teacher's desk.

▶ *To check your answers, go to the Answer Key on page RT-2.*

INFORMATION GAP FOR STUDENT B

Student B, answer your partner's questions. Then ask your partner questions to complete your chart.

Examples: What country has a national holiday on _____? (date)
What month is _____'s national holiday?
What's the date of _____'s national holiday?
What country has a national holiday in _____? (month)
When is _____'s national holiday?

NATIONAL HOLIDAYS AROUND THE WORLD							
COUNTRY		**MONTH**	**DAY**	**COUNTRY**		**MONTH**	**DAY**
Argentina			9	Haiti		January	1
Brazil		September	7			June	2
Denmark		April	16	Japan		December	
		February	27	Lebanon			22
Ecuador		August	10			October	29
Greece		March	25	United States of America			4
Your country's national holiday:							

PART V

Present Progressive; Imperatives; *Can/Could*; Suggestions: *Let's, Why Don't We*

15 The Present Progressive: Affirmative and Negative Statements

Grammar in Context

BEFORE YOU READ

Look at the pictures below. When do you think events 2.–7. are happening? Check your answers on the bottom of the page.

2. a. 1893   **3. a.** 1939   **4. a.** 1960   **5. a.** 1981   **6. a.** 1992   **7. a.** 1989
   b. 1929   **b.** 1959   **b.** 1974   **b.** 1991   **b.** 2002   **b.** 2003

Read about these events.

1. Marcus and Julius **are playing** with yo-yos. It's 100 BC.

2. It's the Chicago World's Fair. Ted and Rose are **riding** the first Ferris wheel. It's the height of a 25-story building.

3. Sue and Ralph Miller **are watching** TV. The Millers are the first on their street to own a color TV.

4. The Suzukis **are visiting** Mexico. They**'re flying** to Cozumel. This year jets **are flying** to Cozumel for the first time.

5. Luis is at a video arcade. He**'s playing** Pac Man. He loves this new game.

6. Berta **is sending** her photo to her boyfriend. She **isn't sending** it by mail. She**'s using** her phone.

7. Yumi **is getting** food from a vending machine. She **isn't using** coins. She **is using** her cell phone to buy the food.

8. Roberto and Marco **are playing** with yo-yos. Yo-yos are over 2,000 years old. It's 2006.

2.a 3.b 4.b 5.a 6.b 7.b

AFTER YOU READ

Match the words on the left and the right to complete the sentences.

_____	**1.** They're playing	**a.**	by jet.
_____	**2.** She's using	**b.**	a Ferris wheel.
_____	**3.** They're visiting	**c.**	Mexico.
_____	**4.** He's riding	**d.**	a camera phone.
_____	**5.** She's buying something	**e.**	with yo-yos.
_____	**6.** They're flying	**f.**	from a vending machine.

Grammar Presentation

PRESENT PROGRESSIVE

Affirmative Statements		
Subject	*Be*	**Base Form of Verb + -*ing***
I	am	
You	are	
He		
She	is	eating.
It		
We		
You	are	
They		

Negative Statements			
Subject	*Be*	*Not*	**Base Form of Verb + -*ing***
I	am		
You	are		
He			
She	is	not	flying.
It			
We			
You	are		
They			

GRAMMAR NOTES

1. Use the **present progressive** (also called the present continuous) to talk about an **action** that is or is not **happening now**.

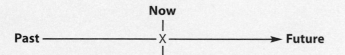

USAGE NOTE: We often use the time expressions *now*, *right now*, and *at the moment* with the present progressive.

▶ BE CAREFUL! We don't usually use non-action verbs in the present progressive.

EXAMPLES

- I **am sending** a fax.
- Their machine **is not working**.

- The machine **isn't working** *now*.
- *Right now* she**'s resting**.
- *At the moment* he**'s talking** on the phone.

  NOT: The textbook ~~is costing~~ $80.

(continued)

2. Use **contractions** in speaking and informal writing.

- **I'm** not working. **I'm** resting.
- Luis **isn't** playing a game. **He's** watching TV.
- We **aren't** flying. **We're** driving.

3. Do not repeat the subject and verb *be* when the subject is doing two things.

- They**'re singing** and **dancing**.

4. We sometimes use the present progressive for an **action** that is taking place **at this time**, **but** may **not** be happening **at this moment**.

```
                    Now
                     |
                     |
Past ───────────────X───────────────► Future
                     |
```

USAGE NOTE: We often use the time expressions *these days*, *this year*, and *nowadays* with the present progressive.

- *These days* many people **are using** camera phones.
- He **is teaching** a basic English and an advanced English class *this year*.
- *Nowadays* many women **are working** outside the home.

Reference Notes
See Unit 27, page 266 for a discussion of non-action verbs.
See Appendix 15, page A-16 for spelling rules for the present progressive.

Focused Practice

1 | DISCOVER THE GRAMMAR

A *Look at Grammar in Context on page 142. There are eight verbs in the present progressive. Write each verb in its base form and **-ing** form.*

1. *play*   *playing*

2.   *riding*

3. *watch*

4.

5.

6.

7.

8.

B *Write the two negative statements about the events.*

_____

_____

2 | ON A PLANE

Grammar Note 1

Complete the sentences in the affirmative or negative of the present progressive. Choose from the verbs in Exercise 1, Discover the Grammar.

1. The Herraras are going to Chile. They _____*are visiting*_____ friends in Santiago, Chile.

2. Their plane _____ at a speed of 1,000 kilometers per hour.

3. It was cold on the plane before. Now it _____ warmer.

4. Mr. Herrara _____ video games.

5. Mr. Herrera (not) _____ the movie. His son _____ the movie.

6. In the movie a man _____ a horse named "Seabiscuit."

7. Mrs. Herrara _____ her BlackBerry®.

8. She _____ a message to her friends in Chile. She (not) _____ a fax.

3 | WHAT'S MARIA DOING NOW?

Grammar Notes 1–3

Write about Maria. Use the words given and use the present progressive.

1. It's 7:00 A.M.

   Maria / exercise / watch the news on TV

   Maria is exercising and watching the news on TV.

2. It's 8:00 A.M.

   She / get on the train

   _____

3. It's 8:15 A.M. Maria is on the train.

   Now / she / check e-mail / eat a roll / drink a cup of coffee

   _____

4. It's 6:00 P.M. Maria is on the train.

   a. She / go home

   _____

   b. She / talk to friends on her cellphone

   _____

(continued)

5. It's 7:00 P.M.

Maria / eat dinner / watch a video

_____

6. It's 9:30 P.M. Maria is meditating.

a. She / not talk

_____

b. She / not think

_____

c. She / not watch TV or videos

_____

d. She / relax

_____

7. It's 11:00 P.M.

She / sleep / dream

_____

---

4 | **IS ITALY CHANGING?**   *Grammar Notes 1–4*

Complete this news article. Use the present progressive of the verb in parentheses.

Is Italy *Changing?*

It's 8:00 in the evening in a small Tuscan town in Italy. Dr. Bresciani ___*is returning*___ home from work. Her husband Francisco
 1. (return)

_____ a delicious salad to go with
 2. (prepare)

the chicken marsala.

In traditional Italy, Francisco is not your usual husband. Mr. Bresciani shops, cooks, and cleans. Mr. Bresciani says, "Italy _____.
 3. (change)

Italians _____ later. Nowadays
 4. (marry)

women _____ home. They
 5. (stay/not)

_____ outside the home. More
 6. (work)

men _____ home. They
 7. (stay)

_____ beds, _____
 8. (make)   9. (do)

the ironing, _____, and
 10. (cook)

_____.
 11. (clean)

Mr. Bresciani wants the government to list his job as "househusband." Mr. Bresciani is the founder of a group called "The Association of Househusbands." Their numbers _____.
 12. (grow)

Today there are over 4,000 members.

Is this just a fad? Is this a real change? Only time will tell.

5 | EDITING

Correct this postcard. There are thirteen mistakes. The first mistake is already corrected.

Dear Eun Young,

　　It was great to hear from you.

I'm sitting on a park bench in Prospect Park and waiting for Sung Hyun. It's a beautiful day. An older man is takes pictures. Two boys is running and is laughing. Some women doing tai chi. A young woman is talks on her cell phone. A father is push his baby in a stroller. The baby holding a bottle. He isn't drinks from the bottle. He playing with it.

　　I hope your work is going well. Sung Hyun is works hard and I studying hard. We're plan a vacation in Hawaii next summer. I hope you can join us.

　　　　Fondly,

　　　　Bo Jeong

To:

　Ms Eun Young Kim

　2543 Palm Blvd. Apt. E4

　Los Angeles, CA 90069

Communication Practice

6 | LISTENING

🎧 *Listen to a telephone conversation. Then listen again and mark the statements* **T** *(true) or* **F** *(false).*

_____1. The mother is calling from a train.

_____2. The mother is calling from a plane.

_____3. The father isn't watching TV.

_____4. The father isn't cooking.

_____5. Emily is doing her homework.

_____6. Emily is helping her father.

_____7. The mother isn't hungry.

_____8. The mother is looking forward to dinner.

_____9. They are preparing lasagna.

7 | INFORMATION GAP: ON THE PLANE

Student B, turn to page 186. Follow the directions on that page.

Student A, look at the picture of people on a plane. First tell Student B about one of the people in your picture. Then Student B will tell you about that person in his or her picture. Use the present progressive. Find five differences.

Example: A: In my picture, the man in 14A is playing a video game.

8 | WRITING

Look at people in a school cafeteria, a park, a mall, or on a train or a bus. Write about four people.

- Where are you? What time is it?

- What are the people doing?

- What are they wearing?

Example: I'm in our school cafeteria. It's 12:30 P.M. Two girls are paying for their food. One girl is very tall. The other is not. The tall girl is wearing black pants and a black t-shirt. The shorter girl is wearing jeans and a red sweater. They're carrying a lot of books. The tall girl isn't smiling. She's carrying a tray with a cup of yogurt and a salad. The shorter girl is carrying a tray with a sandwich, a salad, an apple, and cookies. She's talking a lot. The tall girl is listening. She isn't saying a word. I think they're in the same class. I don't think they're close friends.

9 | ON THE INTERNET

E-mail a friend. Tell where you are. Tell what's happening around you.

Example:

Hi Ricardo,

I'm writing to you from the computer lab at school. Five students are in the lab with me. Ali is on my right. He is Instant Messaging a friend. Ranya is on my left. She is playing games. Boris is next to Ranya. He is doing research. Another student is writing a paper. An older man is not using his computer. He's talking to someone on the phone.

What are you doing? Something fun? I hope so.

Well, I'll see you tomorrow.

Igor

16 The Present Progressive: Yes/No and Wh- Questions

Grammar in Context

BEFORE YOU READ

Check (✔) the kinds of TV shows you like.

comedies ☐	news ☐	sports ☐	reality shows ☐
movies ☐	music television (MTV) ☐	talk shows ☐	documentaries ☐
quiz shows ☐	cartoons ☐	soap operas ☐	cooking shows ☐

What's your favorite TV show? _____

🎧 *Abby has a cold. Her husband, Greg, is calling to see how she is. Read their conversation.*

I'M WATCHING A FUNNY SHOW

ABBY: Hello.

GREG: Hi, Abby. **How're you feeling?** Any better?

ABBY: Uh-huh. I'm not coughing as much.

GREG: Good. **Are you reading?**

ABBY: No. I'm watching TV.

GREG: **What are you watching?**

ABBY: An old *I Love Lucy* show.

GREG: **What's Lucy doing?**

ABBY: She and Ethel are working.

GREG: **Where are they working?**

ABBY: In a chocolate factory.

GREG: **What's happening now?**

ABBY: Lucy isn't working fast enough. So she's eating some chocolates and putting some in her pockets. It's really funny.

GREG: Lucy is good medicine. **Are you taping the show for me?**

ABBY: Why? You're not a Lucy fan.

GREG: No, but I'm catching your cold.

ABBY: Oh no. I'll call you later. Bye.

GREG: Bye, honey.

AFTER YOU READ

Match the questions and the answers.

_____ **1.** Is Abby reading?

_____ **2.** Is Greg watching TV?

_____ **3.** Who's watching TV?

_____ **4.** What's Abby watching?

_____ **5.** Who's catching a cold?

_____ **6.** Where's Lucy working?

_____ **7.** Is Abby enjoying the show?

a. Yes, she is.

b. No, he's not.

c. No, she's not. She's watching TV.

d. At a chocolate factory.

e. Greg is.

f. The *I Love Lucy* show.

g. Abby is.

Grammar Presentation

PRESENT PROGRESSIVE: *YES/NO* QUESTIONS AND *WH-* QUESTIONS

Yes/No Questions		
Be	Subject	Base Form of Verb + *-ing*
Am	I	
Are	you	
Is	he she it	**working**?
Are	we you they	

Short Answers					
Affirmative			Negative		
Yes,	you	**are**.	No,	you**'re**	not.
	I	**am**.		I**'m**	
	he she it	**is**.		he**'s** she**'s** it**'s**	
	you we they	**are**.		you**'re** we**'re** they**'re**	

Wh- Questions				Answers
Wh- Word	*Be*	Subject	Base Form of Verb + *-ing*	
Why	are	you	staying home?	I'm sick.
What	are	you	watching?	The *I Love Lucy* show.
Who	is	he	meeting?	His teacher. He's meeting his teacher.
Where	are	they	going?	To the movies. They're going to the movies.

Wh- Questions about the Subject			Answers
Wh- Word	*Be*	Base Form of Verb + *ing*	
Who	is	reading?	My friend (is).
What	is	happening?	They're making candy.

GRAMMAR NOTES   **EXAMPLES**

1. Use the **present progressive** to ask about **something that is happening now**.

   Reverse the subject and *be* when asking a **yes/no question**.

   - statement
     - He is working.
   - *yes/no* question
     - Is he working?

2. Most **wh- questions** in the present progressive use the same word order as *yes/no* questions.

   Use *whom* only for formal English.

   - Where **is he working**?
   - What **are they doing**?
   - Who **are you meeting**?
   - **Whom** is the president meeting?

3. *Who* and *What* **questions about the subject** use statement word order.

   - statement
     - Lucy is working.
   - *wh-* question
     - Who is working?
   - statement
     - Nothing is happening.
   - *wh-* question
     - What is happening?

Focused Practice

1 | DISCOVER THE GRAMMAR

Read the conversation on page 151 again.

1. Write the two complete *yes/no* questions.

   _____ and _____

2. Write the *wh-* question about the subject. _____

3. Write the three other *wh-* questions in the chart below.

Wh- Word	Be	Subject	Base Form of Verb + -ing
How	are	you	feeling?

2 | YES/NO QUESTIONS

Grammar Note 1

Write yes/no questions in the present progressive. Use the words in parentheses. Then match your questions with the answers below.

_____ **1.** (you / watch / TV) *Are you watching TV?* _____

_____ **2.** (he / look at / the TV Guide?)_____

_____ **3.** (they / enjoy / the talk show) _____

_____ **4.** (we / paying a lot for cable TV)_____

_____ **5.** (the movie / start now) _____

    a. Yes. He's checking the time of the ball game tonight.

    b. Yes, I am. I'm watching the news.

    c. Yes, we are. It's expensive.

    d. No, it isn't. It's too early.

    e. Yes, they are. They watch that show every week.

3 | QUESTIONS

Grammar Notes 1–3

A *Abby and Greg are talking on the telephone. Complete their conversation. Use the words in parentheses and the present progressive.*

GREG: Hello.

ABBY: Hi, Greg. *How are you feeling* ? _____ ?
                         1.(How / you / feel)   **2.(you / feel / any better)**

GREG: No, I'm not.

ABBY: _____ ?
                    3.(you / take / the medicine)

GREG: No.

ABBY: Well, take it. It's good for you.

GREG: _____ ?
                    4.(Where / you / call from)

ABBY: I'm on Fifth Avenue and, listen to this. Renée Zellweger is walking ahead of me.

GREG: No kidding! _____ ?
                           5.(What street / you / walk on)

ABBY: I'm on Fifth Avenue between 55th and 56th Street.

GREG: _____ ?
                    6.(What / she / wear)

ABBY: She's wearing a pink suit. She looks great.

GREG: _____ ?
                    7.(she / talk / to anyone)

ABBY: She's talking to a man and three women. She's giving them her autograph.

_____? _____?
8. (What / you / do)   9. (you / watch / TV)

GREG: I'm looking at Renée Zellweger too. I'm watching the movie *Chicago*.

ABBY: That was a good movie. _____?
10. (What / happen)

GREG: Renée Zellweger and Catherine Zeta-Jones are dancing.

ABBY: Oh. I remember that part. Well, feel better! I'll be home after my class. Bye, hon.

GREG: Bye-bye.

🎧 **B** *Listen and check your work.*

4 | COMMON TWO-WORD VERBS   *Grammar Notes 1–2*

Complete the questions. Use the words in the box and the present progressive.

listen to	look at	look for	wait for

1. **A:** What are you watching?

   B: Nothing now. I _____ the game to come on. My favorite team is playing.

2. **A:** What _____ she _____?

   B: She's looking at the mail.

3. **A:** _____ you _____ your glasses?

   B: Yes, I am. Why? Do you see them?

4. **A:** What _____ they _____?

   B: Mozart's opera *The Magic Flute*.

5 | EDITING

Correct this conversation. There are eight mistakes. The first mistake is already corrected.

A: Are you ~~listen~~ *listening* to the radio?

B: No, I not. I'm watching TV.

A: What you watching?

B: I'm watch a cooking show.

A: Oh. What happening?

(continued)

B: The chef is preparing dinner for six.

A: What he's making?

B: Spinach lasagna and salad.

A: What's he use?

B: Spinach, cheese, tomato sauce, and mushrooms.

A: He making the tomato sauce?

B: No. It's from a can, but it looks good. I'm getting hungry.

Communication Practice

6 | LISTENING

 *Roberto is returning home. He meets his friend Cesar. Roberto is listening to a ball game. Write possible ways to complete the conversation. Then listen and write what you hear.*

ROBERTO: Hey, Cesar. What _____?

    CESAR: The ball game.

ROBERTO: Who _____?

    CESAR: The Red Sox and the Astros.

ROBERTO: Where _____?

    CESAR: In _____.

ROBERTO: _____?

    CESAR: It's a _____. It's the bottom of the ninth. Wait . . . Something's
happening. Everyone's shouting.

ROBERTO: What _____?

    CESAR: It's a _____ run.

ROBERTO: Yes! That's terrific. The _____ won.

7 | INFORMATION GAP: SURFING THE CHANNELS

A *Work in pairs. Student B, turn to the Information Gap on page 186. Student A, look at the programs on channels 2 and 4. Write the* wh- *questions that you need to ask to complete the sentences. Ask your partner your questions. Answer your partner's questions about channels 5 and 7.*

1. A: *Where is the man lying* ? B: *He's lying on the floor* .

2. A: _____ ? B: _____ .

3. A: _____ ? B: _____ .

4. A: _____ ? B: _____ .

5. A: _____ ? B: _____ .

6. A: _____ ? B: _____ .

7. A: _____ ? B: _____ .

- CHANNEL 2: A man is lying _____ . _____
  1.   **2.**
  isn't breathing. The man's wife and housekeeper are _____ .
  3.
  A family friend is calling _____ .
  4.

- CHANNEL 4: Some big men are wearing _____ . They're
  5.
  _____ on a playing field. A tall man is carrying
  6.
  _____ .
  7.

- CHANNEL 5: A woman is sitting at a desk. She's wearing a suit. She is talking about the president's trip to Asia.

- CHANNEL 7: A young couple and an older couple are having dessert in an expensive restaurant. The older woman is smiling. She is throwing a pie in her husband's face.

B *Work with your partner. Match the type of show and the channel.*

Channel	Type of Show
_____ 1. Channel 2	a. a comedy
_____ 2. Channel 4	b. a news show
_____ 3. Channel 5	c. a murder mystery
_____ 4. Channel 7	d. a sports show

8 | WHAT ARE YOU WATCHING?

Work in pairs. Write a telephone conversation with your partner. Student A is watching TV when Student B calls. Student B, ask Student A questions about his or her show. Use the present progressive. Then write more sentences to continue the conversation.

A: Hello.

B: Hi, _____. This is _____. Are you busy?

A: Oh, hi, _____. I _____ TV.
(watch)

B: What _____?
(watch)

A: _____

B: What's happening?

A: _____

9 | ON THE INTERNET

Search for TV shows you like. If you can, print one or two photos of the show. What's the name of the show? What kind of show is it? Who are the stars? What are they doing in the photos?

Example: I like the documentaries on *National Geographic Explorer.* The shows are always different. This summer I saw shows on race cars, elephants, and Afghanistan.

The Imperative

Grammar in Context

BEFORE YOU READ

Do you like contests? What kind?

WIN A PLASMA TV
Write why you love to watch TV.

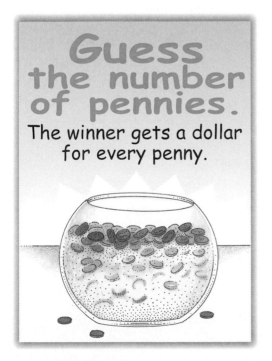

Guess the number of pennies.
The winner gets a dollar for every penny.

Write a paragraph:
Clothes Make the Woman
Win a Day of Shopping at The Wrap

Parents and Children *is a family magazine. Every month the magazine has a contest. It gives readers money for true stories about children. Read about a contest.*

Kids Are Funny! We're not kidding.

Send us your story and **win** a great prize.

Write a true story about your child, or about yourself as a child.

Don't write more than 100 words.

Include your name, address, and phone number with your story.

Don't send a return envelope. We do not return stories.

E-mail it to: PC.com (Click "kids")

or

Write to:

Parents and Children
480 Elk Street
Madison, Wisconsin 53704
*For more information, **visit** our website at PC.com*

AFTER YOU READ

Correct this contest information.

1. Send us a ~~sad~~ *funny* story.

2. Include your name, e-mail address, and phone number with the story.

3. Don't write more than 10 words.

4. Visit our office in Madison for current information.

5. E-mail *Teachers and Children* at p&c.com.

Grammar Presentation

THE IMPERATIVE

Affirmative	
Base Form of Verb	
Write	to the magazine.

Negative		
Don't	Base Form of Verb	
Don't	**send**	money.

GRAMMAR NOTES	EXAMPLES

1. The **imperative** uses the **base form of the verb**.

- **Walk** three blocks and turn right.

2. Use the **imperative** to:

   a. Give directions and instructions.

   b. Give orders.

   c. Give advice or suggestions.

   d. Give warnings.

   e. Make polite requests.

- **Write** to the magazine.
- **Stand** there.
- **Take** the train. **Don't take** the bus.
- **Be** careful! It's hot.
- **Please call** before noon.

3. *Don't* comes before the base form for the negative imperative.

- **Don't call** us after 10:00 P.M.
- **Don't be** late.

4. In an imperative statement, the subject is always *you*, but we don't say it or write it.

- **Ask** for directions.
  (You) ask for directions.

5. Use *please* to make orders, warnings, and requests more polite. *Please* can come at the beginning or the end of the sentence.

- **Please** stand there.
- **Please** be careful.
- **Please** call before noon.
- Call before noon, **please**.

Focused Practice

1 | DISCOVER THE GRAMMAR

Check the sentences that use the imperative.

_____ 1. Write to the magazine.

_____ 2. I'm writing to the magazine.

_____ 3. Win a trip to Florida.

_____ 4. Please visit us online.

_____ 5. They often win contests.

_____ 6. Don't send photos.

_____ 7. You write a funny story and you get $300.

_____ 8. Take the number 6 bus.

_____ 9. Be careful!

2 | GREAT ADVICE!   *Grammar Notes 1–5*

Every month FOG Magazine *gives prizes to people with great ideas. Read this month's "That's a Great Idea!" Complete the sentences. Use the verbs in the box.*

Don't shop	Enter	Please don't write	Send	Wash
Don't use	Make	Point	Shop	

THAT'S A GREAT IDEA!

• **You want to remove a bandage. You don't want it to hurt.**

_____ a hair dryer at the bandage for a
                1.
few seconds.

Ricardo Alvarez

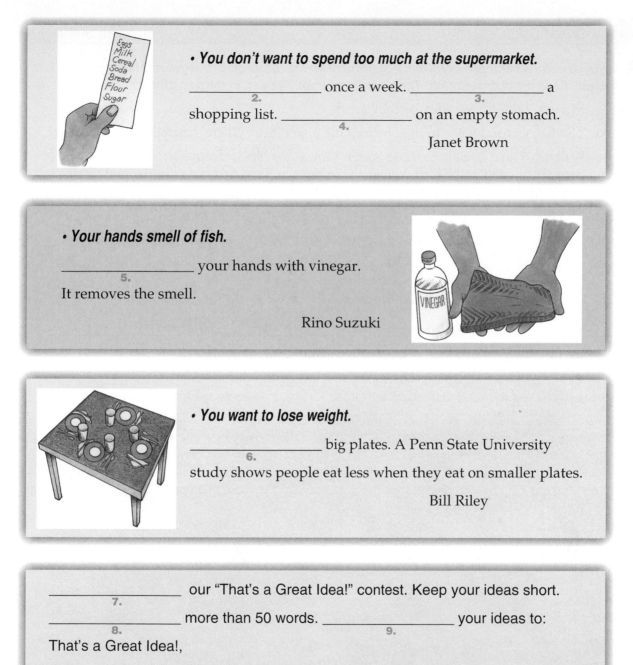

• **You don't want to spend too much at the supermarket.**

_____ once a week. _____ a
2.   3.
shopping list. _____ on an empty stomach.
4.

Janet Brown

• **Your hands smell of fish.**

_____ your hands with vinegar.
5.
It removes the smell.

Rino Suzuki

• **You want to lose weight.**

_____ big plates. A Penn State University
6.
study shows people eat less when they eat on smaller plates.

Bill Riley

_____ our "That's a Great Idea!" contest. Keep your ideas short.
7.
_____ more than 50 words. _____ your ideas to:
8.   9.
That's a Great Idea!,

FOG Magazine, 10 Thinktank Street, Gray Matter, NY 10606

Winners receive a prize.

3 | GIVING DIRECTIONS

A *Miyuki is visiting her friend Carol in her apartment on the corner of 70th Street and 3rd Avenue. Read their conversation. Then look at the map. Put an **x** at the post office.*

CAROL: Miyuki, I think your idea is really great.

MIYUKI: Thanks, Carol. I want to mail it from the post office. Where's the nearest post office?

CAROL: Walk up Third Avenue to 72nd Street. That's two blocks from here. The post office is between Second and Third Avenue. Turn right at 72nd Street. It's in the middle of the block, on the north side of the street.

MIYUKI: Thanks.

CAROL: I need to go to the bank. The post office is on the way. We can walk together.

MIYUKI: Great.

B *Now write directions from Carol's home to the bank.*

_____ up Third Avenue to _____ Street. _____

right. Walk _____ blocks. The bank is on the corner of the street.

4 | POLITE REQUESTS

Grammar Note 5

Complete the requests. Choose from the words or phrases in parentheses.

1. _____*Please mail*_____ this for me when you're at the post office.
   (Please mail / Please don't mail)

2. It's cold in here. Please _____ the window.
   (open / don't open)

3. I like to sleep late. _____ before 11:00 A.M.
   (Please call / Please don't call)

4. The concert starts at 8:00. _____ on time.
   (Please come / Please don't come)

5. We're baking this cake for Grandpa. _____ it, please.
   (Don't eat / Eat)

6. He doesn't understand how your camera works. _____ him
   (Please show / Please don't show)
   how to use it.

7. Those glasses break easily. _____ them.
   (Please touch / Please don't touch)

5 | CONTEST INFORMATION

Grammar Notes 1–2

Complete the sentences with the correct phrasal (two-word) verbs.

Check out	Fill in	Pick up	Send in

JELLY BEAN CONTEST

1. _____ an entry form at Cathy's Candy Store.

2. _____ your name, address, and e-mail address.

3. _____ your entry before March 31.

4. _____ the winning entry at Cathycandy@fog.com

6 | EDITING

Correct the sentences. There are five mistakes. Put a check (✓) next to each of the two correct sentences.

_____ 1. Win a vacation for two.

_____ 2. Please to include your name and address.

_____ 3. For information, visits our website at www.longtrip.com.

_____ 4. Enter here.

_____ 5. Write not more than 100 words.

_____ 6. Don't sends money.

_____ 7. Send your entry please before the end of this month.

Communication Practice

7 | LISTENING

 Listen to the phone messages on Penny and Steve's answering machine. Listen again and complete the chart.

Caller	Message for	Message	Caller's Number
Denise			

8 | AN AD

Prepare a short advertisement for your school. Write no more than 50 words. Hang your ad on the wall. The class selects the best ad.

Example: Come to FOG Language School. Have fun while you learn. Learn to speak, read, and write English. Register early and receive a discount.

9 | WRITING

Look at the map in Exercise 3.

A *Work in pairs. You and your partner are in front of Carol's building. Ask your partner how to get to one of the following places. Then switch roles.*

- the bakery
- the supermarket
- the school
- the drugstore

Example: **A:** How do I get to the nearest bakery?
B: Walk up Third Avenue. The bakery is between 71st and 72nd Streets. It's in the middle of the block.

B *Write directions from Carol's home to two places on the map. Read your directions aloud. The class names the places.*

Example: **A:** Walk up Third Avenue to 71st Street. Turn right. Walk to First Avenue. It's on the corner of 71st Street and First Avenue.
B: A drugstore?
A: Right.

10 | ON THE INTERNET

 *Look up contests on the Internet. Find sentences in the imperative. Read them to the class.*

Can / Could

Grammar in Context

BEFORE YOU READ

Do you or a friend have a parrot? If so, can it talk? What language does it speak?

🎧 *Read about an amazing parrot.*

A Genius Parrot

Everyone knows parrots **can talk.** By "talk" we mean they **can repeat** words. Most parrots **can't** really **express** ideas.

N'kisi is different. N'kisi is an African Gray parrot. He **can say** almost 1,000 words. He **can use** basic grammar. He **can talk** about the present, past, and future. When he doesn't know a form, he **can invent** one. For example, he used the word "flied," not "flew," for the past of the verb "fly."

N'kisi lives in New York City with his owner, Aimee Morgana. He **couldn't talk** much at first. At first he **could** only **say** a few words. But Aimee was a great teacher and N'kisi was a good student. Now N'kisi talks to anyone near him.

Donald Broom, a professor of Veterinary Medicine at the University of Cambridge, is not surprised. He says that parrots **can think** at high levels. In that way, they are like apes and chimpanzees.

Les Rance of the Parrot Society says, "Most African Grays are intelligent. They **can learn** to do easy puzzles. They **can say** 'good night' when you turn the lights off at night. They **can say** 'good-bye' when you put a coat on. But N'kisi **can do** many more things. N'kisi is an amazing bird. He's not just smart. He's a genius."

AFTER YOU READ

Mark these statements **T** *(true),* **F** *(false), or* **?** *(it doesn't say).*

_____ 1. N'kisi can say more than 1,100 words.

_____ 2. N'kisi can't use basic grammar.

_____ 3. N'kisi can talk about the past and the future.

_____ 4. N'kisi can understand Italian.

_____ 5. Parrots can't think at high levels.

_____ 6. N'kisi could only say a few words at first.

Grammar Presentation

CAN/CAN'T FOR ABILITY AND POSSIBILITY;

COULD FOR PAST ABILITY

Affirmative and Negative Statements		
Subject	*Can / Could*	Base Form of Verb
I You He She It We You They	**can** **can't** **could** **couldn't**	**speak** Spanish.

Yes/No Questions		
Can/Could	Subject	Base Form of Verb
Can **Could**	you	**understand**?

Answers
Yes, we can understand. No, we can't understand.
Yes, we could understand. No, we couldn't understand.

GRAMMAR NOTES

EXAMPLES

1. *Can* expresses **ability** or **possibility**. It comes before the verb. The verb is always in the **base form**.	• He **can say** 950 words. • We **can travel** by bus or train.
2. The **negative** of *can* is *can't*. NOTE: *Cannot* is also a correct form of the negative.	• I **can't** understand you. • I **cannot** understand you.

3. Reverse the subject and *can* for *yes/no* questions.	**Q: Can he** speak about the past?
	A: Yes, he can.
	    OR
	    No, he can't.

4. *Could* expresses **past ability**. The **negative** of *could* is *couldn't*. *Could not* is also correct.	• I **could** run fast in high school. • I **couldn't** drive five years ago. • I **could not** drive five years ago.

5. Reverse the subject and *could* for *yes/no* questions.	**Q: Could you** speak English last year? **A:** Yes, I could. OR No, I couldn't.

Pronunciation Note

When *can* is followed by a base form verb, we usually pronounce it /kən/ or /kn/ and stress the base form verb: We can **dánce**. In sentences with *can't* followed by a base form verb, we stress both *can't* and the base form verb: We **cán't dánce**.

Focused Practice

1 | DISCOVER THE GRAMMAR

A *Read the sentences in column A. Underline* **can, can't**, *or* **couldn't** + base **form** *verbs. Circle negative statements.*

B *Match the sentences in column A with the possible reasons in column B.*

A

_____ 1. N'kisi can talk about the past.

_____ 2. We can't understand her.

_____ 3. I'm sorry. I can't help you now.

_____ 4. I can't hear you.

_____ 5. He can lift 50 kilos (110 pounds).

_____ 6. They can't smell the roses.

_____ 7. The boy couldn't reach the button.

B

a. He's very strong.

b. She speaks too fast.

c. He was too short.

d. They have colds.

e. He's a smart bird.

f. I'm busy.

g. It's very noisy here.

2 | CAN AND CAN'T
Grammar Notes 1–2

Complete the sentences. Use **can** *or* **can't** *and the verb in parentheses.*

1. Most African Gray parrots _____can learn_____ to speak. They are very intelligent birds.
   (learn)

2. I _____ the sign. We are too far away.
   (see)

3. My dog _____, but he _____ me my shoe. I'm trying to teach him
   (sit)   (bring)

   to get things.

4. We _____ to our school. It's near our home.
   (walk)

5. They _____ two languages, Spanish and Italian. They're learning English now.
   (speak)

6. My uncle _____. He wants to take driving lessons.
   (drive)

7. He _____ the door. His arms are full.
   (open)

3 | N'KISI WANTS A CAR
Grammar Note 3

N'kisi and Aimee were in a car. After the ride this is what N'kisi said. This is a real conversation. Read the conversation. Then write yes/no *questions and answer the questions.*

N'KISI: Wanna [I want to] go in a car right now.

AIMEE: I'm sorry. We can't right now—maybe we can go later.

N'KISI: Why can't I go in a car now?

AIMEE: Because we don't have one.

N'KISI: Let's get a car.

AIMEE: No, N'kisi, we can't get a car now.

N'KISI: I want a car.

1. Q: _____Can N'kisi talk?_____   A: _____Yes, he can._____
   (N'kisi / talk)

2. Q: _____   A: _____
   (he / ask questions)

3. Q: _____   A: _____
   (he / make suggestions)

4. Q: _____   A: _____
   (Aimee and N'kisi / get a car now)

5. Q: _____   A: _____
   (you / believe this conversation)

4 | PAST ABILITIES

Grammar Notes 4–5

*Complete the sentences with **could** or **couldn't** and the verbs in parentheses.*

1. My cat was not a good hunter. He ____*couldn't catch*____ any mice. _____ your
   a. (catch)

   cat _____ mice?
   b. (catch)

2. Michael was a smart gorilla. He _____ sign language. He _____
   a. (use)   **b. (make)**

   600 different gestures.

3. My dog Charlie was a good watchdog, but he _____ any tricks.
   (do)

4. He was a child genius. He _____ college physics when he was 10 years old.
   (understand)

5. I _____ English well a few months ago. But now I can.
   (speak)

6. Long ago he was on the all-star tennis team. He _____ tennis very well.
   (play)

7. She _____ incredible weights in high school. She was on a weight-lifting team.
   (lift)

5 | EDITING

*Read the sentences. There are six mistakes. The first mistake is already corrected. Add **can***
to fix one mistake.

         come

A: Can you ~~coming~~ to my party? It's next Saturday night.

B: Yes, thanks. How I get to your home?

A: You can to take the train and a taxi.

B: Can you meet me at the train station?

A: I'm sorry I can't. I no can drive. Maybe Bob can meets you. He has a car and he can to drive.

Communication Practice

6 | LISTENING

🎧 *Listen and repeat the sentences. Listen again and complete the sentences. Then listen*
a third time and mark the stress.

1. My friend _____*can séw*_____, but he _____*cán't cóok*_____.

2. My dog _____, but it _____.

3. Kelly _____ 100 kilos, but Nitza _____.

4. José _____ tennis. He _____ basketball, too.

5. Elena _____ English newspapers, but she _____ spoken English well.

7 | FIND SOMEONE WHO CAN . . .

A *Walk around the class. Ask your classmates questions with **can** or **could**. Ask about now and about five years ago. If they answer **yes**, write their names in the box.*

Example: VICTOR: Can you play an instrument?

CAROLINA: Yes, I can. I can play the guitar.

VICTOR: Could you play the guitar five years ago?

CAROLINA: No, I couldn't.

	Now	**Five years ago**
1. play an instrument	*Carolina*	
2. design a web page		
3. fix a car		
4. fly a plane		
5. write with both hands		
6. snowboard		
7. windsurf		

B *Report to your class.*

Example: Erna can play the piano and design a web page. Five years ago she could play the piano, but she couldn't design a web page.

8 | GAME: WHAT CAN YOUR GROUP DO?

Work in small groups. When your group can do one of the following, raise your hand. The first group to do a task wins.

1. Can you say "I love you" in more than five languages?

2. Can you name the colors of the flags of eight countries?

3. Can you name the capitals of ten countries?

9 | WRITING

Write about an interesting pet. What kind of animal is it? What does it look like? Where does it live? Does it have a name? What is it? What can it do? What can't it do?

Example: I have a beautiful green parakeet. His name is Chichi. He is two years old. He lives in a cage in the living room. Sometimes he flies around the room. Chichi can sing very beautifully. Chichi couldn't do anything when he was a baby. But now he can sit on my finger and eat from my hand. He can't speak, but I'm happy about that. I tell him all my secrets and he doesn't tell anyone. That's a wonderful quality. I love my Chichi.

10 | ON THE INTERNET

Find out more about animals who can use or understand language. Search for Koko the gorilla (California, USA) or Rico the border collie (Germany), or learn more about African Grey parrots like N'kisi. Report to the class.

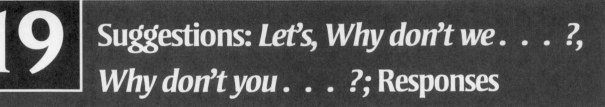

Suggestions: *Let's, Why don't we . . . ?, Why don't you . . . ?*; Responses

Grammar in Context

BEFORE YOU READ

What kind of sports do you like to do?
What kind of sports do you like to watch?

- soccer or football
- rock climbing
- snorkeling or scuba diving
- other sport

🎧 *Four friends are on vacation in Maui. Read their conversation.*

RODICA: The weather is perfect. **Let's spend** the afternoon at the beach.

ARDA: Yeah. **Let's go** snorkeling again.

PAUL: **Why don't we try** scuba diving?

RODICA: Scuba diving? That's not so easy. You need to take lessons. And the tank is heavy.

SHIRA: I have a better idea. **Let's go** Snuba® diving.

ARDA: Snuba diving? What's that?

SHIRA: It's something new. I read a brochure about it. It combines scuba diving and snorkeling. It's pretty safe. They say anyone over eight years old can do it. So, what do you think? Want to try it? Are you game?

RODICA: Sure. Why not? It sounds like fun.

SHIRA: OK. **Why don't we get** a disposable underwater camera? I want pictures of the fish.

RODICA: Me too. Shira, **why don't you get** the camera? Arda and I can get information about Snuba diving at the front desk.

SHIRA: OK. Then **let's meet** back here.

RODICA: Great.

AFTER YOU READ

Change the sentences to match the information in the conversation above.

The weather is ~~bad~~ perfect. Five friends decide to go snorkeling. They also decide to buy phones.

They want to take pictures of themselves. Arda and Rodica get information at the hotel pool.

Grammar Presentation

SUGGESTIONS

Affirmative		
Let's	Base Form of Verb	
Let's	go	to the beach.

Negative			
Let's	*Not*	Base Form of Verb	
Let's	not	go	to the beach.

Suggestions for a Group		
Base Form *Why Don't We*	of Verb	
Why don't we	go	on a bike tour?

Suggestions for Another Person		
Why Don't You	Base Form of Verb	
Why don't you	get	the cameras?

RESPONSES

Agree
OK.
That's a good idea. (Good idea.)
That sounds good to me. (Sounds good to me.)
Sounds like a plan.

Disagree
No, I don't feel like it.
Why don't we . . . instead.
Sorry, not today.
I can't. I . . .

GRAMMAR NOTES	EXAMPLES
1. Use *Let's* or *Let's not* + **the base form** for suggestions that include you and another person.	• **Let's go.** • **Let's not eat** there.
2. Use *Why don't we* and the base form for suggestions that include you and another person. Use *Why don't you* to make a suggestion or give advice to another person. Remember to put a question mark (**?**) at the end of sentences with *Why don't we* and *Why don't you*.	• **Why don't we** go to the pool? • **Why don't you** look on the Internet? • **Why don't we** meet in the lobby**?** • **Why don't you** call home**?**
3. To **agree** to a suggestion we sometimes use, *OK*, *That's a good idea.*, or *That sounds good to me*. To **reject** a suggestion we usually **give a reason** and **make another suggestion**.	**A:** Let's meet at eight o'clock. **B: OK.** OR **That's a good idea.** **A:** Let's meet at eight o'clock. **B: That's too early. Why don't we meet at eight-thirty?**

Focused Practice

1 | DISCOVER THE GRAMMAR

A *Read the statements. Underline the suggestions.*

B *Unscramble the conversation. Write the conversation on the lines below.*

- OK. The prices there are better.
- Let's get some souvenirs.
- That's true, but the prices are high. Why don't we go to the market?
- That's a good idea. Why don't we go to the gift shop? They have some beautiful things.

A: _____

B: _____

A: _____

B: _____

2 | *LET'S AND LET'S NOT*   *Grammar Note 1*

*Complete the sentences. Use **Let's** or **Let's not** and the verb in parentheses.*

1. We're out of film. _____*Let's get*_____ some at the gift shop.
   (get)

2. The taxis here are expensive. _____ a bus.
   (take)

3. The food there was terrible. _____ back.
   (go)

4. It's cold today. _____ swimming in the ocean.
   (go)

5. The store isn't far. _____ there.
   (walk)

6. Snuba diving was fun. _____ it again.
   (do)

7. This is our last day here. _____ late. Let's get up early and see the volcanoes.
   (sleep)

3 | CONVERSATIONS   *Grammar Notes 1–2*

Complete the conversations. Use the sentences below.

> **a.** Why don't we meet at the pool?
>
> **b.** Let's walk to the beach.
>
> **c.** Why don't we try that new Lebanese restaurant?
>
> **d.** Why don't you call the front desk and complain?
>
> **e.** Let's not go to the market for souvenirs.
>
> **f.** Let's ask the receptionist.

1. SHIRA: Let's go to Luigi's Restaurant.

    RODICA: Again? _____

2. ARDA: Let's meet in the gift shop in about 15 minutes.

    SHIRA: It's so nice outside. _____

3. ARDA: _____ Then we can go for a swim.

    SHIRA: It's far. Why don't we drive?

4. RODICA: It's too crowded at the market. _____

    ARDA: OK. We can buy souvenirs at the shopping mall.

5. ARDA: Is there a fitness room at the hotel?

    SHIRA: I don't know. _____

6. RODICA: The TV in my room doesn't work.

    ARDA: _____

4 | MAKE A SUGGESTION

Grammar Notes 1–3

Complete the suggestions. Use the phrasal (two-word) verbs in the box. Then circle the letter of the correct response.

check out	find out	pick up	sit down	turn on

1. A: Let's _____ some sandwiches. We can eat them in the park.

   B: a. Sounds like a plan.

   b. Yes.

2. A: Let's _____ over there. There are two empty seats.

   B: a. I don't feel like it. Why don't we go for a swim or play ball?

   b. No, we aren't.

3. A: Why don't we _____ about a tour for this afternoon?

   B: a. Because I'm busy.

   b. I'm sorry, I can't. I have a scuba diving lesson at 2:00.

4. A: Why don't you _____ the TV? We can hear the news.

   B: a. Good idea.

   b. Yes, I can.

5. A: Why don't we _____ the menu at that fish restaurant? It looks nice.

   B: a. Because I don't like fish.

   b. Sorry. I don't like fish.

5 | EDITING

Correct these conversations. There are five mistakes. The first mistake is already corrected.

1. A: Let's ˄*get* something to eat.

   B: I'm not hungry now. How about in an hour?

2. A: Why don't we go to the movies?

   B: Yes.

3. A: Why do not we help them?

   B: OK.

4. A: Let's us go snuba diving.

   B: That's a good idea.

5. A: Why don't we meet for dinner at 6:00?

   B: That's a little early. Let's at 6:30.

Communication Practice

6 │ LISTENING

🎧 *Rodica, Arda, and Shira are talking about their plans for the afternoon. Listen. Then listen again and check the things they decide to do.*

_____ **1.** go whale watching

_____ **2.** go bike riding

_____ **3.** go windsurfing

_____ **4.** take photos

_____ **5.** go surfing

_____ **6.** take a boat ride

_____ **7.** go to the market

_____ **8.** buy handmade baskets

7 │ ROLE PLAY

Work in pairs (A and B). Student A makes a suggestion. Student B agrees or makes another suggestion and gives a reason why. Continue until you both agree. Take turns.

Example: **A:** Let's have pizza.
  B: I'm tired of pizza. Why don't we have Chinese food?
  A: That's a good idea.

1. Let's have pizza.

2. Let's take a break.

3. Let's play tennis.

4. Let's go Snuba diving.

5. Let's visit Hawaii.

6. Let's study grammar tonight.

8 | SOUVENIRS

*Work in pairs. You and your partner are on vacation in Hawaii. You each want to buy souvenirs for five people. Give each other suggestions. Use **Why don't you** for suggestions.*

Example: A: I want to get souvenirs for my parents, my brother, my best friend, and a coworker.
B: Why don't you buy a basket for your mother?
A: That's a good idea. What about my brother? Any ideas for him?

9 | ON THE INTERNET

A *Find out places you can do one of the following sports:*

- parasailing

- bungee jumping

- surfing

- water skiing

- horseback riding

- ice skating

B *Work in pairs. Have a conversation with your partner. Make a suggestion to do one of the above sports.*

Example: A: Let's go parasailing.
B: Where can we go?
A: I read about a place in South Africa.
B: Really?
A: Uh-huh. It's near Johannesburg. It's . . .

From **Grammar** to **Writing**
Subjects and Verbs

1 | *What's wrong with these sentences?*

A
1. He a handsome man.
2. She a red skirt.
3. I from Argentina.

B
1. Am wearing blue pants.
2. Are tired?
3. Is a cool day.

All sentences in A are missing a verb. All sentences in B are missing a subject.

Study the information about subjects and verbs.

Every sentence needs a subject and verb.

The **subject** is a noun or pronoun. It tells who or what the sentence is about.

The **verb** tells the action or links the subject with the rest of the sentence.

- **John** is running.
- **They** are watching TV.
- It **is raining**.
- He **is** a doctor.

---

2 | *Correct this paragraph. Then underline the subject and circle the verb in each sentence.*

I in Central Park. It a sunny day in September. Is crowded. Some children soccer. They're laughing and shouting. Some people are running. Three older women on a bench. Are watching the runners and soccer players. A young man and woman are holding hands. Are smiling. Are in love. Central Park a wonderful place to be, especially on a beautiful September day.

3 | *Imagine you are in one of these places. Write a paragraph about the people you see.*

1. You are on a busy street.
2. You are in an airport or train station.
3. You are in a park.

Review Test

I *Read each conversation. Circle the letter of the underlined word or group of words that is not correct.*

1. A: What <u>you're</u> <u>doing</u>?
       A   B

   B: <u>We're</u> <u>watching</u> the news on TV.
      C   D

   A B C D

2. A: She's <u>studying</u> Portuguese.
              A

   B: <u>No</u>, she's <u>no studying</u> Portuguese. <u>She's</u> studying Italian.
      B   C   D

   A B C D

3. A: Aunt Jessica <u>is</u> <u>in the hospital</u>.
                    A   B

   B: <u>Let's</u> <u>to send</u> her flowers.
      C   D

   A B C D

4. A: <u>They're</u> <u>playing</u> basketball.
      A   B

   B: <u>Why</u> <u>you don't</u> join them?
      C   D

   A B C D

5. A: How's his English?

   B: Good. Last year he <u>couldn't</u> <u>understand</u> anything. Now he <u>cans</u>
                          A   B   C

   understand and <u>speak</u> well.
                   D

   A B C D

6. A: <u>Those cookies</u> are for the party. <u>Please</u> <u>not to eat</u> them.
      A   B   C

   B: <u>OK</u>. They look delicious.
      D

   A B C D

7. A: How <u>can I</u> <u>get</u> to the bank?
          A   B

   B: <u>Walk</u> two blocks to Second Street. <u>Turns</u> left.
      C   D

   A B C D

II *Read each dialogue. Circle the letter of the correct response.*

1. **A:** Let's have lunch now.

   B: _____

   a. It's too early. Why don't we

      wait until noon?

   b. Yes, you're right.

2. **A:** Why don't you call home?

   B: _____

   a. OK.

   b. Let's call home.

3. **A:** Let's rent a movie.

   B: _____

   a. No, we don't.

   b. That sounds like a good idea.

4. **A:** Are they waiting for us?

   B: _____

   a. No, they aren't.

   b. Yes, we are.

5. **A:** What's he doing?

   B: _____

   a. He's playing.

   b. He can play.

6. **A:** Can you hear me?

   B: _____ Please speak louder.

   a. No, we can't.

   b. No, I couldn't.

7. **A:** Did you enjoy the play?

   B: No, I didn't. _____

   a. I can't see the stage.

   b. I couldn't see the stage.

III *Read each situation. Write one affirmative statement and one negative statement in the imperative. Use the phrases in the box.*

forget your scarf	read the directions	start before 10:00	~~stop~~
take the highway	use the side streets	~~walk~~	wear your jacket

1. The traffic light is red.

   a. *Stop.* _____

   b. *Don't walk.* _____

2. You have a test at 10:00.

   a. _____

   b. _____

3. There are many cars on the highway.

   a. _____

   b. _____

4. It's cold outside.

   a. _____

   b. _____

IV *Complete the paragraph. Use the affirmative or negative present progressive of each verb in parentheses.*

Jen and Jon are at the library, but they _____. Jen
1.(study)

_____ a letter to her grandmother. Jon _____
2.(write)   3.(look)

at a magazine. Their textbooks are open, but they _____ them. They
4.(read)

_____. They _____ a break.
5.(relax)   6.(take)

V *Correct the mistake in each conversation.*

1. **A:** Is it's raining outside?

   B: Yes, it is. I'm not leaving.

2. **A:** Are they play soccer?

   B: No, they're playing baseball.

3. **A:** How is his English?

   B: He speaks well now, but last year he can't speak at all.

4. **A:** Why don't we to take a walk?

   B: OK.

5. **A:** Please you are quiet.

   B: Sorry.

▶ *To check your answers, go to the Answer Key on page RT-2.*

INFORMATION GAP FOR STUDENT B — *Unit 15, Exercise 7*

Student B, look at the picture of people on a plane. First, tell Student A about one of the people in your picture. Then Student A will tell you about that person in his or her picture. Use the present progressive. Find five differences.

Example: B: In my picture, the man in 14A is watching a movie.

INFORMATION GAP FOR STUDENT B

Unit 16, Exercise 7

A *Student B, look at the programs on channels 5 and 7. Write the wh- questions that you need to ask to complete the sentences. Answer your partner's questions about channels 2 and 4. Ask your partner your questions.*

1. B: _Who's sitting at a desk_ ? A: _A woman is sitting at a desk_ .

2. B: _____? A: _____.

3. B: _____? A: _____.

4. B: _____? A: _____.

5. B: _____? A: _____.

6. B: _____? A: _____.

- CHANNEL 2: A man is lying on the floor. The man isn't breathing. The man's wife and housekeeper are crying. A family friend is calling the police.

- CHANNEL 4: Some big men are wearing uniforms. They're running on a playing field. A tall man is carrying a football.

- CHANNEL 5: _____ is sitting at a desk. She's wearing
  _____. She is talking about _____.
        1.   **2.**   **3.**

- CHANNEL 7: A young couple and an older couple are having dessert in
  _____. The _____ is smiling.
                    4.   **5.**
  _____ is throwing a pie in her husband's face.
             6.

The Simple Past

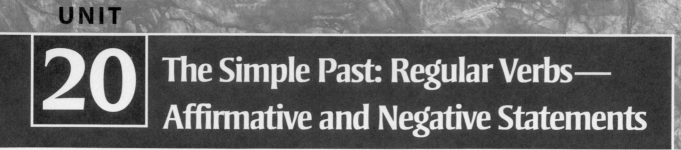

20 The Simple Past: Regular Verbs—Affirmative and Negative Statements

Grammar in Context

BEFORE YOU READ

Look at the chart. Are you from one of these countries? Have you visited any of these countries? Which ones? Which cities did you visit? When?

Example: I'm from Mexico. I was in Canada in 1999. I visited Montreal and Quebec. I was in the United States last summer. I visited San Francisco and Los Angeles.

Most Popular Tourist Places

	Country	2003 (arrivals in millions)	Percent change from 2002
1.	France	75.0	−2.6
2.	Spain	52.3	+0.3
3.	United States	40.4	−3.6
4.	Italy	39.6	−0.5
5.	China	33.0	−10.3
6.	United Kingdom	24.8	+2.6
7.	Austria	19.1	+2.6
8.	Mexico	18.7	−4.9
9.	Germany	18.4	+2.4
10.	Canada	17.5	−12.7

🎧 *Read the postcard. What city did Karen and Gene visit? The answer is at the bottom of the page.*

Dear Dahlia and Jon,

They say everyone loves this city. Now we know why.

Yesterday morning we **watched** foot-volley on Ipanema Beach. It was unbelievable! The players were great. They **didn't miss** the ball. In the afternoon we **visited** Sugarloaf. The view from the top was out of this world. Then in the evening we **enjoyed** a delicious meal at a churrascaria (barbecued meat restaurant).

Our flight here was the only bad part of the trip. We **didn't land** until 11:30 at night, and the flight was very bumpy. But the people at our hotel were helpful and our room is beautiful.

Our body language is still better than our Portuguese, but we are trying.

Ciao!

Karen and Gene

To: Dahlia and Jon Lamb
2909 Northport Trail
Charleston, SC 29401
USA

AFTER YOU READ

Change these false statements to true ones.

1. Dahlia and Jon visited Rio de Janeiro.

2. Karen and Gene played foot-volley on Ipanema Beach.

3. Karen and Gene enjoyed a meal at an Italian restaurant.

4. Karen and Gene's plane arrived in the evening.

5. The people at the hotel were unhelpful.

6. Karen and Gene speak Portuguese well.

Grammar Presentation

THE SIMPLE PAST: REGULAR VERBS—AFFIRMATIVE AND NEGATIVE STATEMENTS

Affirmative Statements	
Subject	**Base Form of Verb + ed**
I You He She It We You They	walk**ed**. arrive**d**. stud**ied**.

Negative Statements		
Subject	*Did Not*	**Base Form of Verb**
I You He She It We You They	**did not** **didn't**	**walk**. **arrive**. **study**.

Common Past Time Markers		
Yesterday	*Ago*	*Last*
yesterday **yesterday** morning **yesterday** afternoon **yesterday** evening	two days **ago** a week **ago** a month **ago** a year **ago** a couple of days **ago**	**last** night **last** Monday **last** week **last** summer **last** year

GRAMMAR NOTES

EXAMPLES

1. Use the **simple past** to tell about **things that are finished**.

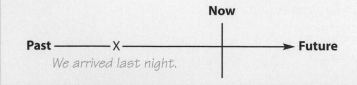

- We **arrived** last night.

2. There are three endings for the regular simple past: **-d**, **-ed**, and **-ied**.

arrive – arrived

land – landed

try – tried

Regular simple past verbs end in three sounds: **/d/**, **/t/**, or **/ɪd/**.

- I **arrived** late.
- We **landed** in Caracas.
- He **tried** to change his flight.

- /d/ – He arriv<u>ed</u> late.
- /t/ – They work<u>ed</u> at a hotel.
- /ɪd/ – We wait<u>ed</u> a long time.

3. In the simple past, the **verb form** is the **same for all persons**.	• **I visited** Seoul. • **She visited** Mexico City. • **They visited** Madrid.

4. For **negative statements** in the simple past, use *did not* **+ the base form of the verb**. Use the contraction *didn't* for negative statements in speaking or informal writing.	• We **did not stay** at a hotel. • They **did not see** the art museum. • We **didn't stay** at a hotel.

5. Time markers usually come at the beginning or at the end of a sentence.	• **Yesterday morning** I studied. • I studied **yesterday morning**.

6. *Today*, *this morning*, *this afternoon*, and *this evening* can be past time markers if they mean "before now."	• I studied grammar **today**. *(It is now 9:00 P.M. I studied grammar in the afternoon.)* • **This morning** I listened to the news. *(It is now the afternoon.)*

Reference Note
See Appendix 17, page A-18 for complete spelling and pronunciation rules for the simple past.

Focused Practice

1 | DISCOVER THE GRAMMAR

Read the sentences. Underline the verbs in the simple past. Write the base form of the verb next to each sentence. Circle six more time markers.

1. We <u>arrived</u> in San Francisco (last Wednesday). ___*arrive*___

2. We visited the Fairmont Hotel on Thursday. _____

3. Yesterday afternoon we walked around Fisherman's Wharf. _____

4. High school friends invited us for dinner last night. _____

5. Dan baked a delicious cake yesterday morning. _____

6. Sheila carried it to the dining room. _____

7. Sheila dropped it and I cried out, "Oh no!" _____ _____

8. After dinner we walked around Chinatown. _____

9. We talked about politics. _____

10. This morning I called and thanked them for a great evening. _____ _____

2 | SPELLING AND PRONUNCIATION

Grammar Note 2

A *Complete the sentences. Use the simple past of the verbs in the box. Then follow the directions for Part B below.*

arrive	borrow	cook	hug	joke	~~miss~~	visit	walk	want	watch

	/t/	/d/	/ɪd/
1. I'm sorry I'm late. I _____*missed*_____ my train.	☑	☐	☐
2. The plane _____ on time.	☐	☐	☐
3. Last night she _____ the art museum.	☐	☐	☐
4. He _____ a delicious meal for us.	☐	☐	☐
5. I'm tired. I _____ up a lot of hills in San Francisco this morning.	☐	☐	☐
6. We _____ to take a tour of Alcatraz in the afternoon, but the tour was filled.	☐	☐	☐
7. We _____ a guidebook from our friends.	☐	☐	☐
8. Two nights ago they _____ a parade.	☐	☐	☐
9. The comedian _____ about the politicians.	☐	☐	☐
10. Everyone _____ and kissed us when we left.	☐	☐	☐

B 🎧 *Now listen to the sentences. Then listen again and check (✓) the final sound of each verb. (See Appendix 17 on page A-18 for pronunciation rules for the regular simple past.)*

3 | NEGATIVE STATEMENTS

Grammar Note 4

Read the first sentence of each item. Underline the verb in the sentence. Complete the second sentence with the negative form of that verb.

1. He <u>stayed</u> with friends. He _____*didn't stay*_____ at a hotel.

2. They arrived at nine at night. They _____ at nine in the morning.

3. I wanted a nonsmoking room. I _____ a smoking room.

4. It rained in the morning. It _____ in the afternoon.

5. She only invited you. She _____ your whole family.

6. He helped you. He _____ me.

7. I wanted an egg. I _____ an egg roll.

4 | TRAVEL LOG   Grammar Notes 1–4

Complete the travel log with the affirmative or negative of the verbs in parentheses. (Two sentences are negative.) Use the simple past.

Carlos and I _____ a car last Wednesday morning. We _____ here
            1. (rent)   **2. (arrive)**

in San Francisco Wednesday night. We _____ the driving so it was easy. The
                                             3. (share)

weather was fine. I like San Francisco. It's a colorful city.

On Thursday it _____, but the weather _____ us from
                   4. (rain)   **5. (stop)**

sight-seeing. We _____ umbrellas and _____ around Fisherman's
                6. (carry)   **7. (walk)**

Wharf and Chinatown. Friday we _____ the University of California at Berkeley.
                                       8. (visit)

Carlos's father _____ Berkeley in the sixties. I think it's an interesting place.
               9. (attend)

Berkeley students are very open.

Friday night Carlos's cousin _____ and _____ us to his home in
                           10. (call)   **11. (invite)**

Long Beach, but we _____ to drive so far. We _____ to see him on
                       12. (want)   **13. (promise)**

our next trip to California. I hope we get back there soon. All in all, it was a great trip.

5 | THEY TRAVEL A LOT   Grammar Note 5

*Complete the conversations. Use **last**, **ago**, or **yesterday**.*

1.   **BEN:** Were you away?

    SAMUEL: Yes, I was in Mexico City _____ week.
                                        a.

    BEN: Oh. I was there a couple of months _____. When did you get back?
                                             b.

    SAMUEL: _____ afternoon. Ian called me _____ night. He wants
            c.   **d.**

    us to meet for lunch.

    BEN: Good. I'll call him today.

2.   **STEVE:** Where is Demetrios?

    ALLY: I don't know. He's always on the road. He was in Montreal _____
                                                            a.

    weekend. He was in Prague _____ month. And two months
                                    b.

    _____ he visited his family in Greece.
          c.

    STEVE: OK, but where is he now?

6 | SIMPLE PAST AND SIMPLE PRESENT   *Grammar Notes 1–6*

Complete the conversations. Use the words in parentheses. Use the simple past and the simple present in each conversation.

1. A: When do you usually travel?

   B: We _____ in the summer, but last summer we _____
            (usually / travel)   **(travel)**
   in the fall.

2. A: Does John like guided tours?

   B: No. He _____ most guided tours, but he _____
               (like / not)   **(like)**
   the one yesterday in San Francisco.

3. A: When does that restaurant open?

   B: It _____ at 7:00 A.M., but it _____ until
            (usually / open)   **(open / not)**
   7:30 yesterday.

4. A: Do you usually travel on business?

   B: I _____ on business, but last month I _____
           (rarely / travel)   **(travel)**
   twice on business.

5. A: When do you start work?

   B: I _____ at 9:00, but I _____ at 8:00
           (usually / start)   **(start)**
   yesterday because I was very busy.

6. A: Does the baby always nap in the afternoon?

   B: She _____ in the afternoon, but this afternoon she
             (usually / nap)
   _____ . She _____ in her crib.
        (nap / not)   **(play)**

7 | EDITING

Correct the postcard message. There are six mistakes. The first mistake is already corrected.

Dear Ilene,

    Paris is magical at night! It's 10 p.m. and I'm writing to you from a café. We arrived here two days ~~before~~ *ago*. Paul's friend Pierre picks us up. We toured the city during the day and at night we did walked along the Seine River. Today we dining in Montmartre and we visited the Louvre Museum. I not like the Mona Lisa, but maybe I understood it not. Now we're at the Eiffel Tower and it looks just like it does in the photo.

    We hope all is well with you. Don't work too hard.

                Love,

                Michelle and Paul

To:

    Ilene Carson
    85 Maple Street
    Plymouth, DE 19905
    USA

Communication Practice

8 | LISTENING

Listen to the conversation. Check (✓) all of the true statements. Change the false statements to true ones.

_____ 1. She didn't stay with friends.

_____ 2. She stayed at a traditional *ryokan*.

_____ 3. She rented a car.

_____ 4. She didn't use public transportation.

_____ 5. She practiced Japanese.

_____ 6. She didn't visit the different parts of Osaka.

_____ 7. She learned how to use chopsticks.

_____ 8. She didn't enjoy the trip.

9 | WHAT I DID LAST WEEKEND

Work in small groups. Tell your group what you did and didn't do last weekend. Then add information to the activities you did.

Example: Last weekend I watched TV. On Friday night, I watched Hitchcock's movie *The Birds*. It was scary. On Sunday, I watched football with some friends.

1. I watched TV.

2. I played a sport.

3. I played a computer game.

4. I listened to music.

5. I used the Internet.

6. I visited friends or relatives.

7. I e-mailed a friend or relative.

8. I worked.

10 | GUESS THE SITUATION

Work in pairs. Read these lines. Describe the situation. Use the verbs in the box. (There are different possibilities.) Write down your answers. Tell your answers to the class.

arrived late	asked for	delivered	dialed	didn't return	returned

Example: "Here's the money. Please keep the change."

Someone delivered a pizza to a man. The man said, "Here's the money. Please keep the change."

1. "Here's the money. Please keep the change."

_____

_____

2. "Sorry, wrong number."

_____

_____

3. "Walk two blocks and turn right."

_____

_____

4. "We missed the first 10 minutes."

_____

_____

5. "I'm getting angry. That's the third time I left a message for him to call back."

_____

_____

6. "Here. And thanks again for letting me use it."

_____

_____

11 | WRITING

Write about a city you know. Pretend you were there last week and write an e-mail message to a classmate. Use at least five of the verbs in the word box in your message.

arrive	rent	stay at	visit	want
enjoy	shop	tour	walk around	watch

Example

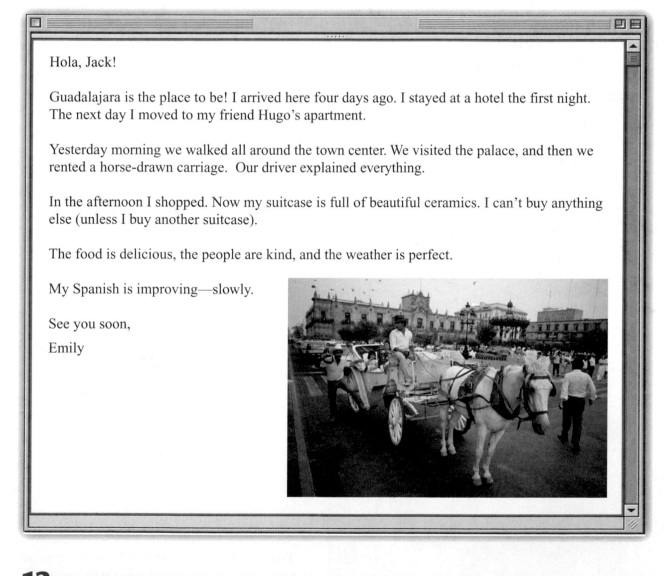

Hola, Jack!

Guadalajara is the place to be! I arrived here four days ago. I stayed at a hotel the first night. The next day I moved to my friend Hugo's apartment.

Yesterday morning we walked all around the town center. We visited the palace, and then we rented a horse-drawn carriage. Our driver explained everything.

In the afternoon I shopped. Now my suitcase is full of beautiful ceramics. I can't buy anything else (unless I buy another suitcase).

The food is delicious, the people are kind, and the weather is perfect.

My Spanish is improving—slowly.

See you soon,

Emily

12 | ON THE INTERNET

Find out about places to see in a city you want to visit. Pretend you were there last week and write a postcard or e-mail message to a classmate.

Grammar in Context

BEFORE YOU READ

	Yes	No
I heard many folktales as a child.	☐	☐

What does the saying "You never know what will happen" mean?

🎧 *Read this Chinese folktale.*

YOU NEVER KNOW WHAT WILL HAPPEN

A long time ago there lived a poor Chinese peasant. One day a beautiful horse appeared on his farm. When the peasant's friends **saw** the horse they **said**, "How lucky you are!"

The peasant answered, "You never know what will happen."

Two days later the horse **ran** away. The peasant's friends **came** and **said**, "What a terrible thing. How unlucky you are! The fine horse **ran** away." The peasant **didn't get** excited. He simply **said**, "You never know what will happen."

Exactly one week later the horse returned. And it **brought** three other horses. When the peasant's friends **saw** the horses they **said**, "Oh. You are so lucky. Now you have four horses to help you." The peasant looked at them and once again **said**, "You never know what will happen."

The next morning the peasant's oldest son **was** in the field. Suddenly one of the horses **ran** into him, and the boy **fell** to the ground. He **was** badly hurt. He **lost** the use of his leg. Indeed, this **was** terrible, and many people **came** to the peasant and

expressed their sadness for his son's misfortune. But again the peasant simply **said**, "You never know what will happen."

A month after the accident, soldiers **rode** into the village. They shouted, "There is a problem along the border! We are taking every healthy young man to fight." The soldiers **took** all the other young men, but they **didn't take** the peasant's son. All the other young men **fought** in the border war, and they all died. But the peasant's son lived a long and happy life. As his father **said**, you never know what will happen.

AFTER YOU READ

Number these events in the order they occurred (1 to 8).

_____ The horse came back with three other horses.

__*1*__ A horse appeared on a peasant's land.

_____ One of the four horses ran into the peasant's son; the son was hurt.

_____ Soldiers rode into the village and took all the healthy young men to fight.

_____ The peasant's son lived a long and happy life.

_____ All the other young men died.

_____ The horse ran away.

_____ The soldiers didn't take the peasant's son.

Grammar Presentation

THE SIMPLE PAST: IRREGULAR VERBS—AFFIRMATIVE AND NEGATIVE STATEMENTS

Affirmative Statements		
Subject	Verb	
I You He She It We You They	**bought** **rode** **saw**	the horses.

Negative Statements			
Subject	*Did not / Didn't*	Base Form of Verb	
I You He She It We You They	**did not** **didn't**	**buy** **ride** **see**	the horses.

Affirmative of *Be*		
Subject	*Was / Were*	
He	**was**	lucky.
They	**were**	unlucky.

Negative of *Be*		
Subject	*Was / Were*	
I	**wasn't**	home.
We	**weren't**	at the library.

GRAMMAR NOTES

1. Many common verbs are irregular. **Irregular past verbs** do not add *-ed*. They often look different from the base form.

BASE FORM	PAST
see	*saw*
go	*went*
come	*came*
bring	*brought*
eat	*ate*

2. For **negative statements** in the past, use *did not +* **the base form of the verb** (except for the verb *be*).

The short form of *did not* is **didn't**. Use *didn't* for speaking and informal writing.

▶ **BE CAREFUL!** Do not use the simple past form after *didn't*.

EXAMPLES

- We **saw** a beautiful horse.
- They **went** to work.
- She **came** late.
- He **brought** a friend to school.
- He **ate** a big lunch.

- They **did not see** him.
- She **did not eat** lunch.

- They **didn't** see him.
- She **didn't** eat lunch.

NOT: They didn't ~~saw~~ him.
 They didn't ~~ate~~ lunch.

3. The **past tense of** *be* is *was* or *were*.

The **negative** of *was* is *was not*, and the negative of *were* is *were not*. Use *wasn't* and *weren't* for speaking and informal writing.

- I **was** at the library last night.
- They **were not** home this morning.
- It **wasn't** late.
- They **weren't** in Mexico City.

4. We use *was* or *were* + *born* to tell when or where people were born.

- I **was born** in Nicaragua.
- She **was born** in Lima.
- They **were born** in 1989.

Reference Notes
See Appendix 7, page A-7 for a list of irregular past forms.
See Unit 3, page 24 for a discussion of the past of *be*.
See Unit 20, page 190, and Unit 22, page 208 for more about the simple past.

Focused Practice

1 | DISCOVER THE GRAMMAR

Circle the verbs in the past. Then write the verb and the base form of that verb in the chart below.

I have two brothers. My older brother (was) a great student. He (brought) home prizes and won awards. My younger brother disliked school. He never did well. My parents worried about him. Then in his second year of high school, he had a great chemistry teacher. He became interested in chemistry. He began to study hard. He's now a chemistry professor at a university. So, you never know what will happen.

Past	Base Form
was	be
brought	bring

2 | RAGS TO RICHES

Complete the sentences with the affirmative or negative of the verbs in parentheses.

John Tu is the cofounder and head of Kingston Technology. He is a billionaire today, but he

_____ always rich. Tu _____ born in China. His family
1. (be / not)   2. (be)

_____ to Taiwan when he _____ a young boy. Tu
3. (move)   4. (be)

_____ school and he _____ well. He _____ different
5. (like / not)   6. (do / not)   7. (feel)

from the other students. He _____ in.
8. (fit / not)

Tu _____ to go to the university in Taiwan, but his grades _____
9. (want)   10. (be)

too low. He _____ to Germany and _____ there. Later he
11. (go)   12. (study)

_____ to the United States. He _____ a gift shop in Arizona and
13. (move)   14. (open)

_____ some real estate. He _____ money in real estate and
15. (buy)   16. (make)

_____ the money to start a computer business. In 1987, Tu _____ a
17. (use)   18. (lose)

lot of money but he _____ up. He and his partner _____ their
19. (give / not)   20. (rebuild)

business into a bigger company with over 500 employees. Today, John Tu has a two-billion-dollar

business.

3 | YOU NEVER KNOW WHAT WILL HAPPEN

Complete the sentences of each paragraph. Use the simple past of the words in the box.
Use each word once.

be	be/not	become	begin	have/not	love	name	study

She _____ born in 1965 in England. Her parents _____ her
1.   2.

Joanne Kathleen. She _____ writing at the age of five. She wasn't interested in
3.

sports and she _____ any athletic ability, but she always _____ to
4.   5.

read. She _____ French at the university and _____ a bilingual
6.   7.

secretary. But she _____ very good at it.
8.

end	have	move	start	teach

At 26 she _____ to Portugal. She became an English teacher and
         9.

_____ English as a foreign language. At this time she first _____
    10.   **11.**

working on a story about a boy with special powers named Harry. She met a journalist in

Portugal. They married and _____ a daughter in 1993. Unfortunately, the marriage
                              12.

_____ in divorce.
    13.

have/not	move	sell	want

She _____ to Scotland to be near a sister. She really _____ to
    14.   **15.**

finish her book. In Scotland life was hard because she _____ much money. After
                                                          16.

many attempts, she finally _____ her book for about $4,000.
                              17.

become	give	write

Several months later, an American company became interested in her writing and

_____ her money to write full-time. Soon her book _____ a
    18.   **19.**

best-seller. She _____ several more Harry Potter books. Today, J. K. Rowling is rich
                    20.

and famous.

So you never know what will happen.

4 | A MISTAKE

Grammar Notes 1–3

*Complete the sentences with the affirmative or negative of the verbs in parentheses. Three
of the sentences are in the negative.*

My grandfather, Ben Brown, _____ a cruise. At dinner the first night, a
                              1. (take)

Frenchman _____ across from my grandfather. Before the man _____
              2. (sit)   **3. (sit)**

down, he _____ at my grandfather and said, "Bon appétit." My grandfather only
            4. (look)

spoke English. He _____ French. He _____ the Frenchman.
                     5. (speak)   **6. (understand)**

My grandfather _____ up and said, "Ben Brown." The same thing
                  7. (stand)

_____ the next two nights.
    8. (happen)

(continued)

My grandfather _____ a Canadian and _____ to the man,
                     9. (meet)   **10. (say)**

"There's a Frenchman at my dinner table. Every night he introduces himself." The Canadian

spoke both French and English. He asked my grandfather some more questions. Soon he

_____ my grandfather's mistake. He _____ the misunderstanding to
11. (understand)   **12. (explain)**

my grandfather. So then my grandfather _____ that "Bon appétit" was not the
                                         13. (know)

man's name, but was French for "Enjoy your meal."

The next night my grandfather _____ to dinner after the Frenchman. This time
                               14. (come)

my grandfather _____ "Ben Brown." Instead my grandfather _____
                15. (say)   **16. (smile)**

and with a perfect French accent said, "Bon appétit." The Frenchman _____ and
                                                                    17. (stand)

replied, with a perfect American accent, "Ben Brown."

5 | EDITING

Correct these sentences. There are nine mistakes. The first mistake is already corrected.

My grandfather born in Peru. He had an older brother and sister. Their dad (my great
          ^{was}

grandfather) were a dreamer. The family have not much money. When he was 13, my

grandfather's mother did died and his dad remarried. My grandfather no like his stepmother.

He move in with his sister and her husband. All three leave for America. They did start a small

business. They worked hard and the business growed. Today my sister and I are running the

business.

Communication Practice

6 | LISTENING

🎧 *Listen to Paul's story. Complete the sentences.*

1. Paul's grandfather gave him a _____.

2. After a couple of years it _____ _____ good.

3. Paul's mother made it into a _____ _____.

4. Then the _____ _____ tore.

5. His mother made it into a _____ _____ .

6. Paul _____ the _____ .

7. He felt _____ .

8. His friends said, "_____ _____ _____ ."

9. Paul didn't _____ about it. He _____ about it instead.

10. Many years later Paul's _____ found the story.

7 | A MEMORY GAME

Sit in a circle. Take notes. The first student tells one thing he or she did last weekend. The next student tells what the first one did and then what he or she did. Continue until every student speaks.

    Example: ANN: I went to the movies.
              JOE: Ann went to the movies, and I read a book.

8 | HOW WAS YOUR DAY?

Work in small groups. Tell about a wonderful day and a terrible day. Use **First**, **Then**, *and* **After that**.

    Examples: I had a wonderful day. First, I saw my grandmother. Then, I went to the park. After that, I rented a video.

             Yesterday I had a terrible day. First, I got to school late. Then, I broke my glasses. After that, I lost my keys.

9 | WRITING

Write your autobiography. The year is now 2066. Where and when were you born? Where did you go to school? What did you do in your free time? What did you become? Why? Where did you live? Did you marry? Did you have children? Did you travel? Did you become rich or famous? Did you make a difference in the world? Were you happy?

or

Write a family story with a surprise ending.

10 | ON THE INTERNET

    Find a short folktale or fable on the Internet that you didn't know before. Tell it to the class.

22 The Simple Past: *Yes/No* and *Wh-* Questions

Grammar in Context

BEFORE YOU READ

Do you know the name J. R. R. Tolkien?

Have you seen The Lord of the Rings *movies?*

Have you read The Lord of the Rings *books?*

What do you know about the author?

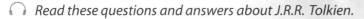

Read these questions and answers about J.R.R. Tolkien.

Q: Where was Tolkien **born? When was** Tolkien **born?**

A: Tolkien's family was English, but J.R.R. Tolkien was born in South Africa in 1892. His father was there on business.

Q: We know him as J.R.R. Tolkien. **What did** his family **call** him?

A: His family and friends called him Ronald. The initials J.R.R. stand for John Ronald Reuel.

Q: Did he **grow up** in South Africa? If not, **where did** he **grow up?**

A: He didn't grow up in South Africa. When he was four, his mother took him and his younger brother back to England. He grew up in the countryside of England, in a place called Sarehole.

Q: What did he **like** to do as a child?

A: He was always good at languages, and he liked to invent new languages with his two young cousins.

Q: What did he **study? Where did** he **study?**

A: He studied Old and Middle English (the languages in England from 500 to 1500) at Exeter College, Oxford.

Q: Did he **marry? Did** he **have** any children?

A: Yes, he did. He married his childhood sweetheart, Edith Bratt. They had four children.

Q: When did he **discover** his gift for storytelling?

A: He discovered his gift when he told his children his stories. They all loved his stories.

Q: Did he **write** full-time?

A: No, he didn't. First he worked on the *New English Dictionary*. Then in 1920 he started teaching, first at the University of Leeds, and later at Oxford. He was a lively and imaginative teacher. He wrote *The Hobbit* in the 1930s.

Q: How long did it **take** Tolkien to write *The Lord of the Rings*?

A: *The Lord of the Rings* novels took 12 years to complete. They did not come out until Tolkien was near retirement.

Q: Did Tolkien **expect** *The Lord of the Rings* to be so popular?

A: No, he didn't. He was very surprised.

Q: When did he **die**?

A: He died in 1973, at the age of 81.

AFTER YOU READ

Circle the letter of the correct answer.

1. Did Tolkien live in South Africa for many years?
   a. Yes, he did.   **b.** No, he didn't.

2. Did Tolkien have any brothers or sisters?
   a. Yes, he did.   **b.** No, he didn't.

3. Did Tolkien's family and friends call him "John"?
   a. Yes, they did.   **b.** No, they didn't.

4. Where did he grow up?
   a. in London   **b.** in Sarehole

5. Did Tolkien write full-time?
   a. Yes, he did.   **b.** No, he didn't.

6. Who first enjoyed his stories?
   a. his children   **b.** his students

Grammar Presentation

THE SIMPLE PAST: *YES/NO* AND *WH-* QUESTIONS AND ANSWERS

Yes/No Questions		
Did	Subject	Base Form of Verb
Did	I you he she it we you they	**start**?

Affirmative Short Answers		
Yes,	you I he she it you we they	**did**.

Negative Short Answers		
No,	you I he she it you we they	**didn't**.

Wh- Questions				Answers
Wh- Word	*Did*	Subject	Base Form of Verb	
What	did	I	**ask**?	You asked about his name.
Where		you	**go**?	I went to the library. (To the library.)
When		he	**write**?	He wrote at night, after work. (At night, after work.)
Why		we	**leave**?	We went someplace else.
Who(m)		you	**call**?	I called my friend. (My friend.)
How long		they	**stay**?	They stayed for an hour. (For an hour.) (An hour.)

Wh- Questions about the Subject			Answers
Wh- Word	Past Form of Verb		
Who	**wrote**	*The Hobbit*?	J. R. R. Tolkien wrote it. (J. R. R. Tolkien.)
What	**happened**?		It became a big success.

GRAMMAR NOTES

1. *Yes/No* questions in the **simple past** have the same form (*Did* + subject + base form) for regular and irregular verbs.

   The verb *be* is the one exception.

EXAMPLES

   regular verb
- **Did** you **want** that book?
   irregular verb
- **Did** you **write** your report?

- **Were** you good at writing?

2. Most *wh- questions in the past* begin with the **question word** followed by *did* + *the subject* + *the base form* of the verb.	• **What did** he **write**? • **Why did** he **write**? • **Where did** he **write**? • **Who did** he **work** for?

3. *Wh-* questions in the past **do not use *did*** when the **question is about the subject**.	subject • Tolkien wrote *The Hobbit*. **Q: Who** wrote *The Hobbit*? **A:** Tolkien. NOT: **Q:** Who ~~did write~~ *The Hobbit*?

4. We usually give **short answers** to *yes/no* and *wh-* questions, but we can also give **long answers**.	**Q:** Did you work yesterday? **A:** Yes. OR Yes, I did. OR Yes, I worked yesterday.

Pronunciation Note

Yes / No questions use rising intonation. *Wh-* questions use falling intonation.

Did you hear the story? What did you think about it?

Focused Practice

1 | DISCOVER THE GRAMMAR

A *Read questions 1–6 in Exercise B below. Underline the base form verbs.*

1. Which questions are *yes/no* questions? _____

2. Which one is a *wh-* question about the subject? _____

B *Match the questions and answers.*

a. I read *The Hobbit*.	**d.** Yes, I saw it three times.
b. J. R. R. Tolkien.	**e.** No, I didn't. I got it at the library.
c. I read most of it.	**f.** Yes, I did. I finished it last night.

1. **A:** Did you finish your book report?

   B: _____

2. **A:** What did you read?

   B: _____

(continued)

3. A: Who wrote it?

   B: _____

4. A: Did you buy the book?

   B: _____

5. A: Did you see the movie?

   B: _____

6. A: Did you read the whole book?

   B: _____

2 | YES/NO QUESTIONS
Grammar Note 1

Write **yes/no** *questions. Use the verb from the first sentence.*

1. I read all his books. ____*Did*____ you ___*read*___ them too?

2. We enjoyed the movie. _____ you _____ it too?

3. It had a good storyline. _____ it _____ a lot of action?

4. I didn't understand everything. _____ she _____ everything?

5. We didn't like the ending. _____ he _____ the ending?

6. I expected a different ending. _____ you _____ a different ending?

7. We saw a review online. _____ they _____ the review online?

3 | SHORT ANSWERS
Grammar Note 4

Write affirmative or negative short answers.

1. **A:** Did you finish your homework?

   B: __*Yes, I did*_____. I finished it before dinner.

2. **A:** Did they go to the movies?

   B: _____. They stayed home and watched TV.

3. **A:** Did I call too late?

   B: _____. I'm usually up at this hour.

4. **A:** Did we get any mail?

   B: _____. We got some bills and a letter from your uncle.

5. **A:** Did the package arrive?

   B: _____. It came in the early mail.

6. A: Did you buy the DVD?

    B: _____. I plan to buy it next weekend.

7. A: Did you rent any DVDs?

    B: _____. I rented a comedy and a romance.

---

4 | INTERVIEW WITH AN AUTHOR

Grammar Notes 1–4

Sherryl Woods is a best-selling romance and mystery writer. Her books are available in over 20 countries. She has written more than 100 books. Read an interview with Sherryl Woods. Complete the questions.

INTERVIEWER: _____ your first book?
                              1. (When / you / write)

SHERRYL WOODS: In 1980. It came out in 1982.

    I: _____ to be a writer?
                  2. (you / always / want)

    SW: No, I didn't. For many years I wanted to be a graphic artist.

    I: _____ always good at writing?
                  3. (be / you)

    SW: Well, my first-grade teacher wrote, "Sherryl is good at everything except making

        up stories."

    I: _____ your first-grade teacher?
                  4. (you / like)

    SW: I can't remember.

    I: _____ to write?
                  5. (When / you / start)

    SW: After I graduated from college, I became a journalist.

    I: _____ as a journalist?
                  6. (How long / you / work)

    SW: I worked for newspapers for fourteen years.

    I: _____ writing romance novels?
                  7. (Why / you / start)

    SW: Romances were new in the '80s. I read one and said, "I can do this too."

    I: _____ the most?
                  8. (Who / help / you)

    SW: My agent did. She was there for me from the beginning.

    I: _____ when your books became popular?
                  9. (How / you / feel)

    SW: It was exciting. I remember the first time I saw someone with my book. I said,

        "That's my book." The woman looked at me and said, "No, it's not. It's mine."

        I said, "No, no, no. It's my book. I wrote it."

5 | EDITING

John Steinbeck was a great American writer. Correct these questions and answers about him. There are 11 mistakes. The first mistake is already corrected.

Q: When John Steinbeck ~~was~~ born?

  <small>was</small>

A: He born in 1902.

Q: Where he was born?

A: He was born in Salinas, California.

Q: Where did he studied writing?

A: He studied writing at Stanford University.

Q: He graduate from Stanford?

A: No, he didn't.

Q: Does he marry?

A: Yes, he did. He married in 1930.

Q: When he published *Tortilla Flat*?

A: In 1936.

Q: What year did he published *The Grapes of Wrath*?

A: In 1938. It was his best book.

Q: What were it about?

A: It was about a family who lost their farm and became fruit pickers in California.

Q: Did he won many prizes?

A: Yes, he did. He won a Pulitzer Prize, a Nobel Prize in Literature, and the U.S. Medal of Freedom.

Q: When did he died?

A: He died in New York in 1968.

Communication Practice

6 | LISTENING

🎧 *Ali is asking Berrin about his grandparents. Listen to their conversation. Mark the statements* **T** *(true) or* **F** *(false).*

_____ **1.** Berrin's grandfather had a large farm.

_____ **2.** Berrin went to the farm every winter.

_____ **3.** Berrin's father had seven sisters and brothers.

_____ **4.** Berrin's grandmother never helped on the farm.

_____ **5.** Berrin's grandmother wrote poetry.

_____ **6.** Berrin's grandparents met at a wedding.

7 | WHAT WAS HE/SHE LIKE?

Work in pairs. Ask your partner about one of his or her grandparents.

Examples: Which of your grandparents do you know best? Where did he/she grow up? What did he/she do? Did he/she live with your family?

8 | WRITING

A *Work in small groups. Complete the chart with names of famous people from the past.*

Artists	Writers	Musicians	Scientists	Actors	Athletes
Andy Warhol					

B *Write 12 questions about one of the people from Exercise A. Use the words in parentheses.*

1. *Where was Andy Warhol born?*
   (Where / he or she / born?)

2. _____
   (When / he or she / born?)

3. _____
   (Where / he or she / grow up?)

4. _____
   (What / he or she / do in his or her free time?)

5. _____
   (he or she / have / a happy childhood?)

6. _____
   (he or she / travel?)

7. _____
   (he or she / work hard?)

8. _____
   (he or she/ make a lot of money?)

9. _____
   (YOUR QUESTION)

10. _____
    (YOUR QUESTION)

11. _____
    (YOUR QUESTION)

12. _____
    (YOUR QUESTION)

9 | ON THE INTERNET

Look on the Internet for information about the person you chose in Exercise 8. Try to answer your questions from Exercise 8B. Read your questions and answers to the class. Do not say the name of the person. Let your classmates guess the person.

Example: Where was he born? He was born in Pittsburgh, Pennsylvania.

From **Grammar** to **Writing**

Punctuation II: The Exclamation Point (!), The Hyphen (-), Quotation Marks (" . . . ")

1 *What's wrong with these sentences?*

1. You're kidding

2. She's twenty one years old

3. He said I love you

4. He worked for many years before he became rich.

Study this information about punctuation.

The Exclamation Point (!)

Use the exclamation point after **strong, emotional statements**. (Don't use it too often.)

- What a surprise!
- You're kidding!
- How wonderful!

The Hyphen (-)

a. Use a hyphen in **compound numbers** from twenty-one to ninety-nine.

b. Use a hyphen **at the end of a line** when dividing a word. Words must be divided by syllables. (Check your dictionary if you are unsure.)

- There were **twenty-two** students in the class.
- We visited them at the **begin-ning** of the year.

Quotation Marks (" . . . ")

Use quotation marks **before** and **after the exact words** of a speaker. Use a comma before the quote.

- She said, "I just love your new sweater."

---

2 *Add the correct punctuation to the sentences in Exercise 1.*

3 | *Read the story. Circle the exclamation marks and hyphens. Add quotation marks where necessary.*

Whose Baby Is It?

Solomon was a king. He lived about 3,000 years ago. Everyone came to Solomon because he was very wise.

One day two women approached King Solomon. One carried a baby. The woman said, We live nearby and had our babies three days apart. Her baby died in the night, and she changed it for mine. This baby is really mine.

The other woman said, No! That woman is lying. That's my baby.

The two women started arguing. They continued until King Solomon shouted, Stop!

He then turned to his guard and said, Take your sword and chop the baby in two. Give one part to this woman and the other to that one. The guard pulled out his sword. As he was about to harm the baby, the first woman screamed, No! Don't do it. Give her the baby. Just don't kill the baby.

King Solomon then said, Now I know the real mother. Give the baby to the woman who has just spoken.

4 | *Work in small groups.*

1. Think about these questions. Take notes.

   What was your favorite story as a child?

   When did you first hear it? Who told it to you? Why did you like it?

2. Tell your story to your group.

3. Write your story. When you are finished, read your story twice. First pay attention to the story. Next pay attention to the grammar and punctuation.

4. Rewrite your story. Hang it on the wall. Go around and read the stories of your classmates.

Review Test

I *Read each conversation. Circle the letter of the underlined word or group of words that is not correct.*

1. **A:** You <u>didn't</u> <u>finished</u> your dinner.
           A   B

   B: That's because <u>it</u> <u>wasn't</u> good.
               C   D

   A B C D

2. **A:** <u>Who(m)</u> <u>you did</u> call?
         A   B

   B: I <u>called</u> John. I <u>wanted</u> Susan's phone number.
         C   D

   A B C D

3. **A:** When <u>did</u> they <u>visit</u> Hawaii?
           A   B

   B: They <u>visit</u> Hawaii last fall. They <u>were</u> there for a week.
         C   D

   A B C D

4. **A:** <u>How long</u> did <u>it took</u> you to get to work?
         A   B

   B: <u>It took</u> me over an hour. <u>Traffic was</u> very heavy.
        C   D

   A B C D

5. **A:** <u>Did</u> she <u>drank</u> a glass of milk?
        A   B

   B: Yes. She <u>drank</u> it with some cookies. Then she <u>did</u> her homework.
           C   D

   A B C D

6. **A:** Where <u>did</u> you <u>see</u> them?
           A   B

   B: I <u>did</u> <u>saw</u> them during the Thanksgiving vacation.
       C D

   A B C D

II *Read each question. Circle the letter of the correct answer.*

1. When did you get up?

   a. At eight-thirty.

   b. Yes, I did.

   c. Because it was early.

2. Who visited us last week?

   a. They do.

   b. They were.

   c. They did.

3. Where did they go yesterday?

   a. To the movies.

   b. At noon.

   c. With their friends.

4. Did they have a good breakfast?

   a. Yes, they do.

   b. Yes, they had.

   c. Yes, they did.

5. How long did they stay?

   a. By bus.

   b. A few hours.

   c. An hour ago.

6. Did she have a good vacation last summer?

   a. No, she hasn't.

   b. No, she didn't.

   c. No, she wasn't.

7. Who did you stay with?

   a. My relatives.

   b. John did.

   c. On Saturday.

8. Did it rain last night?

   a. No, it doesn't.

   b. No, it didn't.

   c. No, it don't.

III *Complete this popular story about George Washington. Use the past of each verb in parentheses.*

George Washington was the first president of the United States. He _____

1. (live)

in a beautiful home in Virginia. His mother _____ a special garden with a

2. (have)

beautiful little cherry tree. Everyone _____ that cherry tree. One day George

3. (love)

_____ a hatchet as a present. He _____ to try the hatchet. He

4. (get)   5. (decide)

_____ to the cherry tree and _____ it down. As soon as he

6. (go)   7. (chop)

_____ the tree fall on the ground, he _____ terrible. He

8. (see)   9. (feel)

_____ sadly back to the house and _____ to his room. He

10. (walk)   11. (go)

_____ that afternoon. He _____ that evening. That night

12. (play, not)   13. (eat, not)

George's father said, "Someone _____ down our cherry tree." George

14. (chop)

_____ to tell his father the truth. He _____ toward his father and

15. (decide)   16. (walk)

said, "I _____ it. I _____ it down with my new hatchet. I cannot

17. (do)   18. (chop)

tell a lie."

"Thank you for telling the truth," his father _____.

19. (say)

IV *Complete the conversations. Use the simple present, present progressive, or simple past form of each verb in parentheses.*

1. A: Why _____ you _____ so late?

a. (arrive)

   B: I _____ to set my alarm clock last night.

b. (forget)

2. A: There aren't any grapes. Who _____ them all?

a. (eat)

   B: I don't know. I _____ them. I _____ grapes.

b. (eat, not)   c. (like, not)

3. A: I _____ a beautiful gift in the mail last week.

a. (get)

   B: Who _____ it? Uncle Sam?

b. (send)

4. A: What _____ his answering machine _____?

a. (say)

   B: It says, "I'm sorry I _____ your call. Please leave your name and a short

b. (miss)

   message. Thank you. Have a nice day."

(continued)

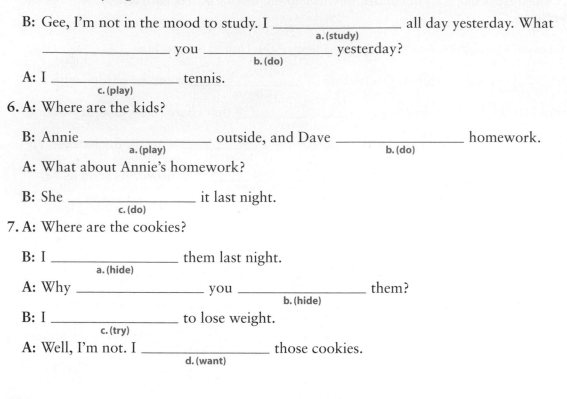

5. A: Let's study together.

   B: Gee, I'm not in the mood to study. I _____ all day yesterday. What
                                              a. (study)
   _____ you _____ yesterday?
                              b. (do)

   A: I _____ tennis.
          c. (play)

6. A: Where are the kids?

   B: Annie _____ outside, and Dave _____ homework.
              a. (play)   b. (do)

   A: What about Annie's homework?

   B: She _____ it last night.
            c. (do)

7. A: Where are the cookies?

   B: I _____ them last night.
          a. (hide)

   A: Why _____ you _____ them?
                                     b. (hide)

   B: I _____ to lose weight.
          c. (try)

   A: Well, I'm not. I _____ those cookies.
                         d. (want)

V   *Circle the correct time marker to complete the sentences.*

1. A week ago / Every Monday I wash my clothes.

2. Did you see your friend this morning / now?

3. We visited them two weeks last / ago.

4. I spoke to the doctor last / ago Thursday.

▶ *To check your answers, go to the Answer Key on page RT-3.*

PART VII

There Is / There Are; Pronouns; Count and Non-Count Nouns

Grammar in Context

BEFORE YOU READ

- *Do you like to shop at malls? Why or why not?*

- *Is there a mall near your school?*

- *What's the largest mall you know?*

⌒ *Read an advertisement for the West Edmonton Mall in Canada.*

Come to Edmonton and see its top attraction,
West Edmonton Mall.

West Ed Mall is a shopper's dream. **There are** more than 800 stores. They include everything from Old Navy to Godiva Chocolates to one-of-a-kind stores. Enjoy the mall's international flavor. **There's** Chinatown, where you can shop in a traditional Chinese marketplace. **There's** Europa Boulevard with its many European specialties. West Ed Mall also has over 110 eating places. And for the young and the young-at-heart **there are** seven world-class attractions including a water park, an amusement park, and an indoor skating rink. So make your travel plans now. **There isn't** a better time to get away.

AFTER YOU READ

Mark these statements **T** *(true),* **F** *(false), or* **?** *(I don't know).*

_____ **1.** West Ed Mall is short for West Edmonton Mall.

_____ **2.** There are more than 8,000 stores.

_____ **3.** There's a Turkish marketplace.

_____ **4.** There's a water park.

_____ **5.** There's an art museum.

_____ **6.** There isn't a skating rink.

_____ **7.** There are things for children to do.

Grammar Presentation

THERE IS / THERE ARE; IS THERE . . . ? / ARE THERE . . . ?

Affirmative			
There	*Be*	Subject	Place/Time
There	**is**	a restaurant	on this level.
		a movie	at 6:30.
There	**are**	two restaurants	near the entrance.
		shows	at 7:00 and 9:00.

Negative			
There	*Be*	Subject	Place/Time
There	**isn't**	a restaurant	on the second level.
There	**aren't**	any movies	at 8:00.

Contractions	
there is	→ there's
there is not	→ there isn't
there are not	→ there aren't

Yes / No Questions			
Be	*There*	Subject	Place
Is	**there**	a pizza place	on Second Street?
Are	**there**	any banks	nearby?

Short Answers	
Affirmative	Negative
Yes, there is.	No, there isn't.
Yes, there are.	No, there aren't.

GRAMMAR NOTES	EXAMPLES
1. Use *there is* or *there's* to state facts about a **person** or **thing**.	• **There is a man** at the door. • **There's a man** at the door.
2. Use *there are* to talk about people or things. We often use *there is* or *there are* to tell the **location** of people or things or the **time** of events. ▶ **BE CAREFUL!** Don't confuse *there are* and *they are*.	• **There are five shoe stores** at the mall. • There's a woman's shoe store **on the second level**. (location) • There are concerts **on Friday and Saturday nights**. (time) • **There are two good restaurants. They are** on the third level.
3. In the negative, use the contractions *isn't* and *aren't*. The full forms, *is not* and *are not*, are rarely used with *there*. ▶ **BE CAREFUL!** Don't confuse *there aren't* with *they aren't*.	• **There isn't** a cloud in the sky. • **There aren't** any gyms near our school. • **There are** two gyms near my home, but **they aren't** open today.
4. We often use *any* with *yes/no* questions about plural nouns.	• Are there **any** malls nearby?
5. **BE CAREFUL!** *Here* and *there* are adverbs of place. *Here* is for something nearby and *there* is for something far. Don't confuse the adverb of place *there* with *there is* or *there are* or with the possessive adjective *their*.	• Last summer we exchanged homes with friends near Banff. We went **there** and they came **here**. • Banff National Park is good for hiking. **There are** high mountains **there**. • **Their** home is in the mountains.
6. We often use *There is* or *There are* the first time we talk about people or things. We use *he, she, it,* or *they* to tell more about the people or things.	• **There's a package** in the mail. **It's** heavy. • **There's a man** at the door. **He** wants to speak to you. • **There are three women** in the flower shop. **They** are choosing flowers for a party.

Focused Practice

1 | DISCOVER THE GRAMMAR

Look at the mall directory. Check (✓) the sentences that are true.

Mall Directory

Third Level	3a	3b	3c	3d	3e	
Food Court	Thai food	Chinese food	Burgers	Sushi bar	Café	

Second Level	2a	2b	2c	2d	2e	2f
	Women's clothes	Shoe store	Art supply store	Furniture store	Children's clothes	Cosmetics store

First Level	1a	1b	1c	1d	1e	1f
	Flower shop	Gift shop	Bookstore	Unisex hair salon	Electronics store	Women's clothes

_____ 1. There's a flower shop on the first level.

_____ 2. There's a café on the second level.

_____ 3. There aren't any toy stores.

_____ 4. There are five places to eat.

_____ 5. There isn't any Thai food at this mall.

_____ 6. There's a bookstore on the first level.

_____ 7. There aren't any office supply stores at the mall.

_____ 8. There aren't any jewelry stores at the mall.

2 | WORD ORDER PRACTICE   Grammar Notes 1–3

Put a check (✓) next to each correct sentence. Change the sentences that don't make
sense.

_____ 1. There's a mall in the Chinese restaurant. _There's a Chinese restaurant in the mall._

_____ 2. There's a second level on the shoe store. _____

_____ 3. There are two women's clothing stores at the mall. _____

_____ 4. There's an electronics store on the first level. _____

_____ 5. There isn't a mall in the men's clothing store. _____

_____ 6. There aren't any furniture stores in the desks. _____

3 | A TERRIBLE PIZZA PLACE   Grammar Notes 3, 5

Complete the sentences. Use **there isn't**, **there aren't**, or **they aren't**.

A: This pizza place is awful. _____ any tablecloths and the placemats are dirty.
                                          1.

B: You're right. _____ any napkins either.
                         2.

A: There are knives and forks, but _____ clean.
                                                 3.

B: There are waiters, but _____ very polite.
                                     4.

A: It's hot, but _____ even a fan.
                        5.

B: Let's leave.

4 | HOW ABOUT SOME MEXICAN FOOD?   Grammar Notes 1–2, 5

Complete the conversation. Use **there's**, **there are**, **they're**, and **there**.

A: How about some pizza?

B: Well, _____ only one pizza place nearby and it's awful.
                  1.

   _____ a lot of other restaurants though.
          2.

A: Today is Sunday. Are they open?

B: _____ all open seven days a week.
        3.

A: Well, _____ a nice Mexican place over _____.
                  4.   5.

B: Where?

A: Over _____ next to the jewelry store.
               6.

B: That's right. I know the place. I was _____ a few months ago. Let's go.
                                                      7.

5 | TELL ME MORE

Grammar Notes 1–2, 6

*Complete the sentences. Use **There's** or **There are** in the first sentence. Use **He's**, **She's**, **It's**, or **They're** in the second sentence.*

1. ___There's___ a restaurant over there. ___It's___ next to the bookstore.

2. _____ a salesman behind the counter. _____ talking to that woman.

3. _____ a lot of wool sweaters. _____ in the back of the store.

4. _____ a scarf on the floor. _____ your new one, isn't it?

5. _____ some parking spaces over there. _____ near the exit.

6. _____ a small mall on Route 4. _____ next to the gas station.

7. _____ a lot of people in that line. _____ buying tickets for the movie.

6 | ENTERTAINMENT

Grammar Notes 1–6

Look at the advertisements. Complete the conversations. Start yes / no *questions with* **Is there** *or* **Are there**.

1. **A:** ___Is there a play tonight?___
   (a play / tonight)
   B: Yes, there is. _____ Theater.

2. **A:** _____
   (a comedy / Main Street Cinema)
   B: Yes, there is. *Modern Times* is playing there.

   A: _____
   (any shows / after 6:00 PM)
   B: Yes, there are two, at 6:30 and 8:30.

(continued)

3. A: _____
   (an art auction / at the Town Plaza Hotel)

   B: Yes, there is. _____ on May 25.

4. A: _____
   (concert / at New City Library on May 24)

   B: No, there isn't. There's a concert there on May 26.

7 | EDITING

Correct this paragraph. There are five mistakes. The first mistake is already corrected.

> Pizzas come in all shapes and sizes. *There* are pizzas with mushrooms, pepperoni, broccoli, and
> tofu. There is also pizzas with curry, red herring, and coconut. In the United States they are
> over 61,000 pizza places. There represent 17 percent of all restaurants. Are popular with
> young and old.

Communication Practice

8 | LISTENING

🎧 *Listen to this conversation between two drivers. Then mark the sentences **Y** (yes), **N** (no), or **?** (I don't know).*

_____ 1. Is there a mall up ahead?

_____ 2. Is the mall crowded?

_____ 3. Is there a pizza place at the mall?

_____ 4. Is the food court on the second level?

_____ 5. Are there at least 10 places to eat?

9 | WHAT'S THE DIFFERENCE?

Work in pairs. Find 10 differences between Picture A and Picture B.

Example: In Picture A there's a shoe repair shop between a bakery and a pizza place. In Picture B the pizza place is between the bakery and the shoe repair shop.

Picture A

Picture B

10 | GAME

*Use the phrases in the boxes and ask your classmates questions. Begin with **Is there** or
Are there any. If a student says "yes," write his or her name in the box. When you have
three across, down, or diagonally, call out, "I've got it!"*

a big mall near your home	an amusement park near your home	a pizza place on your street
twins in your family	an Italian restaurant near your home	a skating rink near your home
photos of friends in your wallet	credit cards in your purse or pocket	a public pool near your home

11 | WRITING

Write about a place where you like to shop.

Example: There's a small store near my home. It's called "Village Gifts." It's on a street with two other small shops. The owners are a husband and wife. They sell crafts from all over the world. There are some great things you can buy—colorful pottery from Mexico, beautiful jewelry from Thailand, frames from China, and baskets from Jamaica. The owners love the things they sell. There's a story behind every item. That's why I like to shop there. There aren't many shops like that.

12 | ON THE INTERNET

Check online for events you would like to attend. Tell your class about one of them.

Example: There's a tennis match at Arthur Ashe Stadium in Flushing Meadows, Queens, in New York City. It's between Roger Federer and Andre Agassi. It's on September 3.

Subject and Object Pronouns; Direct and Indirect Objects

Grammar in Context

BEFORE YOU READ

Read this saying. What does it mean?

Give a man a fish
And you feed him for a day,
Teach a man to fish
And you feed him for life.

🎧 *Were you ever a teacher? What did you teach? Who did you teach? Read the conversation.*

MARIA: Ohayoo, Masako.

MASAKO: Tudo bem, Maria.

KEL: Who was that? And what language was that?

MASAKO: That was Maria. **We** greeted each other in Japanese and Portuguese. **I** met **her** at the library last month.

KEL: That's pretty cool.

MASAKO: **I'm** teaching **her Japanese** and **she's** teaching **me Portuguese**.

KEL: Sounds like fun.

MASAKO: **It** is fun, but **it's** not so easy.

KEL: How are **you** teaching **her Japanese**?

MASAKO: Well, first **I** say **a phrase**. Then **Maria** repeats **it**. Then **I** write **it** down. **She** reads **it** and tries to memorize **it**.

KEL: How is **she** doing?

MASAKO: Great. But **I'm** not. **I** can't remember anything from one day to the next. Yesterday Maria gave **me a tape** and **I** lent **her** a **Japanese phrase book**. Now **I** have a lot of work to do.

KEL: Bonne chance!

MASAKO: What was that?

KEL: French for good luck.

MASAKO: Hey! Don't confuse **me**. English and Portuguese are enough for now.

AFTER YOU READ

Look at the underlined pronoun. Write the person or thing it refers to in the parentheses.

    (Masako)   (Maria)   (Maria)   (Masako)

1. I'm teaching <u>her</u> Japanese and <u>she</u>'s teaching <u>me</u> Portuguese.

               (   )   (   )

2. How are <u>you</u> teaching <u>her</u> Japanese?

     (   ) (   )

3. Then <u>I</u> write <u>it</u> down.

     (   ) (   )   (   )

4. <u>She</u> reads <u>it</u> and tries to memorize <u>it</u>.

            (   )   (   )

5. Yesterday Maria gave <u>me</u> a tape and I lent <u>her</u> a Japanese phrase book.

Grammar Presentation

SUBJECT AND OBJECT PRONOUNS

Singular			
Subject Pronoun and Verb			**Object Pronoun**
I'm **You'**re **He'**s **She'**s	happy.	He likes	**me.** **you.** **him.** **her.**
It's	wonderful.		**it.**

Plural			
Subject Pronoun and Verb			**Object Pronoun**
We're **You'**re **They'**re	happy.	He likes	**us.** **you.** **them.**

DIRECT AND INDIRECT OBJECTS

Subject	Verb	Direct Object	*To*	Indirect Object
She	**sent**	**a tape** **it**	to	**me**.

Subject	Verb	Indirect Object	Direct Object
She	**sent**	**me**	**a tape**.

To Before the Indirect Object			
e-mail	owe	show	throw
give	pass	teach	write
hand	read	tell	
lend	sell		

GRAMMAR NOTES

EXAMPLES

---

1. A pronoun replaces a noun. A **subject pronoun** replaces a noun in subject position.

- subject
Maria teaches.
- **She** teaches.

---

2. An **object pronoun** replaces a noun in object position.

- object
Maria helped **John**.
- Maria helped **him**.

---

3. When you refer to yourself and another person, the other person comes first.

- **Maria and I** helped John.
  NOT ~~I and Maria~~ helped John.

---

4. Some sentences have only a subject and a verb.

Some sentences have a subject, a verb, and an object.

Some sentences have two objects following the verb.

A **direct object** answers the question *whom* or *what*.

An **indirect object** answers the question *to whom* or *to what*.

- subject   verb
Maria taught.
- subject verb   object
She taught **Portuguese**.
- direct object   indirect object
She taught **Portuguese** to **Masako**.
- direct object
What did she teach? **Portuguese**.

- **To whom** did she teach it?
  to indirect object
To Masako.

(continued)

5. For the verbs *e-mail*, *give*, *hand*, *lend*, *owe*, *pass*, *read*, *sell*, *show*, *teach*, *tell*, *throw*, and *write* there are two possible sentence patterns if the **direct object** is a noun.

If the direct object is a pronoun, the pronoun always comes before the indirect object.

direct object   indirect
(noun)   object

• She gave **the book** to **her**.

OR

indirect   direct object
object   (noun)

• She gave **her** **the book**.

direct object   indirect
(pronoun)   object

• She gave **it** to **her**.

Reference Note
See Appendix 14, page A-15 for verbs that follow other patterns.

Focused Practice

1 | DISCOVER THE GRAMMAR

*Read the sentences. Underline the direct and indirect objects. Write **d** above the direct object and **i** above the indirect object.*

1. He gave me a dictionary.
   (i above "me", d above "a dictionary")

2. Show your work to your partner.

3. She taught me some Spanish greetings.

4. I e-mailed a note to her in Spanish.

5. He sent me an answer in French.

6. Who taught you that word?

7. We owe it to them.

2 | DIRECTIONS AND HELP   *Grammar Note 2*

*Complete the sentences. Use **me**, **him**, **her**, **it**, or **them**.*

1. Find the pronouns. Then circle _____.

2. Write the word. Then circle _____.

3. Read the story. Then tell _____ to a partner.

4. Complete the sentences. Then memorize _____.

5. Arwa and Ali are good at grammar. Ask _____ for help.

6. Carol knows some Portuguese. Ask _____ for help.

7. I'm confused. Please help _____.

8. Her uncle speaks Japanese. Ask _____ to translate the message.

9. Study these words. Then teach _____ to a partner.

10. They were very kind. We owe _____ a lot.

3 | CONVERSATIONS   *Grammar Notes 1–2*

Complete the conversations. Use subject or object pronouns.

1. A: Paul and Erna borrowed our camera. They're having trouble with _____*it*_____.
 a.

   Please show _____ how it works.
   b.

 B: No problem.

2. A: I was absent yesterday. Please tell _____ what happened in class.
 a.

 B: _____ learned some idioms. I'll give _____ my notes.
   b.   **c.**

3. A: Excuse _____. I'm waiting for the express train. Can you tell _____ what time it
   a.   **b.**

   is now?

 B: It's 5:30. The express train stops here at 5:31. Look! Here _____ comes.
   c.

 A: Thanks.

4. A: _____ forgot my dictionary. Please lend _____ your dictionary.
   a.   **b.**

 B: Sorry. _____ forgot my dictionary too.
   c.

5. A: What did you learn in class yesterday?

 B: First Mr. Brown taught _____ about pronouns. Then _____ asked _____
   a.   **b.**   **c.**

   questions about our last vacation.

4 | WORD ORDER   *Grammar Notes 1–5*

Write sentences using the words in parentheses.

1. (me / show / your homework / Please)
   Please show me your homework.

2. (me / taught / He / a song)
   _____

3. (my dictionary / gave / I / her)
   _____

4. (showed / My friend / your / work / him / and I)
   _____

5. (to me / Don't / e-mail / it)
   _____

(continued)

6. (it / Send / by regular mail / to me)

_____

7. (I / a letter / him / wrote)

_____

8. (gave / to them / He / the book)

_____

9. (gave / the money / me / They)

_____

10. (I / read / it / My husband / and / yesterday)

_____

---

5 | IN OTHER WORDS   _Grammar Note 5_

Underline the direct object in each sentence. Then complete the conversations. Use **it** or **them** in place of the direct object. (Remember: When the direct object is a pronoun, it always comes before the indirect object.)

1. A: I gave my friend <u>my notes</u>.

   B: Who did you give your notes to?

   A: _I gave them to my friend._ _____

2. A: I handed my teacher my composition.

   B: Who did you hand the composition to?

   A: _____

3. A: She owes her roommate a lot of money.

   B: Who does she owe a lot of money to?

   A: _____

4. A: Please pass Ranya the rolls.

   B: What do you want me to do with the rolls?

   A: _____

6 | EDITING

Correct these conversations. There are eight mistakes. The first mistake is already corrected.

1. **A:** I hate to lend or borrow money. Last month I ~~Sue lent~~ *lent Sue* $10. She still owes I the money. I reminded she last week and she promised to pay me back. I see her in school, but now she doesn't want to look at I.

   B: That's too bad.

2. **A:** Who's teaching boxing you?

   B: Sachiko is.

   A: Really? Who taught her it?

   B: Her brother's friend. He's a champion boxer.

3. **A:** I and my cousin are learning Italian.

   B: That's great. Who's your teacher?

   A: Fiore. He's teaching to us useful phrases.

Communication Practice

7 | LISTENING

Listen to the conversations. Then complete the sentences.

1. You buy a car with a lot of problems. You say, "I bought a _____."

2. Someone caused you to worry a lot. You say, "He nearly _____ me a _____ attack."

3. You are angry at someone. You decide to _____ that person a _____.

4. The little girl told a _____ tale when she said the monster ate the cookies.

5. You can't do a job alone. You ask a friend to _____ you a _____.

8 | TEACH YOUR CLASSMATES SOMETHING

Work in groups. Teach your group something you know and they don't. It can be a magic trick, words in a new language, a dance, etc. Report to the class.

Example: Rodika taught us a traditional Romanian dance.
Ali taught us a few words in Arabic.
Angel taught us a card trick.

9 | WRITING

Write about a special teacher. What did the person teach? Where did the person teach? Why was this teacher special?

Example: I had a great math teacher in junior high school. The beginning of eighth grade was a hard time in my life. That year my family moved to a new neighborhood, and I didn't have any friends. Also, my dad was out of work. I was very unhappy. And I didn't understand eighth grade math. Ms. Johnson had a lot of patience with me. She stayed after school. She taught me math tricks. She helped me with my homework. She gave me confidence. By the end of the year I was a strong math student. I also made a couple of friends. I owed it all to Ms. Johnson. She was about 65 years old at the time and it was her last year in the school. I wanted to call her or write to her, but I never did. I'm sorry I didn't.

10 | ON THE INTERNET

 *The following movies are about teachers. Choose one you haven't seen. Look it up on the Internet. Tell the class three or four things about the movie.*

Mr. Holland's Opus

Stand and Deliver

Dead Poet's Society

The Emperor's Club

School of Rock

Example: *Mr. Holland's Opus* stars Richard Dreyfus.
It's about a musician and music teacher, Mr. Holland.
Mr. Holland first teaches music just to pay the rent while he tries to compose something great. He ends up becoming a great teacher.

Count and Non-Count Nouns; Articles

Grammar in Context

BEFORE YOU READ

*What do you usually look for in a restaurant? Check (✓) the three most important things for you. Put an **X** next to the three least important things.*

_____ unusual food   _____ a quiet place

_____ polite service   _____ a lively place

_____ fast service   _____ low prices

_____ a beautiful atmosphere _____ food I like

_____ an unusual atmosphere   _____ big portions

⌒ *Read these restaurant reviews and the conversation between two friends.*

Green Grill ★ ★ ★

Vegetables from nearby **farms** are **the draw** at **Green Grill**. Try **the squash** and goat cheese **dumplings** or **the** zucchini **cakes** with **potatoes** and **onions**. Both were delicious. We had **the soup** of **the day**, **a** vegetable **soup**. It was outstanding. There isn't **much meat** or **fish** on the menu. The grilled **chicken** was OK, but it needed **a little salt**. Some **desserts** were unexciting, but **the** apple **pie** was excellent. There aren't **many tables**, so be sure to make **a reservation** well in advance.

Ali Baba ★ ★ ★

Ali Baba serves Middle Eastern **food** in **a** colorful **atmosphere**. **The** vegetable **combo** is **a** great **way** to begin. **The** pita **bread** with **hummus**, **yogurt**, and **tahini** is excellent. For **the** main **course** we suggest **the** lamb **kebab** with **rice** and **salad**. **The** best **dessert** is **the** almond **cake**. There is wonderful **music**. We waited **a few minutes** for our **table** even with **a reservation**, but when we sat down, **the service** was outstanding.

A: Do you have **some time** now? We need to make **a reservation** and send out **the invitations**. **The party** is only **a few weeks** away.

B: I have **time**. Did you get **any information** about **the restaurants**?

A: Yes, and I read **some reviews**. I like **Ali Baba**.

B: Good. How are **the prices** there?

A: Not bad.

B: Is there **room** for all of us?

A: Yes, but we need to be there by 5:45. They're busy later.

B: That's OK. Let's go with **Ali Baba**.

A: Great. I can make **the reservation** and send **the invitations**. Can you collect **the money**?

B: No **problem**.

AFTER YOU READ

Write **GG** *for Green Grill or* **AB** *for Ali Baba next to the restaurant it describes.*

_____ 1. The vegetables come from nearby farms.

_____ 2. They have delicious almond cake.

_____ 3. The apple pie was delicious.

_____ 4. The atmosphere is colorful.

_____ 5. There are only a few tables.

_____ 6. The food is Middle Eastern.

_____ 7. There's music.

Grammar Presentation

COUNT AND NON-COUNT NOUNS; ARTICLES

AFFIRMATIVE STATEMENTS

Singular Count Nouns		
	Article or *One*	Singular Noun
She wants	a	banana.
	an	apple.
	one	banana. apple.

Plural Count Nouns		
	Number or Quantifier	Plural Noun
He has	seven	friends. books.
	a few	
	some	
	a lot of	
	many	

Non-count Nouns		
	Quantifier	Non-count Noun
Carol needs	a little	help.
	some	
	a lot of	

NEGATIVE STATEMENTS

Singular Count Nouns		
	Article or *One*	Singular Noun
I didn't buy	a	pear.
	an	apple.
	one	pear. apple.

Plural Count Nouns		
	Number or Quantifier	Plural Noun
I didn't buy	two	pears.
	any	
	many	
	a lot of	

Non-count Nouns		
	Quantifier	Non-count Noun
I didn't buy	any	milk.
	much	
	a lot of	

The Definite Article *The*		
Count Noun	Non-Count Noun	Plural Count Noun
I need **the menu**.	He has **the butter**.	She has **the napkins**.

GRAMMAR NOTES

1. There are two kinds of nouns: **count nouns** and **non-count nouns**.

Count nouns are ones that we can count. **Examples:** *a salad, an onion,* and *one olive.*

Use *a*, *an*, or *one* before a singular count noun. Use *a* before a **consonant sound**. Use *an* before a **vowel sound**.

EXAMPLES

- He made **a salad**.
- He put **an onion** in the salad.
- He used **one olive**.

(continued)

2. We cannot count **non-count nouns**.

Examples: *milk, water, salt*

Do not put *a, an*, or a number before a non-count noun. Do not add *-s* or *-es* to a non-count noun.

- There's **salt** on the table.
  NOT: There's ~~a salt~~ on the table.
  NOT: There's ~~salts~~ on the table.

3. *The*, *a*, and *an* are articles. *A* and *an* are indefinite articles.

The is a definite article.

We use *the* when it is clear which person or thing you mean.

- You're hungry. You are looking for a restaurant. You see one and say, "There's **a** restaurant."

- You are looking for a particular restaurant. You see it and say, "There's **the** restaurant."
- We ate chicken and rice. **The chicken** was good, but **the rice** was bad.

4. You can use the definite article *the* before singular count nouns, plural nouns, and non-count nouns.

- **The restaurant** is here.
- **The menus** are there.
- **The soup** is delicious.

5. Use *some* before plural count nouns and non-count nouns in affirmative statements.

Use *any* before plural count nouns and non-count nouns in negative statements.

- He wrote **some invitations**.
- He drank **some juice**.
- He didn't mail **any invitations**.
- He didn't drink **any soda**.

6. Use *a few* for small amounts and *many* for large amounts with count nouns.

Use *a little* for small amounts and *much* for large amounts with non-count nouns.

▶ **BE CAREFUL!** *Much* is not usually used in affirmative statements. We usually use *a lot of* instead.

- I ate **a few peanuts**.
- I ate **many grapes**.

- I used **a little salt**.
- I didn't use **much pepper**.

- I drank **a lot of water**.
  NOT: I drank ~~much water~~.

7. Some nouns can be <u>both</u> **count** and **non-count nouns**.	*count noun* • He bought three **cakes** for the party. *non-count noun* • He ate some **cake**.
USAGE NOTE: In informal speaking, some non-count nouns are used as count nouns.	• I'd like **two coffees** and **two sodas**. *(I'd like two cups of coffee and two cans of soda.)*

Reference Notes

See Unit 4, page 40 for count nouns, *a*, and *an*.
See Appendix 9 on page A-10 for rules about plural nouns.
See Appendix 11 on page A-12 for a list of common non-count nouns.
See Unit 33, page 336, and Unit 34, page 346 for more about count and non-count nouns.

Focused Practice

1 | DISCOVER THE GRAMMAR

A *Read the sentences. Circle the noun in each sentence. Then check (✓) whether the noun is a singular count noun, a plural count noun, or a non-count noun.*

	Singular Count Noun	Plural Count Noun	Non-count Noun
1. We ate a little (chicken.)	☐	☐	☑
2. I need some information.	☐	☐	☐
3. There's a menu over there.	☐	☐	☐
4. There aren't many customers.	☐	☐	☐
5. We ate some bread.	☐	☐	☐
6. We need one more napkin.	☐	☐	☐
7. There was one server there.	☐	☐	☐
8. It's 10 kilometers from here.	☐	☐	☐
9. The coffee is expensive.	☐	☐	☐
10. There aren't any rolls.	☐	☐	☐
11. There isn't any food left.	☐	☐	☐
12. Those people came before us.	☐	☐	☐

B *Read the situations. Circle the letter of the correct answer.*

1. You're in a restaurant. You need a napkin. Your friend sees one and says,
   a. "Here's a napkin."
   b. "Here's the napkin."

2. You ask about a person's job. Someone says,
   a. "He's a teacher."
   b. "He's the teacher."

3. It's your child's birthday. She says,
   a. "Please bake a cake."
   b. "Please bake some cake."

4. You are planning a party at your house. You say,
   a. "I need a help."
   b. "I need some help."

2 | BILL'S PARTY   *Grammar Notes 3, 4*

*Complete the conversation. Use **a**, **an**, or **the**.*

A: Where's _____ party?
            1.

B: At Ali Baba Restaurant.

A: Are _____ Garcias coming?
           2.

B: Yes, they are.

A: Tell me, is Rob Garcia _____ dentist?
                                  3.

B: Yes, he is. His wife is _____ dentist too.
                                4.

A: Did you buy Bill _____ gift?
                          5.

B: Uh-huh. I bought him _____ photo album.
                              6.

A: _____ album? That was _____ great idea. He's always taking photos. . . . Hey! That
        7.   8.

gives me _____ idea. I can buy him _____ leather camera case. He doesn't
          9.   10.

have one.

B: Leather camera cases are usually expensive.

A: Yes, but _____ ones at Camera Mart are not.
                11.

3 | A FOOD CRITIC

Add **a**, **an**, or **the** to correct this passage about a lucky college student. There are 10 more missing articles.

Kel Warner is a college student. He's English major. He has great part-time job. He writes for school paper. He's food critic. Kel goes to all restaurants in town and writes about them. He can take friend to restaurants and school newspaper pays bill. Kel really has wonderful job.

4 | GUESTS

Complete the conversation. Use **some** or **any**.

A: I bought _____ cookies and fruit for dessert. What else do we need?

B: We don't have _____ milk or cream for the coffee.

A: I can get some.

B: Gideon doesn't drink _____ soda. Let's buy _____ lemonade for him.

A: OK.

B: Here are _____ flowers. There weren't _____ roses so I bought _____ dahlias.

A: They're beautiful. Let's put them on the table.

5 | MANY OR ANY

Complete the sentences. Use **many** or **any**.

1. We're out of milk. There isn't _____ milk in the refrigerator.

2. Let's get the tickets soon. There aren't _____ tickets left.

3. _____ people go to that restaurant. The food is delicious.

4. I can help with the dishes. It isn't _____ trouble.

5. There aren't _____ desserts on this menu. Maybe there's a separate dessert menu.

6 | MANY OR MUCH
Grammar Note 6

Complete the sentences. Use **much** or **many** and the words in the box.

history books	people	restaurants	traffic
homework	pots	~~time~~	water

1. I don't have _____ *much time* _____. My class starts in 10 minutes.

2. We like to eat out. Are there _____ in that area?

3. There wasn't _____, but it still took us an hour to get there.

4. I don't have _____. I can finish that assignment in 20 minutes.

5. There aren't _____ there. Go in that line.

6. He likes history. He has _____.

7. That plant doesn't need _____. It's a cactus.

8. They have a beautiful kitchen and _____ and pans, but they never cook.

7 | A FEW, A LITTLE, MUCH, OR MANY
Grammar Note 6

Complete the sentences. Use **a few**, **a little**, **much**, or **many**.

1. We need to get some more apples. We only have _____ left.

2. There's just _____ milk. We need to stop for more.

3. Please hurry. There isn't _____ time. The concert starts in 15 minutes.

4. There aren't _____ people in that restaurant. I hope the food is good.

5. We don't have _____ information about that place. Where can we get some?

6. I had _____ minor problems with my computer, but my friend was able to fix them in no time.

7. There's _____ soup in the refrigerator. I didn't finish it all.

8. Could we have _____ more rolls? They're delicious.

8 | EDITING

Correct these sentences. There are 12 mistakes. The first one is already corrected.

1. My friend is a waiter. He works at ^an^ Italian restaurant.

2. He doesn't earn many money.

3. I have problem with my car. I think it's a battery.

4. This soup needs a few salt.

5. We bought a apple pie.

6. We don't have some napkins.

7. There weren't much people at the party.

8. There was a lot traffic on the highway.

9. We finished the yogurt. There isn't some left.

10. We bought a pie and a cake. A pie was good, but a cake was terrible.

Communication Practice

9 | LISTENING

🎧 *Listen to a conversation. Boris helps Theresa prepare for a party.*

1. Circle the food Boris buys.

bread	chips	ice cream	salsa	tuna
cheese	ice	nuts	soda	

2. What's the problem? _____

3. Why is Boris upset? _____

10 | OUR CITY: THE GOOD AND THE BAD

A Work in small groups. Write 10 good or bad things about the city or town you are in. Use the words in the box or add your own words. Use a quantifier (**a**, **one**, **a few**, **some**, **many**, **a lot of**, **any**, **a little**, or **much**) in each sentence.

concert halls	job opportunities	schools and universities
crime	museums	sports facilities
good hospitals	parks and gardens	taxis
good restaurants	pollution	traffic
inexpensive restaurants	poverty	

Examples: There's a wonderful concert hall here.
There isn't much pollution here.
There are only a few parks and gardens in this city.

B Write four sentences on the board. Compare your sentences with those of your classmates. Were your ideas about the city or town the same as theirs?

11 | A RESTAURANT

First work alone. Think of a restaurant. Complete the sentences with true statements about the restaurant. Use the suggestions in the box or your own ideas. Then work in small groups. Tell your group about the restaurant.

big selection	flowers	music	tablecloths
candles	free parking	servers	tables outside
desserts	garden	placemats	vegetarian choices

Name of restaurant: _____

There's a _____

There aren't any _____

There aren't many _____

There isn't any _____

There isn't much _____

It doesn't have any _____

It has a lot of _____

Example: Name of restaurant: Tiramisu Restaurant
There's a beautiful garden in the back of Tiramisu Restaurant.
There aren't any rooms for private parties.

12 | WRITING

Write a review of the restaurant you described in Exercise 11 or any other restaurant, coffee shop, or cafeteria. Rate the restaurant and give the address and phone number. Tell about the food, the atmosphere, and the prices.

Rating scale

★★★★ = excellent
★★★ = good
★★ = fair
★ = poor

Example: ★★ *State University Cafeteria, 40 Union Square, Middletown, 909-459-0909*
You're hungry. You don't have much time. You don't have much money. Try our school cafeteria. It's a self-service restaurant. There are a lot of choices and a lot of tables. There's never a long wait. Unfortunately, the food varies. Sometimes the vegetables are overcooked and the desserts are always the same. But the sandwiches are excellent. The bread is always fresh and the fillings are delicious. So for a cheap, satisfying meal, go to State University Cafeteria.

13 | THE SOUP OF THE DAY

Work in pairs. Look at the cartoon and discuss the question. What is the man really saying?

"Exactly what day is this the soup of?"

14 | ON THE INTERNET

Many restaurants have their menus on the Internet. Find the menu of a restaurant you like. Choose a meal. Tell the class about it.

Example: I like The Cheesecake Factory®. There are so many choices on the menu. My favorite meal is the Grilled Portabella on a Bun. It has a big mushroom, other vegetables, and melted cheese, on a bun. It comes with french fries too. Of course, the best part of the meal is dessert—a big slice of strawberry cheesecake!

VII From **Grammar** to **Writing**
Noun–Noun Constructions

We often use a noun to describe (modify) another noun.

1 *Underline the noun-noun constructions in the sentences below.*

1. There's a shoe store on the corner.

2. There are two shoe stores on the street.

3. There's a maple tree near my home.

4. There are some maple trees near my home.

	Yes	No
When a noun is plural, is the noun that modifies (describes) it plural too?	☐	☐

In noun-noun constructions, only the second noun can have a plural ending.

2 *Rewrite the sentences. Replace the word **a** with the number in parentheses. Add the noun modifier. Make other changes if necessary.*

1. (two / shoe) They own a store.

   They own two shoe stores.

2. (three / Sunday) There's a newspaper on his desk.

   _____

3. (three / movie) There's a theater on Main Street.

   _____

4. (two / rock) We went to a concert last month.

   _____

5. (two / music) There's a festival in the city today.

   _____

3 | *Look at this paragraph. Underline the noun-noun constructions. Draw a picture of your favorite city street. Write a paragraph about the street. Include five noun-noun constructions.*

Example

My favorite street is Edgehill Street between First and Second Avenue. It's an unusual street. It's long and crooked. There are two shoe stores, a coffee shop, and a fruit and vegetable market on the north side of the street. On the south side there's an Italian bakery, a bookstore, and a Chinese restaurant. There's a traffic light on one corner and a stop sign on the other. There are two apartment buildings. Only one thing is missing from the street—a music store. Then it would have all the things I like. I know the street very well because my grandparents live there. Every time I go to that street these days, it brings back happy childhood memories.

VII Review Test

I *Read each conversation. Circle the letter of the underlined word or group of words that is not correct.*

1. **A:** <u>There are</u> a lot of <u>difficult words</u> in this article.
         A   B

   B: <u>Are there</u> a dictionary <u>on the shelf</u>?
       C   D

       A B C D

2. **A:** <u>Are you busy</u>?
       A

   B: <u>Me and John</u> are going to the computer lab. He's <u>showing me</u>
       B   C

   how to use a new program. <u>Why don't you</u> join us?
                                  D

       A B C D

3. **A:** <u>I'm learning</u> Spanish.
       A

   B: <u>Who's</u> <u>teaching</u> <u>you</u> <u>it</u>?
       B   C   D

       A B C D

4. **A:** <u>How did you do</u> on the test?
       A

   B: Not so <u>well</u>. <u>I made</u> <u>much</u> <u>mistakes</u>.
             B   C   D

       A B C D

5. **A:** Did you buy <u>a camera</u>?
             A

   B: Yes, <u>I did</u>, but <u>a camera</u> <u>didn't work</u>.
         B   C   D

       A B C D

II *Circle the correct words to complete the **yes / no** questions and short answers.*

1. **A:** <u>Are there / Are they</u> any soda machines in the building?

   B: Yes, <u>there are / they are</u>.

2. **A:** <u>Are there / Are they</u> any malls near your school?

   B: No, <u>there aren't / they're not</u>.

3. **A:** <u>Is it / Is she</u> the teacher?

   B: Yes, <u>she's / she is</u>.

4. **A:** <u>Are there / Are they</u> new students?

   B: No, <u>they aren't / she isn't</u>.

5. **A:** <u>Are there / Is there</u> a men's room on this floor?

   B: No, <u>they aren't / there isn't</u>.

III *Use **a, an**, or **the** to complete the conversations.*

1. **A:** Is there _____ elevator in this building?

   B: Yes, there's _____ elevator down the hall.

2. **A:** What did you get for grandpa?

   B: We bought him _____ CD and _____ tie.

   A: Did he like the gifts?

   B: I think he liked _____ CD. I'm not sure he liked _____ tie.

3. **A:** Where's _____ president's office?

   B: Her office is on _____ top floor.

4. **A:** Do you have _____ exact time?

   B: Yes. It's nine forty-three.

5. **A:** Do you have _____ match?

   B: Sorry. I don't.

6. **A:** What are you looking for?

   B: I lost _____ earring.

IV *Circle the correct word(s) to complete the sentences.*

1. There isn't <u>any / some</u> yogurt in the refrigerator.

2. He found <u>a little / a few</u> stamps at home so he mailed all the letters.

3. We didn't have <u>many / much</u> time. We only had a half hour for the test.

4. There are <u>any / some</u> good sales at that store.

5. He bought <u>a / the</u> beautiful tie for his father.

6. Is there <u>a / the</u> water fountain on this floor?

7. It's inexpensive. It doesn't cost <u>many / much</u> money.

8. They took <u>many / much</u> photos of their trip.

V *One sentence is correct. The other is wrong. Circle the letter of the correct sentence.*

1. **a.** Who's teaching boxing you?

   b. Who's teaching you boxing?

2. **a.** Give it to her.

   b. Give it to she.

3. **a.** It's near we.

   b. It's near us.

4. **a.** I and my friend are helping them.

   b. My friend and I are helping them.

5. **a.** Please send an e-mail to Ron.

   b. Please send an e-mail Ron.

▶ *To check your answers, go to the Answer Key on page RT-3.*

Review and Contrast— Verbs

Grammar in Context

BEFORE YOU READ

You have a personal problem. Who do you talk to?

☐ *a friend or relative*

☐ *a teacher*

☐ *a psychologist*

☐ *a radio talk show psychologist*

☐ *other _____*

🎧 *Do you listen to talk shows on the radio or TV? What do you think about them? Read a transcript of the radio talk show,* Tell Tal Your Troubles.

JOSH: Good morning. This **is** Josh Tal on *Tell Tal Your Troubles*. Right now we **are speaking** to Neat Nita and Bob the Slob. Last week Nita wrote, "My boyfriend, Bob, **is** a slob. He **never puts** his things away. He **never cleans** his apartment. He **has** time for fun and time for work, but he **never has** time to clean. We **plan** to marry in June. **Are** we in trouble?"

And Bob wrote, "Nita's a nut about neatness. She **always cleans**. She **doesn't leave** her apartment until everything **is** in place. **Every day** she **cleans**. I think she's **wasting** her time. Life **is** too short to spend so much time cleaning. What **do** you **think**?"

I **think** Nita and Bob **need** our help. They're on the phone now.

BOB: Morning, Josh.

JOSH: Hi, Bob. Hello, Nita.

NITA: Hi, Josh.

JOSH: Bob, Nita **says** you **almost never clean**. Is that true?

BOB: Hmm. **I don't know** about that.

JOSH: So, Bob, **how often do** you **clean** your apartment?

BOB: **Once in a while.**

JOSH: And how **does** your apartment **look**?

BOB: Not so good, but **I'm almost never** there. **I'm usually** at work or **I'm** out with friends.

JOSH: How's Nita's place?

BOB: It's clean, but she **spends** hours cleaning.

JOSH: Nita, **is** that true? **Do** you **spend** a lot of time cleaning your home?

NITA: Yes, **I do**. A clean home **is** important to me. And I **want** Bob to clean with me when we're married. **Right now I'm dusting** and **polishing** all my furniture. It **looks** great.

JOSH: What **do** you **think** about that, Bob?

BOB: I **don't want** to clean.

JOSH: Well, **do** you **want** to marry Nita?

BOB: Yes, I **love** her.

JOSH: Let's see what our audience **thinks**.

AFTER YOU READ

Write **T** *(true) or* **F** *(false). Change the false statements to true ones.*

_____ 1. It's the afternoon.

_____ 2. Bob and Nita are talking to Tal on a TV show.

_____ 3. Nita spends a lot of time cooking.

_____ 4. Bob spends a lot of time cleaning.

_____ 5. Bob's a slob.

_____ 6. Bob and Nita plan to marry.

_____ 7. Bob loves Nita.

_____ 8. Nita and Bob often clean together.

_____ 9. Bob stays home every weekend.

Grammar Presentation

THE SIMPLE PRESENT AND PRESENT PROGRESSIVE; *HOW OFTEN* . . . ?

The Simple Present
I **eat** at eight o'clock.
He **eats** at eight too.
She **doesn't eat** with me.
They **don't eat** with us.
Does he **eat** meat?
Do you **eat** in the cafeteria?

The Present Progressive
I**'m eating** now.
He**'s eating** now.
She **isn't eating** with him.
They **aren't eating** with us.
Is he **eating** chicken?
Are you **eating** chicken?

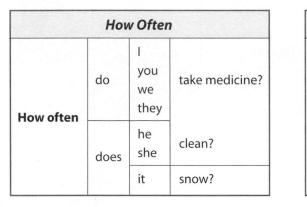

How Often			
How often	do	I you we they	take medicine?
	does	he she	clean?
		it	snow?

Answers
Three times (a day).
Once (a week).
Every (Sunday).
Rarely.
Once in a while.
Never.

ADVERBS AND EXPRESSIONS OF FREQUENCY

Adverbs of Frequency			
Subject	Adverbs of Frequency	Verb	
I You	**always** **almost always** **frequently** **usually/often** **sometimes** **rarely/seldom** **almost never** **never**	**work**	on Tuesdays.
He She It		**works**	
We You They		**work**	

Adverbs of Frequency with *Be*			
Subject	*Be*	Adverbs of Frequency	
I	am	**always** **almost always** **frequently** **usually/often** **sometimes** **rarely/seldom** **almost never** **never**	busy.
You	are		
He She It	is		
We You They	are		

Adverbs of Frequency	
always	100%
almost always	
frequently	
usually/often	
sometimes	50%
rarely/seldom	
almost never	
never	0%

Expressions of Frequency	
Emiko shops	every (day).
	twice (a day).
	three times (a month).
	several times (a year).
	once in a while.

GRAMMAR NOTES

EXAMPLES

1. Use the **simple present** to tell or ask about **habits, customs, regular occurrences, routines,** or **facts**.

Past ———————ooooo———————→ Future

Now

I listen to the radio every morning.

- I **listen** to the radio every morning.
- **Do** you **listen** to the news?

2. Use the **present progressive** to tell or ask about an action that is happening **right now** or **these days**.

Past ——————————X——————————→ Future

Now

I'm listening to the radio right now.

- **I'm listening** to the radio right now.
- **Is** Enrique **watching** TV?
- Jon **is taking** a photography course this year.

3. *How often* asks questions about **frequency**. *How often* is usually used with the simple present or simple past. It is rarely used with the present progressive.

- **How often** do you clean your room?

  NOT: How often ~~are you cleaning~~ your room?

4. **Adverbs** and **expressions of frequency** tell **how often** we do something.

Adverbs and expressions of frequency are often used with the simple present. They rarely occur with the present progressive.

- Tim **always** prepares breakfast.
- Marta goes to class **every day**.
- They **usually** open the store at nine.

  NOT: They ~~are usually opening~~ the store at nine.

(continued)

5. Adverbs of frequency usually come **after the verb** *be*.

They usually come **before other verbs** in the simple present.

Sometimes, *usually*, and *often* can also come at the beginning of a sentence.

▶ **BE CAREFUL!** Don't begin a sentence with *never* or *always*.

▶ **BE CAREFUL!** Don't use negative adverbs of frequency (*rarely, seldom, almost never*) in negative sentences.

- Yoko **is usually** on time. She **isn't usually** late.

- She **rarely listens** to the radio.
- She **doesn't often watch** TV.

- He **sometimes goes** to concerts.
- **Sometimes** he **goes** to concerts.

- I **never** play golf.
  NOT: ~~Never~~ I play golf.

  NOT: I ~~rarely don't~~ play golf.

6. Expressions of frequency are time markers. They usually come at the beginning or at the end of a sentence.

- He plays soccer **every day**.
- **Every week** she goes to the movies.

Reference Notes

See Unit 8, page 71, Unit 9, page 80, and Unit 10, page 89 for a more complete discussion of the simple present.

See Unit 15, page 143 and Unit 16, page 153 for a more complete discussion of the present progressive.

Focused Practice

1 | DISCOVER THE GRAMMAR

Read the sentences. Write the simple present verbs and the present progressive verbs in the chart.

Simple Present Verbs	Present Progressive Verbs
listen	'm listening

1. I usually listen to *Tell Tal Your Troubles*, but today I'm listening to another program.

2. Today she's eating out, but she almost always eats at home.

3. Every Thursday morning psychologist Josh Tal appears on a radio talk show. It's Wednesday afternoon and Josh is preparing for his show.

4. They're studying and listening to music now. They often study and listen to music.

2 | LETTER TO PSYCHOLOGIST JOSH TAL

Grammar Notes 1–2

Complete the letter. Use the simple present or the present progressive.

Dear Josh,

My girlfriend and I __have__ a great relationship in every way but one. I'm romantic,
1. (have)

but she is not. Every week I _____ her flowers. She usually _____, "Don't buy
2. (buy)   3. (say)

flowers. You're wasting money." Every time I _____ her a love poem, she _____,
4. (write)   5. (say)

"Don't write poems. You _____ time." Sometimes I _____ a candlelit dinner. After
6. (waste)   7. (prepare)

five minutes she _____, "I _____ on the lights now. I want to see my food."
8. (say)   9. (turn)

What's wrong with her? Or is there something wrong with me?

Ronnie the Romantic

3 | COMPLAINTS AND COMPLIMENTS

Grammar Notes 1, 4–5

*Complete the sentences. Use **never** or **always** and the simple present form of the verb in parentheses.*

1. (listen) He talks too much. He __never__ __listens__ to me.

2. (plan) She does her work at the last minute. She _____ _____ ahead.

3. (help) He's very thoughtful. He _____ _____ other people.

4. (ask) The young boy is very curious. He _____ _____ good questions.

5. (be) He never comes late. He _____ _____ on time.

6. (take) Josh Tal works hard. He _____ _____ a day off.

7. (wear) My aunt loves bright colors and looks good in them. She _____ _____ yellow, orange, or red.

8. (look) She has great taste in clothes. She _____ _____ good.

9. (stop) There's something wrong with this clock. It _____ _____ at 6:30.

10. (buy) He's not very romantic. He _____ _____ me flowers.

4 | QUESTIONS OF FREQUENCY
Grammar Notes 3–6

Write questions. Begin with **How often**. Use the words in the box. Then answer the
questions. Use the frequency expressions in the box or your own.

Activities	Expressions of Frequency
you / go to the movies	every day
you / e-mail friends	once a day / twice a day / three times a day
your family / have dinner together	once a week / twice a week / three times a week
your best friend / call you	once a month / twice a month / three times a month
your relatives / get together	once in a while

1. Q: _How often do you go to the movies?_____

   A: _I go once in a while._ OR _Once in a while._____

2. Q: _____

   A: _____

3. Q: _____

   A: _____

4. Q: _____

   A: _____

5. Q: _____

   A: _____

5 | A BROTHER AND SISTER
Grammar Notes 1–2, 4–5

A Complete the conversation between a sister and brother. Use the simple present or the
present progressive of the verb in parentheses.

MIKE: Michelle, what _____are_____ you _____doing_____?
                                          1. (do)

MICHELLE: I _____ Janet.
              2. (call)

MIKE: But you _____ my phone.
                  3. (use)

MICHELLE: That's because you _____ a lot of free minutes left, and I
                              4. (have / always)

_____. Dad said I can't go over my limit this month.
   5. (do / not)

MIKE: I _____ you. You and Janet _____ on the phone at least
         6. (understand / not)   **7. (talk)**

five times a day.

MICHELLE: No, we _____.
                        8. (do / not)

MIKE: Yes, you do.

MICHELLE: Well, you _____ people all the time.
                            9. (e-mail)

MIKE: That's different.

MICHELLE: I just _____ to make one phone call. Please. It's really important. You
                    10. (need)

can use my iPod®.

MIKE: Can I borrow your jean jacket too?

MICHELLE: Oh, OK . . . Hi, Janet. This is Michelle. What _____ you

_____?
       11. (do)

B 🎧 *Now listen and check your work.*

6 | EDITING

Correct these conversations. There are 10 mistakes. The first mistake is already corrected.

1. **A:** Are you busy?

    B: Yes, I am. I'm really ~~work~~ *working* hard these days.

2. **A:** Can I help you?

    B: Yes, thank you. I call about my new air conditioner. It not work.

3. **A:** How often you see them?

    B: About once a month.

4. **A:** Can I see the doctor on Tuesday?

    B: Sorry. He doesn't works on Tuesdays.

5. **A:** Is she play tennis at West Park?

    B: No, she's not. Never she plays there.

6. **A:** Where you calling from?

    B: Downtown. I walk along Second Street.

7. **A:** Do you eat there often?

    B: No. I don't rarely eat there. It's too expensive.

Communication Practice

7 | LISTENING

∩ *Listen to the conversation. Complete the sentences by circling the letter of the correct answer.*

1. John usually _____.
   a. drinks water   b. drinks coffee

2. Today John is drinking _____.
   a. water   b. coffee

3. John usually _____ apples.
   a. eats   b. doesn't eat

4. Today John _____.
   a. is eating a donut   b. isn't eating a donut

5. John is trying _____.
   a. to change his habits   b. to change Anne

8 | SURVEY: HOW OFTEN DO YOU . . . ?

Work in groups of three. Ask each person in your group five questions that begin with **How often**. *Choose an idea from each box. Use adverbs or expressions of frequency in your answers.*

Habits	Chores	Fun Activities	Good Deeds	Sports
eat out	clean	go to the movies	visit the sick	play tennis
wear a suit	do laundry	go to concerts	give to the poor	swim
get up early	cook	go shopping	help the elderly	play soccer
eat pizza	sew	go to a museum	call lonely people	ski
eat raw fish	fix things	play computer games		play baseball
go to the gym				

	Student #1	Student #2
1. How often do you eat pizza?	Once a week.	Almost never.
2.		
3.		
4.		
5.		

Report the results to the class.

9 | HOW OBSERVANT ARE YOU?

Work in pairs (A and B).

Student A, study your classmates for one minute. Then close your eyes.

Student B, ask your partner questions about the people in your class. Use the present progressive and the simple present. Use adverbs of frequency and the verbs **wear**, **sit**, *and* **do**.

Example: A: What's Enrique wearing?
B: He's wearing jeans and a black t-shirt.
A: Does Enrique often wear jeans and a black t-shirt?
B: He often wears jeans, but he rarely wears a black t-shirt.

10 | WRITING

Imagine a private investigator is watching you. He or she is writing a report about your actions this month. Write the investigator's report. Include several habits and at least one special event.

Example: Every weekday, Paula leaves her house at 7:15. She drives to her office. She takes the same road every morning. She usually arrives at work by 8:00. She rarely goes out for lunch, but she often shops at the mall during her lunch hour. She leaves work at 4:30 and she sometimes stops for gas on the way home. Now she is coming out of a mysterious building. She is carrying two large bird cages . . .

11 | ON THE INTERNET

Write six questions for a celebrity that you want to interview. Look up that celebrity on the Internet. See how many of your questions you can answer with the information you find. Write an imaginary interview. Role-play the interview with a classmate.

Examples: Where do you live?
Where do you go on vacations?
Do you have any special hobbies? What are they?
What are you working on at this time?

27 | Non-Action Verbs

Grammar in Context

BEFORE YOU READ

Look at the photo. Is this a place you would like to visit? Why or why not?

🎧 *Read the conversation.*

HEATHER: Any mail?

RICK: A postcard from Bora Bora.

HEATHER: No kidding. Who's there?

RICK: Aunt Janet and Uncle Fred.

HEATHER: Really? **Is** Bora Bora in the Pacific?

RICK: Uh-huh. **It's** part of French Polynesia. Take a look at this photo.

HEATHER: Wow! It **looks** like paradise. Look at that white sand!

RICK: Yeah, it **seems** like the perfect vacation spot. Read this card. Aunt Janet and Uncle Fred **are** crazy about it. They **like** everything there.

HEATHER: It **sounds** great.

RICK: I **agree**. So . . . let's go there too.

HEATHER: To Bora Bora? **Are** you serious? It probably **costs** half a year's salary.

RICK: But, Heather, my new invention will make us rich. You **believe** in me, don't you?

HEATHER: I **guess** so. . . . But, Rick, **remember** . . . that's what you said about your last invention . . . and the one before that too.

AFTER YOU READ

Change all these false statements to true ones.

1. Bora Bora is part of French ~~West Africa~~. *Polynesia*

2. Bora Bora looks like Paris to Heather.

3. Bora Bora sounds terrible.

4. Rick doesn't want to go to Bora Bora.

5. Rick doesn't believe in his invention.

Grammar Presentation

NON-ACTION (STATIVE) VERBS

State of Being	Emotion	Sense / Appearance	Need / Preference	Mental State	Possession	Measurement
be	love hate like dislike	hear see feel taste smell sound look	want need prefer	agree disagree guess understand know remember believe think mean	have own belong	cost weigh owe

GRAMMAR NOTES

EXAMPLES

1. Some verbs do not describe actions. These verbs are called **non-action** or **stative verbs**.

- I **have** a great idea.
- This **belongs** to me.
- They **love** Bora Bora.

2. Non-action verbs do the following:

  a. express emotion

  b. describe sense or appearance

  c. express a need or preference

  d. describe a thought

  e. show possession

  f. give a measurement

  g. *Be* expresses a state of being.

- We **like** the beach.
- The music **sounds** romantic.
- I **prefer** black coffee.
- Jennifer **knows** you.
- It **belongs** to me.
- It **costs** a lot of money.
- I **am** tired now.

3. We usually do not use non-action verbs in the present progressive (*-ing*) form.

- I **own** a car.
- It **costs** a lot.
  - NOT: I'm owning a car.
  - It's costing a lot.

(continued)

4. Some non-action verbs can have non-action and action meanings.

Examples: *have, taste, smell, feel, look, think*

non-action verb
• I **have** (own) a new car.

action verb
• I**'m having** (experiencing) trouble with the engine.

non-action verb
• He **looks** (appears) sad.

action verb
• The boy **is looking** (searching) for his mother.

non-action verb
• I **think** (in my opinion) it's interesting.

action verb
• I**'m thinking about** English grammar.

Focused Practice

1 | DISCOVER THE GRAMMAR

Underline the non-action verbs in the questions. Then match the questions with the answers.

___d___ 1. Do you <u>like</u> golf?

_____ 2. Do you love me?

_____ 3. Do you smell smoke?

_____ 4. Does the pineapple taste good?

_____ 5. Do you hear the birds?

_____ 6. What do you see?

_____ 7. Does she have time this morning?

_____ 8. Do you know those men?

a. Nothing. It's too foggy.

b. Yes. They sound beautiful.

c. Yes. They're servers at Star Café.

d. I prefer tennis.

e. Of course I do. My heart belongs to you.

f. No. I have a cold.

g. No. I think she's busy.

h. Yes. It's delicious.

2 | ALL ABOUT BORA BORA

Grammar Notes 1–2

Complete the questions and answers with the correct form of the verbs in the box. Verbs may be used more than once.

be	belong	cost	have	like	prefer

1. **Q:** _Does_ it _cost_ a lot to visit Bora Bora?

a.

   A: Yes. Bora Bora is the second most expensive place to visit. Japan is the most expensive.

   Everything in Bora Bora _____ a lot.

b.

2. **Q:** _____ Bora Bora _____ a tropical climate?

a.

   A: Yes, it does. It _____ two seasons: the wet season and the dry one.

b.

3. **Q:** _____ there a lot of mosquitos?

a.

   A: During the wet season, there _____ plenty.

b.

4. **Q:** What can I do in Bora Bora that's different from in other places?

   A: It depends on what you like. If you _____ swimming, there's the lagoonarium. There

a.

   you can swim with turtles, dolphins, sharks, and tropical fish. If you _____ to see a

b.

   show, you can see traditional dancers.

5. **Q:** Is Bora Bora a country?

   A: No, it's not. It _____ to France. It's part of French Polynesia.

a.

3 | A POSTCARD FROM BORA BORA

Grammar Notes 1–3

Complete the postcard message. Use the simple present or present progressive.

Dear Heather and Rick,

   I can't _____believe_____ we're here. I _____ on my terrace at the hotel

1.   2. (sit)

and _____ a fresh pineapple. Uncle Fred _____ in the ocean. He

3. (eat)   4. (swim)

_____ 10 years younger. He _____ about work.

5. (look)   6. (worry / not)

   I _____ 20 years younger. I _____ about Uncle Fred.

7. (feel)   8. (worry / not)

   We really _____ it here. We can see the ocean and beach from our terrace

9. (love)

and the weather _____ perfect.

10. (be)

Our love to all!

Aunt Janet and Uncle Fred

4 | PRESENT AND PRESENT PROGRESSIVE FORM
Grammar Notes 1–4

Write sentences with the words in parentheses. Use the simple present or the present progressive form of the verbs.

1. **A:** Whose camera are you using?

   B: Mine. *This camera belongs to me.*
   (to / camera / This / belong / me)

2. **A:** What are you doing?

   B: Nothing much. _____
   (think / vacation / our / I / about)

3. **A:** Does he need help?

   B: Yes, he does. _____
   (French / He / understand / not)

4. **A:** Do you have any information about French Polynesia?

   B: _____. We can lend it to you.
   (about French Polynesia / We / a good guidebook / have)

5. **A:** Are they there?

   B: Yes, hurry! _____
   (us / They / wait for)

6. **A:** What do you want to do?

   B: _____. The water looks inviting.
   (want / to go / to the beach / I)

7. **A:** Where are you?

   B: I'm at the department store in the mall. _____
   (look / I / for / a swimsuit)

8. **A:** Is that Mario?

   B: I don't know. _____
   (his name / I / remember / don't)

9. **A:** What are you doing?

   B: _____
   (I / the / soup / taste)

10. **A:** How is it?

    B: _____
    (It / delicious / taste)

5 | EDITING

Correct these short conversations. There are seven mistakes. The first mistake is already corrected.

1. **A:** Do you ~~having~~ *have* the key to the room?

   B: Yes. It's in my bag.

2. **A:** How much is it cost to get to the airport?

   B: I don't know.

3. **A:** Do you wants a double bed or two twin beds?

   B: A double bed.

4. **A:** Hurry. The shuttle bus is leaving now.

   B: I come.

5. **A:** Do you wearing sunscreen? The sun is very strong.

   B: Yes, I am.

6. **A:** Are you needing a beach towel?

   B: No. I have one.

7. **A:** How much cost these pearls?

   B: They're $200.

Communication Practice

6 | LISTENING

🎧 *Listen to a conversation among two couples. One person makes five complaints. Check (✓) the complaints.*

_____ **1.** There are a lot of bugs.

_____ **2.** The hotel is too expensive.

_____ **3.** It's too noisy.

_____ **4.** The food is too plain.

_____ **5.** The food is too pricey.

_____ **6.** The food is too spicy.

_____ **7.** The people are not friendly.

_____ **8.** The people don't speak English.

7 | OPINIONS

Work in pairs. Read these opinions. Respond with a phrase from the box. Then add a sentence.

Example: **A:** Vacations are good for your health.
B: It depends. My friend often comes home from a vacation with a cold. How do you explain that?

I agree.	I don't agree. (I disagree.)	I think so too.	I don't think so.	It depends.

1. Vacations are good for your health.

2. It's important to learn a few words of the language when you travel to a foreign country.

3. Two short vacations are better than one long one.

4. I believe, "When in Rome, do as the Romans do."

8 | EMOTIONS

A *Work in pairs. Tell each other how you feel about the items in the box. Use* **I love**, **I like**, **I don't like**, *or* **I hate**.

chocolate	laptops	opera	romantic movies	this city
English grammar	modern art	reality shows	soap operas	warm weather

Example: **A:** How do you feel about this city?
B: I like it. It's exciting.

B *What do you now know about your partner? In what ways are you and your partner alike? Tell the class.*

Example: We both like this city.

9 | SURVEY

A *Complete the questions. Use the ideas in parentheses or your own ideas.*

Do you know _____? (karate)

Do you like _____? (water-skiing)

Do you remember the movie _____? (*Star Wars*)

Do you understand _____?
(sign language)

B *Survey five classmates. Report the results to the class.*

10 | WRITING

Describe an object, but don't tell what it is. Your class guesses the object. Use non-action verbs in your description.

Example: I think it tastes good with a hamburger. Some people like it with ketchup. Sometimes it's French. Sometimes it's baked. Sometimes it's fried. Sometimes it's boiled. It has eyes. Its skin is brown or red. What is it?

11 | ON THE INTERNET

Choose A or B.

A *Download a picture of a vacation spot. Pretend you are on vacation there. Show the picture to your class and describe the place in 10 sentences. Use non-action verbs in each sentence. Ask your classmates to guess where you are.*

OR

B *Many famous people have visited French Polynesia. Find out about one of these people: Herman Melville (author), Paul Gauguin (artist), Charles Darwin (scientist), or James Michener (author). Pretend you are that person. You are in French Polynesia for the first time. What do you see and feel?*

Grammar in Context

BEFORE YOU READ

Look at the photos. Why do people become surgeons? carpenters? clowns?

🎧 *To get the right job and be successful, you need to know yourself. Read these people's comments and the jobs that match their needs.*

> I **like to learn**. I **hope to continue** learning throughout my career.

Software Developer
Scientist
Diplomat
Doctor
Writer

1.

> I **enjoy working** with my hands.

Carpenter
Auto Mechanic
Dentist
Farmer
Chef

2.

> I **expect to do** something different every day. I **like things** to be unpredictable.

Small Business Owner
Police Officer
Musician
Advertising Executive
Actor

3.

> I'm very competitive. I **hate losing**. People say I have a type A personality.

Attorney
Investment Banker
Politician
Professional Athlete
Stockbroker

4.

I **can't stand wearing** a suit. I **avoid wearing** formal clothes whenever possible.

Farmer
Artist
Computer Programmer
Anthropologist
5. Child Care Worker

I **love meeting** people. I **enjoy talking** to and **helping** others.

Teacher
Guidance Counselor
Psychologist or Social Worker
Physical Therapist
6. Hotel Manager

AFTER YOU READ

Circle the letter of the career that doesn't belong.

1. You expect to make a lot of money. You always want to win.

    a. lawyer   **b.** investment banker   **c.** social worker

2. You often need to wear a suit.

    a. banker   **b.** farmer   **c.** lawyer

3. You're a "people person." You enjoy interacting with others.

    a. teacher   **b.** physical therapist   **c.** computer programmer

Do you disagree with any of the matches?

Grammar Presentation

GERUNDS AND INFINITIVES

Subject	Verb	Gerund (Verb + -*ing*)
I	**enjoy**	**dancing**.

Subject	Verb	Infinitive
I	**want**	**to sing**.

Subject	Verb	Infinitive or Gerund
I	**like**	**painting**. **to paint**.

Verbs + Gerund	Verbs + Infinitive		Verbs + Infinitive or Gerund
avoid	agree	refuse	hate
enjoy	decide	want	like
finish	expect		love
keep	hope		prefer
keep on	intend		
regret	need		
think about	plan		

GRAMMAR NOTES   **EXAMPLES**

1. A **gerund** is a noun that is formed by the **base form of a verb + -ing**. Some verbs, such as *enjoy*, *finish*, and *keep*, can be followed by a gerund.	gerund • I **enjoy singing**. • We **finished studying** at eight. • She **keeps asking** about the job.

2. An **infinitive** is *to* + **the base form of the verb**. Some verbs, such as *want*, *need*, and *try*, can be followed by an infinitive.	infinitive • I **want to work**. • She **needs to write** a resume. • He**'s trying to get** an interview.

3. Some verbs, such as *like* and *hate*, can be followed by a gerund (*-ing* form) or an infinitive (*to* + base form).	• I **like writing**. • I **like to write**.

Focused Practice

1 | DISCOVER THE GRAMMAR

Mark each sentence **I** *(Verb + Infinitive) or* **G** *(Verb + Gerund).*

_____G_____ **1.** I enjoy working with people.

_____ **2.** He needs to get a job.

_____ **3.** She prefers to work at night.

_____ **4.** I prefer working in the daytime.

_____ **5.** I avoid wearing a suit.

_____ **6.** He refused to work late.

_____ **7.** They hope to take a vacation in July.

_____ **8.** They finished eating at 10.

2 | FAME

Bob hopes to be a successful actor. Complete the conversation with the gerund or the infinitive of the verbs in parentheses. In one case there are two possible correct answers.

ELENA: Do you enjoy _____*acting*_____ ?
    1. (act)

BOB: Yes. I love _____ .
    2. (act)

ELENA: Is it hard to find work as an actor?

BOB: Very hard. Many people want _____ actors. You need _____
    3. (become)   **4. (have)**

talent, patience, and luck.

ELENA: Do you ever want _____ careers? Do you ever regret _____
    5. (change)   **6. (spend)**

so much time at such a hard job?

BOB: No. I refuse _____ my dream. I keep _____ for new parts. I
    7. (give up)   **8. (try out)**

think I'm a great actor and I plan _____ the world!
    9. (show)

3 | ABOUT WORK

Complete the sentences. Choose verbs from the box. Use an infinitive or gerund.

find	get	look	meet	study	tell	~~work~~

1. Do you enjoy _____*working*_____ with children?

2. Do you plan _____ an advanced degree?

3. He hoped _____ with the president of the company. Instead he met with the vice president.

4. I regret _____ him about my problem with my previous employer.

5. We're trying _____ a time when everyone can meet.

6. He keeps _____ at his watch. I hope he isn't bored.

7. Many people decide _____ law after watching courtroom dramas.

4 | EDITING

Correct this letter. There are seven mistakes. The first mistake is already corrected.

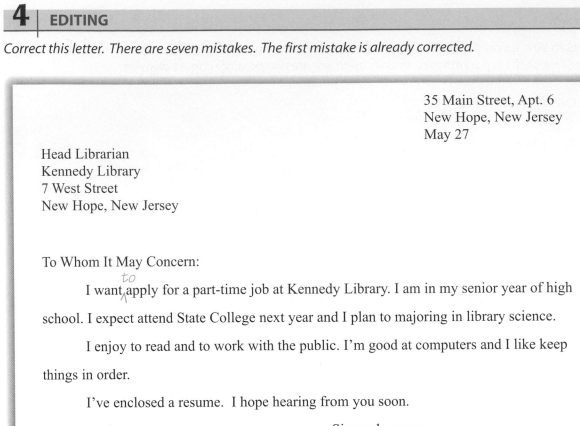

35 Main Street, Apt. 6
New Hope, New Jersey
May 27

Head Librarian
Kennedy Library
7 West Street
New Hope, New Jersey

To Whom It May Concern:

     I want *to* apply for a part-time job at Kennedy Library. I am in my senior year of high school. I expect attend State College next year and I plan to majoring in library science.

     I enjoy to read and to work with the public. I'm good at computers and I like keep things in order.

     I've enclosed a resume. I hope hearing from you soon.

               Sincerely yours,

               Joe Reed

Communication Practice

5 | LISTENING

🎧 *Listen to a conversation between two friends who meet after several years. Mark the statements **T** (True) or **F** (False). Change the false statements to make them true.*

_____ **1.** Ken plans to go back to school for more training.

_____ **2.** Cindy got tired of working for a big company.

_____ **3.** Cindy decided to open a store.

_____ **4.** Cindy enjoys planning conventions.

_____ **5.** Cindy likes to work with animals.

_____ **6.** Ken wants to have lunch with Cindy on Saturday.

6 | LIKES

Work in pairs. Write something you like to do or enjoy doing for each category. Read your sentences to your partner. Your partner then agrees or names something he or she prefers. Use an infinitive or gerund in your answer.

Example: **A:** I like to play golf.
 B: I do too.   OR   I prefer to play tennis.

1. sports: _____*golf*_____   3. books: _____   5. desserts: _____

2. movies: _____   4. music: _____   6. cars: _____

7 | GAME: WHAT DO I DO?

Work in small groups. Each group thinks of an occupation and gives the other groups hints. Use only the verbs in the chart on page 275.

Example: MOHAMMED: You want to help people.
 TATIANA: You need to study for many years.
 MAKI: You care about health.

 HECTOR (Student from another group): Are you thinking about a doctor?
 MOHAMMED: Yes, we are.

8 | THE RIGHT JOB

Work in pairs. Ask your partner the following questions. Talk about possible jobs.

- Do you enjoy working with people?
- Do you want to be rich?
- Do you want to be famous?
- Do you want to help others?

- Do you want to make a difference in the world?
- Do you dislike traveling?
- Do you dislike wearing "business clothes"?
- Do you like to "do you own thing"?

9 | WRITING

Write a two-paragraph letter. Apply for a part-time job near your home or school. Look at Exercise 4. Explain who you are and why you want the job.

10 | ON THE INTERNET

Think of an unusual job. Look for information about it on the Internet. Write a description of the job. Where did you find information about it? Share the information with your classmates.

Example: I found out about the job of a zookeeper. I went to a site called "ABC Career Information."
      Zookeepers usually enjoy working with animals. To become a zookeeper, you need to study biology or zoology, and you need to get experience taking care of animals, maybe as a volunteer. The pay is not very high and it's hard to take care of animals, but most zookeepers like their job and keep it for a long time.

29 Review of the Simple Past

Grammar in Context

BEFORE YOU READ

The artist Andy Warhol said, "Everybody will be world famous for 15 minutes." Is fame important to you? What would you like to be famous for?

🎧 *Read the story of Michael Larsen and his 15 minutes of fame.*

Michael Larsen **was** an ice cream truck driver. In 1983, he **lost** his job. He **began** to watch quiz shows, including one called *Press Your Luck. Press Your Luck* **was** a game of luck. You **pushed** a button and it **landed** on one of several squares: prizes, vacations, or whammies. Whammies **were** bad. You **lost** everything if you **landed** on a whammy. Most people on *Press Your Luck* **lost**, but some people **won** a few thousand dollars.

Larsen **had** several TVs and VCRs. He **recorded** and **studied** all the episodes of *Press Your Luck*. He **discovered** that there **were** different patterns. The game **wasn't** really a game of chance. He **went** on the show and **kept** winning. Everyone **was** amazed. How **did** he **do** it? **Was** it a trick? How much **did** he **win**? He **won** over $100,000 and vacations to wonderful places.

The TV producers **were** unhappy. They **thought** Larsen had cheated, so they **hired** lawyers. Finally, they **admitted** Larsen had figured out the game and **won** fairly. After that the TV producers **changed** the game. It **became** a true game of chance.

But what **happened** to Larsen? What **did** he **do** with his money? **Did** he **enjoy** it? Unfortunately, his life **did not get** better. He **lost** some of his money in bad business deals. He **lost** the rest when he was robbed. And in 1999 he **died**.

AFTER YOU READ

A *Put the sentences in the correct order. Label the events 1–4.*

_____ **a.** He had a lot of free time and watched a lot of TV.

__1__ **b.** Larsen lost his job.

_____ **c.** He studied the show *Press Your Luck.*

_____ **d.** He figured out a way to win.

B *Label the events 5–8.*

_____ **a.** The TV producers were unhappy, but decided that Larsen won honestly.

_____ **b.** He went on the show.

_____ **c.** Larsen was not rich for long. He lost all his money, and died soon after.

_____ **d.** He won over $100,000.

Grammar Presentation

THE SIMPLE PAST

Affirmative (All Verbs Except *Be*)		
Subject	**Verb**	
I	**stayed**	home.
We	**went**	

Affirmative of *Be*		
Subject	**Verb**	
I	**was**	home.
We	**were**	

Negative (All Verbs Except *Be*)			
Subject	*Did Not (Didn't)*	**Base Form of Verb**	
I	**did not (didn't)**	**stay**	with them.
We		**go**	

Negative of *Be*		
Subject	**Verb**	
I	**was not (wasn't)**	at work.
We	**were not (weren't)**	

Yes / No Questions (All Verbs Except *Be*)		
Did	**Subject**	**Base Form of Verb**
Did	she	**leave?**
	they	

Yes / No Questions with *Be*		
Was / Were	**Subject**	
Was	he	home last night?
Were	they	

(continued)

Wh- Questions			
Wh- Word	Did	Subject	Base Form of Verb
When		they	**arrive**?
Where		he	**work**?
How	did	it	**begin**?
Why		he	**leave**?
Who(m)		you	**help**?

Wh- Questions with Be			
Wh- Word	Past Form	Subject	
When	**were**	you	there?
Where	**was**	he	from?
How	**was**	his	test?
Why	**were**	they	late?
Who(m)	**were**	they	with?

Wh- Questions About the Subject		
Wh- Word	Past Form	
Who	**invented**	the game?
What	**happened**	to him?
How many people	**watched**	the show?

Wh- Questions About the Subject with Be		
Wh- Word	Past Form	
Who	**was**	his friend?
What	**was**	his last name?
How many people	**were**	there?

GRAMMAR NOTES

EXAMPLES

1. Use the **simple past** to tell about **something that happened in the past**. For all verbs except *be*, the simple past form is the same for all persons.

- **He liked** that show.
- **We liked** that show.
- **I liked** that show.

2. **Regular verbs** end in *-d*, *-ed*, or *-ied*.

   Many common verbs are **irregular** in the past. See Appendix 7 for a list of common irregular past forms.

   regular
- They **changed** the game.
- He **pushed** a button.
- She **studied** the game.
   irregular
- He **had** two TVs.
- He **lost** his money.

3. For **negative statements** use *did not (didn't)* + the base form of the verb.

- He **did not have** a job.
- He **didn't have** a job.

4. For *yes/no* questions use *Did* + the subject + the base form of the verb.

	Did	subject	base form	
•	**Did**	you	**watch**	the show?
•	**Did**	they	**go**	to work?

5. Most *wh-* **questions** use a *wh-* question word and *yes/no* question order.

wh- word	*did*	subject	base form	
• **What**	did	he	do?	
• **Where**	did	she	go?	
• **Who**	did	he	work	for?
• **How**	did	he	do	it?

6. Questions about the subject use statement word order. They do not use *did*.

subject	verb		subject
• Who	helped	him?	His friend did.

7. The verb *be* has **different forms** from all other verbs.

STATEMENTS
- He **was** happy.
- They **weren't** happy.

QUESTIONS
- **Was** he on TV?
- **Were** you in the audience?
- When **was** the show on TV?
- Where **were** they? Who **was** on TV?

Not: ~~Did~~ they were famous?

Not: He was ~~be~~ a fan of the show.

► **BE CAREFUL!** Do not use *did* or the base form of the verb for questions or negative statements with *be*.

Reference Notes

For a more complete discussion of the past, see Unit 3, page 24, Unit 20, page 190, Unit 21, page 200, and Unit 22, page 208.

For a list of irregular verbs see Appendix 7, page A-7.

For pronunciation and spelling rules for the simple past of regular verbs, see Appendix 17, page A-18.

Focused Practice

1 | DISCOVER THE GRAMMAR

Read a conversation about famous leaders. Then write four statements or questions with **be** *in the past and four statements or questions with other verbs in the past.*

BORIS: Who's the man in the picture?

TEACHER: George Washington. He was the first president of the United States.

BORIS: When was that?

TEACHER: He became the president in 1789.

RODRICA: How long was he president?

TEACHER: For eight years.

RODRICA: Was he a good leader?

TEACHER: Yes, he was. And before he became president, he led the army during the American Revolution.

BEKIR: He sounds a lot like Ataturk. Kemal Ataturk was the father of modern Turkey. He was also a great soldier and leader. He led from 1923 to 1938. He gave Turkey many things including a modern alphabet. Now spelling is easy in Turkish.

TEACHER: Well, George Washington didn't do anything about the English alphabet. Spelling is still hard in English.

EUN YOUNG: King Sejong gave Korea an alphabet. He was one of Korea's greatest leaders.

JOSÉ: In South America, Simon Bolivar was the father of half a dozen countries. He led many countries to independence. He didn't change our alphabet, but spelling is not so hard in Spanish.

Sentences with *Be* in the Past

1. _____

2. _____

3. _____

4. _____

Sentences with Other Verbs in the Past

1. _____

2. _____

3. _____

4. _____

2 | A RECLUSE

Recluses *are people who live alone. They don't want other people in their lives. Read a newspaper article about a recluse. Complete the sentences with the correct form of the simple past.*

Recluse Leaves Millions to Help Poor Women Get an Education

Anne Schreiber _____*was*_____ a recluse. She never _____.
                       1. (be)   2. (marry)

She never _____ close friends. She _____ alone in a tiny
              3. (have)   4. (live)

studio apartment and _____ the same outfit every day—a black coat and a
                          5. (wear)

black hat. For many years she _____ for the tax department of the U.S.
                                    6. (work)

government. She _____ an auditor. She _____ sure people
                     7. (be)   8. (make)

paid their taxes. However, she _____ to pay taxes. She _____
                                    9. (like, not)   10. (like, not)

to pay for anything.

As a young woman, Anne _____ the suggestions of a brother and
                            11. (follow)

_____ all her money in his company. His company _____
    12. (invest)   13. (go)

bankrupt and she _____ her life savings. She _____ her
                      14. (lose)   15. (forgive, not)

brother. Anne _____ investing again in 1944 when she _____
                   16. (start)   17. (be)

49 years old. This time she _____ her own ideas. By investing well, she
                                 18. (use)

_____ $5,000 into $22,000,000. She _____ better than the
    19. (turn)   20. (do)

biggest businessmen. But she _____ her relatives to know she had so much
                                  21. (want, not)

money because she _____ to give them any of it. And she didn't. Anne
                       22. (want, not)

Schreiber _____ in 1995 at the age of 101. She _____ her
               23. (die)   24. (leave)

money to universities to help poor, bright women get an education.

3 | A MAN OF MANY TALENTS

Grammar Notes 1–7

Read the following article.

A *Write the questions that the underlined words answer.*

When you think of basketball, do you think of Michael Jordon, Shaquille O'Neal, or Dr. James Naismith. Dr. Naismith? Who was he? What did he do for basketball?

James Naismith was born <u>in Ontario, Canada</u>, <u>in 1861</u>. He
1.   2.
was a good athlete and a good student. He always loved <u>school</u>.
3.
He had <u>four</u> degrees. <u>In 1887</u> he received a philosophy degree
4.   5.
from McGill University in Montreal. In 1890 he received

<u>a degree in religion</u> from Presbyterian College in Montreal. He then moved to the United States.
6.
In 1890 he got a degree in physical education from the YMCA Training School in Springfield, Massachusetts, and in 1898 he got <u>a medical degree</u> from the University of Colorado. But
7.
<u>in the winter of 1891</u> he made his biggest contribution to the world. At that time he was a
8.
physical education instructor in Massachusetts. His students were active and hard to control. He

wanted them to play an indoor sport, <u>because it was too cold to play outdoors</u>. He invented the
9.
game of <u>basketball</u>. It became an instant success in the United States. Soon it spread to other
10.
countries. In 1936, <u>basketball became a sport in the Berlin Olympics</u>.
11.

1. *Where was James Naismith born?* _____

2. _____

3. _____

4. _____

5. _____

6. _____

7. _____

8. _____

9. _____

10. What game _____

11. What happened _____

B *Now write yes/no questions about Naismith. Then give the short answer.*

1. be / he good at sports?

   Q: _Was he good at sports_ ?   A: _Yes, he was._

2. be / he a good student?

   Q: _____ ?   A: _____

3. he / finish college?

   Q: _____ ?   A: _____

4. he / become a lawyer?

   Q: _____ ?   A: _____

5. he / invent the game of volleyball?

   Q: _____ ?   A: _____

4 | EDITING

Correct the questions or answers. There are 11 mistakes. The first one is already corrected.

1. Q: Who ^was^ Elizabeth Blackwell?

   A: She was the first woman physician in the United States.

2. Q: Where she was born?

   A: She was born in England.

3. Q: When was she born?

   A: She born in 1821.

4. Q: When she did come to the United States?

   A: She did come to the United States in 1833.

5. Q: Was it hard for her to become a doctor?

   A: Yes, it were. Most medical schools didn't want women.

6. Q: How was her grades in medical school?

   A: She was an outstanding student. Her grades were excellent.

7. Q: When she graduate?

   A: In 1849.

8. Q: What did Dr. Blackwell fight for?

   A: She did fight for the admission of women to medical schools.

(continued)

9. Q: Where did she goes in 1869?

   A: She returned to London. She worked and wrote there for many years.

10. Q: When she die?

    A: She died in 1910.

Communication Practice

5 | LISTENING

🎧 *Two people are watching a quiz show,* Win a Fortune. *Listen to their conversation and the quiz show. Then complete the questions and answers.*

1. Q: Who _____ *The Night Watch?*   A: Rembrandt.

2. Q: In what century _____?   A: The _____.

3. Q: Where _____?   A: In _____.

4. Q: What is _____?   A: Rembrandt van Rijn.

5. Q: Who _____ Yoko Ono?   A: _____.

6. Q: What _____ of John Lennon's   A: _____.
      _____?

7. Q: Where _____?   A: _____.

8. Q: When _____ their last appearance   A: _____.
   together?

6 | A QUIZ SHOW

Work in small groups. Prepare a quiz show. Write questions in the past. Choose a host or hostess from your group. Choose contestants from classmates in other groups.

Examples: Who starred in the *Matrix* movies?

What was the *Titanic*?

Who wrote *One Hundred Years of Solitude*?

7 | WHAT WERE YOU LIKE AS A CHILD?

Work with a partner. Ask your partner what he or she was like as a child. Use boxes A and B for ideas.

Example: **A:** When you were a child, were you talkative?
B: Yes. Once my teacher wrote a note to my mother. "Bernie never stops talking. He's smart, but he needs to give other children a turn." What about you? What were you like? Did you study hard?
A: No, I didn't. I began to study hard in high school.

A. Were you _____?	**B. Did you _____?**
athletic / uninterested in sports?	study hard
naughty / well behaved	listen to your teachers / your parents
stubborn / easygoing	watch a lot of TV
talkative / quiet / shy	play a lot of computer games
cheerful / moody	like music / art / dance

8 | INFORMATION GAP

Student A, look at this page.

Student B, turn to page 297.

A *Use the words given to write questions in the past.*

1. When / he / born _____

2. Where / he / born _____

3. What / be / his / occupation _____

4. Where / he / begin his career _____

5. Who / discover him _____

6. Where / be / he from 1958 to 1960 _____

7. What / he / appear in after that _____

8. When / die _____

B *Read the biography below. Your partner will ask you questions about the person. Answer your partner's questions. Your partner guesses who the person is.*

He was born in Albany, Georgia in 1930. His family was very poor. He became blind at the age of seven. He learned to read Braille and play music at the St. Augustine School for the Deaf and the Blind in Florida. His mother died when he was a teenager. He left school at 15 and began his career as a musician. He moved to Seattle and started his rise to fame. He started out as a jazz and blues pianist and singer, but over more than 50 years, he built a career that combined many types of music. In June of 2004, he died of liver disease in Beverly Hills, California. He was 73 years old at the time.

(Ray Charles)

C *Ask your partner the questions in Exercise A. Guess who the person is.*

9 | WRITING

Write a short biography of a musician you like. If possible, bring the person's music to class. Play a song. Then read the biography.

10 | ON THE INTERNET

James Naismith invented basketball. Do you know what these people invented? Go online and find out what things they invented and when they invented them.

1. Mary Anderson

2. Edward Binney and Harold Smith

3. Willis Carrier

4. William Keith Kellogg

5. Walter Frederick Morrison

6. Steve Russell

7. Thomas Sullivan

Example: Mary Anderson invented the windshield wiper in 1903.

From **Grammar** to **Writing**
Organization: Time Sequence Markers

1 Look at these sentences. Which words show the time?

1. He studies at home in the evening.
2. At present I live on Bleeker Street.

Time Sequence Markers

You can organize your writing by using **time sequence markers**. Some common markers for the time of day are: **in the morning**, **in the afternoon**, **in the evening**, **at night**.

Some common markers for the past, present, and future are: **in the past**, **at present**, **in the future**.

• Monique works **in the morning**.

• **At present**, I'm a student.

---

2 Read this story about a country doctor. Underline the time sequence markers. Then write about a day in the life of someone you know well.

A COUNTRY DOCTOR

Michelle Hirch-Phothong is a country doctor. Her day begins at six-thirty in the morning. At seven o'clock she is at the hospital. She visits her patients and discusses their problems with the nurses and other doctors. Michelle enjoys talking to her patients. She listens to them carefully and never rushes them.

In the afternoon Michelle works at a clinic. The clinic is busy, and patients are often worried about their health. Michelle and the other doctors try to help them.

At six o'clock in the evening Michelle leaves the clinic. She goes home and relaxes. Every evening at seven o'clock Michelle goes to "Bangkok in the Boondocks." That's my restaurant, and Michelle is my wife. Michelle and I enjoy a delicious Thai dinner alone.

Sometimes, however, people come to the restaurant and tell Michelle their medical problems. I say, "Tell them to go to the clinic." But Michelle never sends them home without listening to their problems and offering advice. Michelle is a wonderful doctor.

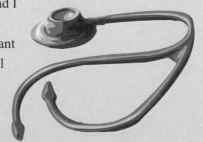

VIII Review Test

I *Read each conversation. Circle the letter of the underlined word or group of words that is not correct.*

1. **A:** I <u>don't know</u> him very well. <u>Does he work</u> on Mondays?   **A B C D**

        A   B

   B: I <u>don't think</u> so. He <u>works usually</u> on Tuesdays and Thursdays.

       C   D

2. **A:** Does she <u>like black coffee</u>?   **A B C D**

             A

   B: No, <u>she doesn't</u>. She <u>prefers</u> <u>drink</u> coffee with milk and sugar.

       B   C   D

3. **A:** <u>How often</u> <u>do you changing</u> the oil?   **A B C D**

      A   B

   B: <u>Every three months</u>. I <u>usually check</u> my tires too.

       C   D

4. **A:** What <u>did he</u> <u>do</u> after the concert?   **A B C D**

      A   B

   B: <u>He met</u> some friends and <u>go to a club</u>.

    C   D

II *Circle the letter of the correct word(s) to complete the sentences.*

1. Where _____ last night?   **A B C D**

(A) you went

(B) are you going

(C) did you go

(D) did you went

2. Who _____ you at the airport yesterday?   **A B C D**

(A) did meet

(B) is meeting

(C) met

(D) meets

3. _____ to you?   **A B C D**

   (A) Is this book belonging

   (B) Does this book belong

   (C) Did belong this book

   (D) Belongs this book

4. _____ on Monday.   **A B C D**

   (A) She almost always works

   (B) Almost she works always

   (C) Almost always she works

   (D) She almost works always

III *Match the questions with the answers.*

_____ 1. What are they doing?   **a.** At his friend's apartment.

_____ 2. What do they usually do on Sunday afternoon?   **b.** They're painting their bookcases.

_____ 3. Are they working hard?   **c.** About twice a week.

_____ 4. Do they usually work hard?   **d.** His friend Juan.

_____ 5. Where is her brother studying?   **e.** Yes, they do.

_____ 6. Who is he studying with?   **f.** Because it's quiet there.

_____ 7. Why is he studying there?   **g.** Yes, they are.

_____ 8. How often do they study together?   **h.** They relax.

IV *Rewrite each sentence. Use the adverb or expression of frequency in parentheses.*

1. (every week) They go to the bank.

_____

2. (rarely) She wears jeans.

_____

3. (always) They watch TV at night.

_____

4. (several times a year) We go to rock concerts.

_____

5. (often) He is late.

_____

V *Write questions with* **How often**. *Use the simple present.*

1. (Ellen / call her parents)

   A: _____

   B: Once a week.

2. (We / get a free lunch)

   A: _____

   B: There are no free lunches.

VI *Circle the correct words to complete the conversations.*

1. A: How's the food?

   B: The chicken is terrible, but this pasta <u>tastes / is tasting</u> delicious.

2. A: Why <u>do / are</u> you <u>wear / wearing</u> a suit and tie?

       a.

   B: I have a job interview this morning. I <u>want / am wanting</u> to look good.

                                              b.

3. A: <u>Are / Do</u> you <u>remember / remembering</u> your first date?

   B: Yes, I do. What about you?

4. A: <u>Is / Does</u> he <u>eat / eating</u> dinner now?

       a.

   B: No. He <u>likes / is liking</u> to eat dinner later.

           b.

5. A: How <u>do / are</u> you <u>spell / spelling</u> your name?

   B: It's J-E-A-N-N-E.

VII *Complete the letter with the correct form of the verb in parentheses.*

Dear Grandma,

How _____ things in Miami?
　　　　1. (be)

The newspaper _____ it's 80 degrees and sunny there today. Here it's 15
　　　　　　　　　2. (say)

degrees. The weather here is not always great, but I _____ this school. I really enjoy
　　　　　　　　　　　　　　　　　　　　　　　　　3. (love)

_____ in the International House and _____ people from all over the
　　4. (live)　　　　　　　　　　　　　　　　　　　　　　5. (meet)

world. I _____ a great roommate, and most of the kids on my floor are cool.
　　　　6. (have)

My favorite class is American literature. This month we _____ *Moby Dick*. It's
　　　　　　　　　　　　　　　　　　　　　　　　　　　　　　　7. (read)

a book about the hunt for a big whale. Next summer I plan _____ whale watching
　　　　　　　　　　　　　　　　　　　　　　　　　　　　8. (go)

with friends. I also want _____ another course with this professor.
　　　　　　　　　　9. (take)

Chemistry is hard, but I _____ OK. I need _____ it because I
　　　　　　　　　　　　　10. (do)　　　　　　　　11. (take)

_____ to go to medical school.
　　12. (want)

Every evening, I _____ to the library for a few hours. I _____ all
　　　　　　　　　13. (go)　　　　　　　　　　　　　　　　　14. (study, not)

the time. After a couple of hours, I usually _____ a break and _____
　　　　　　　　　　　　　　　　　　　15. (take)　　　　　　　　　　16. (talk)

with Jonathan. He's my best friend here. I hope _____ you to him this summer.
　　　　　　　　　　　　　　　　　　　　　　17. (introduce)

Thanks again for the beautiful sweater. I _____ the color. I _____
　　　　　　　　　　　　　　　　　　18. (love)　　　　　　　　　19. (wear)

it now. I _____ warm and close to you. I can't wait to see you.
　　　　20. (feel)

Please write or e-mail me.

　　　　　　　　　　　　　　　　　　　　　　　　　Love,
　　　　　　　　　　　　　　　　　　　　　　　　　Dara

VIII *Read the information in the box. Then complete the questions.*

- Thomas Jefferson—1743–1826
- Born—Virginia
- Wrote—the Declaration of Independence in 1776
- (Third) U.S. president—1801–1809
- Wife—Martha

1. A: _____*Who was*_____ the third president of the United States?

   B: Thomas Jefferson.

2. A: _____?

   B: In 1743.

3. A: _____?

   B: In 1826.

4. A: _____?

   B: In Virginia.

5. A: _____?

   B: In 1776.

6. A: _____?

   B: For eight years.

7. A: _____ his wife's name?

   B: Martha.

▶ *To check your answers, go to the Answer Key on page RT-4.*

INFORMATION GAP FOR STUDENT B

A *Use the words given to write questions in the past.*

1. Where / he / born _____

2. When / he / born _____

3. What / happened to him at the age of seven _____

4. Where / he / go to school _____

5. What / he / learn at school _____

6. Where / he / move _____

7. How many years / he / be / in the music business _____

8. When / he / die _____

B *Read the biography below. Your partner will ask you questions about the person. Answer your partner's questions. Your partner guesses who the person is.*

He was a popular singer. He was born in Tupelo, Mississippi in 1935. He began singing in a local church and he taught himself to play the guitar. Sam Phillips, the president of Sun Records, discovered him in 1953. By 1956 he was the most popular performer in the United States. Soon after that he became popular all over the world. His music combined country and western music with rhythm and blues. He spent two years, from 1958 to 1960, in the army. He appeared in several movies, but none were very successful. He died in 1977. He is known as the King of Rock and Roll.

(Elvis Presley)

C *Ask your partner the questions in Exercise A. Guess who the person is.*

PART

IX

The Future

Grammar in Context

BEFORE YOU READ

Do you ever read the letters to the editor in newspapers? Did you ever write a letter to the editor? What was it about?

Read these letters from students to the editor of their school newspaper.

LETTERS TO THE EDITOR

To the Editor:

Last week President Clark talked about plans for a new fitness center for our college. The center sounds great. It**'s going to have** a beautiful gym, a track for running, an Olympic-size pool, saunas, steam rooms, a basketball court, exercise machines, and weight-lifting equipment.

But, this fitness center **is going to cost** a lot of money. **Where is** the money **going to come** from? You guessed it. Most of the money **is going to come** from us. Our tuition **is going to increase**. That's why I'm against the plan. With a tuition increase, more students **are going to need** to work while they go to school. We**'re not going to have** time to enjoy the fitness center. We**'re not going to have** time to study.

Why is President Clark doing this? He only wants a fitness center because other schools have them. He thinks more students **are going to come** to our school if we have a fancy fitness center. But we're here for a good education, not to enjoy a state-of-the-art fitness center.

Sincerely,
Joe Molina

To the Editor:

A week ago President Clark announced plans for a new fitness center for our college. I love the idea. It**'s going to give** us a chance to relax and unwind before and after classes.

College is not just a time to sit in a library and study. It's a time for us to make our bodies *and* our minds stronger.

When the gym is built, I**'m going to go** there every day. I**'m going to study** harder and do better. Yes. We**'re going to pay** for it. There **is going to be** a tuition hike. But in my opinion it's worth it. It**'s going to improve** our lives. Last month a study showed that most students gain 10 pounds in their freshman year. I'll bet that**'s not going to happen** once we have our new fitness center.

Yours truly,
Alison Meadows

AFTER YOU READ

Read the sentences in a–f. Write the letter in the correct box.

For the Fitness Center	Against the Fitness Center
	a

a. It's going to cost a lot of money.

b. It's going to be a place to relax and unwind.

c. It's going to keep students in good shape.

d. More students are going to need to work during the school year.

e. Tuition is going to increase.

f. It's going to attract more students.

Grammar Presentation

BE GOING TO FOR THE FUTURE

Affirmative / Negative Statements

Subject + *Be*	(Not)	*Going to*	Base Form of Verb	
I'm				
You're				
He's	(not)	going to	study	tomorrow.
We're You're They're				
It's	(not)	going to	rain	tomorrow.

Yes / No Questions

Be	Subject	*Going to*	Base Form of Verb	
Am	I			
Are	you	going to	drive	tomorrow?
Is	he			

Short Answers

Affirmative	Negative
Yes, you are.	No, you're not.
Yes, I am.	No, I'm not.
Yes, he is.	No, he's not.

Wh- Questions

Wh- Word	*Be*	Subject	*Going to*	Base Form of Verb
What	is	she		do?
Where	are	they	going to	go?
How	am	I		get there?

Short Answers

Meet her friend.
To the library.
By plane.

GRAMMAR NOTES	EXAMPLES
1. There are different ways to express **the future**. USAGE NOTE: In speaking, *be going to* is more common than *will*.	• We **are going to buy** a car. • We **are buying** a car next month. • We **will buy** a car.
2. One way to express the future is with a form of *be* + *going to* + **the base form of the verb**. Use **contractions** of *be* in speaking and informal writing. Remember to use a form of *be* before *going to*. Remember to use the base form of the verb after *going to*.	• He **is going to start** at 9:00. • They **are going to start** at 9:00. • He**'s going to start** at 9:00. • They**'re going to start** at 9:00. NOT: ~~He going~~ to start at 9:00. NOT: He's going to ~~starts~~ at 9:00.
3. Use *be going to* + base form to • **state facts about the future**. • **make predictions**. • **talk about plans**.	• The politicians **are going to meet** in Rome. • There **is going to be** a change in the climate. • I can't go to the restaurant. **I'm going to take** my friend to the airport.
4. Use *probably* with *be going to* to say that something is **not definite**.	• We're **probably** going to start at 9:00. • It's **probably** going to rain.
5. Future time markers usually come at the beginning or the end of a sentence. Some common future time markers are: *tomorrow*, *next week*, *next month*, *this weekend*, *in 2100*.	• They are going to start construction **next week**. • **Next week** they are going to start construction.
6. Sometimes we use **the present progressive + a future time marker** to talk about the future. This is especially true with the verb *go* and with other words of movement or transportation. We do not use the present progressive with non-action verbs to talk about the future.	• We**'re going** there **next week**. • He**'s driving** to the country **this weekend**. • He**'s going to need** a new car next year. NOT: He's ~~needing~~ a new car next year.

Focused Practice

1 | DISCOVER THE GRAMMAR

A *Read the sentences. Underline all examples of* **be going to** *for the future. Then match the sentences on the left with those on the right.*

_c_ 1. Last week Mayor Jonas talked about building a sports stadium.

_____ 2. They're going to build a garage for the stadium.

_____ 3. The mayor is giving a speech on Wednesday afternoon here in our school.

_____ 4. They're going to build stores around the stadium.

_____ 5. Some people don't want the city to build a new stadium.

_____ 6. I'm against the new stadium.

a. It's going to have spaces for 5,000 cars.

b. I'm probably going to write a letter to the editor.

c. It's going to seat 30,000 people.

d. They're against it because the city is going to destroy some historic buildings when they build the stadium.

e. Those stores are going to provide jobs for a lot of people.

f. She's going to talk about raising money for the stadium.

B *Which sentence in Exercise A uses the present progressive for the future?* _____

2 | WHAT'S GOING TO HAPPEN? *Grammar Notes 1–3*

Write statements or questions. Use **be going to** *for the future and the words given.*

1. _Tomorrow it's going to be warm and humid._
   (Tomorrow / it / be / warm and humid.)

   _____
   (It / rain / not.)

2. _____
   (We / move / to a bigger apartment / next weekend.)

   _____
   (Our friends / help us move.)

3. _____
   (They / build / a new high school next year.)

   _____
   (They / raise / taxes to pay for the school.)

4. _____
   (I / write / not / to the school paper.)

   _____
   (I / talk / to the student leaders.)

5. There's a good show on TV tonight at 8:00.

   _____
   (you / be / home?)

   _____
   (you / watch the show?)

6. Gino is in the hospital.

   _____
   (you / visit / him / tonight?)

3 | A LETTER TO THE EDITOR

The West Street Association is against the construction of a new building on West Street.
*Complete their letter to the editor with the affirmative or negative of **be going to**.*

To the Editor:

    Mr. Romp wants to build a 20-story building on West Street. The West Street

Association is against the plan.

    It *'s going to change* _____ the area. All the buildings on West Street are four or
               1. (change)

five stories high. A very tall building _____ good. The new
                                  2. (look)

building _____ garage spaces for 50 cars, but there
                 3. (have)

_____ 200 apartments. There _____
          4. (be)   **5. (be)**

enough parking spaces. There _____ a lot more traffic in the area.
                                   6. (be)

    The new building _____ over all the other buildings in the
                                  7. (tower)

area. It _____ terrible. Let's work together to keep West Street
               8. (look)

beautiful. Stop construction of the Romp Tower!

                                                  West Street Association

4 | PAST, PRESENT, FUTURE

Complete the sentences with the correct form of the verb. Use the simple past, the simple present, or **be going to** *for the future.*

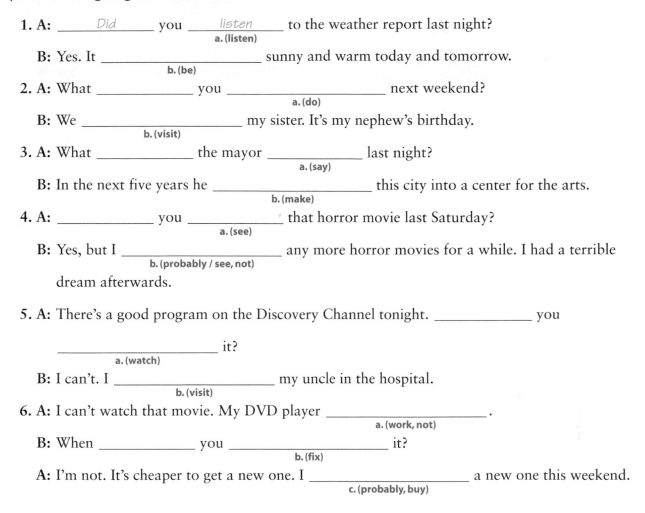

1. **A:** _____*Did*_____ you _____*listen*_____ to the weather report last night?
   a. (listen)

   B: Yes. It _____ sunny and warm today and tomorrow.
   b. (be)

2. **A:** What _____ you _____ next weekend?
   a. (do)

   B: We _____ my sister. It's my nephew's birthday.
   b. (visit)

3. **A:** What _____ the mayor _____ last night?
   a. (say)

   B: In the next five years he _____ this city into a center for the arts.
   b. (make)

4. **A:** _____ you _____ that horror movie last Saturday?
   a. (see)

   B: Yes, but I _____ any more horror movies for a while. I had a terrible
   b. (probably / see, not)

   dream afterwards.

5. **A:** There's a good program on the Discovery Channel tonight. _____ you

   _____ it?
   a. (watch)

   B: I can't. I _____ my uncle in the hospital.
   b. (visit)

6. **A:** I can't watch that movie. My DVD player _____ .
   a. (work, not)

   B: When _____ you _____ it?
   b. (fix)

   A: I'm not. It's cheaper to get a new one. I _____ a new one this weekend.
   c. (probably, buy)

5 | PLANS   *Grammar Note 5*

Look at the mayor's schedule for next Monday and Tuesday. Write questions and answers.
Use the present progressive for the future.

November 12	November 13
MONDAY —————————	**TUESDAY** —————————
10:00 A.M. Senior Center—Speech	8:00 A.M. American Airlines- Flight #41
	to LAX (Los Angeles Airport)
Noon Lunch with Community	Noon Mayors' Meeting
Leaders	
2:00 P.M. State University—Speech	2:00 P.M. Return flight-AA#46
	5:00 P.M. Arrive home
	7:30 P.M. Dinner for Police Chief—
	Grand Hotel

1. When / she speak to the senior citizens?

   Q: *When is she speaking to the senior citizens?*

   A: *On Monday at 10:00 A.M.*

2. Who / she / have lunch with on Monday?

   Q: _____

   A: _____

3. What / she / do / Monday afternoon?

   Q: _____

   A: _____

4. she / fly / to Los Angeles on Monday?

   Q: _____

   A: _____

5. What / she / do / in Los Angeles?

Q: _____

A: _____

6. What time / she / fly home from Los Angeles?

Q: _____

A: _____

7. she / go / to a dinner for the police chief?

Q: _____

A: _____

6 | EDITING

Correct the newsletter article. There are five mistakes. The first mistake is already corrected.

PEACEFUL PLACE APARTMENTS

Dear Residents:

Last week the mayor talked about building a sports stadium in our neighborhood. I think it's a terrible idea.

It's going ^to cost taxpayers millions of dollars. It going to mean traffic jams. Parking is being difficult, and it's going to bringing noise and dirt to the area.

Next Monday at 7:00 P.M. the mayor is goes to answer questions at the public library. I ask everyone from Peaceful Place Apartments to come and speak out about the new stadium.

Sincerely,

Dale Ortiz

President, Residents' Association

Communication Practice

7 | LISTENING

🎧 *Listen to a conversation about a new building. Answer the questions.*

1. What are two reasons for building it?

   a. _____

   b. _____

2. What are two reasons against building it?

   a. _____

   b. _____

3. Is the man for or against the new building? _____

8 | CHANGES

Work in pairs. Take turns. Tell about an upcoming change in your life or the life of someone you know well. For example, tell about a marriage, a graduation, a move, a new job, or a new baby. Your partner asks you questions about the change.

Example: **A:** My sister is getting married.

B: When is she getting married?
Is she going to have a big wedding? Where is it going to be?
How many people is she going to invite? Where is she going to live?

9 | CLASS PRESIDENT

Someone gave your school $200,000. You are a school leader. You must use the money before the end of this month. You can use it any way you want to improve your school. Write down five things you are going to do. Tell your class your ideas.

Examples: I'm going to have free snacks all year for all the students.
I'm going to put really comfortable chairs in the Student Center lounge.

10 | WRITING

Write a letter to the editor. Explain why you are for or against one of these changes. Explain what the change is going to mean.

School Changes	City Changes
Computer courses to replace half the teachers	No cars on University Ave on weekends
No tests, just written reports	A new jail in your neighborhood
New school dress code: No jeans or T-shirts	Higher taxes to pay for better schools
	A no smoking law in all public places

Example

Dear Editor:

Last week the mayor spoke about a law to ban cars on University Ave on weekends. I think that's a great idea. The street is going to be safer for people. The air is going to be cleaner. It's going to be quieter.

The change is going to make the campus area a friendlier place for walking, shopping, and dining.

Sincerely,
Bill Mann

11 | ON THE INTERNET

*Read today's news online. Make predictions based on three news items. Use **be going to** in each prediction.*

Examples: John Doe gave a good speech. I think he's going to be president one day.
The Gators won three games. They're probably going to win the championship.

31 *Will* for the Future; Future Time Markers

Grammar in Context

BEFORE YOU READ

Do you like to read about the future? What do you think will be different by the year 2020? 2050? 2100?

Tomorrow Magazine *asked a group of scientists to make predictions for the year 2050. What will we eat? How will we look? How will we travel? Where will we go? How long will we live? Read their predictions.*

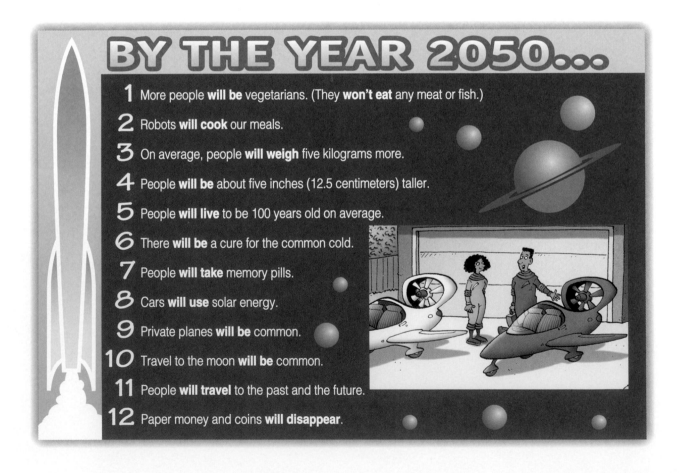

BY THE YEAR 2050...

1 More people **will be** vegetarians. (They **won't eat** any meat or fish.)

2 Robots **will cook** our meals.

3 On average, people **will weigh** five kilograms more.

4 People **will be** about five inches (12.5 centimeters) taller.

5 People **will live** to be 100 years old on average.

6 There **will be** a cure for the common cold.

7 People **will take** memory pills.

8 Cars **will use** solar energy.

9 Private planes **will be** common.

10 Travel to the moon **will be** common.

11 People **will travel** to the past and the future.

12 Paper money and coins **will disappear**.

AFTER YOU READ

Answer the questions based on the article in Tomorrow Magazine. *There may be more than one correct answer.*

1. How will people look?
   a. taller   b. shorter   c. heavier   d. thinner

2. Where will people travel?
   a. to the moon   b. to Mars   c. to the past   d. to the future

3. What will increase?
   a. the number of vegetarians   b. the average life span   c. the number of colds   d. the number of private planes

4. What will be common in 2050?
   a. coins   b. solar energy   c. travel to the moon   d. travel by private plane

Grammar Presentation

WILL FOR THE FUTURE

Affirmative Statements			
Subject	*Will*	Base Form of Verb	Time Marker
I			
You			
He			
She			
It	**will**	**leave**	tomorrow.
We			
You			
They			

Negative Statements			
Subject	*Will Not*	Base Form of Verb	Time Marker
I			
You			
He			
She			
It	**will not**	**leave**	tonight.
We			
You			
They			

Contractions	
Affirmative	Negative
I'**ll**	I
you '**ll**	you
he '**ll**	he
she'**ll**	she **won't**
it'**ll**	it
we'**ll**	we
you'**ll**	you
they'**ll**	they

(continued)

Yes / No Questions			
Will	Subject	Base Form of Verb	Time Marker
Will	I you he she it we you they	**arrive**	**tomorrow**?
Will	it	**rain**	**tonight**?

Short Answers	
Affirmative	Negative
Yes, you **will**. Yes, I **will**. Yes, he **will**. Yes, she **will**. Yes, it **will**. Yes, you **will**. Yes, we **will**. Yes, they **will**.	No, you **won't**. No, I **won't**. No, he **won't**. No, she **won't**. No, it **won't**. No, you **won't**. No, we **won't**. No, they **won't**.
Yes, it **will**.	No, it **won't**.

Future Time Markers	
today	
tonight	
tomorrow	
this	morning afternoon evening
tomorrow	morning afternoon evening night
next	week month year Monday weekend
in	2010 the 22nd century twenty years two weeks a few days

GRAMMAR NOTES

EXAMPLES

---

1. Use *will* + **the base form of the verb** to talk about things that will take place in the future.

▶ **BE CAREFUL!** Use the base form of the verb after *will* or *won't*. Remember the base form does not change.

- The class **will begin** on November 2.
- We **will meet** tomorrow at 10:00 A.M.
- The plane will **arrive** at 6:00 P.M.
  NOT: The plane will ~~to arrive~~ at 6:00 P.M.
  The plane will ~~arrives~~ at 6:00 P.M.

---

2. Use **contractions** of *will* **with pronouns** in speaking and informal writing.

▶ **BE CAREFUL!** Do not use contractions in affirmative short answers.

- **We'll** be there before 3:00.

A: Will they be there?
B: Yes, they **will**.
  NOT: Yes, ~~they'll~~.

---

3. Use *will* to make **predictions**.

USAGE NOTE: In writing, we often use *will* in one sentence and *be going to* in the next sentence.

- In 2050 there **will be** more mega-cities.
- Those cities **are going to be** very crowded.

---

4. Use *will* to make a **promise** or **give assurance**.

- **I'll be** back in five minutes.
- I **won't do** that again.

---

5. Use *will* to **ask for** or **offer** something.

A: **Will** you **help** me?
B: Don't worry. **I'll help**.

---

6. *Won't* is the contraction of *will* + *not*. It has two meanings.
Use *won't* to mean the **negative future**.

Use *won't* to mean "**refuse(s) to**."

- He **won't be** in school tomorrow.

- The child **won't eat** carrots.

---

7. To say that something is not definite, use *probably* with *will* for the future.

- People will **probably** take more vacations.

---

8. Some **time markers** are used only for the future. Other time markers can be used for the past or the future.

- She won't be home **tomorrow**.
  ^{future}
- She'll be home **this afternoon**.
  ^{future}
- She was at the library **this afternoon**.
  ^{past}

Focused Practice

1 | DISCOVER THE GRAMMAR

Read the sentences. Write the letter that explains the meaning.

__b__ 1. I won't do it. I think it's wrong.

_____ 2. Will you show me how to use that computer?

_____ 3. I'll be back by 9:00.

_____ 4. There won't be any meeting on February 8.

_____ 5. By 2020 people will fly to the moon for fun.

a. predicts something

b. states refusal

c. promises to do something

d. asks for something

e. tells about something that is not going to happen

2 | CONVERSATIONS
Grammar Notes 1–8

Complete the conversations with **will** or **won't** and the verb in parentheses.

1. **A:** Listen to that rain. When ___will___ it ___stop___?
   a. (stop)

   B: Don't worry. It _____ long.
   b. (last)

   A: What's the forecast for this afternoon?

   B: It's going to be warm and sunny.

   A: Then I _____ my report today. I _____ it tomorrow. Let's go
   c. (finish)   d. (finish)

   to the park.

   B: OK. I _____ you there at 2:00. I _____ that book I told you
   e. (meet)   f. (bring)

   about.

   A: Great. I _____ a basketball. Maybe we can shoot some hoops.*
   g. (bring)

2. **A:** I'm hungry. When _____ dinner _____ ready?
   a. (be)

   B: It _____ ready until 7:00.
   b. (be)

   A: I guess I _____ a candy bar.
   c. (have)

   B: Don't. It _____ your appetite.
   d. (spoil)

   A: No, it _____. Nothing spoils my appetite. Remember, I'm a growing boy.

---

*Shoot some hoops: play basketball

3 | COMMON PHRASES WITH *WILL*   *Grammar Notes 1–8*

Write statements or ask questions. Use the words in parentheses and put them in the correct order. Then match the sentences with the situation.

_e_ **1.** _Someone will be with you shortly._
(shortly / Someone / be with you / will)

____ **2.** _____
(you / Will / me / marry)

____ **3.** _____
(I / be / long / won't)

____ **4.** _____
(I'll / them / forget / never)

____ **5.** _____
(hurt / It / won't / much)

____ **6.** _____
(bring the hamburgers. / I'll / You bring the rolls.)

____ **7.** _____
(quiet / you / be / please / Will)

Situation

a. Someone planning a picnic says this.

b. You say this about special people.

c. You say this to a talkative person at a library.

d. You say this when someone is waiting for you and you are almost ready.

e. Two people are sitting at a table in a restaurant. A host says this to them.

f. A nurse says this when he or she gives a patient a shot.

g. This is a common marriage proposal.

4 | FOGVILLE 2010   *Grammar Notes 2–8*

Look at the chart of predictions. Write questions and short answers about Fogville. Use the words in parentheses.

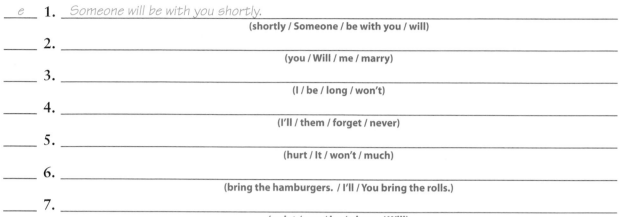

Predictions for Fogville in 2010				
The cost of Housing	↓	Crime	→	
Taxes	↓	The percent of people under 25	↑	
The cost of health care	↓	The percent of people over 65	→	

Key		
Increase	=	↑
Stay the Same	=	→
Decrease	=	↓

1. A: _Will the cost of housing increase?_
(the cost of housing / increase)
  B: _No, the cost of housing will decrease._

2. A: _____
(taxes / stay the same)
  B: _____

(continued)

3. A: _____
(the cost of health care / stay the same)

   B: _____

4. A: _____
(the percent of people under 25 / decrease)

   B: _____

5. A: _____
(the percent of people over 65 / decrease)

   B: _____

5 | REVIEW OF PRESENT, PAST, FUTURE
Grammar Notes 3–4, 6–8

Complete the sentences. Use the present, the past, or the future with **will**. *Use the verbs in parentheses.*

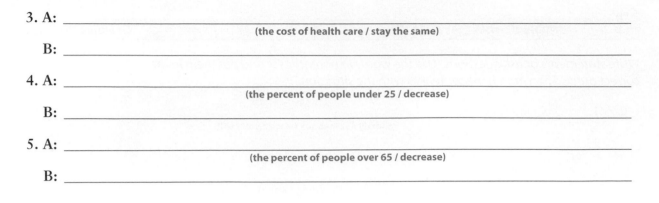

A: _____*Did*_____ you _____*hear*_____ the lecture last week?
                    1. (hear)

B: No, what _____ it about?
            2. (be)

A: The future. According to Professor Johns, by the year 2100 there _____ cities in
                                          3. (be)

the ocean, we _____ trips to the moon, and we _____ everything
               4. (take)   **5. (learn)**

from computers.

B: By 2100? We _____ all _____ gone by then. _____ the people _____ his
                         6. (be)   **7. (like)**

lecture?

A: Yes, they did. They always do. He _____ how to make any subject fascinating.
                                  8. (know)

6 | EDITING

Correct the conversation. There are six mistakes. The first mistake is already corrected.

A: What did he say?

B: He said there *^will* be an increase in the population. Many young people will moves to the area.

Taxes will increases. The value of homes will also to increase.

A: How about crime? Will it increases?

B: No, it doesn't.

A: Well, it sounds like a great place to live.

Communication Practice

7 | LISTENING

⌒ *Listen to a conversation between a TV news anchor and two lottery winners.*

1. What will the woman do with her winnings?

   a. _____

   b. _____

   c. _____

2. What will the man do with his winnings?

   _____

8 | CLASS SURVEY

Work in small groups. Look at the statements in the Grammar in Context on page 310. Do you agree? What are your predictions? Discuss your answers. Report to the class.

Example: We all think paper money will disappear. People will use credit cards or check cards to pay for everything. Coins are heavy and bills are not clean. These cards are the way of the future.

9 | SURVEY: IN THE FUTURE

Complete the questions. Then survey five classmates.

1. Write the name of something that is very popular today. _____

   Ask five classmates if it will be popular in the future.

   Will _____ still be popular in _____?

2. Write the name of a country and a time in the future. Ask if it will be a popular tourist destination in the future.

   Will _____ be a popular tourist destination in _____?

Report your results to the class.

Example: I asked six people this question: "Will DVDs still be popular in ten years?" Four out of six students said, "Yes."

10 | WONDERFUL FORTUNES

Be a fortune teller. Write a fortune you would love to get. Use **will** *for the future. Hang your fortune on the wall for the class to read.*

> **Example:** You will make a difference in the world. You will become rich and famous. You will invent something great.

Number all the fortunes. Go around and read each fortune. Choose your favorite fortune. Did many students choose the same fortune?

11 | WRITING

Work with a partner. Look at the sentences in Exercise 3. Write short role plays which include those sentences. Make them funny. Act them out in front of the class.

> **Example:** A: Will you marry me?
> B: What? We hardly know each other. We just met this afternoon.
> A: But . . .

12 | ON THE INTERNET

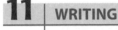 Do you have a favorite

- actor?
- athlete or team?
- author or artist?
- musician, music group, or singer?
- politician?

Read recent news online about that person or group. Make three predictions about what that person or group will do next year.

> **Example:** I like the music group U2. I predict they will perform around the world next year.

May or *Might* for Possibility

Grammar in Context

BEFORE YOU READ

1. How do you know how the weather will be?

   a. I watch TV **or** I listen to the radio.

   b. I check my computer.

   c. I look in the newspaper.

   d. I look out the window.

2. In your opinion, how often is the weather report wrong?

   a. rarely

   b. sometimes

   c. often

   d. almost always

∩ *Read a conversation and TV weather report.*

STAY INDOORS WITH A GOOD BOOK

MOTHER: Shh. The weather report is coming on.

METEOROLOGIST: Good evening, everyone. This is Luis Scheraga with today's weather report. Anyone with plans to be outdoors tomorrow or Tuesday will not welcome this news. The weather will continue to be unseasonably cold and windy. And heavy rain will begin tonight or tomorrow. For the morning commute, there **may be**

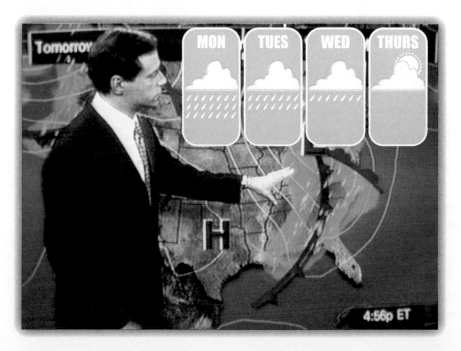

flooding on the highways. So, if you can, take public transportation. And don't put away those umbrellas too soon. There will be more rain on Wednesday. By Thursday the weather **may become** milder with only a 20 percent chance of showers. We **might** even **see** some sun. But until then, my friends, my best advice is: Stay indoors with a good book or movie.

ALEX: I guess that means no soccer tomorrow.

MOTHER: Don't be too sure. You **may** still **have** a game. The meteorologist is often wrong. Remember last Friday. He predicted a beautiful day, but it was awful. And last week he said we **might have** a major storm. It turned out to be sunny and dry.

ALEX: Maybe.

MOTHER: I just hope you don't play in the rain.

ALEX: We **might**. The last time it rained we played the entire game. Playing in the mud was great! And we won!

AFTER YOU READ

1. Alex and his mother are having a conversation on _____.

   a. Sunday   **b.** Monday   **c.** Tuesday

2. The rain may begin on _____.

   a. Sunday   **b.** Tuesday   **c.** Wednesday

3. Check (✓) the two true statements.

   _____ **a.** Alex's team won't play soccer in the rain.

   _____ **b.** Alex's team will play soccer in the rain.

   _____ **c.** Alex's team may play soccer in the rain.

   _____ **d.** Alex's team might play soccer in the rain.

Grammar Presentation

MAY OR MIGHT FOR POSSIBILITY

Affirmative / Negative Statements				
Subject	*May / Might*	*(Not)*	Base Form of Verb	
I You He She We You They	**may** **might**	**(not)**	**play**	soccer.
It	**may** **might**	**(not)**	**rain**	this afternoon.

GRAMMAR NOTES	**EXAMPLES**
1. Use *may* or *might* to express **possibility** about the present or the future. *May* and *might* have almost the same meaning, but *may* means something is a little more possible than *might*.	**A:** Where's John? **B:** I don't know. He **may be** on vacation. **A:** What are you going to do this weekend? **B:** We **might go** to a movie. • It **might** rain. *(It's possible.)* • It **may** rain. *(It's more possible.)* • It**'ll probably** rain. *(It's likely.)* • It **will** rain. *(It's definite.)*
2. *May* and *might* are **followed** by the **base form of the verb**. There are no contractions for *may* or *might*.	• We **might go** to the movies. NOT: We might ~~to go~~ to the movies. NOT: He might ~~goes~~ to the movies. NOT: He ~~mightn't~~ go to the movies.
3. USAGE NOTE: We usually use *will* or *be going to*, not *may* or *might*, to **ask yes/no questions about the future**.	**A:** Will you go to the party? **B:** I might. OR I may. **A:** Are you going to see that movie tonight? **B:** We might. OR We may. NOT: ~~May~~ you go to the party?
4. We use *I think I might* or *I think I may* for possibility. We use *I'm sure* + subject + *will* for certainty.	• **I think I might** buy that book. • I'm sure I will be there. NOT: I'm sure I ~~might~~ buy that book.
5. *May* and *might* are modal verbs. *Maybe* is an adverb. It means "there's a possibility." *Maybe I will* has a similar meaning to *I might* or *I may*.	• **Maybe I'll go** to the party. OR **I might go** to the party. OR **I may go** to the party. **A:** Are you going to the game? **B: Maybe**. OR **I may**. OR **I might**.

Focused Practice

1 | DISCOVER THE GRAMMAR

Match the sentences in column A with the sentences in column B.

A

_____ 1. It's definitely going to rain.

_____ 2. There's an 80 percent chance of rain.

_____ 3. There's about a 50 percent chance of rain.

_____ 4. There's a 10 percent chance of rain.

_____ 5. It's definitely not going to rain.

B

a. It probably won't rain.

b. It'll probably rain.

c. It won't rain.

d. It will rain.

e. It may rain.

2 | POSSIBILITIES

Grammar Notes 1–2

Complete the conversations with the affirmative or negative of **may** *or* **might** *and a verb from the box.*

be	have	need	~~rain~~	return	see

1. **A:** Take your umbrella. It _____ *might rain* _____ this afternoon.

   B: Really? The forecast was for sun.

2. **A:** Start dinner without me. I _____ back home before 9:00.

   B: That's OK. I'll wait.

3. **A:** Sandy looks upset.

   B: She is. She _____ an operation.

4. **A:** I don't understand him. Why is he studying part-time?

   B: He _____ enough money to study full-time.

5. **A:** Here's a small gift. I _____ you before your birthday.

   B: Thanks.

6. **A:** Are you flying home on Sunday?

   B: We're not sure. We _____ on Saturday night.

3 | DEFINITE OR POSSIBLE

Grammar Notes 1–2 , 4

Choose the correct words to complete the conversation.

1. **A:** Look at those clouds.

   B: I'm sure it _____ *will rain* _____.
   (may rain / will rain.)

2. **A:** Remember, the movie begins at seven o'clock. Please don't be late.

   B: Don't worry. We _____ there on time.
   (may be / 'll be)

3. **A:** I wonder why Jack isn't here.

   B: He looked pale yesterday. He _____ sick.
   (may be / is)

4. **A:** Do you think that man's OK?

   B: I don't know. Let's go see. He _____ our help.
   (might need / needs)

5. **A:** Uh-oh. The car _____. What's wrong?
   (may not start / won't start)

   B: Keep trying. The engine _____.
   (will be cold / may be cold)

4 | IN OTHER WORDS

Grammar Note 5

Replace **maybe** *with* **may** *or* **might**. *In some cases you may need to add a subject or a subject and a verb.*

1. **A:** Are you going to the park?

   B: ~~Maybe~~. *We may.* Do you want to come with us?

2. **A:** Is there a restroom nearby?

   B: I don't know. Maybe there's one in that library.

3. **A:** Are the Smiths going to the party?

   B: Maybe. I don't know.

4. **A:** How long will the test take?

   B: Maybe two or three hours.

5. **A:** Are they relatives?

   B: I'm not sure. Maybe they're good friends.

5 | EDITING

Correct the conversations. There are five mistakes. The first mistake is already corrected.

1. **A:** Where's Bill?

   B: ~~I'm sure~~ *I think* he may be on vacation.

2. **A:** We maybe go to the park. Do you want to join us?

   B: Thanks. I'd love to.

3. **A:** May you take another course next term?

   B: Yes, I may.

4. **A:** Are you going to finish your report today?

   B: I want to, but I mightn't have enough time.

5. **A:** What's the weather report?

   B: It's sunny now, but it may to rain this afternoon.

Communication Practice

6 | LISTENING

🎧 *A couple is going on a trip. Listen to their conversation.*

What reason does the man give for packing these things in his suitcase?

1. boots *They may go mountain climbing.*_____

2. a raincoat _____

3. two hats _____

4. two books _____

5. a sports jacket _____

7 | TONIGHT

Work with a partner. Take turns asking about plans for tonight.

Example: A: Are you going to _____?
B: Yes, I am.
Yes, I'll probably . . .
I may . . .
I might . . .
OR
No, I'm not.

Use the ideas in the box or your own. Explain your answer.

cook dinner	go running	listen to the weather report	watch TV
eat out	go to the movies	study	work

8 | WRITING

You are a reporter for UpToDateWeather.com. Write a weather report for your region. Look at pages 319–320 for ideas.

Example: Good evening. This is Hye Won Paik with today's weather report. You might want to take out your tennis rackets. We're going to have perfect weather tomorrow. It's going to be sunny and warm. Temperatures will be a few degrees above normal with very little wind.

9 | ON THE INTERNET

Check the weather forecast for your city for the next weekend. Write possible plans based on the forecast. Use **may** or **might** in each sentence.

Example: It's going to be warm and sunny on Saturday. I might play soccer with some friends.

From **Grammar** to **Writing**
Time Clauses with When

1 | *How can you combine these sentences using* **when**?

1. I was six years old. I loved to play with dolls.

_____

2. I will graduate next year. I will work for a newspaper.

_____

TIME CLAUSES WITH *When*

1. Time Clauses We can combine two sentences that tell about time by using a **time clause** and a **main clause**. *When I was six years old* is a **time clause**. It is not a sentence and can never stand alone. It needs a main clause.	• I was six years old. I started school. time clause • **When** I was six years old, main clause I started school.
2. Present Time Clauses When we use **present time clauses**, both parts of the sentence are written in the **present**.	present present • When I **get** home, I **have** dinner.
3. Past Time Clauses When we use **past time clauses**, both parts of the sentence are written in the **past**.	past past • When I **got** home, I **had** dinner.
4. Future Time Clauses When we use a **future time clause**, the future time clause uses the **simple present**. The main clause uses the **future**.	present future • When I **get** home, I **will have** dinner. (First I'll get home. Then I'll have dinner.)
5. You can begin a sentence with the time clause or the main clause. When the time clause begins the sentence, you need a **comma** before the main clause. There is no comma when the main clause begins the sentence.	• When I got home**,** I had dinner. • I had dinner when I got home. • When I get home**,** I will have dinner. • I will have dinner when I get home.

2 | *Rewrite this paragraph using three time clauses.*

My Dream

I was a child. I loved to play "make-believe" games. Sometimes I was a cowboy, and sometimes I was a prince. I became a teenager. I got a job at a video store. I saw many movies. I also made a couple of videos and I acted in all the school plays. Now I'm studying film and acting at school. I will finish college next year. I will move to Hollywood. I hope to become a movie star.

3 | *Write a paragraph about yourself at different times of your life. Include a part about your future.*

Review Test

I | *Circle the letter that best completes each sentence.*

1. Where _____ tomorrow night?   A B C D

   (A) you going

   (B) will you going

   (C) are you going

   (D) you go

2. Will she _____ the car?   A B C D

   (A) to take

   (B) takes

   (C) going to take

   (D) take

3. Is he _____ his house?   A B C D

   (A) going to sell

   (B) going to sells

   (C) will sell

   (D) sell

4. She _____ to the library.   A B C D

   (A) might to go

   (B) might go

   (C) may goes

   (D) mayn't go

II *Circle the letter of the correct sentence to complete the conversation.*

1. A: What are you going to buy him?

    B: I'm not sure. _____

        a. I'll buy him a sweater.

        b. I buy him a sweater.

        c. I may buy him a sweater.

2. A: Will he write a letter to the editor?

    B: _____

        a. No, he will.

        b. No, he won't.

        c. No, he isn't.

3. A: Are you going to return that TV?

    B: _____

        a. I maybe.

        b. Maybe I'll.

        c. Maybe.

4. A: When are you going to start?

    B: _____

        a. Yesterday.

        b. Tomorrow.

        c. Yes, I am.

III   *Circle the correct word(s) to complete the conversations.*

1. **A:** Is he busy all day?

   B: I'm not sure. He <u>may / 'll</u> be free in the afternoon.

2. **A:** These boxes are heavy.

   B: I <u>may / 'll</u> help you carry them.

   A: Thanks.

3. **A:** Would you explain that math problem to me?

   B: I <u>might / 'll</u> try to help you.

4. **A:** What kind of vegetables are you planning to grow this year?

   B: I'm not sure. I <u>may / won't</u> grow tomatoes. They usually do well. One thing is certain. I

a.
   <u>may / won't</u> grow carrots. They never do well.

b.

5. **A:** Where's Joe?

   B: Don't worry. He <u>'ll / won't</u> be back in a few minutes. He just went to the store.

6. **A:** What class is Professor Okun going to teach next semester?

   B: He <u>may / 'll</u> probably teach the same course he taught last spring—International Relations.

7. **A:** Do you have any coins for the meter?

   B: I don't have any in my pocket, but I <u>might / will</u> have some in my bag.

IV *Circle the correct word(s) to complete the conversations.*

1. **A:** I'm tired of all the rain. It <u>rains / rained</u> yesterday. It <u>'s raining / rains</u> right now, and the
   a.b.

   weather report says tomorrow it <u>rains / 's going to rain</u> too.
   c.

   B: Oh no.

2. **A:** Do you want to go to that art exhibit this afternoon?

   B: I'm sorry, I can't. I <u>help / 'm going to help</u> my cousin move.
   a.

   A: How about on Wednesday?

   B: Wednesday I <u>got / 'm getting</u> a haircut. I'm free on Thursday. Is that good for you?
   b.

   A: Yes, it is. So, let's make it for Thursday.

3. **A:** <u>Do / Did</u> you <u>hear / heard</u> the news about James? He <u>won / 's going to win</u> first prize
   a.b.

   for one of his photographs.

   B: I know. I <u>'m thinking / think</u> that's great. What <u>is / does</u> he <u>going to do / do</u> with the
   c.d.

   prize money?

   A: He <u>'s going to visit / visits</u> Kenya.
   e.

   B: Why Kenya?

   A: He <u>'s going to take / takes</u> pictures of the animals.
   f.

4. **A:** Haru, <u>do / did</u> you <u>return / returned</u> the video?
   a.

   B: Not yet. I <u>return / 'll return</u> it after dinner.
   b.

   A: Well, don't forget. The store <u>closes / closing</u> early on weekdays.
   c.

   B: Don't worry. I <u>don't / won't</u>.
   d.

V   *Read the questions and complete the answers. Use the correct verb forms. There may be more than one possible answer.*

1. **A:** What did you say? Where are you going to go this afternoon?

    B: I _____ to the bank and the post office.

2. **A:** When will you be back?

    B: We _____ on Sunday.

3. **A:** Do you have plans for the long weekend?

    B: We're not sure. We _____ go to the movies or we

    _____ watch videos at home.

4. **A:** Are you meeting them Wednesday morning?

    B: No, I'm not. I _____ Wednesday afternoon.

VI   *Correct the sentences.*

1. They're going to tomorrow start the job.

2. He's going to sees the art exhibit this afternoon.

3. How you will travel?

4. She won't is home this evening.

5. I think they might to buy a car.

6. We maybe will go to the early show.

▶ *To check your answers, go to the Answer Key on page RT-4.*

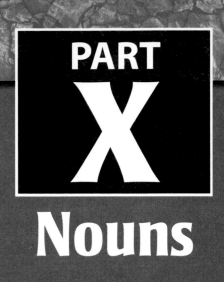

PART

X

Nouns

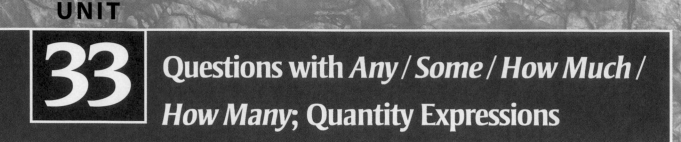

Grammar in Context

BEFORE YOU READ

About how many hours do you sleep each night? About how much exercise do you do each week?

🎧 *Read the following from* Health and Fitness *magazine.*

HEALTH AND FITNESS

This week's *Health and Fitness* magazine has a questionnaire by Dr. Diane Stone. Complete the questionnaire and calculate your score. Send us your answers and receive a free copy of our newsletter, "News on Health and Fitness."

RATE YOUR HEALTH

Measure your health and fitness. Circle the number next to your answer. Then add the numbers. This is your score. The higher the number, the healthier you are.

1. **How much time** do you exercise?
   - 5 at least an hour every day
   - 4 about an hour three times a week
   - 1 about an hour a week
   - 0 I don't exercise.

2. **How much coffee** do you drink?
   - 0 four or more cups of coffee a day
   - 2 three cups a day
   - 4 two cups a day
   - 4 I don't drink any coffee.

3. **How many vacations** do you take in a year?
   - 4 a lot, at least four
   - 4 two or three
   - 1 one
   - 0 I don't take any vacations.

4. **How much candy** do you eat each day?
   - 0 a lot
   - 2 some
   - 3 a little
   - 4 none

5. **How many servings of vegetables** do you eat each day?
   - 5 six or more servings
   - 4 about three servings
   - 2 only two servings
   - 0 I don't eat any vegetables.

AFTER YOU READ

A *Read about the health habits of two people. According to this questionnaire, which person has the higher score, Steve or Jackie? Add the numbers to the left of the questions.*

STEVE: I spend about an hour a day exercising. I don't take any vacations. I drink four cups of coffee a day. I eat six or more servings of vegetables. I don't eat any candy.

JACKIE: I spend about an hour a week exercising. I take one vacation a year. I drink two cups of coffee a day. I don't eat vegetables. I eat some candy.

B *Who has the highest score in your class?*

Grammar Presentation

QUESTIONS WITH *ANY* / *SOME* / *HOW MUCH* / *HOW MANY*; QUANTITY EXPRESSIONS

Articles and Numbers		
	Quantity Expressions	Singular Count Noun
Do you want	**a**	pear?
	an	apple?
	one	banana?

Some and *Any*		
	Quantity Expressions	Plural Count Noun or Non-count Noun
I want	**some**	apples. water.
I don't want	**any**	pears. tea.
Do you want	**any** **some**	apples? water?

Questions with *How Much*		
How Much	Non-count Noun	
How much	**milk**	do you need? did she buy?

Answers
Quantity Expressions
A lot. (A lot of milk.)
Two quarts. (Two quarts of milk.)
A carton. (A carton of milk.)
A glass. (A glass of milk.)
A little. (A little milk.)

Questions with *How Many*		
How Many	Plural Count Noun	
How many	**apples**	do we need? did he buy?

Answers
Quantity Expressions
A lot. (A lot of apples.)
One bag. (One bag of apples.)
Two pounds. (Two pounds of apples.)
One or two. (One or two apples.)
A few. (A few apples.)

(continued)

Enough + Nouns			
		Enough	Noun (Plural Count or Non-count)
We	have	**enough**	**vegetables**.
	don't have		**meat**.

GRAMMAR NOTES

EXAMPLES

1. Use *a*, *an*, and *one* before **singular count nouns**. Use *a* before **consonant sounds** and *an* before **vowel sounds**.

- I want **a pear**.
- I have **an apple**.
- I bought **one apple** and **one banana**.

2. *Some* and *any* refer to an amount, but they don't say *how much* or *how many*.

- Use *some* with **affirmative statements**.

- Use *any* with **negative statements**.

- Use *some* and *any* with **plural count nouns** and **non-count nouns**.

- We usually use *any* in *yes/no* questions.

- We can also use *some* in *yes/no* questions when we **offer** something or **ask for** something.

AFFIRMATIVE STATEMENTS
- I bought **some** tea.
- I bought **some** rolls.

NEGATIVE STATEMENTS
- I did**n't** buy **any** coffee.
- I did**n't** buy **any** donuts.

plural count noun
- I need **some apples**.
- I don't need **any pears**.

non-count noun
- I need **some coffee**.
- I don't need **any milk**.

YES / NO QUESTIONS
- Did you buy **any** milk?
- Did you buy **any** bananas?

AN OFFER
- Would you like **some** juice?

A REQUEST
- Can I have **some** more milk, please?

3. Use *how much* or *how many* to ask about quantity.	**A: How much** juice do you have?
	B: A little. OR
Use *how much* with non-count nouns.	I have **a little juice**.
Use *how many* with count nouns.	
Use *a little* with non-count nouns.	**A: How many** onions do you need?
Use *a few* with count nouns.	**B: A few.** OR
	We need **a few onions**.

4. It is not necessary to repeat the noun after *how much* or *how many* if the noun was named before.	**A:** I need some **money**.
	B: How much do you need? *(How much money do you need?)*
	A: I bought some **magazines**.
	B: How many did you buy? *(How many magazines did you buy?)*

5. You can **count non-count nouns** by using **measure words** or **containers**.	
Measure words: *a quart, a liter, an ounce, a kilogram*	• Please get me **one quart of milk**.
Containers: *a cup, a glass, a can, a box*	• He drank **two glasses of water**.

6. *Enough* means the amount you need. Use *enough* before plural count nouns and non-count nouns.	• We have **enough eggs**. *(We need six eggs, and we have six eggs.)*
	• We have **enough juice**.
Not enough means less than the amount you need. Use *not enough* before plural count nouns and non-count nouns.	• There **aren't enough apples**.
	• There **isn't enough milk**.

Reference Notes

See Unit 42, page 430 for a more complete discussion of *enough* after an adjective.
See Appendix 11, page A-12 for a list of quantity expressions.

Focused Practice

1 | DISCOVER THE GRAMMAR

Read the sentences. Underline the nouns. Complete the chart. Write the noun in the proper category.

1. She ate an <u>apple</u>. He ate a pear.

2. I bought one apple and two pears.

3. I need some water and some eggs.

4. Do you need any cheese or vegetables?

5. How much meat do they want?

6. How many carrots did he use?

7. There wasn't enough salt in the soup.

8. There weren't enough onions in the soup either.

9. We used a lot of potatoes.

10. It takes a lot of time to cook.

	Singular Count Noun	Plural Count Noun	Non-count Noun
a			
an	*apple*		
one			
two			
some			
any			
How much			
How many			
enough			
a lot of			

2 | **PLANNING A PARTY** *Grammar Notes 1, 3, 5*

Write questions and answers. Use the words in parentheses.

1. **A:** *Do we need any more soda?*
   (more / we / any / soda / Do / need)
   B: *No, we have enough.*
   (have / enough / No, / we)

2. **A:** _____
   (water / we / enough / Do / have)
   B: _____
   (we / Yes, / ice / enough / but / have / don't)

3. **A:** _____
   (some / you / yogurt / more / Do / want)
   B: _____
   (thanks. / No / full / I'm)

4. **A:** _____
   (there / Are / glasses / more / any)
   B: _____
   (top / They're / Yes. / shelf / on the)

5. **A:** _____
   (you / the gym / Did / go / this morning / to)
   B: _____
   (No. / time / wasn't / enough / There)

6. **A:** _____
   (bake / a pie / going to / you / Are)
   B: _____
   (have / Yes, / but / flour / don't / any / we)

7. **A:** _____
   (to get / I / need / napkins / some)
   B: _____
   (yet / store / open / Is / the)

8. **A:** _____
   (some / milk / need / We)
   B: _____
   (we / need / much / How / do)

3 | **RATE YOUR JOB** *Grammar Note 2*

*Complete the sentences with **How much** or **How many**.*

1. _____ hours a day do you work?

2. _____ time does it take you to get to work?

3. _____ vacation days do you get a year?

4. _____ sick days do you get?

5. _____ work do you bring home?

6. _____ people do you report to?

7. _____ times a week does someone say, "Nice job"?

8. _____ money do you make?

4 | *A FEW AND A LITTLE*

Grammar Note 2

Complete the sentences with **a few** *or* **a little***.*

1. The new gym is _____ miles up ahead on your right.

2. She's out of shape. She can only run for _____ minutes.

3. We know _____ good exercises for the back.

4. They served a lot of fruit and vegetables, but just _____ meat.

5. We need _____ more time.

6. They found _____ coins in their pockets.

7. Do you need _____ more minutes?

8. Add _____ water and the soup won't taste so salty.

9. He had _____ good ideas.

10. We're having _____ problems with our new exercise bike.

5 | CONTAINERS

Grammar Note 4

Complete the conversations. Use one of the words in the box.

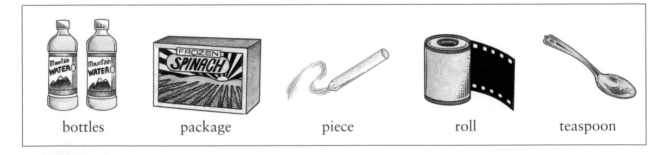

| bottles | package | piece | roll | teaspoon |

1. **A:** How much sugar do you take?

   B: One _____, please.

2. **A:** How much water did he drink?

   B: Two _____. He was very thirsty.

3. **A:** There's no chalk in our classroom.

   B: Maybe there's an extra _____ of chalk next door.

4. **A:** Where can I get a _____ of film?

   B: At the drugstore on the corner.

5. **A:** How much spinach do you need for the lasagna?

   B: One _____ of frozen spinach.

6 | EDITING

Correct the conversations. There are eight mistakes. The first mistake is already corrected.

1. **A:** How ~~much~~ *many* gyms are there in this area?

   B: Only one.

2. **A:** How many time do you spend at the gym?

   B: About an hour, three times a week.

3. **A:** Do we have water enough for everyone?

   B: Yes, we have six bottles of water.

4. **A:** How much yoga classes do they offer at the gym?

   B: They offer two classes every day.

5. **A:** Is there treadmills enough?

   B: There are three treadmills, but one never works.

6. **A:** Are there any clean towels?

   B: There are any near the swimming pool.

7. **A:** Do you need any towel?

   B: Yes, thanks.

Communication Practice

7 | LISTENING

🎧 *Listen to a conversation. Complete the shopping list.*

Shopping List

1. six _____
2. five _____
3. a head of _____
4. a few _____
5. a can _____
6. a bunch _____

8 | FUN FACTS ABOUT THE HUMAN BODY

*Work in small groups. Complete the questions with **How much** or **How many**. Then try to answer the questions. Check your answers below.*

1. _____ times do people blink each year?
   a. 6,205   **b.** 6,205,000   **c.** 62,500

2. _____ time does it take to digest milk?
   a. 10 minutes   **b.** 60 minutes   **c.** 3 hours

3. _____ nerve cells does the average brain have?
   a. one hundred billion   **b.** ten million   **c.** one hundred thousand

4. _____ muscles does a person use to speak?
   a. 7   **b.** 17   **c.** 72

5. _____ does the average head weigh?
   a. 8 pounds   **b.** 18 pounds   **c.** 28 pounds

6. _____ bones are there in the human body?
   a. about 200   **b.** about 300   **c.** about 400

7. _____ body parts have three letters? (for example, *ear*)
   a. 5   **b.** 10   **c.** 15

8. _____ body parts can you name with three letters?

9 | A WEEK'S GROCERIES

Work in small groups. Your group is going to buy food for one week. Make a list of all the items you will need. Next to each item, write the amount you will buy.

Meat and Fish	Vegetables and Fruit	Bread and Cereals	Dairy Products and Eggs
tuna—4 cans	bananas—2 bunches	bread—1 loaf	yogurt—10 containers

1. b 2. b 3. a 4. c 5. a 6. a 7. b 8. arm, ear, eye, gum, hip, jaw, leg, lip, rib, toe

Compare your list with other groups' lists. Which group bought the most food? Which group bought the healthiest food? Did your group forget to buy anything important?

Example: A: How much bread did you buy?
B: One loaf.
A: That's not enough for four people. I think you'll need two or three loaves.

10 | SURVEY YOUR CLASSMATES

Write two questions that begin with **How much** *or* **How many**. *Show your teacher your questions. Survey ten classmates.*

Examples: How much time do you spend watching TV in the evening?
How many hours do you sleep each night?
How much money does it cost to take a bus in your city?

Report the results.

11 | WRITING

Write a report about your survey.

Example: I prepared a class survey. I asked ten students the following questions:

How long does it take you to get to school?
How many times did you come late to class in the last month?

These were the results: It takes four students over an hour. It takes three students about 40 minutes. It takes two students 20 minutes and one student can get to school in less than 10 minutes. In answer to the second question, I found out that only three students came late to class last month. I also discovered that all the students who came late live near school.

12 | ON THE INTERNET

 *Look up Olympic champions. Choose three champions and prepare a quiz about their accomplishments.*

Example: How many gold medals did Ian Thorpe win in the 2004 Olympics? How many did he win in 2000?

Quiz your classmates.

34 *Too Much / Too Many / Too + Adjective*

Grammar in Context

BEFORE YOU READ

Does your city or town have any of these problems?

❑ There is too much noise.
❑ There is too much traffic.
❑ There is too much crime.
❑ There are not enough jobs.
❑ There are not enough schools.

❑ There are too few parks.
❑ There are too few parking spaces.
❑ It's too hot.
❑ It's too cold.
❑ It's too humid.

On a scale of 1 to 10, how do you rate where you live? _____ Why?

🎧 *Read a magazine article called "Finding the Right Place to Live."*

Finding the Right Place to Live

Where do you want to live?

Most people want to live in a safe place with great schools, a warm sunny climate, inexpensive housing, good jobs, and a lot of activities. But in the real world, we can't have everything we want.

Read what people say about where they live. How important is each category for you? Rank them from 1 to 6. It will help you find the best place for you.

___Climate

"The climate here is awful. It gets **too hot** in the summer and **too cold** in the winter. There's **too much snow**. The winters are **too long**. But, I have a great job, so I don't plan to move."

___Employment (Jobs)

"I need to move. There are **too few jobs** in this area. The unemployment rate is always high. My family and friends are here, and I don't want to leave them, but I can't stay here without a job."

___Culture & Leisure (Free-Time Activities)

"This place is boring. There aren't enough things to do. There's only one movie theater, a pizza place, and one sports stadium. There's not even a good museum. I have a nice home, and a good job, but I'd like to move to a more exciting place."

___Health

"There are **too few doctors** in this area and there isn't a good hospital. Sometimes I worry about it, but I'm young and healthy and I like other things about this town."

___Environment

"There's **too much air pollution** here. But where else can you find good jobs, inexpensive homes, and a great nightlife?"

___Education

"There are **too few schools**. The ones we have aren't very good. They're too crowded. I'm thinking about moving away when my children are ready for school."

AFTER YOU READ

Write the letter of the phrase in the right category.

Climate	Employment	Culture & Leisure	Health	Environment	Education

a. too few teachers

d. too few restaurants

b. too few businesses

e. too much noise

c. too many rainy days

f. too few nurses

Grammar Presentation

TOO MUCH / TOO MANY / TOO + ADJECTIVE

		Too Many / Too Few	Plural Count Noun
There	are	**too many**	**cars.**
		too few	**parking spaces.**

		Too Much / Too Little	Non-count Noun
There	is	**too much**	**noise.**
		too little	**light.**

	Too	Adjective
It's	**too**	**hot.**
		cold.

GRAMMAR NOTES

1. *Too many* and *too much* mean "more than the right amount." They usually have negative meanings. Use *too many* before plural count nouns. Use *too much* before non-count nouns.

Too few is the opposite of *too many*.

Too little is the opposite of *too much*.

Both *too few* and *too little* mean "not enough." They usually have negative meanings. Use *too few* with count nouns. Use *too little* with non-count nouns.

2. Use *too* + **adjective** to say that something has a negative result.

EXAMPLES

- **Too many** students registered for that course. *(There was room for ten students. Fifteen people registered.)*

- It costs **too much** money. *(We can't afford it.)*

- There were **too few** books. *(There were books for five people, but seven people needed books.)*

- There was **too little** time. *(We couldn't finish.)*

- The water is **too cold.** *(We can't swim here.)*

Reference Note
See Unit 42, page 430 for more about *too* + adjective.

Focused Practice

1 | DISCOVER THE GRAMMAR

Underline the adjectives that follow **too**. *Circle the nouns that follow* **too much**, **too many**, **too few**, *and* **too little**. *Then match the statement with the reason.*

___b___ 1. The weather was terrible.
We stayed indoors.

_____ 2. Classes are crowded.

_____ 3. I won't go back to that restaurant.

_____ 4. Don't take the expressway at this hour.

_____ 5. Let's move to another picnic spot.

_____ 6. They're not going to fix the computer.

_____ 7. I can't watch TV.

_____ 8. He didn't take the job.

a. The food was too expensive and the service was awful.

b. It was too cold and too windy to do anything outside.

c. I have too much homework.

d. There are too few teachers. The school needs to hire more.

e. They offered him too little money.

f. It's too crowded. Wait until after rush hour.

g. It has too many problems. They're going to buy a new one.

h. There are too many bugs here.

2 | PERSONAL PROBLEMS

Grammar Note 1

Complete the sentences with **too many** *or* **too much***.*

1. I'm getting _____ phone calls. I can't do my work.

2. He gets _____ e-mail. He can't answer all of it.

3. She has _____ work. She needs an assistant.

4. She did _____ exercise. Her body hurts all over.

5. He drank _____ coffee. He can't sleep.

6. There are _____ cars on the highway. I'm going to drive through the city.

7. There is _____ work left. We can't finish the job today.

3 | IN OTHER WORDS

Grammar Note 1

Complete the conversations. Use **There is***,* **There are***, or* **There was***, and* **too few** *or* **too little** *and the ideas in parentheses.*

1. **A:** What's the problem?

   B: *There are too few doctors*_____. They need to hire more.
   (not enough doctors)

2. **A:** Why is the grass brown?

   B: _____ this past summer.
   (not enough rain)

3. **A:** Why are so many people moving?

   B: _____ in this area.
   (not enough jobs)

4. **A:** Why are all those people moving so far out?

   B: _____ in the center of town.
   (not enough affordable homes)

5. **A:** Why do so many students study in other countries?

   B: _____ at the university here.
   (not enough spaces)

6. **A:** Where are you going?

   B: To the store. _____ for the party.
   (not enough food)

4 | PROBLEMS

Add **too** *before the adjective in each sentence.*

1. Don't go running. It's $\overset{too}{\wedge}$ hot outside.

2. I didn't enjoy the movie. It was violent.

3. Am I late for the movie?

4. I don't eat there because it's dirty.

5. I can't reach those shelves. They're high for me.

6. Is it far to walk to the beach?

7. Homes are expensive in that area.

8. They can't lift it. It's heavy.

5 | FINDING THE RIGHT HOME

Read about this family.

The Stones want to rent a house. There are eight people in the family. They want a four-bedroom, three-bathroom house with a two-car garage. They also want to be near public transportation. They can afford to pay $2,000 per month.

Now read these ads for houses. Circle the ad for the best house for the Stones. Write the problem next to the other ads.

Key

ba = bathroom   nr = near

br = bedroom   trans = transportation

mo = month

4br/3ba/2-car garage/nr trans $3,000 mo	1. *This house is too expensive.*
3br/3ba/2-car garage/nr trans $2,000 mo	2. _____
3br/3ba/2-car garage/nr trans $3,000 mo	3. _____
4br/3ba/1-car garage/nr trans $2,000 mo	4. _____
4br/3ba/2-car garage/nr trans $2,000 mo	5. _____
4br/2ba/2-car garage $2,000 mo	6. _____

6 | COMPLAINTS

Complete the conversations with **too**, **too many**, **too much**, **too few**, *or* **too little**.

1. **A:** How was the restaurant?

   B: It was _____ dark. I wasn't able to read the menu or see my food. There was
         a.
   _____ light.
      b.

2. **A:** Do you go to that beach?

   B: Not in the summer. It's _____ far and there are _____ people.
            a.   **b.**
   I don't like crowds.

3. **A:** How was the weather?

   B: There was _____ rain and it was _____ humid.
          a.   **b.**

4. **A:** Did you take a psychology class?

   B: I wanted to, but the class was canceled. _____ people
   registered for it.

5. **A:** Did you take the job?

   B: No. The salary was _____ low and there were
            a.
   _____ holidays and sick days.
      b.

6. **A:** Am I _____ late for the movie?

   B: Yes, it began an hour ago.

7. **A:** What's wrong?

   B: We bought _____ grapes. They're beginning to go bad.

8. **A:** His class was _____ hard.
         a.

   B: And we got _____ homework.
         b.

9. **A:** Which car did you buy, the green one or the red one?

   B: Neither. The green one was _____ expensive and the red one had
            a.
   _____ problems.
      b.

7 | EDITING

Correct these conversations. There are seven mistakes. The first mistake is already corrected.

1. **A:** I'd like to change my class. It's ~~to~~ *too* hard. And there's too many homework.

   B: But the other class will be too easy.

2. **A:** What's wrong with that company?

   B: There are too many bosses and too little workers.

3. **A:** Did you buy that computer?

   B: No. It was too money and too very complicated.

4. **A:** Don't go by bus. It will take too many time. Take the train. It's a lot faster.

   B: Yes, but it's a lot expensive. The bus is half the price.

Communication Practice

8 | LISTENING

A couple looked at three apartments. Listen to their conversation with a real estate salesperson. Then complete the chart.

	What They Liked	**What They Didn't Like**
First apartment		
Second apartment		
Third apartment		

9 | ROLE PLAY

Act out a situation with a partner. Use **too**, **too much**, *or* **too many** *in your conversations.*

Situations

Host and diner: diner complains about a table in a restaurant

Hotel manager and guest: guest complains about a room in a hotel

Teacher and student: student asks to change seats in a class

Salesperson and customer: customer wants to exchange a gift

Two friends: one friend tells why he or she wants to move

(continued)

Examples: HOST: Is this table OK?

DINER: I think it's too noisy. And it's right next to the kitchen.

HOST: How about that table over there? It's quieter and it looks out on the garden.

DINER: Thanks. That would be great.

OR

(At a store)

CUSTOMER: Excuse me. I'd like to exchange these pants. They're too large.

SALESPERSON: Certainly. What size are you looking for?

CUSTOMER: Size small.

SALESPERSON: No problem.

CUSTOMER: Thanks.

10 | OUR CITY: THE GOOD AND THE BAD

Work in small groups. Write four good and four bad things about the city or town you are in. Use an article or quantifier **(a, one, a few, some, many, much, a lot of, any, a little, too many, too much,** *or* **not enough)** *in each sentence.*

Example: **Good**   **Bad**

There's a wonderful concert hall here.   There aren't enough jobs.
There isn't much pollution here.   There are too many cars on the highway.

11 | WRITING

Write a review about a movie, a TV show, or a book that you didn't like. Use **too, too many, too much, too few,** *or* **too little** *in your review.*

Example: Yesterday night I watched the movie *Jurassic Park 3* starring Sam Neill on TV. The TV review said it was fun and not too scary. I disagree. The first part was too long. And there was too much blood. The second half was a little better, but all in all I did not enjoy the movie. I don't recommend this movie.

12 | ON THE INTERNET

Look up facts about a city you've heard about but never visited. Pretend you are in that city. Use the categories in the magazine article on pages 344–345 and write about the city.

Example: Buffalo, New York

Climate: It gets very cold in Buffalo in the winter. There's too much snow for me. But it's nice the rest of the year.

Possessives

Grammar in Context

BEFORE YOU READ

Look at the bicycles. How many differences can you find?

🎧 *Read the conversation between Jasmine and her friend Dora.*

THEY LOOK ALIKE

DORA: Jasmine, **your** family's bikes are all the same. How can you tell them apart?

JASMINE: They look the same because we bought them at a huge sale. But they're not exactly alike. Look. **Mine** has a basket in the front.

DORA: Oh, I see it now. But the others are the same.

JASMINE: No. That one is **my** brother Johnny's bike. **His** has a small license in the back.

DORA: Oh yeah. And **his** has a higher seat. But the other two are the same.

JASMINE: Look carefully. That one, the one next to Johnny's bike is Amy's. She's **my** sister. **Hers** has a bag in the back. The rest of **ours** don't.

DORA: You're right. Whose is the last one?

JASMINE: That one belongs to **my** two uncles, Roger and Ted. They don't ride much, so they share the bike. **Theirs** has a horn.

AFTER YOU READ

Write the name of the owners above their bicycles.

Jasmine   Johnny   Amy   Roger and Ted

Grammar Presentation

POSSESSIVES

Possessive Adjective	Possessive Pronoun
This is **my** bike.	**Mine** is red.
That is **your** bike.	**Yours** is green.
Is that **his** pen?	No. **His** is black.
Is that **her** book?	No. **Hers** is at home.
This isn't **our** classroom.	**Ours** is on the second floor.
That's not **their** car.	**Theirs** is in a garage.
Its name is Goldy.	

Review of Pronouns and Adjectives			
Subject Pronoun	Object Pronoun	Possessive Adjective	Possessive Pronoun
I	me	my	mine
he	him	his	his
she	her	her	hers
it	it	its	
we	us	our	ours
you	you	your	yours
they	them	their	theirs

GRAMMAR NOTES	EXAMPLES

1. A **possessive adjective** shows **belonging**.	• This is a bike. *(We don't know whose bike it is.)*
	
	         possessive
	         adjective
	 • This is **my** bike. *(It belongs to me.)*
	 • This is **her** bike. *(It belongs to her.)*

2. A **possessive pronoun** replaces a **possessive adjective and a noun**. ▶ **BE CAREFUL!** A noun never follows a possessive pronoun.	possessive possessive adjective noun pronoun • This isn't **my umbrella**. **Mine** is blue. *(My umbrella is blue.)* • This is my hat. This is **mine**. NOT: This is mine ~~hat~~.
3. The verb that follows a possessive pronoun agrees with the noun it replaces.	• Her **notebook** is blue. = **Hers is** blue. • Her **notebooks** are red. = **Hers are** red.

Reference Notes
See Unit 12, page 114 for a discussion of possessive adjectives.
See Unit 24, page 233, and Unit 1, page 6 for a discussion of subject and object pronouns.

Focused Practice

1 | DISCOVER THE GRAMMAR

Read an ad for Best Bike Tours. Write the underlined words in the correct place in the chart.

Join <u>us</u> on Best Bike Tours. No other bike tours are like <u>ours</u>.

<u>Our</u> tour leaders are experts in the areas <u>they</u> take <u>you</u> to.

<u>We</u> offer <u>you</u> five tours to choose from.

For more information about the tours and <u>their</u> leaders, visit <u>us</u> at bestbiketours.com.

Subject Pronouns (2)	Object Pronouns (4)	Possessive Adjectives (2)	Possessive Pronoun (1)
	us		

2 | WHOSE IS IT?

Grammar Note 2

Replace the underlined words with a possessive pronoun.

1. **A:** Is that your notebook?

   B: No, it's not ~~my notebook~~ *mine*. It's his notebook. My notebook is in my book bag.
                 a.   **b.**   **c.**

2. **A:** Is this their house?

   B: No. Their house is next door.
            a.

   A: Whose house is this?

   B: It's our house.
           b.

   A: Your house?
        c.

   B: Yes, our house.
          d.

3. **A:** Are those your sunglasses?

   B: No, they're her sunglasses. My sunglasses are in my bag.
            a.   **b.**

3 | POSSESSIONS

Grammar Notes 1–2

Choose the correct word to complete the conversations.

1. **A:** I think you are taking my umbrella.

   B: No. This is _____ umbrella. _____ is over there. It's next to _____ bag.
                 a. (my / mine)   **b. (You / Yours)**   **c. (her / hers)**

   A: Oh, excuse me.

2. **A:** Your bags are alike.

   B: No. _____ bag has many pockets. _____ has only one.
          a. (Her / Hers)   **b. (My / Mine)**

3. **A:** Where is _____ car?
             a. (their / theirs)

   B: _____ car is in the garage.
     b. (Their / Theirs)

   A: Is _____ there too?
          c. (your / yours)

   B: No. _____ is on the street.
          d. (Our / Ours)

4 | REVIEW OF PRONOUNS AND POSSESSIVES   *Grammar Notes 1–2*

Choose the correct word to complete the sentences.

1. It's _____. Please give it to _____.
   a. (I / my / me / mine)   b. (I / my / me / mine)

   _____ need it.
   c. (I / My / Me / I)

2. I think _____ missed _____ train. I don't see
   a. (he / him / his)   b. (he / him / his)

   _____.
   c. (he / him / his)

3. Our family is from Edmonton. _____ is from Vancouver.
   a. (They / Their / Theirs / Them)

   _____ moved to Edmonton two years ago. We live next door to
   b. (They / Their / Theirs / Them)

   _____.
   c. (they / their / theirs / them)

5 | SINGULAR OR PLURAL   *Grammar Note 3*

Complete the sentences. Choose from the words in parentheses.

1. These are my shoes. His _____ over there.
   (is / are)

2. Whose key is this? _____ it yours?
   (Is / Are)

3. _____ that their classroom?
   (Is / Are)

4. Their homework is missing. _____ yours missing too?
   (Is / Are)

5. Her friends have mountain bikes. _____ yours?
   (Do / Does)

6. His notes are messy. Mine _____ neat.
   (is / are)

7. Her name has ten letters. Mine _____ seven.
   (has / have)

8. My parents live in Asia. Hers _____ in Europe.
   (live / lives)

6 | EDITING

Correct these conversations. There are 10 mistakes. The first one is already corrected.

1. **A:** Is their class in room 304 today?

   B: No. ~~Our~~ *Ours* is in room 304. Theirs are in 306.

2. **A:** I like yours watch.

   B: Thanks, but it isn't my. It's my uncle's. He lent it to my. Mine watch is broken.

3. **A:** Where are yours keys?

   B: In my pocket.

(continued)

4. **A:** Can I use your phone? Mine phone doesn't work here.

   B: Sure. Here.

   A: Your doesn't work either.

   B: Try Mary's. Hers phone works everywhere.

Communication Practice

7 | LISTENING

🎧 *Listen to a young man's dream. Then complete the sentences.*

The young man's dad gives _____ the _____

to a new _____ _____ car. It's a _____

for _____ for _____ _____ birthday.

8 | GUESSING GAME

Student A, go to the front of the class and close your eyes.

Student B, choose five objects that belong to different students and put them in front of Student A.

Student A, open your eyes and guess whose they are. Point to an object and use a possessive pronoun. You get one point for a correct guess, and one point for the correct use of the possessive pronoun.

Example: **A:** I think this pen is **his**. (A points to C.)
                 B: That's right. You get two points.

                 A: I think this bag is **yours**. (A points to B.)
                 B: That's wrong. It isn't **mine**. It's **hers**. You get one point.

9 | WRITING

Write about a place you are sharing or have shared with someone. Include at least one possessive pronoun.

Example: I share an apartment with my cousin. We each have our own room. My room is smaller, but has more light. Mine has a big closet and a big window. His has a tiny window and a small closet, but his has enough space for a TV and a computer, so I spend a lot of time in there.

10 | ON THE INTERNET

Write an ad for something you would like to have. Look online to get details about it. Include a subject pronoun, object pronoun, possessive adjective, and possessive pronoun.

Example: Buy a sports car from our sleek new line of sports cars. Other carmakers say their sports models have all the extras, but ours really do.

They're beautiful, reasonably priced, and loaded with features. You are sure to love everything about them.

They have a powerful 6-cylinder engine, a 6-speaker stereo/CD system, front and side airbags, and a 10-year/100,000-mile warranty. Hurry! Don't miss this opportunity.

PART X

From **Grammar** to **Writing**
A Business Letter

1 | *Work in pairs. Look at the business letter on the next page and answer the questions. Read the rules and check your work.*

1. Where does your address belong?

_____

2. Where does the date belong?

_____

3. Where does the name and the address of the person you are writing to belong?

_____

4. How do you address the person you are writing to?

_____

5. What do you do in the first sentence?

_____

6. What does the last full line of the letter often say?

_____

7. How do you end the letter?

_____

8. What do you write last?

_____

When we write a business letter, we follow a certain form. Use this form for all letters that are not to friends or relatives.

1. Write your address at the top left of the page.

2. Write the date below your address.

3. Skip at least two lines. Write the name and address of the person you are writing to on the left margin below the date.

4. When you write a letter, it's best to write to a person by name. If you don't know the person's name, you may write "Dear Sir/Madam:" or "To Whom It May Concern:"; be sure to use a colon (:) after the name.

5. Explain what you want in your first sentence.

6. In the last line of your letter you usually thank the person you are writing to.

7. You may end a letter with "Sincerely yours" or "Yours truly."

Rua Rio de Janeiro 12 —————————————— 1.
Saõ Paulo, Brasil

March 12, _____ ————————————— 2.

Ms. Alison Rice ————————————— 3.
Director
International English Language Institute
Hunter College
New York, New York 10021

Dear Ms. Rice: ————————————— 4.

I am interested in attending Hunter College's ———— 5.
International English Language Institute in the fall.

Would you please send me an application and a catalog of your courses?

Thank you for your prompt attention to this request. ——— 6.

Sincerely yours, ————— 7.

Joaõ Lima
Joaõ Lima ————— 8.

8. Finally, write your signature, and write your name below your signature.

2 | *Write one of the following business letters. Follow the form of the letter above.*

1. Ask for a bulletin of courses and an application for a language program.

2. Ask for a list of moderately priced apartments near the college.

PART

X

Review Test

I *Read each conversation. Circle the letter of the underlined word or group of words that is not correct.*

1. **A:** Why is the <u>pool empty</u>?

               A

   B: The water is <u>too much</u> <u>cold</u>.

                 B   C

   A: Really? It was warm <u>yesterday</u>.

                        D

                                                       A   B   C   D

2. **A:** Is there <u>enough meat</u>?

              A

   B: I think so. <u>How much</u> <u>people</u> do you expect?

                      B   C

   A: <u>About ten</u>.

      D

                                                         A   B   C   D

3. **A:** Where is your family?

   B: <u>Mine parents</u> are here, but <u>my brother</u> is in Spain.

       A   B

   A: What's <u>he doing</u> there?

              C

   B: He's teaching <u>English</u>.

                    D

                                                         A   B   C   D

4. **A:** <u>How many</u> <u>man</u> are there in your class?

        A   B

   B: Fourteen.

   A: <u>There are</u> only two in <u>mine</u>.

       C   D

                                                         A   B   C   D

II *Complete the conversation. Use* **How much** *or* **How many**.

A: This French toast is delicious. Can you tell me how you made it?

B: Sure. What do you want to know?

A: _____ eggs did you use?
   1.

B: Two or maybe three.

A: _____ slices of bread?
   2.

B: Two.

A: _____ butter?
   3.

B: About half a teaspoon. I'm not really sure.

A: _____ salt?
   4.

B: Just a pinch.

A: Your French toast is good, but your directions are awful!

III *Circle the correct word(s) to complete the sentences.*

1. He met <u>a few / a little</u> <u>friend / friends</u> at the concert. After the concert they all went out
           a.   b.

   for <u>some / any</u> ice cream.
        c.

2. Is there <u>some / any</u> <u>ice / ices</u> in the freezer?
         a.   b.

3. He bought <u>some / any</u> <u>stamp / stamps</u> at the post office.
          a.   b.

4. There is only <u>a few / a little</u> <u>time / times</u> left.
           a.   b.

5. <u>How much / How many</u> <u>mail / mails</u> did they get?
       a.   b.

6. <u>How much / How many</u> <u>bottle / bottles</u> of milk did the baby drink?
       a.   b.

7. I'm leaving. There are <u>enough cooks / cooks enough</u> in the kitchen.

8. I couldn't finish my homework. I didn't have <u>many / enough</u> time.

9. <u>How much / How many</u> vacation <u>day / days</u> do you get?
       a.   b.

10. He doesn't feel well. He ate <u>too much / too many</u> hot dogs.

11. I can't drive. I'm <u>too / too much</u> young.

12. The class was canceled because <u>too little / too few</u> students registered.

IV Use the nouns in the box to complete the sentences.

bowl	cup	carton	jar	piece	pound

1. He bought a _____ of milk.

2. I usually have a _____ of cereal.

3. He always drinks a _____ of tea with his dinner.

4. I'm washing the floor because I dropped a _____ of jam.

5. I bought a _____ of chicken for the barbecue, but I need to get more.

6. He wrote the number on a _____ of paper, but he can't find it.

V Use the words in the box to complete the conversations.

1. | you your yours |

 A: Do _____ need an umbrella?
                 a.

 B: Yes.

 A: Here's mine.

 B: I don't want to use _____.
                             b.

 A: It's OK. I'm wearing _____ rain hat.
                              c.

2. | I me mine my |

 A: What's wrong?

 B: This sweatshirt is _____. Mom gave it to _____. It belongs in
                             a.   b.
 _____ closet. _____ want to wear it now, but you wore it
          c.   d.
 yesterday and it's dirty.

3. | our ours us we |

 A: Do you and your wife live alone in that big house?

 B: No, _____ don't. _____ married son and his wife live with
         a.   b.
 _____. Their rooms are on the second floor. _____ are on the
        c.   d.
 first.

4. | it   its |

    A: Is that your rabbit?

    B: Yes. _____ name is Lucky. _____ has a home in our garden.
                      a.   **a.**

5. | their   them   they |

    A: Do _____ drive that big van?
                    a.

    B: Yes, but it doesn't belong to _____. It's _____ grandparents'
                                        b.   **c.**
    van.

VI   *Correct the sentences.*

1. We didn't buy some bread.

2. They need a little more days to finish.

3. We don't have chairs enough for everyone.

4. He has too many homework. He can't go out.

5. We can't see that movie today. It's very too late.

6. This isn't my jacket. Mine jacket is in the closet. It's probably hers.

▶ *To check your answers, go to the Answer Key on page RT-5.*

Modals: Permission / Requests; Desires; Offers; Advice; Necessity

Grammar in Context

BEFORE YOU READ

Foods are mainly protein, carbohydrates, and fat. Some foods like chicken are high in protein. Foods like rice are high in carbohydrates. Foods like cream cheese are mostly fat.

In which category do these foods belong? (Check your answers on the next page.)

Protein	Carbohydrate	Fat
chicken	rice	cream cheese

beef   bread   cake   fish   oil   pasta   potatoes

🎧 *Read the magazine article about diets.*

Health and Nutrition Magazine

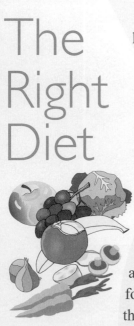

The Right Diet

Marita gained ten pounds during her first year of college. She tried to lose the weight on her own, but couldn't. Two years later she joined Weight Watchers™. Many people like Marita want to lose weight. Most nutritionists say that exercise and a program based on calorie reduction is the best way to do it. The Weight Watchers diet is an example of such a program. It uses a point system. You **can eat** any food, but you **may not eat** more than a certain number of points each day. Different foods have different numbers of points. For example, an orange has 1 point. A piece of chocolate cake has 7 points. Dieters **can follow** Weight Watchers by joining a weekly class. They meet other dieters, exchange ideas, and get support and advice from the class organizer. But you **can** also **do** the program at home online. Marita is happy. She has lost five pounds in three months. She hopes to lose the other five within six months.

Bill Morgan is a businessman. He works long hours and eats many meals out. He's twenty-five pounds overweight. He says, "I tried Weight Watchers a few years ago, but it wasn't for me. I'm not good at counting points." Bill is following the Atkins™ diet. The Atkins diet is different from usual ideas of healthy eating. In this diet you **may eat** foods high in protein and fat, such as red meat and cheese, but you **can't eat** carbohydrates such as bread, cereal, pasta, and rice. The first two weeks are especially strict. You **can't have** any fruit, grains, cereals, bread, or vegetables such as potatoes, peas, corn, and carrots. You **can't drink** any milk or juice. Even after the first two weeks, dieters **can add** only 5 grams of carbohydrates to their diet. Bill has lost ten pounds in the first three weeks. He's thrilled.

Many people, like Marita and Bill, lose weight on diets, but they don't keep it off.

So they have to start all over again. Dieters don't always agree on the best diet, but almost every dieter would like to take a pill one day, become slim the next, and never regain the weight.

AFTER YOU READ

Answer **T** *(true),* **F** *(false), or* **?** *(It doesn't say).*

_____ **1.** You can eat small portions of everything on the Weight Watchers diet.

_____ **2.** You can't eat meat on the Atkins diet.

_____ **3.** You may follow the Weight Watchers diet online.

_____ **4.** You can't eat cereal in the first two weeks of the Atkins diet.

_____ **5.** An overweight person can take a pill and become slim the next day.

_____ **6.** You may not drink coffee on the Atkins diet.

Protein: beef, fish; Carbohydrates: bread, cake, pasta, potatoes; Fat: oil

Grammar Presentation

CAN or MAY FOR PERMISSION

Statements			
Subject	Can / May Can't / May Not	Base Form of Verb	
You	can may	start	today.
He	can't may not	eat	nuts.

Yes / No Questions			
Can / May	Subject	Base Form of Verb	
Can May	I	have	the day off?
Can May	I	help	you?

Answers
Yes, you can. **Yes, you may.** **Sure.** **Of course.** **I'm sorry. We're too busy.**
Yes, thanks. **No, thanks. I'm just looking.**

Wh- Questions				
Wh- Word	Can	Subject	Base Form of Verb	
When	**can**	I	**borrow**	the car?
Where	**can**	we	**park**?	

GRAMMAR NOTES

1. Use **can** or **may** to **give permission**. (It's OK to . . .) *Can* and *may* are followed by the base form of the verb.

Use **can't** or **may not** to **deny permission**. (Something is not OK.)

There is no contraction for *may not*.

EXAMPLES

- You **can see** the doctor now.
- You **may eat** fish.

- You **can't drive** a truck on this road.
- You **may not drive** a car without a license.

  NOT: You ~~mayn't~~ drive a car without a license.

2. Use *can* or *may* to **ask for permission**. *May* is more formal than *can*.

We respond:
Yes, you may.
Sure.
Of course.
OR
I'm sorry. + a reason

A: **May** I see the doctor this afternoon?

B: **Yes, you may.**

A: **Can** I tell my friends about this?

B: **No, I'm sorry. I don't want anyone to know.**

3. We use **Can I help you?** or **May I help you?** to offer help to someone.

We respond:
Thank you.
Thanks.
Yes, thank you.
OR
No thanks. + a reason

A: **Can I help you**?
OR
May I help you?

B: **Thanks**. I'm looking for a winter jacket.
OR
No thanks. **I'm just looking**.

Focused Practice

1 | DISCOVER THE GRAMMAR

Read the conversations. Then write the speakers next to the questions and answers.

Student A / Student B	Driver / Police Officer	Salesperson / Customer
Patient / Dentist	Student / Teacher	

1. a. _Patient_ : When can I eat regular food?

b. _Dentist_ : Take liquids today. Tomorrow you can eat soft foods—no carrots or apples. Wednesday you can return to a normal diet.

2. a. _____ : Can I borrow your eraser?

b. _____ : Sure. Here it is.

3. a. _____ : May I help you?

b. _____ : Yes. I'm looking for a laptop.

4. a. _____ : Can I see your license and registration?

b. _____ : Sure, officer. Is something wrong?

5. a. _____ : Can I use my dictionary?

b. _____ : Sorry. No dictionaries during the test.

2 | PERMISSION

Complete the conversations with the items in the box.

> **a.** Can I have a salad instead?
>
> **b.** Can I wear jeans?
>
> **c.** Can I watch it?
>
> **d.** May I help you?
>
> **e.** ~~OK. May I have the dressing on the side?~~
>
> **f.** Sorry. My Internet connection is down right now.
>
> **g.** Can we use a pencil?
>
> **h.** Yes, thanks. I'd like to buy a cell phone.
>
> **i.** Great. When can I return to work?

1. A: The salad comes with Italian dressing.

    B: *OK. May I have the dressing on the side?*

2. A: The dinner comes with wonton soup.

    B: I don't want the soup. _____

3. A: The test is one hour long. We'll begin in three minutes.

    B: _____

4. A: May I use your computer to check my e-mail?

    B: _____

5. A: The ceremony is on Tuesday evening. You don't have to wear a suit.

    B: _____

6. A: You're doing very well, Mr. Smith. The operation was a success.

    B: _____

7. A: There's a good show on TV at 8:00. _____

    B: Sorry, Cindy. It's a school night. The movie ends at 11:00.

8. A: _____

    B: Yes. Do you have this sweater in medium?

9. A: Can I help you?

    B: _____

3 | QUESTIONS FOR A NUTRITIONIST

Write questions. Use **can** *or* **may** *and the information in parentheses.*

DR. LEE: OK, Nuray. Here's your diet. Any questions?

NURAY: (Can) _____
1. (Is it OK to drink coffee?)

DR. LEE: Yes, but don't drink more than three cups a day.

NURAY: (Can) _____
2. (Is it OK to eat ice cream?)

DR. LEE: No, you can't, but you can have lowfat yogurt instead.

NURAY: (May) _____
3. (Is it OK to call you with questions?)

DR. LEE: Certainly. But don't worry. Everything is on these papers. Just read the diet and follow

the directions. You will look and feel better in no time.*

NURAY: Thanks, Dr. Lee.

* *in no time*: very quickly

4 | EDITING

Correct these conversations. There are five mistakes. The first mistake is already corrected.

1. A: Can we ~~paid~~ *pay* in two installments?

   B: Yes, you can pays half now and half next month.

2. A: May I speaks to the doctor?

   B: I'm sorry. He's with a patient now. Tell me your number and he'll call you back.

3. A: Is it OK to use a dictionary during the test?

   B: Sorry. You can't to use a dictionary.

4. A: How much time do we have?

   B: Fifty minutes. You mayn't continue after two o'clock.

Communication Practice

5 | LISTENING

 Listen to a telephone conversation. A patient calls a doctor. Then answer the questions.

1. What's the woman's problem? _____

2. What can she do for the swelling and pain? _____

3. What activities can she do? _____

4. What activities can't she do? _____

6 | INFORMATION GAP: ROLE PLAY

Student B, look at the Information Gap on page 409.

Student A, read the information about Central Tennis Courts. Answer your partner's questions.

> **Example:** **B:** When can you use the courts?
> **A:** You can use the courts from April until October.

CENTRAL TENNIS COURT INFORMATION

1. You can use the courts from April until October.

2. You can't play tennis without a permit.

3. You can play one hour of singles or two hours of doubles.

4. You can't wear leather shoes on the courts. You need athletic shoes.

5. You can buy a permit on the website or at the tennis courts from 8:00 A.M. to 6:00 P.M.

Ask Student B these questions about Central Ice Skating Rink.

1. Is the rink open every day?

2. Do I need to have my own skates?

3. Can I race?

4. Is there a place to eat nearby?

7 | WRITING

Write rules to a game you know well. Include what you can and can't do. Read the rules to the class. The class guesses the game.

Example: STUDENT A: In this game there are two teams of 11 people. The aim is to get a ball into a goal. You can use your feet to kick the ball and you can use your head, but you can't use your hands.

STUDENT B: Are you talking about soccer?

STUDENT A: Yes, I am.

8 | ON THE INTERNET

🌐 *Look online for information about Weight Watchers, Atkins, South Beach™, Zone®, or some other diet. Tell the class what you can or can't eat.*

Grammar in Context

BEFORE YOU READ

Read these requests for favors. Which ones are OK to ask a friend?

	OK	Depends	Not OK
Would you please get my mail while I'm on vacation?			
Could you help me move to a new apartment?			
Can you drive me to the airport?			
Can you lend me $500?			

What does the expression "Your friend has a lot of nerve" mean?

🎧 *Read the letter to an advice columnist and read her response.*

Dear Connie,

Last month my friend Gina said, "Monique, **can you do** me a favor? **Can you drive** me to the airport tonight? I have a nine o'clock flight."

I said, "**Sure**, Gina. **I'd be glad to**. **Would you like** me to pick you up at 7:00?"

Then yesterday Gina said, "Monique, **could you help** me out? I'm going away for a few days next month. **Could you water** my plants and walk my dog?" Again I said, "**Sure**."

Well, yesterday I needed a favor. I called Gina and said, "Gina, I'm going to paint my bedroom tomorrow afternoon. **Would you help me?**" She said, "Oh, Monique. **I'd like to help you, but I'm going to go shopping**." I didn't say anything, but I was angry and hurt. What do you think? Was I right to be hurt?

Hurt and Angry Monique

Dear Monique,

Your friend has a lot of nerve. It's OK to ask for favors if you return them. Some people almost never ask or do favors for friends. But other people consider favors a part of friendship. In that case, when one friend asks, "**Would you do** me a favor?" the other should answer, "**Of course**."

Tell Gina how you feel and see what happens.

Good luck,
Connie

AFTER YOU READ

Who Is **She***? Write* **G** *(Gina) or* **M** *(Monique) next to each statement.*

_____ **1.** She would like a ride to the airport.

_____ **2.** She offered to pick her friend up at 7:00.

_____ **3.** She would like her friend to water her plants.

_____ **4.** She asked her friend to help paint her bedroom.

_____ **5.** She would like to help, but she can't.

_____ **6.** She would like advice from Connie.

Grammar Presentation

REQUESTS, DESIRES, AND OFFERS

Polite Requests		
Would You / Could You / Can You (Please)	*Base Form of Verb*	
Would you **Could you** **Can you**	help	me?

Short Answers	
Affirmative	**Negative**
Sure. Of course. OK. I'd be glad to.	Sorry, I can't. I have to work. I'd like to, but I can't. I have a class.

Desires		
Subject	*Would Like*	
I		
You		
He		
She	**would like**	some help. to move.
We		
You		
They		

Contractions
I would = **I'd**
you would = **you'd**
he would = **he'd**
she would = **she'd**
we would = **we'd**
you would = **you'd**
they would = **they'd**

Offers			
Would	*Subject*	*Like*	
Would	you	**like**	some blueberries? to join us?

Short Answers	
Affirmative	**Negative**
Yes, thank you. Yes, I would.	No, thanks.

GRAMMAR NOTES	**EXAMPLES**
1. In Unit 17 you learned how to make requests using *Please* + a base form verb.	**A:** Please help me carry these books. OR **Would you (please)** help me carry these books?
Would you, **Could you**, and **Can you** are three other ways of making **requests**.	
When we agree to a request, we say: **Sure**. **Of course**. **OK**. or **I'd be glad to**.	**B:** **Sure**. **A:** **Could you (please)** help me carry these books? **B:** **Of course**.
Can you is the most common and most informal.	**A:** **Can you (please)** help me? **B:** **I'd be glad to**. OR **Sorry, I can't. I have to work.**
When we don't agree to a request, we say *sorry* and **give a reason**.	

2. *Would like* is a polite way of saying *want*.
 	
USAGE NOTE: Use the contraction in speaking and informal writing.
 	
Would like can be followed by **a noun** or **an infinitive**.
	• **I'd like** some advice.
	• **We'd like** to see you.
	
	      noun
	• I'd like **an apple**.
	     infinitive
	• I'd like **to buy** an apple.

3. Use **Would you like** for offers or invitations.	• **Would you like** some help? • **Would you like** to dance?

4. We don't usually use *would like* in short answers to invitations with *Would you like*.	**A:** Would you like some coffee? **B:** Yes, thank you. OR No, thanks. NOT: No, I ~~wouldn't like~~ any, thank you.

Pronunciation Note
You never pronounce the letter *l* in the word *would*. *Would* is pronounced like the word *wood* /wʊd/.
We pronounce *Would you* /wʊdyə/.

Focused Practice

1 | DISCOVER THE GRAMMAR

Next to each sentence write **R** *(request),* **O** *(offer), or* **D** *(desire).*

_____ 1. Would you give me a ride?

_____ 2. We'd like to see you again soon.

_____ 3. Would you like some more lemonade?

_____ 4. Could you lend me your car?

_____ 5. I'd like some more fruit.

_____ 6. Can I please see your homework?

_____ 7. Would you like another dumpling?

2 | A NEW FRIENDSHIP
Grammar Notes 1–3

Complete the conversation. Use the sentences below.

> **Mary**
> - Thanks so much.
> - Steve, I love to listen to your music, but sometimes I can't get to sleep. Could you please stop practicing by 11:00?
> - Dinner? Sure. I'd love to.

> **Steve**
> - Listen Mary, I'd like to do something for you. Would you like to have dinner together sometime?
> - Nice to meet you, Mary. I'm Steve Kaufman.

MARY: *Excuse me, I'm Mary Brown. I live next door.* _____

STEVE: _____

MARY: _____

_____

STEVE: Oh, I'm so sorry. Of course.

MARY: _____

STEVE: _____

_____

MARY: _____

3 | REQUESTS, DESIRES, AND OFFERS   *Grammar Notes 1–3*

Read the questions in the box. Then complete the conversations with the correct question.

a. Can you do me a favor and return this book this afternoon?	**e.** How many bottles of soda would you like me to get for the party?
b. What would you like to drink?	**f.** What would you like us to do with the dirty glasses?
c. Would you please pass the salt?	**g.** Would you like some help with the homework?
d. Would you like a lift? I have my dad's car today. I can drive you home.	

1. A: *Can you do me a favor and return this book this afternoon?*

   B: I'm not going to the library today. I'm going there tomorrow. Can it wait until then?

2. A: _____

   B: Oh, yes, thanks. I'm terrible at math.

3. A: _____

   B: Some lemonade, please.

4. A: _____

   B: Thanks. That would be great. The train is terrible at this hour.

5. A: _____

   B: Sure, here.

6. A: _____

   B: You can put them on the counter. I'll wash them later.

7. A: _____

   B: Four bottles, please.

4 | RESPONSES   *Grammar Notes 1–2, 4*

Read the questions. Choose and write the correct response to complete the conversation.

1. A: Can you help me with these books?

   B: _____
   (Sure. / Yes, thanks.)

2. A: Could you get the mail?

   B: _____
   (No, thanks. / Sorry, I can't right now.)

3. A: Would you like some more lemonade?

   B: _____
   (I'd like to. / Thanks.)

4. A: Could I borrow your dictionary?

   B: _____
   (Sure. / I'm sure.)

5. A: Can you do me a favor? Can you drive me to the airport?

   B: _____
   (I could. / Of course.)

5 | AT THE RESTAURANT   *Grammar Notes 1–3*

Complete the conversation with **I'd like**, **would you like**, *or* **would you please**.

   SERVER: Ready to order?

CUSTOMER: Yes, _____ two eggs, scrambled, and a large orange juice.
                              1.

   SERVER: _____ toast with the eggs?
                        2.

CUSTOMER: Yes, please. I'd like rye toast.

   SERVER: Sure. _____ something to drink?
                           3.

CUSTOMER: Yes, thanks. _____ some tea.
                                4.

   SERVER: _____ the tea now or with the eggs?
                        5.

CUSTOMER: With the eggs. And _____ bring some extra napkins?
                                      6.

   SERVER: Sure.

6 | EDITING

Correct these conversations. There are five mistakes. The first mistake is already corrected.

1. A: Could ~~please I~~ ^{I please} borrow the car next Saturday?

   B: Sure, son.

2. A: He'd likes to go to a concert.

   B: When?

3. A: Would you like come for dinner?

   B: Yes, thank you.

4. A: May I to help you?

   B: No, thanks. I'm just looking.

5. A: Could I see your math notes?

   B: Yes, you could.

Communication Practice

7 | LISTENING

🎧 *Listen to a conversation between Robert, a business manager, and his assistant, John.*

What does Robert tell John to do?

1. Call _____ and get _____.

2. Write_____.

3. Look _____.

4. Contact me if _____.

8 | WHAT'S OK TO ASK A FRIEND?

Ask five students if it is OK to ask a friend these favors. Write their answers.

    Example: **A:** Is it OK to ask a friend, "Would you lend me your car?"
                B: I don't think so—not unless it's an emergency.

1. Would you lend me your car?

2. Could you help me with the homework?

3. Can I see your answers on the test?

4. I'd like to have a birthday party. Could you plan one for me?

5. I'd like to save some money. Can I live with you for awhile?

6. Would you drive me to the airport next Monday night?

7. Could you show me how to use this printer?

Report the results to the class. Then as a class discuss what you would do for a friend and what you would ask a friend to do for you.

9 | MAKING POLITE REQUESTS

Work in pairs. Read the situations. Take turns making polite requests. Answer the requests.

Example: You're in a restaurant with your friend. You want the sugar, which is near your friend.
A: Maki, can you please pass the sugar?
B: Here you go.

1. You're in a restaurant with your friend. The salt and pepper is in front of your friend. You would like the salt and pepper.

2. You're in class. You forgot your eraser. Your partner has an eraser.

3. You need to move your sofa. Your friend is at your home.

4. You want to hang a painting on the wall. You'd like your friend to help you.

5. Your neighbor's parrot wakes you up at five o'clock every morning.

6. Your co-worker always borrows your stapler but never returns it.

7. Your teacher gives you too much homework.

10 | INVITATIONS

Work in pairs. Take turns. Extend invitations to your partner. Your partner can accept or refuse. Use the suggestions given or your own.

Example: A: Would you like to come over for dinner tonight?
B: Sure. What time?
OR
I'd like to, but I can't. I have too much homework.

go roller skating	go fishing	see a horror movie	study calculus together

11 | WRITING

Write three short requests: to a classmate, a company, and a person you live with. Use the ideas in the box or your own ideas.

A Classmate	A Company	A Person You Live With
• help you with some work	• send you something	• buy some food
• lend you something	• return your money	• feed the fish
• explain something to you		• water the plants
		• get the mail

(continued)

Examples

> To whom this may concern:
>
> I bought a D.E. telephone last month. I'm enclosing a copy of my receipt. I lost the User's Guide that came with the phone. Could you please send me another one?
>
> Thank you.
>
> Sincerely yours,
> Bill Smiley

> Juan,
>
> I missed writing class
> yesterday. Could you please
> lend me your notes?
> Thanks a lot.
> Bill

> Mark,
> I won't be home until late
> tonight. Could you please feed
> the cat?
> Thanks a lot.
> Bill

12 | ON THE INTERNET

 *E-mail an invitation to a friend. Ask for a favor in your invitation.*

> Dear Suki,
>
> I hope you can come to my birthday party. It's this Saturday. The party will be at Hunan Palace at eight o'clock. Could you please send me Maki's e-mail address or phone number? I'd like to invite her too, but I don't have any way to reach her.
>
> Thanks so much. I look forward to seeing you.
> Sali

Advice: *Should, Shouldn't, Ought to, Had Better,* and *Had Better Not*

Grammar in Context

BEFORE YOU READ

Discuss this situation.

Imagine you're planning a business trip to Chile. When should you go? Imagine you're at a business meeting in Chile. Six people are at the meeting. Should you shake hands with everyone? Should you greet everyone, but not shake hands? Should you hug anyone?

🎧 *Read advice to people doing business in Chile, Egypt, and Hungary.*

GL🌐BAL BUSINESS

Doing Business in Chile

Chileans usually take vacations in January and February. You **should not plan** a business trip during those two months. Many offices will be closed for the summer vacation.

When attending a business meeting in Chile, you **ought to greet** and **shake hands** with everyone. At business dinners and receptions, men sometimes greet other men with hugs. Women often hug and touch cheeks while kissing the air. You **should not be** surprised to get a hug or kiss from a Chilean you know. When you eat, you **should keep**

your hands on the table, not in your lap.

In Chile, an open palm with the fingers separated means "stupid." You **should avoid** making this

gesture. And beware! Slapping your right fist into your left open palm is very impolite. You**'d better not make** that gesture, or you may insult or anger someone.

Doing Business in Egypt

In Egypt, you **should not expect** to do business on Fridays. It is the Muslim day of rest. Throughout the Arab world, people use the Arabic and the Western calendar. To avoid confusion, you **should put** two dates on paperwork —the Gregorian (Western) date and the Hijrah (Arabic) date.

If you're invited for a meal, you **should eat** with your right hand since the left hand is considered unclean. Leaving a little food is a sign that you are full, so you **shouldn't eat** everything on your plate. You**'d better not add** salt to your food, or you might insult the cook.

You **should** never **sit** with legs crossed or **show** the sole of your shoe. In Arab culture, it is an insult to show the bottom of the foot.

Doing Business in Hungary

You **should avoid** planning a business trip to Hungary during July and August and from mid-December to mid-January. These are holiday and vacation periods.

In Hungary, you **should be** on time in all business matters: You **should not be** late for appointments; you **should**

always **pay** on time, and you **should make sure** you keep the date you promise for deliveries.

You **should address** all adults by their titles and family names, unless you are asked not to. In Hungary, the family name is listed before the first name. For example, in Hungary the musician Béla Bartók is Bartók Béla. Foreign names, however, are listed in the order that is customary in their country of origin.

It **shouldn't surprise** you to get an invitation to go horseback riding. Horseback riding is a popular sport in Hungary.

AFTER YOU READ

Read the statements. Mark **C** *(Chile),* **E** *(Egypt), or* **H** *(Hungary).*

_____ **1.** You don't plan business meetings on Friday.

_____ **2.** You shake the hands of all the people in a room.

_____ **3.** You don't say, "Please pass the salt."

_____ **4.** You see the name Juhasz Francis. You address the person, Mr. Juhasz.

_____ **5.** You leave a little food on your plate.

_____ **6.** You don't plan a trip in July.

Grammar Presentation

MODALS

SHOULD, *SHOULDN'T*, AND *OUGHT TO*

Affirmative and Negative Statements			
Subject	***Should/Ought to***	**Base Form of Verb**	
I You He She We You They	**should** **should not** **(shouldn't)** **ought to**	**shake**	hands.
It		**be**	a surprise.

Yes / No Questions			
Should	**Subject**	**Base Form of Verb**	
Should	we he they	**wear**	a suit?

Short Answers					
Affirmative			**Negative**		
Yes,	you he they	**should.**	No,	you he they	**shouldn't.**

Wh- Questions			
***Wh-* Word**	***Should***	**Subject**	**Base Form of Verb**
What	**should**	I	**do?**
When		we	**go?**

(continued)

HAD BETTER AND *HAD BETTER NOT*

Affirmative and Negative Statements			
Subject	*Had Better*	Base Form of Verb	
We	**had better** ('d better)	**take**	an umbrella.
You	**had better not** ('d better not)	**wear**	jeans.

Contractions	
I had better → **I'd better**	we had better → **we'd better**
you had better → **you'd better**	you had better → **you'd better**
he had better → **he'd better**	they had better → **they'd better**
she had better → **she'd better**	

GRAMMAR NOTES

EXAMPLES

1. Use *should* to **give advice** or **talk about what is right to do**.

Should is followed by the base form of the verb.

Use *should not* for the negative.

Use the contraction *shouldn't* in speaking and informal writing.

- We **should bring** flowers.

- He should **bring** them a gift.
  NOT: He should ~~to bring~~ them a gift.
  NOT: He should ~~brings~~ them a gift.
- We **should not** bring roses.

- We **shouldn't** bring roses.

2. We use *should* to talk about the **present** or **future**.

- You **should** do the report **now**.
- You **should** turn in the report **tomorrow**.

3. *Ought to* means the same as *should*.

Ought to is not usually used in questions or negatives. We use *should* instead.

USAGE NOTES: To sound more polite, use *I think* or *Maybe* before saying, "you should" or "you ought to."

- You **ought to read** that book. It's very helpful.
- Should I wear a suit?
- **I think you should** bring a small gift.
- **Maybe you ought to** ask him first.

4. Use *had better* to **give advice**. *Had better* is stronger than *should*. It implies that something bad might happen if you don't follow the advice.

Had better is followed by the base form of the verb.

The negative of *had better* is **had better not**.

We often use the short form *'d better* in speaking and informal writing.

- You had better **call** before you go to the store. (*It may be closed.*)
- He **had better not** forget his passport. (*He needs it to get into that country.*)
- We**'d better ask** the doctor.

5. *Had better* is used to talk about the **present** or the **future**. (The *had* in *had better* does not refer to the past.)

- I**'d better** finish my homework now.
- She**'d better not** miss the test tomorrow.

Focused Practice

1 │ DISCOVER THE GRAMMAR

Business cards are important in Japan. They are generally presented at a first business meeting.

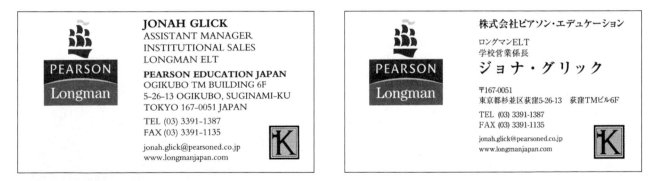

Read the questions and answers about business cards in Japan. Underline **should**, **had better**, **ought to**, *and the base form of the verb. Write the letter of the answer that matches the questions. Check your answers below.*

_____ 1. When should I present my business card?

_____ 2. Should I translate my card into Japanese?

_____ 3. What should I do when I get my colleague's card?

_____ 4. Is it OK to write on a colleague's business card?

a. Read it carefully and try and remember the information on it.

b. Right after you shake hands or bow.

c. No. You'd better not write on a business card. It isn't polite. You ought to handle a business card carefully and treat it with respect.

d. Yes. It's a good idea to have English on one side and Japanese on the other.

1.b 2.d 3.a 4.c

2 | CULTURAL DIFFERENCES

Grammar Notes 1–2

*International students at a North American school are talking about customs in their countries. Complete the sentences. Use **should** or **shouldn't** and the verb in parentheses.*

1. I was in the cafeteria with a group of students. A guy had a cold. He blew his nose at the table. In my country you _____ your nose at the table. It's very impolite.
   (blow)

2. In my country, you _____ people.
   (touch)
   Many people feel uncomfortable when others touch them. Here I notice people touch more often.

3. I think that people here don't like silence. Someone always speaks. I guess you
   _____ quiet.
   (be)

4. When we want a waiter to come, we usually clap our hands. My friend said I _____
   (do)
   that here. I think here you _____
   (wait)
   until the waiter looks at you. But sometimes the waiter never looks at me.

5. Here people often say, "We'll have to get together," or "I'll see you later." But they don't plan to meet me or see me later. In my opinion, they _____ that.
   (say)

6. In Poland, I walk arm in arm with my girlfriends. Here people don't do that. My friend said I _____ that here. It
   (do)
   may look funny, but I still do it. It's my custom.

3 | GOOD IDEAS

Grammar Note 3

Complete the sentences with **ought to**. *Choose from the verbs in the box.*

| become | ~~bring~~ | buy | congratulate | get | sell | send |

1. We're going to the Chens for dinner tomorrow night. We _____ *ought to bring* _____ a gift.

2. We had a wonderful time at their home. We _____ them a thank-you note.

3. I _____ Mr. Chen. His son graduated from law school last week.

4. We _____ the recipe for that soup. It was delicious.

5. She _____ a party planner. She's so good at giving parties.

6. They _____ their car. They hardly ever use it and it costs a lot to keep.

7. He _____ a laptop. Then he'll be able to work while he travels.

4 | ADVICE WITH *HAD BETTER*

Grammar Notes 4–5

Complete the sentences with **'d better** *or* **'d better not**.

1. He doesn't want to decide now on a return date for his flight. He _____ *'d better* _____ get an open-ended ticket.

2. It will cost a lot to fix the car. You _____ tell Dad about the accident now.

3. You _____ mail the letter from the post office. It has to be postmarked today.

4. I _____ forget my cell phone. I'm lost without it.

5. You _____ leave now. You don't want to miss the train.

6. We _____ hug them. They might feel uncomfortable. It's not their custom.

7. You _____ call and tell him that you're going to be late.

8. We _____ stop for gas. The tank is almost empty.

9. We _____ stop for gas. We don't have time now, and we don't want to be late.

5 | EDITING

A *Correct these conversations by adding **should** or **shouldn't** to each conversation. There are five mistakes. The first mistake is already corrected.*

1. A: Is that your watch?

    B: No, it's John's. I ^should^ return it. He may need it.

2. A: We're almost out of juice. We get some on the way home.

    B: You're right.

3. A: Careful. You have a bad back. You lift that heavy chair.

    B: You're right. I won't lift it.

4. A: When we leave for the party?

    B: At 9:00. The invitation is for 8:30, but we don't want to be the first ones there.

5. A: Those kids are throwing stones in the water. It's dangerous, because people are swimming.

    B: You're right. Someone tell them.

B *Correct these conversations by adding **'d better** or **'d better not** to each conversation. There are three mistakes.*

1. A: I missed the train this morning.

    B: You leave earlier tomorrow.

2. A: You leave town. We may want to speak to you again.

    B: Yes, officer.

3. A: What time does she go to sleep?

    B: Early. You call her after 10:30 at night.

Communication Practice

6 | LISTENING

 Listen to the conversation. Max is traveling to Japan. He asks his Japanese friends Sho and Kaori four questions. What are his questions? What are their answers?

1.   MAX: Should I bring _____?

     ANSWER: _____

2.   MAX: Should I _____?

     ANSWER: _____

3.   MAX: Should_____?

     ANSWER: _____

4.   MAX: _____?

     ANSWER: _____

7 | INFORMATION GAP: RESPONSES

Work in pairs.

Student B, turn to page 409.

Student A, read statements 1–3. Student B will respond.

Then Student B will read three statements. Choose the correct response from those below.

Statements

1. I never know what to say when someone sneezes.

2. He's a really nice guy. I'm going to get him a sympathy card.

3. When should I say, "Congratulations?"

Responses

a. You ought to say, "Excuse me."

b. You should say, "Where's the restroom?" It's more polite.

c. You should say, "Check, please."

8 | WRITING

A person wants to do business in a culture you know well. Give the person advice. You may want to write about the topics in the box.

asking questions	greetings / titles / forms of address
business cards	punctuality (being on time)
dress	saying "yes" or "no"
eating habits	tips
gifts	

Example

Tips for Doing Business in the United States

Managers and presidents of companies in the United States often tell people to call them by their first names. You shouldn't think it means you are close. It is a part of the culture. In a business relationship, you should first call a person by a title (Dr., Ms., or Mr.) with the last name, and wait for that person to tell you how he or she wants to be called.

In business, people often shake hands when they first meet. You should always give a firm handshake. The handshake should last about three seconds. Being on time is important in the United States. You ought to arrive on time for all business meetings, and you ought to try to meet deadlines.

Business people often go to restaurants. You'd better not whistle, clap hands, or snap fingers when you want to call a server in a restaurant. In the United States those gestures are rude. Instead, you should try to make eye contact.

9 | ON THE INTERNET

Look up information about business etiquette (manners) in a country other than your own. Compare a business practice from that country to one in your own culture. Report to the class.

Example: In Brazil you shouldn't give someone anything black or purple. These are colors of mourning. In my country it's OK to give someone something black or purple.

Necessity: *Have to, Don't Have to, Must, Mustn't*

Grammar in Context

BEFORE YOU READ

What do you have to do for your English class? Do you have to _____?

  a. do homework

  b. wear a uniform

  c. sit in the same seat for each class

  d. take tests

  e. answer questions in class

  f. do a class presentation

🎧 *Read about the requirements for a college history course.*

PROFESSOR: Welcome to American History 102. I'm Rich Anderson. This course covers the period from the American Civil War to the present day. There will be a midterm and a final exam. You **have to score** an average of 65 percent or above on both tests to pass this course. In addition there is a term paper. The term paper **must be** at least 10 pages, and you **have to include** a bibliography. The handout I'm passing out will explain the term paper. Now, are there any questions? . . . Yes?

STUDENT A: When is the term paper due?

PROFESSOR: You **have to hand** it **in** by the last day of class. That's December 15th. It **must not be** late. You should hand in an outline by the fourth week of the term. You can e-mail the outline. My e-mail address is on the board and on your handout. You **don't have to give** me a hard copy of the outline, but I would like a hard copy of your paper. Any other questions? . . . Yes?

STUDENT B: Last semester, we **didn't have to buy** a textbook. Is there a textbook for this course?

PROFESSOR: Yes. The textbook is called *American History from the Civil War to Today.*

STUDENT B: Who's the author?

PROFESSOR: I am.

STUDENT B: Do we **have to buy** the book?

PROFESSOR: Only if you want to pass.

AFTER YOU READ

Check (✓) what students in Professor Anderson's class have to do and don't have to do.

	1. Students have to:	2. Students don't have to:
a. take a quiz every week		
b. take a midterm and final exam		
c. give an oral report		
d. hand in an outline		
e. read four books for their term paper		
f. buy the textbook		

Grammar Presentation

MODALS

HAVE TO AND *DON'T HAVE TO*

Affirmative Statements			
Subject	*Have to / Has to*	**Base Form of Verb**	
I You	**have to**	take	a history class.
He She	**has to**		
We You They	**have to**		
It	**has to**	be	a three-credit class.

Negative Statements				
Subject	*Do Not / Does Not*	*Have to*	**Base Form of Verb**	
I You	**don't**	**have to**	take	a math class.
He She	**doesn't**			
We You They	**don't**			
It The report	**doesn't**	**have to**	be	10 pages long.

Yes / No Questions					Short Answers	

Do / Does	Subject	Have to	Base Form of Verb	
Do	I You			
Does	he she	**have to**	**read**	the whole book?
Do	you we they			
Does	It		**be**	a five-page report?

Affirmative	Negative
Yes, you do. Yes, I do.	No, you don't. No, I don't.
Yes, he does. Yes, she does.	No, he doesn't. No, she doesn't.
Yes, we do. Yes, you do. Yes, they do.	No, we don't. No, you don't. No, they don't.
Yes, it does.	No, it doesn't.

MUST AND MUSTN'T

Affirmative and Negative Statements			
Subject	**Must**	**Base Form of Verb**	
I You He She It We You They	**must** **must not** **(mustn't)**	**arrive**	early.

Past of *Have to* and *Must*			
Subject	**Had to**	**Base Form of Verb**	
I You He She It We You They	**had to**	**leave**	early.

GRAMMAR NOTES

EXAMPLES

1. Use **have to** and **must** to talk about things that are **necessary**. Both *have to* and *must* are followed by the base form of the verb.

   Must is stronger than *have to*.

   USAGE NOTE: We usually use *have to* in speaking and informal writing.

▶ BE CAREFUL! *Have to* is different from the verb *have*.

   NOTE: The past of *must* and *have to* is *had to*.

- I **have to take** a test next week.

- Students **must take** a three-credit history course.

- I **have** a psychology class.
- I **have to read** 50 pages for my psychology class.
- Last week I **had to buy** a lot of books for school.

(continued)

2. Use *don't have to* or *doesn't have to* when there is no necessity. You have a **choice**.

- I **don't have to sit** in the same seat every day. I can sit wherever I want.

- He **doesn't have to wear** a suit to work. He can wear slacks and a shirt.

3. *Must not* or the contraction *mustn't* means that you are **not allowed** to do something. You don't have a choice. You can't do it.

USAGE NOTE: We rarely use *mustn't* in conversation except when talking to small children or telling rules.

- You **must not take** scissors on a plane.

- Children, you **mustn't cross** the street when the signal is red.

Focused Practice

1 | DISCOVER THE GRAMMAR

Complete the sentences.

_____ 1. To drive,

_____ 2. To work here,

_____ 3. To be a writer,

_____ 4. To be an interpreter at the United Nations,

_____ 5. To practice medicine,

a. you must have a good ear for language.

b. you must have a medical degree, but you don't have to know Latin.

c. you must have a driver's license, but you don't have to know how to change a tire.

d. you need to have a college degree, and two years of experience.

e. you must speak three languages, but you don't have to have a degree in international affairs.

2 | THE VALUE OF TESTS

Grammar Note 1

Complete the conversation with **have**, **have to**, *or* **had to**.

A: Would you like to see that new Jim Carrey movie after lunch?

B: I can't. I _____ a test tomorrow. I _____ study this afternoon.

              1.   **2.**

A: What do you _____ study?

                     3.

B: Grammar. I _____ review the modals *can*, *could*, *would*, *might*, and *must*. We

              4.

_____ a test every Thursday.

  5.

A: Do you _____ memorize rules?
                    6.

B: No. We _____ use the grammar to answer questions. We really
                   7.

_____ understand it.
        8.

A: Do you get a lot of tests?

B: Uh-huh. We _____ a quiz after every unit. Actually, I like tests. I
                       9.

_____ review whatever we learn.
        10.

A: Well, to each his own. I don't like tests. Last year I _____ take a test every week
                                                                    11.

and I was always worried. It was terrible.

---

3 | IS THERE A CHOICE?   *Grammar Notes 1–2*

Complete the sentences with **have to**, **has to**, **don't have to**, *or* **doesn't have to** *and the verbs in the box.*

be	buy	do	hand in	~~pay~~	use	wear

1. We don't take checks. You _____*have to pay*_____ by credit card or cash.

2. You can't wear casual clothes to the interview. You _____ a suit.

3. This ticket is good any time this year. You _____ it today.

4. We _____ any homework tonight. Tomorrow is a school holiday.

5. He'd like to stay out later, but he _____ home before midnight.

6. She _____ the book. She can borrow it from the library.

7. Our term paper is due on the last day of class. We _____ our paper by December 15th.

4 | UNDERSTANDING SIGNS

Read these signs. Then explain them. Use the words in the box and begin with **You have to***,* **You must***, or* **You mustn't***.*

- drink the contents of this bottle
- enter this room
- ~~show identification to get in~~

- smoke on the train
- wear shoes in the restaurant

 I.D. Required

  No Smoking

1. *You have to show identification to get in.* OR

You must show identification to get in.

2. _____

_____

 Do Not Enter

Bay Beach Cafe No Bare Feet Allowed

3. _____

_____

4. _____

_____

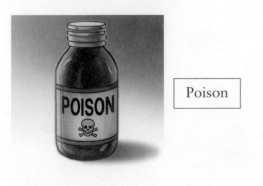 Poison

5. _____

_____

5 | EDITING

Correct these sentences. There are six mistakes. The first mistake is already corrected.

1. They never understand me. I ~~must~~ *have* to repeat everything three times.

2. Now that they are managers, they had to work late several times a week.

3. You mustn't sit in the last row. You can sit anywhere you like.

4. To get to the university, you have turn left at the third traffic light on this road.

5. You mustn't exceeds the speed limit. They give out a lot of traffic tickets here.

6. She have to finish her term paper this weekend. It's due on Monday.

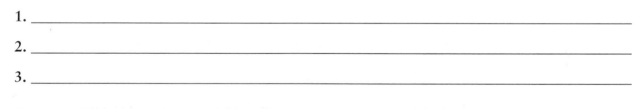

Communication Practice

6 | LISTENING

🎧 *Bill is in his third year of college. He is speaking to an advisor about graduate school. Listen to the conversation. Then write down what you have to do to get an MBA.*

1. _____

2. _____

3. _____

7 | THINGS TO DO

Complete the chart. Compare with a partner.

Things I have to do this month	Things I want to do this month	Things I don't have to do, but I should do this month
a.	a.	a.
b.	b.	b.
c.	c.	c.

8 | RULES

Work in small groups. Make a list of rules at different schools or workplaces. Use **have to**, **don't have to**, **must**, *and* **mustn't**.

Examples: At Kennedy Elementary School (grades 1–6), children have to wear uniforms.

At Public School 6, children mustn't run in the hallways.

At IBC company, the employees don't have to wear suits.

At IBC, employees must use all their vacation days in one year. They can't carry over their vacation days to the next year.

9 | WRITING

Write about an elementary school in the area where you grew up.

Example

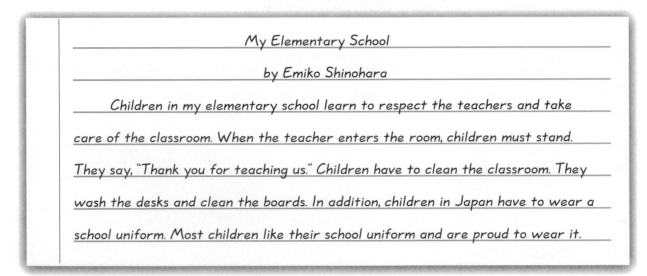

My Elementary School

by Emiko Shinohara

Children in my elementary school learn to respect the teachers and take care of the classroom. When the teacher enters the room, children must stand. They say, "Thank you for teaching us." Children have to clean the classroom. They wash the desks and clean the boards. In addition, children in Japan have to wear a school uniform. Most children like their school uniform and are proud to wear it.

10 | ON THE INTERNET

Choose a college or university in an English-speaking country. Look up the admission requirements for a bachelor's or graduate program, or a professional program (master's program, law school, or medical school). Report to the class.

From **Grammar** to **Writing**
Expressing and Supporting an Opinion

1 | *Read the following sentences. Write* **O** *next to sentences that express an opinion and* **F** *next to sentences that express a fact.*

_____ **1.** The average age at which people get married is increasing.

_____ **2.** I believe young children forget things quickly.

_____ **3.** The Himalayas are the highest mountains in the world.

_____ **4.** John was looking for a gift for his father all day Sunday.

_____ **5.** Children shouldn't watch violent videos.

Study the information about expressing and supporting an opinion.

EXPRESSING AND SUPPORTING AN OPINION

1. When you express your opinion, you can use: **In my opinion** **I believe** **I think** **better than /** **It's better to . . . than to** **should / shouldn't**	• **In my opinion**, it's wrong to spank a child. • **I believe** tests are harmful. • **I think** tests are helpful. • Some tests are **better than** others. • **It's better to** give **than to** receive. • Parents **shouldn't** spank their children.

2. After you express your opinion, give reasons to support your opinion. For example:

Opinion	Support
In my opinion, it's wrong to spank children.	When adults use physical force, children think physical force is okay.

2 Read the e-mail message and the response.

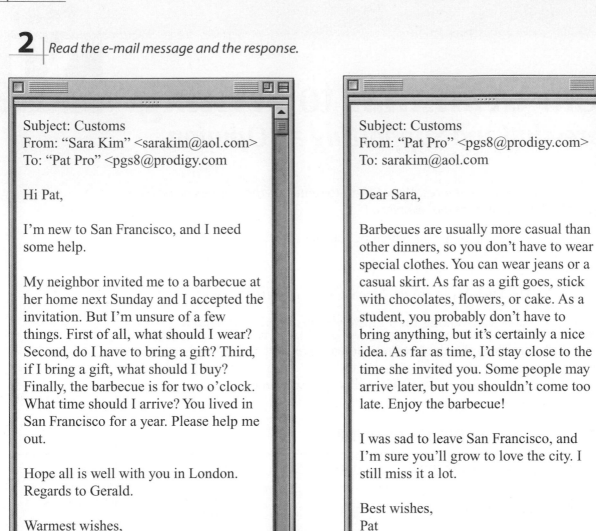

Subject: Customs
From: "Sara Kim" <sarakim@aol.com>
To: "Pat Pro" <pgs8@prodigy.com

Hi Pat,

I'm new to San Francisco, and I need some help.

My neighbor invited me to a barbecue at her home next Sunday and I accepted the invitation. But I'm unsure of a few things. First of all, what should I wear? Second, do I have to bring a gift? Third, if I bring a gift, what should I buy? Finally, the barbecue is for two o'clock. What time should I arrive? You lived in San Francisco for a year. Please help me out.

Hope all is well with you in London. Regards to Gerald.

Warmest wishes,
Sara

Subject: Customs
From: "Pat Pro" <pgs8@prodigy.com>
To: sarakim@aol.com

Dear Sara,

Barbecues are usually more casual than other dinners, so you don't have to wear special clothes. You can wear jeans or a casual skirt. As far as a gift goes, stick with chocolates, flowers, or cake. As a student, you probably don't have to bring anything, but it's certainly a nice idea. As far as time, I'd stay close to the time she invited you. Some people may arrive later, but you shouldn't come too late. Enjoy the barbecue!

I was sad to leave San Francisco, and I'm sure you'll grow to love the city. I still miss it a lot.

Best wishes,
Pat

3 Now read this e-mail message and respond to it. Give your opinion along with reasons to support it.

Subject: A birthday gift for a 15 year-old
From: "Joe Perry" <joeperry@aol.com>

Hi Ron,
I have a problem. It's my cousin's 15th birthday. He wants a new video game, and I want to get it for him, but his mother is very much against it. She thinks violent video games have a bad effect on young people. There is a lot of violence in this game. But my cousin is one of the most nonviolent young people I know. He never gets into fights. He's a good student. He has lots of friends. I think there's no reason not to get him what he wants. On the other hand, I don't want to get his mom angry. What do you think I should do?

Thanks for the advice.
Joe

Review Test

I *Circle the letter of the correct response.*

1. **A:** I lost my passport.   **A   B   C**

   B: _____

   (A) You'd like to report it right away.

   (B) You can report it right away.

   (C) You'd better report it right away.

2. **A:** I'd like to get a driver's license.   **A   B   C**

   B: _____

   (A) You have to pass a written test and a road test.

   (B) You should pass a written test and a road test.

   (C) You can pass a written test and a road test.

3. **A:** That medicine is important for my health.   **A   B   C**

   B: _____

   (A) You mustn't forget to take it every day.

   (B) You don't have to forget to take it every day.

   (C) You might forget to take it every day.

4. **A:** I don't have a computer.   **A   B   C**

   B: That's OK. _____

   (A) You mustn't use one for your composition.

   (B) You don't have to use one for your composition.

   (C) You might not use one for your composition.

(continued)

5. A: There's a No Parking sign on both sides of this street.   **A B C**

  B: _____

  (A) Where can we park?

  (B) Where ought we to park?

  (C) Where had we better park?

6. A: What do you want?   **A B C**

  B: _____

  (A) May you pass the butter?

  (B) Would you like to pass the butter?

  (C) Could you please pass the butter?

II   *Add **to** to the sentences if necessary.*

1. Would you like _____ try some of my pasta?

2. He ought _____ see a doctor.

3. She shouldn't _____ take so many pills.

4. He has _____ go to the dentist on Thursday.

5. You'd better not _____ wait for me. I won't be ready for a while.

6. When can I _____ return to work?

7. She has _____ two children.

8. He doesn't have _____ cook. There are many restaurants nearby.

9. We mustn't _____ use that computer.

10. You cannot _____ eat for 24 hours.

III *Complete the sentences. Use the affirmative or negative form of the words in parentheses.*

1. We _____ take the test now. We can take it next month if we prefer.
(have to)

2. His sister is in trouble. He _____ help her.
(should)

3. You _____ put metal in a microwave oven.
(must)

4. She _____ work this Sunday, but she will be off next Monday.
(have to)

5. I _____ buy a present today. The stores will be closed tomorrow.
(had better)

6. We _____ call and wish them a happy anniversary.
(ought to)

7. His old boots have holes. He _____ get some new ones.
(should)

8. You _____ forget to pay that bill. You don't want to pay a late fee.
(had better)

9. I _____ wear a suit. I can come in jeans.
(have to)

10. You must wear shoes in the lobby. You _____ go barefoot.
(can)

IV *Circle the correct word(s) to complete the conversation.*

ALI: What's the problem, Kemal?

KEMAL: It's my English homework. I <u>may / have to</u> write a three-page essay.
1.

ALI: When is it due?

KEMAL: We <u>have to / don't have to</u> hand it in until Thursday, but I'd like to finish it today.
2.

I <u>have / have to</u> a big soccer game tomorrow and I won't have much time for homework.
3.

ALI: What are you writing about?

KEMAL: That's the problem. I <u>can / had better</u> write about almost anything, and I <u>shouldn't / can't</u>
4.   5.

decide on a topic.

ALI: Write about soccer.

KEMAL: I <u>can / can't</u>. I wrote about it twice before. My teacher wants a new theme.
6.

ALI: Write about your trip to Alaska.

KEMAL: OK. That's a good idea.

V *Circle the correct sentence to complete the conversations.*

1. **A:** Could you help me with these math problems?

   B: I'd be glad to. / Yes, I could.

2. **A:** Would you like some more coffee?

   B: No, thanks. I'm full. / No, I wouldn't.

3. **A:** Would you lend me five dollars?

   B: No, I wouldn't. / I'm sorry. I can't right now.

4. **A:** Would you like some more lemonade?

   B: Yes, thanks. / I'd be glad to.

5. **A:** Can you please help me carry these boxes?

   B: Yes, thanks. / Sure.

VI *Correct the sentences.*

1. What should we doing about the missing book?

2. She ought to finds a better job.

3. May I to help you?

4. You mustn't talked about that in front of him.

5. Yesterday we have to work late.

6. Would please you help me?

7. When do we have be there?

▶ *To check your answers, go to the Answer Key on page RT-5.*

INFORMATION GAP FOR STUDENT B

Student B, ask Student A questions about playing tennis at Central Tennis Courts.

Example: STUDENT B: When can you use the courts?
STUDENT A: You can use the courts from April until October.

1. When can you use the courts?

2. Can anyone use the courts?

3. How many hours can I play?

4. Do I need special clothes?

5. Can I get a permit online?

Student B, read the information about Central Ice Skating Rink. Answer your partner's questions.

CENTRAL ICE SKATING RINK INFORMATION

1. The rink is open six days a week. It's closed on Mondays.

2. You can rent skates or bring your own.

3. You can't race in the rink.

4. You can watch the skaters and enjoy a delicious meal at the rink's coffee shop, but you may not bring food on the ice.

INFORMATION GAP FOR STUDENT B

Student A will read three statements. Choose the correct response from those below. Then read statements 1–3. Student A will respond.

Responses

a. We say it when someone graduates, gets married, or wins something.

b. You'd better not send him that type of card. We only send a sympathy card when a friend or relative of someone dies.

c. You should say, "Bless you."

Statements

1. What should I say when I want the bill in a restaurant?

2. When I'm in a restaurant and I don't know where the bathroom is, can I say, "Where's the toilet?"

3. When I want to interrupt someone, what should I say?

PART

XII

Comparisons

Grammar in Context

BEFORE YOU READ

Where would you prefer to live? In a big city? A small city? A suburb? The countryside? Why?

🎧 *Read about two U.S. cities called Portland. Which Portland would you prefer?*

A Tale of Two Portlands

Two U.S. cities are called Portland. One is in Maine and the other is in Oregon. Maine is on the East Coast of the United States, and Oregon is on the West Coast. Both Portlands have ports. Portland, Oregon is a little **farther from** the ocean. At 173 feet above sea level, it is also **higher** in elevation. Both cities are not very big, but they are **bigger than** any other city in their states. Portland, Maine has a population of about 64,000, whereas Portland, Oregon has a population of about 540,000. Winter in Oregon is a little **milder than** winter in Maine, but both cities have comfortable climates.

Portland, Maine is located on the coast, but the mountains are just 45 minutes away by car. So it's

Portland, Maine

easy to ski in the mountains or sunbathe on the beaches. Portland, Oregon is located on a river. It's a city of different neighborhoods with different personalities. It's **more diverse than** the other Portland.

Portland, Maine (founded in 1632), is a lot **older than** Portland, Oregon (founded in 1845). Why do the two cities have the same name? There's a very good reason. The two founders of Portland, Oregon wanted to name their new city after their hometowns. One man came from Boston, Massachusetts. The other came from Portland, Maine. They tossed a coin and the man from Portland, Maine won.

Portland, Oregon

AFTER YOU READ

Check (✓) the right Portland.

	Portland, Maine	Portland, Oregon
Which Portland has a bigger population?		
Which Portland is older?		
Which Portland has more diverse neighborhoods?		
Which Portland has warmer winters?		

Grammar Presentation

COMPARATIVES

ADJECTIVES

Comparative Forms of Adjectives				
		Comparative Adjective	*Than*	
Portland, Oregon	is	**bigger** **busier** **more crowded**	**than**	Portland, Maine.

Comparative Forms of Irregular Adjectives				
		Irregular Comparative Adjective	*Than*	
My map	is	**better** **worse**	**than**	yours.
My new office	is	**farther**		my old one.

QUESTIONS WITH *WHICH*

Which + Noun			
Which	Noun	Verb	Comparative Adjective
Which	city	is	bigger?
Which	restaurant	is	more expensive?

Which		
Which	Verb	Comparative Adjective
Which	is	bigger?
Which	is	more expensive?

GRAMMAR NOTES	**EXAMPLES**
1. Use the **comparative form of an adjective** + *than* to compare two people, places, or things.	• Alaska is **bigger than** Maine.

2. To form the comparative of most **short (one-syllable) adjectives**, add *-er* to the adjective. Add only *-r* if the adjective ends in *e*.	
long—longer	• The Mississippi River is **longer** than the Hudson River.
large—larger	
Exceptions:	
tired—more tired	• Today I'm **more tired** than I was yesterday.
bored—more bored	
fun—more fun	

3. To form the comparative of adjectives that end in a **consonant** + *y*, change the *y* to *i* and add *-er*.	
busy—busier	• Today the stores are **busier** than they were yesterday.
easy—easier	
heavy—heavier	

4. To form the comparative of most adjectives of **two** or **more syllables**, add *more* before the adjective.	
expensive—more expensive	• The train is **more expensive** than the bus.
intelligent—more intelligent	
Exceptions:	
quiet—quieter	• Is life in the countryside really **simpler** and **quieter**?
simple—simpler	

5. *Less* is the opposite of *more*.	• A car is more expensive than a bicycle. • A bicycle is **less** expensive than a car.

6. The adjectives *good*, *bad*, and *far* have irregular comparative forms. *good—**better*** *bad—**worse*** *far—**farther***	 • Our new apartment is **better** than our old one. • The book was bad, but the movie was **worse**. • The bus stop is **farther** than the train station.

7. Use *much* to make comparisons stronger.	• A two-bedroom apartment is **much** more expensive than a one-bedroom apartment. • He's **much** older than his brother.

8. USAGE NOTES: In formal English, use the subject pronoun after *than*. In informal English, you can use the object pronoun after *than*. ▶ BE CAREFUL! Always compare the same things. ▶ BE CAREFUL! Do not use two comparative forms together.	<div align="center">subject pronoun</div>• Steve's younger **than he** is.<div align="center">OR</div>• Steve's younger **than he**.<div align="center">object pronoun</div>• Steve's younger **than him**. • **John's home** is larger than **William's**.<div align="center">OR</div>• **John's home** is larger than **William's home**. NOT: John's home is larger than ~~William~~. NOT: John's home is ~~more~~ larger than William's.

9. Use *which* to ask about a comparison of **people**, **places**, or **things**.	• **Which city** is larger? • **Which** is larger, **Tokyo** or **Seoul**?

Reference Notes
See Unit 42, page 43 for a discussion of *not as* + adjective + *as*.
See Appendix 18, page A-19 for spelling rules for the comparative.

Focused Practice

1 | DISCOVER THE GRAMMAR

A *Read the conversations. Underline the comparative form of the adjectives.*

1. **A:** Which restaurant do you recommend, Trattoria or Amore?

   B: The food at Trattoria is <u>better</u>, but the service is worse.

2. **A:** Why do you want to live near the ocean?

   B: It's cooler in summer and warmer in winter.

3. **A:** They're looking for a less expensive place to live. Should they look in the city or the suburbs?

   B: Around here, apartments are usually less expensive in the suburbs.

4. **A:** Should I go to the post office today or tomorrow?

   B: Today. It's always busier on Saturday than it is on Friday.

5. **A:** Which park is bigger, East Park or West Park?

   B: East Park is bigger than West Park.

6. **A:** Which movie is more interesting, this drama or this documentary?

   B: The documentary is more interesting.

B *Write the eight adjectives used in the conversations.*

1. _____*good*_____   4. _____   7. _____

2. _____   5. _____   8. _____

3. _____   6. _____

2 | TWO CITIES
Grammar Notes 1, 3, 4, 8

Look at the chart. Compare these two cities. Use the words in parentheses.

	Middletown	Lakeville
number of people	100,000	50,000
average household income	$45,000	$42,000
average rent for a two-bedroom apartment	$1,100	$900
cost of a cup of coffee	$1.00	$.80
percent unemployed	4.5	5.8
number of hospitals	5	1
average summer temperature	78°F	70°F

1. (average household income / high)

The average household income in Middletown is higher than the average household income in Lakeville.

2. (two-bedroom apartment / expensive)

_____

3. (a cup of coffee / expensive)

_____

4. (probably / hard to find work)

_____

5. (probably / health care / bad)

_____

6. (summers / warm)

_____

3 | **QUESTIONS ABOUT GEOGRAPHY**   *Grammar Notes 2, 4, 6, 9*

Write comparative questions. Use a form of **be** *and the words given.*

1. be / Bangalore / big / London

Is Bangalore bigger than London?

2. Which / river / long / the Yangtze or the Nile / be

_____

3. be / Texas / big / Alaska

_____

4. Which country / far north / Korea or Thailand / be

_____

5. be / Which country / far west / France or Germany

_____

6. Which city / be / old / St. Petersburg, Russia or Brasilia, Brazil

_____

7. be / the Indian Ocean / big / Pacific Ocean

_____

8. be / Luxembourg / much / small / Argentina

_____

4 | APARTMENTS FOR RENT

A Look at these ads for apartments and look at the abbreviations (shortened spellings of some words).

APT 1- Main Street	**APT 2- Cedar Lane**
3rms/ lg bdrm/ older bldg/ center of town, walk to all, $1,000 mo.	4rms/ 2 bdrms, 2bths/ modern bldg/ quiet loc/ nr schools and parks, $1,300 mo.

B Write the abbreviations next to the word.

1. rooms _____*rms*_____

2. large _____

3. building _____

4. bedrooms _____

5. baths _____

6. near _____

7. month _____

8. location _____

C Write questions comparing the two apartments. Begin with "Which." Use the words in parentheses. Then answer the questions.

1. (large)

   Q: _Which apartment is larger?_____

   A: _The one on Cedar Lane._____

2. (expensive)

   Q: _____

   A: _____

3. (quiet)

   Q: _____

   A: _____

4. (modern)

Q: _____

A: _____

5. (close to schools and parks)

Q: _____

A: _____

D *Write questions comparing the two apartments. Give your opinion. Then give a reason why.*

1. (good for a couple with a child)

Q: _____

A: _____

2. (good for a single person)

Q: _____

A: _____

5 | EDITING

Correct these sentences. There are eight mistakes. The first one is already corrected.

1. Our new apartment is much more comfortable than our old one.

2. Florida is more hotter than Maine.

3. Oregon is far north than California.

4. A motorcycle is more fast than a bicycle.

5. These days I'm busier then I was last year at this time.

6. The climate in Tokyo, Japan is mild than the climate in Anchorage, Alaska.

7. Elephants are big than tigers.

8. Jake's apartment is more convenient than his sister.

Communication Practice

6 | LISTENING

 Listen to a man talk about his new home. Write three advantages and three disadvantages of the new home.

Advantages (Good Things)	Disadvantages (Bad Things)
1.	**1.**
2.	**2.**
3.	**3.**

7 | PREFERENCES AND REASONS

Work with a partner. Complete the chart. Tell your partner which you prefer. Explain why in a sentence with a comparative.

1. Two ways to travel	*bike*	*motorcycle*
2. Two kinds of movies		
3. Two kinds of restaurants		
4. Two kinds of _____ (your category)		

Example: A: Do you prefer to travel by bike or by motorcycle?

B: I prefer a motorcycle. It's faster and more exciting. What about you?

A: I prefer a bike. It's safer and better for the environment.

8 | COMPARING CITIES

Compare cities. Follow the steps.

1. Each student names a city he or she knows well. The teacher writes the names on the board. (Do not name the city you are in.)

2. The students say adjectives that describe cities, people, and climates. The teacher writes the adjectives on the board.

Examples

Cities	People	Climates
clean	friendly	warm
dangerous	polite	dry
exciting	relaxed	humid

3. Each student writes questions comparing the cities on the board to the city you are in. Students can use the adjectives on the board or choose their own. Then students ask each other questions comparing the cities.

Examples: (You are now in San Francisco)

    A: Is Paris cleaner than San Francisco?
    B: I don't think so. In my opinion, San Francisco is cleaner than Paris.

    C: Does Sapporo have a warmer climate than San Francisco?
    D: No, it doesn't. Sapporo has a colder climate than San Francisco.

9 | WRITING

Compare two movies with the same theme or compare a movie and its sequel. Which one do you prefer? Why?

    Example: The movie *Shrek 2* is better than *Shrek 1*. I prefer *Shrek 2* because the Antonio Banderas character, Puss in Boots, is funny and makes the movie more enjoyable.

10 | ON THE INTERNET

Look online for answers to the questions in Exercise 3.

Grammar in Context

BEFORE YOU READ

You are about to give a public speech. How do you feel?

_____ nervous but confident

_____ calm and confident

_____ nervous and not very confident

_____ I refuse to do it.

🎧 *Read an article about public speaking.*

Public Speaking
by Johnny Jones

Fifteen years ago I gave my first speech in front of a large audience. I wanted to sound smart, so I told a lot of facts. I used big words and long sentences. I spoke **seriously** and **fast**. I was afraid to tell a joke. I worked **hard** and I received polite applause, but I knew my speech was awful.

The next time I gave a speech, I asked a friend for help. She helped me to focus on three ideas and to give good examples. In my next speech I spoke **slowly** and **clearly**. I thought **carefully** about everything I wanted to say. I spoke **honestly** and I gave personal examples. I only said things I really believed. This time the applause was long and loud. I connected with the audience and I felt good. People gave me their time, and I gave them a speech to remember.

AFTER YOU READ

Check (✓) the advice you get from this article.

_____ 1. Speak quickly.

_____ 2. Speak slowly.

_____ 3. Use big words.

_____ 4. Sound serious.

_____ 5. Use humor.

_____ 6. Don't use humor.

_____ 7. Have many ideas, not just three or four.

_____ 8. Speak briefly.

Grammar Presentation

ADVERBS OF MANNER

Adjective + *-ly*	
Adjective	Adverb
accurate	**accurately**
bad	**badly**
careful	**carefully**
clear	**clearly**
fluent	**fluently**
free	**freely**
loud	**loudly**
neat	**neatly**
nervous	**nervously**
quick	**quickly**
quiet	**quietly**
sarcastic	**sarcastically**
serious	**seriously**
slow	**slowly**

Same Adjective and Adverb Form	
Adjective	Adverb
early	**early**
fast	**fast**
hard	**hard**
late	**late**
long	**long**

Irregular Adverb Form	
Adjective	Adverb
good	**well**

GRAMMAR NOTES

EXAMPLES

1. Adverbs of manner describe action verbs. They say **how** or in what manner something happens. The adverb often comes at the end of the sentence.

- She spoke **slowly**.
- He walked **fast**.

(continued)

2. Most adverbs of manner are formed by adding **-ly** to an adjective.	adjective • She's a **careful** driver. adverb • She drives **carefully**.
▶ **BE CAREFUL!** Some words that end in *-ly* are adjectives, not adverbs. Examples: *lively, lovely, ugly, lonely,* and *friendly.* These adjectives have no adverb form.	adjective • She's a **friendly** person. • It's a **lonely** job.

3. Some **adverbs** of manner have the **same form** as **adjectives**.	• She's a **hard** worker. She works **hard**.

4. *Well* is the adverb for the adjective *good*. *Well* is also an adjective that means "in good health." USAGE NOTE: In very informal speaking, when people ask, "How are you?" some people respond, "I'm good."	adjective • She's a **good** speaker. adverb • She speaks **well**. adjective • I feel **well**.

5. Linking verbs are followed by **adjectives**, not adverbs. Common linking verbs are: *appear, be, become, feel, look, seem, smell, sound,* and *taste*.	linking verb adjective • These eggs **taste good**. NOT: The eggs taste ~~well~~. • She **seems sad**. • It **sounds beautiful**.

Focused Practice

1 | DISCOVER THE GRAMMAR

Read the paragraph. Underline four more adverbs in the paragraph.

A public speaker should remember three things: to entertain, to instruct, and to inspire. Author Bob Rosner likes to say, "It's ha-ha, and ah-hah." When you instruct, speak briefly and clearly. Don't speak too long. And don't speak too fast. Use humor frequently. It helps your audience relax. And remember that great speeches inspire and move an audience. Know your audience and touch their emotions.

2 | HOW?

Underline the adverb in each sentence. Then write the adjective form.

1. He spoke <u>quickly</u>. _____*quick*_____

2. Sally writes well. _____

3. They speak Spanish fluently. _____

4. She dresses neatly. _____

5. He drove fast. _____

6. Did he drive dangerously? _____

7. Who sang badly? _____

8. The story began slowly. _____

9. It rained hard last night. _____

10. How carefully does he work? _____

3 | ADJECTIVE OR ADVERB?

Complete each conversation. Choose the correct adjective or adverb in parentheses.

1. **A:** How was the debate?

   B: Good. Both sides spoke _____.
   (good / well)

2. **A:** How's the melon?

   B: It tastes _____.
   (good / well)

3. **A:** That's a _____ picture.
   (beautiful/beautifully)
   B: Thanks.

4. **A:** How did he do on the last test?

   B: Not _____.
   (good / well)

5. **A:** Please open the door _____.
   (slow / slowly)
   B: OK.

6. **A:** How was the play?

   B: The first act was very _____, but the second act was better.
   (slow / slowly)

7. **A:** How did she sound?

   B: _____.
   (Nervous / Nervously)

4 | EDITING

Correct these conversations. There are six mistakes. The first mistake is already corrected.

1. **A:** How did he do?

   B: He did ~~good~~. *well*

2. **A:** Was the food OK?

   B: Everyone loved it. It really tasted well.

3. **A:** Is Harry a good driver?

   B: I don't think so. He drives too slow.

4. **A:** How did they do?

   B: They worked hardly and did well.

5. **A:** How did she seem after her speech?

   B: She seemed excited.

6. **A:** Did you hear him?

   B: No, I didn't. He spoke too soft.

7. **A:** How's the audience?

   B: They seem friendly.

8. **A:** How did she sound?

   B: A little nervously.

Communication Practice

5 | LISTENING

🎧 *In English, the way you speak can change the meaning of a sentence. Do you know what the words in the box mean? If not, use your dictionary. Then listen to the speakers. How is each one talking? Choose from the words in the box.*

angrily	convincingly	questioningly	sadly	sarcastically

1. He is speaking _____.

2. She is speaking _____.

3. He is speaking _____.

4. She is speaking _____.

5. He is speaking _____.

6 | INTONATION AND MEANING

Work with a partner. Take turns reading the sentence: **I love English grammar**. *Read it in the manner listed.*

1. fast	**6.** questioningly
2. slowly	**7.** convincingly
3. nervously	**8.** loudly
4. angrily	**9.** sarcastically
5. happily	**10.** sadly

7 | WRITING

A *Work in pairs. Tell about a speech you've heard.*

Who was the speaker?

What was the speech about?

How did the person speak?

How did the audience respond?

B *Now write about the speech. Use three or more adverbs of manner.*

Example: Two years ago my high school soccer team lost the championship. It was because of one player. The team was unhappy about losing. The team treated that player badly. Our coach, Al Greene, gave a speech about winning and losing. In his speech he told us about his own high school soccer team. The score was tied. He made a big mistake and the other team scored the winning goal. He never wanted to play again. But his team's captain spoke up. He said, "Al played well. He was just unlucky." Our coach spoke sincerely. He reminded us that winning isn't everything. He gave a great speech. I'll never forget it because I was the player who lost the game for our team.

8 | ON THE INTERNET

C *Look up a recent sports event such as the World Cup in soccer, the Wimbledon tennis tournament, the Kentucky Derby, the Tour de France bicycle race, or the Boston Marathon. How did different people, teams, or animals perform? Report to the class.*

Grammar in Context

BEFORE YOU READ

A perfectionist tries to do a perfect job. It's good to try to do one's best, but being a perfectionist may not always be good. Why?

🎧 *Read a conversation between friends. Sally and Penny are at a fruit and vegetable store. Sally is trying to pick a honeydew melon.*

YOU'RE MUCH TOO FUSSY

PENNY: Sally, are you ready? It's getting late.

SALLY: Just a minute. I can't find a good melon.

PENNY: Why not? There are so many. They all look good to me. Here's a nice one.

SALLY: No. That one's way **too small**.

PENNY: What about this one here?

SALLY: No. It's about **the same size as** the other one.

PENNY: Well, here's one. Is it **big enough**?

SALLY: It's **too big**.

PENNY: Take the one in the corner. It's the right size.

SALLY: Hmm. You're right, but feel it. It's **very soft**. Actually, I think it's **too soft**. It may be overripe.

PENNY: OK. Here. This one is harder.

SALLY: It's **too hard**.

PENNY: Sally, you're **much too fussy**. After all, it's just a melon!

AFTER YOU READ

Sally finds problems with some melons. Check (✓) her complaints.

_____ **1.** One is not big enough.

_____ **2.** One is too big.

_____ **3.** One is too late.

_____ **4.** One is not hard enough.

_____ **5.** One is too expensive.

_____ **6.** One is too soft.

_____ **7.** One is too fussy.

Grammar Presentation

ENOUGH; TOO / VERY; AS + ADJECTIVE + *AS; SAME / DIFFERENT*

Adjective + *Enough*			
	Adjective	*Enough*	**(Infinitive)**
The melon is	**ripe**	**enough**	(to eat).
It wasn't	**dark**		(to see the stars).

Very + **Adjective**		
	Very	**Adjective**
It's	**very**	**expensive**.

Too + **Adjective**			
	Too	**Adjective**	**(Infinitive)**
That job was	**too**	**difficult**	(to do).

As + **Adjective** + *As*			
	As	**Adjective**	*As*
This melon is	**as**	**small**	**as** an orange.
This melon isn't		**tasty**	the other one.

The Same As		
My first name is	**the same as**	yours.
My initials are		his.

Different From		
The new edition is	**different from**	the old one.
These books are		those.

(continued)

The Same + Noun (Noun Phrase) + As				
	The Same	Noun	*As*	
My bag is		**size**		yours.
My hair is		**length**		his.
My eyes are		**color**		my brother's.
My suitcase was	**the same**	**weight**	**as**	theirs.
My brother is		**height**		my father.
Irene Stone has		**initials**		Inez Sanchez.
Jim likes		**kind of movies**		I do.

GRAMMAR NOTES

EXAMPLES

1. ***Enough*** means "sufficient." It has a positive meaning.

Use *enough* after an adjective.

Use *enough* before a noun.

> adjective
> • He's **old enough** to drive.

> noun
> • There are **enough chairs**.

2. ***Too*** means "more than necessary." It has a negative meaning. Use *too* before an adjective.

Much too or ***way too*** makes the meaning stronger.

USAGE NOTE: We use *way too* in informal speaking and writing.

A: What's wrong?
B: The coffee is **too hot**. I burned my tongue.
• The soup was **much too cold**. We sent it back.
• This sweater is **way too big**. I wear size small. This one is a large.

3. An **infinitive** can follow **an adjective +** *enough*.

An **infinitive** can follow *too* **+ an adjective**.

> infinitive
> • He's **old enough to drive**.

> • She's **too tired to drive**.

4. *Very* makes the meaning of an adjective stronger. *Very* comes before an adjective.

- He's **very tall**.

▶ BE CAREFUL! *Too* has a negative meaning, but *very* doesn't.

- He's **very young**. *(He's really young. He's 16 and the other students are 18.)*
- He's **too young**. *(He's too young to do something—to drive, to work, etc.)*

---

5. Use *as* + **adjective** + *as* to show how two people, places, or things are alike.

- Sally is **as tall as** Paula. They're the same height.

Use *not as* + **adjective** + *as* to show how two people, places, or things are not alike.

- Sally is **not as tall as** Mike. Mike is taller.

---

6. Use *the same as* for things that are alike.

- His family name is **the same as** hers. *(He's Robert Lee and she's Jennifer Lee.)*

Use *different from* for things that are not alike.

- My book is **different from** yours. *(I have a new edition.)*

Focused Practice

1 | DISCOVER THE GRAMMAR

Match the sentences.

__d__	**1.** I couldn't wear that sweater. I wear a large. It was a medium.	**a.** He's different from his wife.
_____	**2.** He complains about everything.	**b.** It isn't as hard as it seems.
_____	**3.** They didn't like the soup.	**c.** He's too fussy.
_____	**4.** Adam Rusk and Ali Rogers have just one thing in common.	**d.** It was too small.
_____	**5.** They say that opposites attract.	**e.** It wasn't spicy enough.
_____	**6.** Try that puzzle.	**f.** They have the same initials.

2 | WORD-ORDER PRACTICE

Grammar Notes 1–3

Write sentences using the words given.

1. to vote / She isn't / enough / old

She isn't old enough to vote.

2. hot / swimming / to go / It isn't / enough

_____

3. too / This steak / is / to eat / tough / much

_____

4. to see / you / The doctor / busy / is / too / today

_____

5. weren't / the sofa bed / They / enough / strong / to move

_____

6. much / restaurant / too / That / expensive / is

_____

7. too / was / to miss / That meeting / important

_____

8. before the movie / have / don't / time / enough / We / to eat

_____

9. clear / wasn't / to read / His address / enough

_____

10. long / The / too / movie / was / way

_____

11. seats / weren't / enough / There

_____

3 | **HOW ARE THEY ALIKE?**   *Grammar Note 6*

Look at the licenses. Find five similarities. Choose from the items in the box.

city	expiration date	height	license number	weight
~~color eyes~~	family name	initials	state	

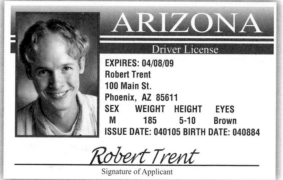

1. _____Russ Tran_____ and _____Robert Trent_____ have _____the same color eyes_____.

2. _____ and _____ are _____.

3. _____ and _____ have _____.

4. _____ and _____ come from _____.

5. _____'s and _____'s licenses have _____.

4 | TOO OR VERY?

Complete the sentences with **too** *or* **very**.

1. Don't wear that skirt. It's ___*too*___ short to wear to a job interview.

2. That's a great painting. The faces are _____ interesting.

3. He can't reach the shelf. He's _____ short. Ask Ali. He's _____ tall.

4. Your composition is _____ well written. You did a great job.

5. I can't lift the sofa. It's _____ heavy. I'll ask Barry. He's _____ strong and _____ helpful.

6. We can't vote. We're _____ young.

7. It's _____ cold outside. Wear a warm jacket.

8. It's _____ difficult to get into that school. Only a small number of the applicants are accepted.

9. This jacket doesn't fit. It's _____ tight in the shoulders.

5 | LOU DIDN'T GET A PROMOTION

Lou is a graphic artist at an advertising agency. He is upset because he did not get a promotion. He is talking to his friend Sally. Complete the conversation between Sally and Lou. Use the phrases in the box.

> as fast and dependable
>
> as hard as she does
>
> as talented as she is
>
> the same amount of experience as she does
>
> the same university as Mary

SALLY: Lou, what's wrong?

LOU: I'm really angry. I didn't get a promotion and Mary did. I work _____.
                                                  1.

SALLY: And you really are talented.

LOU: Thanks. I'm certainly _____.
                                             2.

SALLY: That's true.

LOU: And I hand in every project on time. I'm just _____.
                                             3.

SALLY: What about her background and experience?

LOU: We've got the same degrees. I even went to _____. And I
have _____. I think she got the promotion because she's
a woman.

SALLY: What? That's a switch. It's usually just the opposite.

6 | EDITING

Correct these sentences. There are 10 mistakes. The first mistake is already corrected.

1. Is your new book bag ~~enough big~~ *big enough* for all your books?

2. My new apartment isn't as quiet than my old one.

3. She's very different than her sister.

4. We're very young to vote. You have to be 18 years old. We're 17.

5. She has the same sweater than I do.

6. I'm as taller as my father.

7. Dan's weight is the same as his brother.

8. She wasn't enough old to drive.

9. Sally isn't friendly as Penny.

10. He doesn't have money enough to pay for all those things.

Communication Practice

7 | LISTENING

🎧 *Two managers are talking about their employees Mary and Lou. Listen to their conversation. Read the statements. Then listen again and write **M** (Mary) or **L** (Lou) next to the person they are talking about.*

_____ 1. This person got a promotion.

_____ 2. This person is bright and confident.

_____ 3. This person is too critical of others.

_____ 4. This person thinks nobody's work is good enough.

_____ 5. This person's word is as good as gold.

_____ 6. This person is very fair.

_____ 7. This person is a team player.

8 | ALL ABOUT YOU

Work in pairs. Write sentences about yourself. Choose from the words in the boxes and the sentences below.

Example: I'm not too proud to ask my friends for help.

Read them to your partner.

busy	lazy	proud	shy	tired

I'm too _____ to _____

I'm not too _____ to _____

old	smart	strong	tall	young

I'm _____ enough to _____

I'm not _____ enough to _____

9 | EXPRESSIONS

A *Complete the sentences. Check your answers.*

a. mouse

b. horse

c. gold

d. honey

e. feather

f. cucumber

1. She's bright, but she never says a word. She just sits and smiles. She's as quiet as a
   ____mouse____.

2. That furniture is very heavy. You have to be as strong as a _____ to lift it.

3. He never shouts or gets angry. He's as cool as a _____.

4. That girl is rude and out of control, but her little brother is just the opposite. He's as sweet as

_____.

5. She doesn't weigh much at all. She's as light as a _____.

6. You can believe her. She's very honest. Her word is as good as _____.

B *Write sentences about people you know. Use the phrases* **as . . . as . . .** *Read your sentences to the class.*

10 | SIMILARITIES

Take five minutes. Walk around your classroom. Find classmates who are like you in some way. Take notes. Report to the class. The person who finds the most similarities wins.

Examples: Cecilia and I were born in the same month.
Julio and I have the same color eyes.
Ming and I like the same kind of movies.
Pierre and I have the same number of sisters.
Jasmine and I have the same lucky number.

Suggestions

Born	Looks	Likes	Families	Your Ideas
same month same year same day	same color eyes same color hair same height	same kind of movies/music/ sports	same number of brothers/sisters	?

11 | WRITING

Look around your classroom. Describe an object. The class guesses the object. Use **as . . . as . . .** , **very**, **too**, **enough**, *and* **the same as**.

Example: A: This is something you use to hold things. It comes in different sizes and colors. This one is not as big as our grammar book, but it's big enough to hold two carrots. This one is the same color as Philippe's jacket, a dark brown. It's very old and worn, but it's not too old to use. It's made of soft leather and it's practical. Can you guess what it is?
B: Is it Yosef's pencil case?
A: Yes, it is.

12 | ON THE INTERNET

 *Look up biographies of famous people who were born in the same year as you. Are there any other similarities between you and those people?*

43 | The Superlative

Grammar in Context

BEFORE YOU READ

What do you know about penguins? Answer **T** (true) or **F** (false).

_____ They live south of the equator.

_____ They can weigh up to 90 pounds.

_____ English explorers were the first to see them.

🎧 *Read an article about penguins from* Science Magazine.

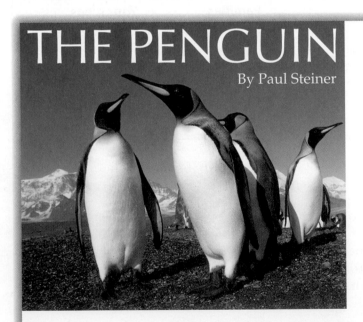

THE PENGUIN
By Paul Steiner

The penguin is one of **the funniest** birds and one of **the easiest** birds to recognize. Penguins have black backs and white bellies. They look fat. They stand upright and they waddle. Unlike most other birds, penguins can't fly, but they can swim very fast.

The name *penguin* came from Spanish explorers. The explorers saw penguins when they sailed around South America in 1519. They thought this type of bird was one of **the strangest** birds in the world. To them, the penguins looked like another strange bird, the great auk of Greenland and Iceland. The great auk was a large black and white bird that did not fly. The Spanish word for great auk is *pinguis* which means "fat."

There are 17 kinds of penguins. They all live below the equator. Little blue penguins (sometimes called fairy penguins) are

the smallest of all. They are 16 inches (about 41 centimeters) tall and weigh only 2 pounds (about 1 kilogram). They got their name because of their indigo-blue feathers. These penguins live in the warm waters off southern Australia and New Zealand.

The largest penguin is the emperor penguin. It stands almost 4 feet (about 1.2 meters) tall and weighs from 70 to 90 pounds (about 32 to 41 kilograms). The emperor penguin lives on the ice around the Antarctic continent. This is **the coldest** climate on earth.

People say penguins are **the cutest, the funniest,** and **the most loved** birds. They also say they're **the most formal**. Do you know why? It's because they look as if they're wearing tuxedos.

AFTER YOU READ

Write the answer next to the phrase. Use the words in the box.

the Antarctic	emperor penguins	Greenland and Iceland	little blue penguins

1. The biggest penguins: _____

2. The smallest penguins: _____

3. The coldest place on earth: _____

4. Home of the great auk: _____

Grammar Presentation

SUPERLATIVE FORMS OF ADJECTIVES

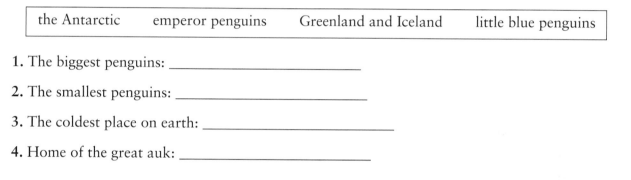

Superlative Forms of Adjectives			
		Superlative Adjective	
The emperor penguin		**the biggest**	of all the penguins.
That photo	is	**the funniest**	of all.
That program		**the most interesting**	one on TV.

Superlative Forms of Irregular Adjectives			
		Superlative Adjective	
This	is	**the best**	photo of all.
We	had	**the worst**	weather on Saturday.
Her home	is	**the farthest**	of all.

GRAMMAR NOTES	EXAMPLES
1. Use the **superlative** form of adjectives to compare three or more people, places, or things.	• The Dead Sea is **the lowest** place on earth.

2. To form the superlative of **short (one-syllable) adjectives**, add *the* before the adjective and *-est* to the adjective. *fast—the fastest* *long—the longest* If the adjective ends in *e*, add *-st*. *large—the largest*	• The cheetah is **the fastest** animal on earth. • Alaska is **the largest** state in the United States.

3. To form the superlative of **two-syllable adjectives that end in y**, add *the* before the adjective, then drop the *y* and add *-iest* to the adjective. *funny—the funniest*	• The penguin is **the funniest** bird in the zoo.

4. To form the *superlative of* **long adjectives**, use *the most* before the adjective. *interesting—the most interesting* *dangerous—the most dangerous*	• The bird section was **the most interesting** part of the zoo.

5. These adjectives have **irregular comparative** and **superlative** forms: 	ADJECTIVE	COMPARATIVE FORM	SUPERLATIVE FORM
---	---	---
good	*better (than)*	*the best*
bad	*worse (than)*	*the worst*
far	*farther (than)*	*the farthest*		• It is **the best** time of year for hiking. • That was **the worst** time of his life. • His home is **the farthest** from school.

6. After the superlative, we often use a **prepositional phrase** to identify the group we are talking about.	• He's the tallest **in the class**. • He's the strongest **of all the animals**.

7. *One of the* often comes before a **superlative adjective**. The adjective is followed by a **plural noun**.	• It is **one of the largest animals** in the world. • It is **one of the most intelligent animals** of all. Not: It is one of the largest ~~animal~~.

8. **Be careful!** Do not use two superlative forms together.	• It's the biggest. Not: It's the ~~most~~ biggest. • It's the most important. Not: It's the most ~~importantest~~.

Reference Note
See Appendix 18, page A-19 for spelling rules with the superlative.

Focused Practice

1 | DISCOVER THE GRAMMAR

Read the statements in Exercise A.

A *Underline the superlative form of the adjectives.*

1. The Berlin Zoo is <u>the largest</u> zoo in the world.

2. The cobra is one of the most venomous snakes.

3. In northern countries, winter is the coldest season of the year.

4. The Nile River is the longest river in the world.

5. Pluto is usually the farthest planet from the sun.

6. Mount Everest is the highest mountain in the world.

B *Write the adjectives.*

1. *large*   3. _____   5. _____

2. _____   4. _____   6. _____

C *Write two prepositional phrases that identify the group.*

1. *in the world* _____

2. _____

2 | ANIMAL FACTS

Complete the sentences with the superlative adjective form. Then guess the animal from the choices in the box. Check your answers below.

a. the African elephant	**d.** the giraffe	**f.** the macaroni penguin
b. apes and monkeys	**e.** the hummingbird	**g.** the sailfish
c. the blue whale		

_____ 1. It is both _____the biggest_____ and _____ animal in the
                              (big)   (loud)

world.

_____ 2. It is _____ land animal.
                      (large)

_____ 3. It is _____ animal today.
                     (tall)

_____ 4. It is _____ bird. It is as small as 6.2 centimeters (2.5 inches) long
                      (small)

and weighs only 1.6 grams (.06 ounces).

_____ 5. It is _____ fish. It swims up to 110 kilometers per hour (68 miles
                     (fast)

per hour).

_____ 6. It is the _____ of all the penguins. It has bright yellow feathers
                        (colorful)

on its head. English explorers gave it its name. In the mid-18th century a young man with

a flashy feather in his hat was called a "Macaroni."

_____ 7. Most scientists say that after humans, they are _____ animals,
                                                               (intelligent)

followed by dolphins and whales.

3 | IT'S ONE OF THE BEST ZOOS

Grammar Notes 1–5, 7

Complete the conversations. Use **one of the** with the superlative adjective and plural noun. Use the adjective and noun in parentheses.

1. **A:** Where were they?

   B: At the San Diego Zoo. It's _____*one of the most popular zoos*_____ in the United States.

(popular / zoo)

2. **A:** Is that a gorilla?

   B: Yes. It's _____ of all.

(smart / animal)

3. **A:** Did you enjoy the movie?

   B: Very much. It was _____ of the year.

(good / movie)

4. **A:** Traffic here is terrible.

   B: Not just here. Traffic is _____ in cities everywhere.

(big / problem)

5. **A:** I think it's below freezing.

   B: It is. It's _____ of the year.

(cold / day)

6. **A:** Does everyone in this town play soccer?

   B: Almost everyone. It's _____.

(popular / sport)

7. **A:** Do you do most of your business in December?

   B: Yes, we do. It's _____ of the year.

(busy / month)

4 | COMPARATIVE AND SUPERLATIVE

Grammar Notes 1–2, 4–6

Complete the sentences with the comparative or superlative form of the adjectives.

1. There are African elephants and Asian elephants. The Asian elephants have

   _____*smaller*_____ ears and _____ tusks than African ones. The

a. (small)   b. (short)
   African elephants are _____ and _____.

c. (big)   d. (tall)

2. Bear's milk is _____ of all milk from animals. It is 46 percent fat. This rich

(rich)
   milk allows the tiny baby to grow very fast.

3. _____ snake in the world is the blind snake. It reaches just 13 centimeters

(small)
   (slightly more than 5 inches) in length and weighs less than 2 grams (less than 0.1 ounce).

4. _____ snakes are the anaconda and the python. They grow as long as 10

(large)
   meters (about 33 feet) and can weigh up to 250 kilograms (about 550 pounds).

(continued)

5. Most female snakes are _____ than male snakes.
(large)

6. A snake's body temperature is about the same as the temperature of the surroundings. When

the temperature warms up, snakes are _____ and when it gets
a. (active)

_____, they are less active.
b. (cold)

7. Many people think the great white shark is _____ and _____ of
a. (dangerous)   b. (aggressive)

all sharks. Studies show that it's not true. White sharks mostly attack when they confuse

humans with seals or sea lions.

5 | EDITING

Correct these conversations. There are seven mistakes. The first mistake is already corrected.

1. A: Is the king cobra the ~~more~~ *most* venomous of all the snakes?

   B: No, but it's the largest of the venomous snakes.

2. A: I read that Pluto is *usually* the most farthest from the sun. Why?

   B: Neptune is farther from the sun 20 years out of every 248 years.

3. A: What's the most small state in the United States?

   B: Rhode Island. It's in the northeast United States.

4. A: I think the cell phone is one of the best inventions in the last 25 years.

   B: Really? I think it's one of the baddest. My boss can always reach me.

5. A: What's the busier day of the week for you?

   B: Wednesday. I work all day and go to school at night.

6. A: What's the most shortest day of the year?

   B: December 21st. June 21st is the most long.

Communication Practice

6 | LISTENING

 *Listen to a quiz show. Write the answers to the questions.*

1. What's the lightest planet? _____

2. What's the brightest planet? _____

3. What's the largest planet? _____

4. What planet has the largest volcano? _____

7 | SURVEY

A *Write superlative questions with the words.*

1. what / good way to relax

   What's the best way to relax?

2. what / easy way / to earn a lot of money

   _____

3. what / interesting show / on TV now

   _____

4. who / powerful person / in the world

   _____

5. when / good time to go to college

   _____

6. what / good restaurant / near your school

   _____

7. what / interesting animal to look at

   _____

B *Choose three questions. Survey five students. Report interesting results to the class.*

> **Example:** A: What's the best way to relax?
> B: I think the best way to relax is to take a 40-minute bubble bath.

8 | COMPLIMENTS

Work in pairs. Use superlatives to say something nice about each person in your class. Give a reason why.

Examples: Marcia is the most helpful person in our class. She always collects the papers.
Chun Che is the funniest. He has the best sense of humor.

9 | CITIES

Each student writes on the board the name of a city he or she knows well. Other students ask questions about that city. Use the superlative form of the words in the box.

popular sport	good university / restaurant / hospital
important holiday	important industry
rainy / hot / cold month	beautiful section
interesting area	

Example: A: What's the most important industry in Taipei?
B: I'm not sure, but I think electronics is one of the most important industries.

10 | WRITING

Write about an unforgettable day. Include at least three uses of superlative adjectives.

Example: Last August I was in New York on business. On a free afternoon I visited the Bronx Zoo. This zoo is one of the best zoos in the world. It covers 265 acres and is home to over 6,000 animals. I enjoyed the Butterfly Zone and the World of Birds, but the most interesting part was the "Congo" exhibit. I saw a rain forest and a lot of gorillas. The funniest gorilla imitated one of the visitors. The people laughed a lot. I started to laugh, but stopped when I realized I was the one he was imitating!

11 | ON THE INTERNET

Work in small groups. Research interesting facts with superlatives. Write a five-question trivia quiz using superlatives. Ask your classmates your questions. Try and answer their questions.

Examples: What is the tallest building in the world?
What country has the highest income tax?

From **Grammar** to **Writing**
The Order of Adjectives Before Nouns

1 | *Complete the sentence with the words in parentheses.*

1. I saw a _____ on Main Street.
   (funny / monkey / brown / little)

2. Maria wore a _____.
   (red / dress / beautiful / silk)

The Order of Adjectives before Nouns							
1. Opinion	**2. Size**	**3. Shape**	**4. Age**	**5. Color**	**6. Origin**	**7. Material**	**8. Noun**
beautiful	big	square	new	red	French	silk	scarf

1. We use adjectives to describe nouns. Decriptions make writing more lively. They also help the reader form mental pictures. When **several adjectives** come before a noun, they follow a **special order**.	• I saw a **beautiful young** woman. Not: I saw a ~~young beautiful~~ woman.

2. Use ***and*** to connect adjectives from the same category.	• The shirt was *cotton* **and** *polyester*. • The blouse was *red* **and** *white*.

2 | *Write the words in parentheses in the correct order.*

1. He ate a _____ pear.
   (brown / big / Asian)

2. His cashmere coat was not as expensive as her _____ jacket.
   (Italian / new / leather / black)

3. They bought three _____ bowls.
   (silver / Mexican)

3 | *Read the story.*

Detective Work

Several years ago I was walking down the street when I saw my father's brand new shiny blue car. I expected to see my father, but to my surprise a young woman with short, curly bright red hair was behind the wheel of the car. I saw an empty taxi nearby and I got in quickly. I said dramatically to the driver, "Follow that new blue car." And I told the driver why.

The taxi driver had a car phone, and I told him to call the police. Soon we heard the siren of the patrol car and a loudspeaker. The police told the woman to pull over. We pulled over too. I immediately said to the woman, "That's not your car. It's my father's."

The woman smiled calmly and said, "Oh. You're Mr. Abbot's younger son. I recognize you from your picture."

Before I could say another word, the woman explained that she was my father's new assistant. My father had asked her to take his computer to the main office to get it fixed. He lent her his car. We called my father and he confirmed her story. The police laughed and the taxi driver laughed. I was too embarrassed to laugh. That was the beginning and the end of my career as a detective.

Now write your own story.
Begin,

I was walking down the street when I saw _____

Review Test

I · *Circle the letter of the correct word(s) to complete the conversations or sentences.*

1. **A:** Did you buy the red coat or the beige one?   **A B C**

   B: The beige one. The red coat was _____.

   (A) too expensive

   (B) as expensive

   (C) much expensive

2. **A:** Why do you prefer to work at night?   **A B C**

   B: It's _____.

   (A) more quieter than during the day

   (B) much quieter than during the day

   (C) as much quiet as the day

3. **A:** How does she work?   **A B C**

   B: _____.

   (A) Very careful

   (B) Much more careful

   (C) Very carefully

4. **A:** Did you compare the two motorcycles?   **A B C**

   B: Yes. The black one is _____ the blue one.

   (A) as expensive than

   (B) more expensive than

   (C) expensive enough

5. **A:** Why can't he get a driver's license?   **A B C**

   B: He isn't _____.

   (A) too old

   (B) old enough

   (C) enough old

6. **A:** Grandpa, you look great. How do you feel?   **A B C**

   B: Fine. They say, "You're only _____.

   (A) as old as you feel

   (B) older as you feel

   (C) old enough as you feel

(continued)

7. A: Which day is better for you, Monday or Tuesday?   A   B   C
   B: Monday. I'm _____.
      (A) more busy on Tuesday
      (B) busier on Tuesday
      (C) too much busy on Tuesday

8. A: Is my hair as long as Paula's?   A   B   C
   B: No. It's _____.
      (A) shorter than Paula
      (B) shorter than Paula is
      (C) shorter than Paula's

9. A: Why did they choose him?   A   B   C
   B: _____ in the class.
      (A) He's the best speaker
      (B) He's the more better speaker
      (C) He's the most best speaker

10. The ending is _____.   A   B   C
       (A) the most important of the book part
       (B) the most important part than the book
       (C) the most important part of the book

11. I can't decide. Should I get the DVD player or the digital camera?   A   B   C
       (A) What one is cheaper?
       (B) Which one is cheaper?
       (C) Which ones is cheaper?

II   *Circle the correct word(s) to complete the sentences.*

1. He thought careful / carefully about his project and did a great job.

2. Don't let him drive. He drives too slow / slowly.

3. Who painted that beautiful / beautifully picture?

4. She sang beautiful / beautifully.

5. He writes very good / well.

6. That's a very / too interesting ring. Where did you get it?

7. It's impossible to walk there. It's very / too far to walk.

8. Something smells very good / well. Is it the soup?

III   *Use **than**, **as**, or **from** to complete the sentences.*

1. Is love more important _____ money?

2. Money isn't as important _____ love.

3. Are dogs very different _____ cats?

4. Is your first name the same _____ your father's?

5. Is your new apartment farther from downtown _____ your old one?

6. Are you the same height _____ your brother?

IV   *Use the superlative or comparative form of the adjective in parentheses to complete the sentences.*

1. It was _____ storm of the century.
               (bad)

2. Today he felt _____ he felt yesterday.
                   (bad)

3. Who is _____ runner on the team?
              (fast)

4. What was _____ section of the museum?
             (interesting)

5. He is a lot _____ his brother.
               (funny)

6. That is _____ show of the season.
            (funny)

7. What is _____ cell phone in the store?
            (good)

8. She is one of _____ people in the company.
              (industrious)

9. Are you _____ your cousin?
           (old)

V   *Correct the sentences.*

1. He is one of the best student in the school.

2. Who's the most tallest one in their family?

3. The next level is a lot more harder than this one.

4. We're busier in December as we are in January.

5. The workbook isn't as expensive the CD.

6. He works hardly.

7. Taxes are highest than last year.

8. It tastes deliciously.

▶ *To check your answers, go to the Answer Key on page RT-6.*

APPENDICES

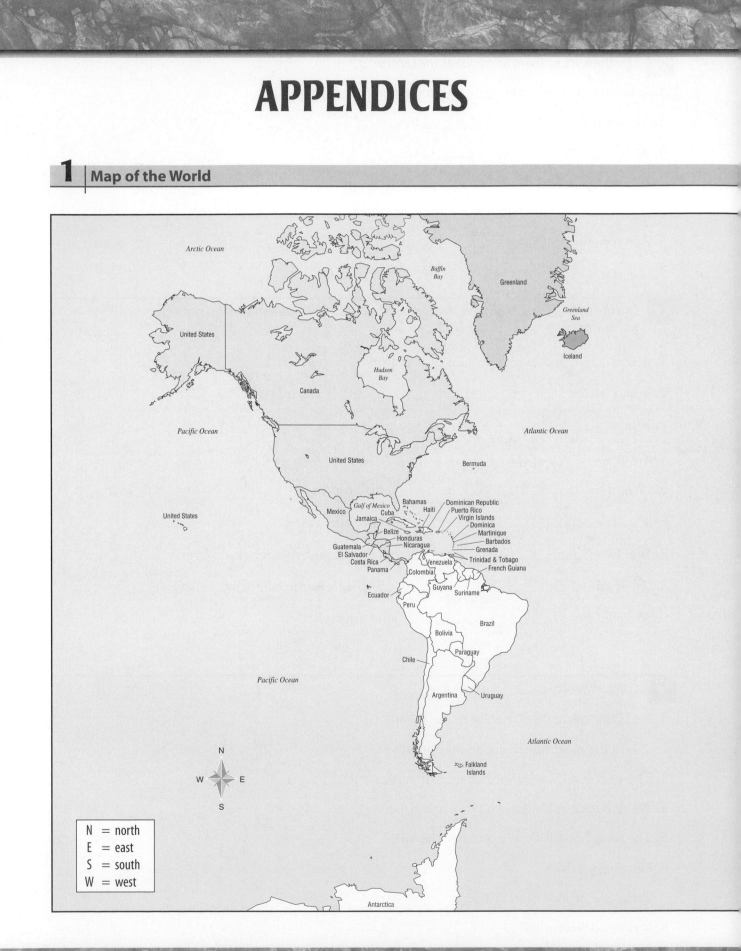

N = north
E = east
S = south
W = west

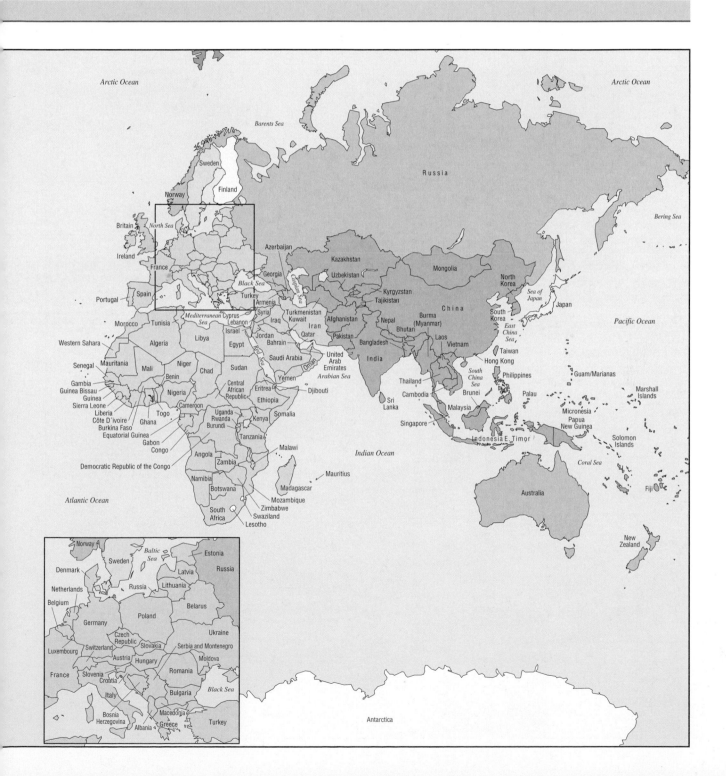

Arctic Ocean

Arctic Ocean

Barents Sea

Bering Sea

Russia

Sea of Japan

Sweden

Finland

Norway

Britain

North Sea

Ireland

Azerbaijan

Kazakhstan

Mongolia

North Korea

France

Georgia

Uzbekistan

Kyrgyzstan

South Korea

Japan

Pacific Ocean

Portugal

Spain

Black Sea

Caspian Sea

Turkey

Armenia

Tajikistan

China

East China Sea

Syria

Turkmenistan

Kuwait

Afghanistan

Nepal

Burma (Myanmar)

Taiwan

Mediterranean Sea

Cyprus

Lebanon

Iraq

Iran

Laos

Hong Kong

Morocco

Tunisia

Israel

Jordan

Qatar

Bahrain

Pakistan

Bhutan

Vietnam

Guam/Marianas

Western Sahara

Algeria

Libya

Egypt

Red Sea

Saudi Arabia

United Arab Emirates

Oman

India

Bangladesh

South China Sea

Philippines

Marshall Islands

Senegal

Mauritania

Mali

Niger

Chad

Sudan

Yemen

Arabian Sea

Thailand

Brunei

Micronesia

Gambia

Benin

Eritrea

Djibouti

Cambodia

Malaysia

Papua New Guinea

Solomon Islands

Guinea Bissau

Guinea

Nigeria

Central African Republic

Ethiopia

Sri Lanka

Singapore

Sierra Leone

Liberia

Togo

Cameroon

Uganda

Rwanda

Kenya

Somalia

Indonesia

E. Timor

Côte D'ivoire

Ghana

Burkina Faso

Equatorial Guinea

Gabon

Burundi

Tanzania

Coral Sea

Congo

Angola

Malawi

Indian Ocean

Fiji

Democratic Republic of the Congo

Zambia

Mauritius

Namibia

Botswana

Madagascar

Australia

Atlantic Ocean

Mozambique

Zimbabwe

South Africa

Swaziland

Lesotho

New Zealand

Norway

Baltic Sea

Estonia

Denmark

Sweden

Russia

Latvia

Russia

Netherlands

Russia

Lithuania

Belgium

Belarus

Germany

Poland

Luxembourg

Czech Republic

Ukraine

Switzerland

Slovakia

Serbia and Montenegro

Austria

Hungary

Moldova

France

Slovenia

Romania

Croatia

Italy

Bulgaria

Black Sea

Bosnia Herzegovina

Macedonia

Turkey

Albania

Greece

Antarctica

CARDINAL NUMBERS

1 = one	11 = eleven	21 = twenty-one
2 = two	12 = twelve	30 = thirty
3 = three	13 = thirteen	40 = forty
4 = four	14 = fourteen	50 = fifty
5 = five	15 = fifteen	60 = sixty
6 = six	16 = sixteen	70 = seventy
7 = seven	17 = seventeen	80 = eighty
8 = eight	18 = eighteen	90 = ninety
9 = nine	19 = nineteen	100 = one hundred
10 = ten	20 = twenty	200 = two hundred
		1,000 = one thousand
		1,000,000 = one million
		10,000,000 = ten million

EXAMPLES:

That building has **seventy-seven** floors.
There are **thirty** days in April.
There are **six** rows in the room.
She is **twelve** years old.
He has **four** children.

ORDINAL NUMBERS

1st = first	11th = eleventh	21st = twenty-first
2nd = second	12th = twelfth	30th = thirtieth
3rd = third	13th = thirteenth	40th = fortieth
4th = fourth	14th = fourteenth	50th = fiftieth
5th = fifth	15th = fifteenth	60th = sixtieth
6th = sixth	16th = sixteenth	70th = seventieth
7th = seventh	17th = seventeenth	80th = eightieth
8th = eighth	18th = eighteenth	90th = ninetieth
9th = ninth	19th = nineteenth	100th = one hundredth
10th = tenth	20th = twentieth	200th = two hundredth
		1,000th = one thousandth
		1,000,000th = one millionth
		10,000,000th = ten millionth

EXAMPLES:

He works on the **seventy-seventh** floor.
It's April **thirtieth**.
He's in the **sixth** row.
It's her **twelfth** birthday.
Bob is his **first** child. Mary is his
    second. John is his **third**, and
    Sue is his **fourth**.

TEMPERATURE

We measure the temperature in degrees (°).

Changing from degrees Fahrenheit to degrees Celsius:

$$(F° - 32) \times 5/9 = °C$$

Changing from degrees Celsius to degrees Fahrenheit:

$$(9/5 \times °C) + 32 = F°$$

MONTHS OF THE YEAR

Month	Abbreviation	Number of Days
January	Jan.	31
February	Feb.	28*
March	Mar.	31
April	Apr.	30
May	May	31
June	Jun.	30
July	Jul.	31
August	Aug.	31
September	Sept.	30
October	Oct.	31
November	Nov.	30
December	Dec.	31

DAYS OF THE WEEK

Weekdays	Weekend
Monday	Saturday
Tuesday	Sunday
Wednesday	
Thursday	
Friday	

*February has 29 days in a leap year, every four years.

THE SEASONS

Spring: March 21st–June 20th

Summer: June 21st–September 20th

Autumn or Fall: September 21st–December 20th

Winter: December 21st–March 20th

TITLES

Mr. (Mister) /mɪstər/ unmarried or married man

Ms. /mɪz/ unmarried or married woman

Miss /mɪs/ unmarried woman

Mrs. /mɪsɪz/ married woman

Dr. (Doctor) /daktər/ doctor (medical doctor or Ph.D.)

4 | Time

It's one o'clock.
(It's 1:00.)

It's five after one.
(It's 1:05.)

It's one-ten.
It's ten after one.
(It's 1:10.)

It's one-fifteen.
It's a quarter after one.
(It's 1:15.)

It's one twenty-five.
It's twenty-five after one.
(It's 1:25.)

It's one-thirty.
It's half past one.
(It's 1:30.)

It's one forty-five.
It's a quarter to two.
(It's 1:45.)

It's one-fifty.
It's ten to two.
(It's 1:50.)

TALKING ABOUT TIME

1. You can ask about time this way:	**A: What time is it?** **B:** It's one o'clock.
2. A.M. means before noon (the hours between midnight and noon).	It's 10:00 **a.m.**
P.M. means after noon (the hours between noon and midnight).	It's 10:00 **p.m.**
▶ BE CAREFUL! When people say 12:00 A.M., they mean midnight. When people say 12:00 P.M., they mean noon.	
3. We often write time with numbers.	It's one o'clock. = It's **1:00**. It's two-twenty. = It's **2:20**.

1. face
2. hair
3. eye
4. ear
5. nose
6. mouth
7. tooth (teeth)
8. lip
9. chin
10. throat
11. neck
12. shoulder
13. arm
14. elbow
15. hand
16. finger
17. stomach
18. waist
19. hip
20. thigh
21. leg
22. knee
23. foot (feet)
24. ankle
25. toe
26. back

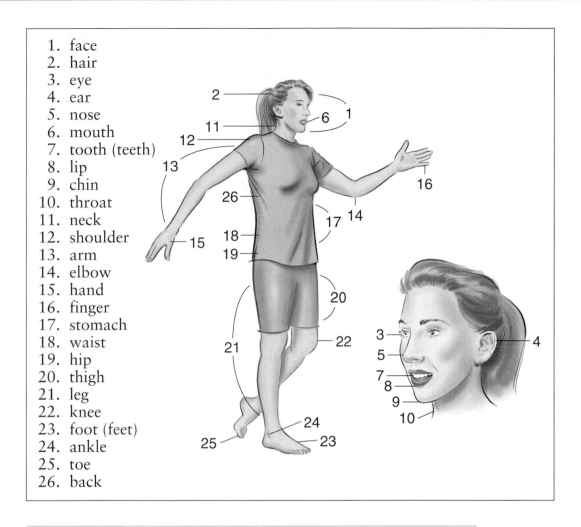

MEDICAL PROBLEMS

I have a backache.
I have an earache.
I have a headache.
I have a sore throat.
I have a stomachache. (I'm nauseous; I have diarrhea; I'm constipated.)
I have a fever.
My nose is running.
I have a cough.
I have a pain in my back.
My neck hurts.

U.S. HOLIDAYS (FEDERAL AND LEGAL HOLIDAYS AND OTHER SPECIAL DAYS)

January
*New Year's Day	January 1st
*Martin Luther King, Jr.'s Birthday	January 15th (observed on the closest Monday)

February
Valentine's Day	February 14th
*George Washington's Birthday	February 22nd (observed on the closest Monday)

March

April
April Fools' Day	April 1st

May
Mother's Day	the second Sunday in May
*Memorial Day	May 30th (observed on the last Monday in May)

June
Flag Day	June 14th

Father's Day	the third Sunday in June

July
*Independence Day	July 4th

August

September
*Labor Day	the first Monday in September

October
*Columbus Day	October 12th (observed on the closest Monday)
Halloween	October 31st

November
Election Day	the first Tuesday after the first Monday in November
*Veterans' Day	November 11th
*Thanksgiving	the fourth Thursday in November

December
*Christmas	December 25th
New Year's Eve	December 31st

*federal legal holidays

CANADIAN HOLIDAYS (LEGAL AND PUBLIC HOLIDAYS)

January
New Year's Day	January 1st
Sir John A. Macdonald's Birthday	January 11th

February
Valentine's Day	February 14th

March
† St. Patrick's Day	the Monday nearest March 17th

March or April
† Good Friday
† Easter Monday

April
April Fool's Day	April 1st

May
Mother's Day	the second Sunday in May
Victoria Day	the Monday preceding May 25th

June
Father's Day	the third Sunday in June

St. John the Baptist's Day	the Monday nearest June 24th (only in Quebec)

July
Canada Day	July 1st

August
Civic Holiday	the first Monday in August (celebrated in several provinces)
Discovery Day	the third Monday in August (only in the Yukon)

September
Labor Day	the first Monday in September

October
Thanksgiving Day	the second Monday in October
Halloween	October 31st

November
Remembrance Day	November 11th

December
Christmas Day	December 25th
Boxing Day	December 26th

†Many Americans in the United States observe these religious holidays too. However, these days are not official U.S. holidays.

BASE FORM	PAST FORM	BASE FORM	PAST FORM
become	became	leave	left
begin	began	lend	lent
bite	bit	lose	lost
blow	blew	make	made
break	broke	meet	met
bring	brought	pay	paid
build	built	put	put
buy	bought	quit	quit
catch	caught	read*	read*
choose	chose	ride	rode
come	came	ring	rang
cost	cost	run	ran
do	did	say	said
draw	drew	see	saw
drink	drank	sell	sold
drive	drove	send	sent
eat	ate	shake	shook
fall	fell	shoot	shot
feed	fed	shut	shut
feel	felt	sing	sang
fight	fought	sit	sat
find	found	sleep	slept
fly	flew	speak	spoke
forget	forgot	spend	spent
get	got	stand	stood
give	gave	steal	stole
go	went	swim	swam
grow	grew	take	took
hang	hung	teach	taught
have	had	tear	tore
hear	heard	tell	told
hide	hid	think	thought
hit	hit	throw	threw
hold	held	understand	understood
hurt	hurt	wake	woke
keep	kept	wear	wore
know	knew	win	won
lead	led	write	wrote

*Pronounce the base form / rid /. Pronounce the past form / rɛd /.

THE PRESENT OF *BE*

Singular		
Subject	*Be*	
I	**am**	
You	**are**	a student.
He She	**is**	
It	**is**	in the United States.

Plural		
Subject	*Be*	
We You They	**are**	in the United States.

THE PAST OF *BE*

Singular			
Subject	*Be*		**Time Marker**
I	**was**		
You	**were**	at a restaurant	last night.
He She It	**was**		

Plural			
Subject	*Be*		**Time Marker**
We You They	**were**	at a restaurant	last night.

THE PRESENT PROGRESSIVE

Subject	*Be*	**Base Form of Verb + *-ing***
I	**am**	
You	**are**	
He She It	**is**	working.
We You They	**are**	

THE SIMPLE PRESENT AND THE SIMPLE PAST

The Simple Present	
Subject	Verb
I You We They	**work**.
He She It	**works**.

The Simple Past	
Subject	Base Form of Verb + *-ed* / *-d* / *-ied*
I You He She It We You They	**worked**. **arrived**. **cried**.

THE FUTURE

Will for the Future			
Subject	*Will*	Base Form of Verb	
I You He She It We You They	**will**	**work**	tomorrow.

Be Going to for the Future				
Subject	*Be*	*Going to*	Base Form of Verb	Time Marker
I	**am**			
You	**are**			
He She	**is**	**going to**	**work**	tomorrow.
You We They	**are**			
It	**is**	**going to**	**rain**	tomorrow.

SPELLING RULES

1. Add -s to form the plural of most nouns.	student chief picture	student**s** chief**s** picture**s**
2. Add **-es** to form the plural of nouns that end in **ss,** **ch, sh**, and **x**. (This ending adds another syllable.)	class watch dish box	class**es** watch**es** dish**es** box**es**
3. Add **-es** to form the plural of nouns that end in o preceded by a consonant. **EXCEPTION:** Add **-s** to plural nouns ending in o that refer to music.	potato piano soprano	potato**es** piano**s** soprano**s**
4. Add **-s** to form the plural of nouns that end in o preceded by a vowel.	radio	radio**s**
5. To form the plural of words that end in a consonant + **y**, change the **y** to **i** and add **-es**.	dictionary fly	dictionar**ies** fl**ies**
6. To form the plural of words that end in a vowel + **y**, add **-s**.	boy day	boy**s** day**s**
7. To form the plural of certain nouns that end in **f** or **fe**, change the **f** to **v** and add **-es**.	half loaf knife wife	hal**ves** loa**ves** kni**ves** wi**ves**
8. Some plural nouns are **irregular**.	woman child person mother-in-law man foot tooth	women children people mothers-in-law men feet teeth
9. Some nouns **do not have a singular form**.	(eye) glasses clothes pants scissors	
10. Some plural nouns are the same as the singular noun.	Chinese fish sheep	Chinese fish sheep

∩ PRONUNCIATION RULES

1. The **final sounds** for regular plural nouns are / s /, / z /, and / ɪz /.	
2. The plural is pronounced / s / after the **voiceless sounds** / p /, / t /, / k /, / f /, and / ø /.	cups hats works cuffs myths
3. The plural is pronounced / z / after the **voiced sounds** / b /, / d /, / g /, / v /, / m /, / n /, / ŋ /, / l /, / r /, and / ð /.	crabs cards rugs
4. The plural *s* is pronounced / z / after all **vowel sounds**.	day days toe toes
5. The plural *s* is pronounced / ɪz / **after the sounds** / s /, / z /, / ∫ /, / ʒ /, / ʧ /, and / ʤ /. (This adds another syllable to the word.)	races causes dishes

10 | Possessive Nouns

1. Add *'s* to form the possessive of singular nouns.	Lulu**'s** last name is Winston.
2. To form the possessive of plural nouns ending in *s*, add only an **apostrophe (')**.	The girl**s'** gym is on this floor. The boy**s'** locker room is across the hall.
3. In hyphenated words (*mother-in-law, father-in-law,* etc.) and in phrases showing joint possession, only the last word is possessive in form.	My sister-in-law**'s** apartment is big. Elenore and Pete**'s** apartment is comfortable.
4. To form the possessive of plural nouns that do not end in *s*, add *'s*.	The men**'s** room is next to the water fountain.
5. To form the possessive of one-syllable singular nouns that end in *s*, add *'s*. To form the possessive of words of more than one syllable that end in *s*, add an **'** or an *'s*.	**James's** apartment is beautiful. **McCullers's** novels are interesting. OR **McCullers'** novels are interesting.
6. Be careful! Don't confuse possessive nouns with the contraction of the verb *be*.	**Carol's** a student. = **Carol** *is* a student. **Carol's** book is open. = **Her** book is open.

COMMON NON-COUNT NOUNS*

Liquids
milk
coffee
oil
juice
soda
water
beer

Food
bread   ketchup
cheese   jam
lettuce   jelly
broccoli   fish
ice cream   meat
butter   sour cream
mayonnaise   soup

Too Small to Count
sugar
salt
pepper
cinnamon
rice
sand
baking powder
cereal
spaghetti
wheat
corn

School Subjects
math
history
geography
biology
chemistry
music

City Problems
traffic
pollution
crime

Weather
snow
rain
ice
fog

Gases
oxygen
carbon
dioxide
nitrogen
air

Abstract Ideas
love
beauty
happiness
luck
advice
help
noise
time

Others
money
mail
furniture
homework
information
jewelry
garbage
toothpaste
paper

*Some nouns can be either count or non-count nouns.

I'd like some **chicken**. (non-count)
There were three **chickens** in the yard. (count)

Did you eat any **cake**? (non-count)
I bought a **cake** at the bakery. (count)

QUANTIFIERS: CONTAINERS, MEASURE WORDS, AND PORTIONS

a bottle of (milk, soda, catsup)
a bowl of (cereal, soup, rice)
a can of (soda, beans, tuna fish)
a cup of (hot chocolate, coffee, tea)
a foot of (snow, water)
a gallon of (juice, gas, paint)
a head of (lettuce)
an inch of (snow, rain)
a loaf of (bread)

a pair of (pants, skis, gloves)
a piece of (paper, cake, pie)
a pint of (ice cream, cream)
a quart of (milk)
a roll of (film, toilet paper, paper towels)
a slice of (toast, cheese, meat)
a tablespoon of (flour, sugar, baking soda)
a teaspoon of (sugar, salt, pepper)
a tube of (toothpaste, glue)

METRIC CONVERSION

1 liter	= .26 gallons or 1.8 pints	1 mile	= 1.6 kilometers	1 ounce	= 28 grams
1 gallon	= 3.8 liters	1 kilometer	= .62 mile	1 gram	= .04 ounce
		1 foot	= .30 meter or 30 centimeters	1 pound	= .45 kilogram
		1 meter	= 3.3 feet	1 kilogram	= 2.2 pounds
		1 inch	= 2.54 centimeters		

1. *The* is the **definite article**. You can use *the* before **singular count nouns**, **plural count nouns**, and **non-count nouns**.

The hat is red.
The hats are red.
The coffee is hot.

2. Use *the* for **specific things** that the listener and speaker know about.

A: How was **the test**?
B: It was easy.

A: Would you like to read **the paper**?
B: Yes, thanks.

3. Use *the* when the speaker and listener know there is **only one** of the item.

A: Is there a cafeteria in this school?
B: Yes, **the cafeteria** is on the third floor.

4. Use *the* when you are talking about **part of a group**.

Meat is usually expensive, but **the meat** at Ron's Butcher Shop is cheap and delicious.

5. Use *the* when you talk about something for the **second time**.

A: What did you buy?
B: Some apples and some pears. **The apples** were bad, but **the pears** were delicious.

6. Use *the* before the **plural name** of a whole family.

The Winstons live in New York City.

7. Use *the* before the names of **oceans**, **rivers**, **mountain ranges**, **seas**, **canals**, **deserts**, and **zoos**.

The Pacific Ocean is on the West Coast.
The Mississippi River is the longest river in the United States.
We visited **the Rocky Mountains**.
Where is **the Dead Sea**?
The boat went through **the Suez Canal**.
The Sahara Desert is growing.
We visited **the San Diego Zoo**.

8. Use *the* with phrases with *of* when there is **only one** of the item that follows *the*.

Paris is **the capital of France**.
I attended **the University of Michigan**.
BUT
He drank **a** cup of tea.

1. A **phrasal verb** consists of a verb and a particle. *Away, back, down, in, off, on, out,* and *up* are common particles.* A particle usually changes the meaning of a verb.	He **took** the coat. *(He removed the coat from where it was.)*
	He **took off** the coat. *(He removed the coat from his body.)*
	He **took back** the coat. *(He returned the coat.)*
2. Some phrasal verbs have **direct objects**. When the direct object is a noun, it can go after the particle or between the verb and the particle.	verb particle direct object He took off **the coat**.
	verb direct object particle He took **the coat** off.
When the direct object is a pronoun, it always goes between the verb and the particle.	object verb pronoun particle He took **it** off.
	NOT: He took ~~off it~~.
3. Some phrasal verbs don't take an object.	His car **broke down** in the middle of the street. Please **come in**.

*Some particles can also be prepositions or adverbs in other sentences. In the sentence, "He walked *up* the hill," *up* is a preposition.

COMMON PHRASAL VERBS THAT TAKE OBJECTS

Phrasal Verb	Meaning	Example
bring out	present; show	He **brought out** the wedding cake.
give away	give as a gift	He **gave away** many books when he moved.
give back	return	The sweater was too big, so I **gave** it **back**.
hand in	give some work to a teacher or boss	I **handed in** a ten-page report.
hand out	distribute	They **handed out** papers about the candidates.
put away	return to the place where something is usually kept	Please **put** your clothes **away**.
put off	do later; postpone	We're very busy now, so let's **put off** our vacation for a few weeks.
put on	cover the body with clothes	When I **put** my new boots **on**, I felt a lot warmer.
take back	return	I'd like to **take** those shirts **back**. They're a little tight.
take off	remove from one's body	He **took** his sweater **off** because he was hot.
throw away	put in the garbage	She's sorry that she **threw** those papers **away**.
turn down	lower the volume	The TV is too loud. Please **turn** it **down**.
turn off	stop a machine or electrical item from working	Don't forget to **turn** all the lights **off** before you go to sleep.
turn on	make a machine or electrical item work	The radio is next to you. Please **turn** it **on**.
wrap up	complete	We'll **wrap** the meeting **up** before noon.

COMMON PHRASAL VERBS THAT DON'T TAKE OBJECTS

Phrasal Verb	Meaning	Example
break down	stop working	His car **broke down** in the middle of the street.
catch on	become popular; learn	That new style **caught on** very quickly.
		The new worker **caught on** quickly.
clear up	become clear	In the morning it was foggy, but the weather **cleared up** by noon.
come in	enter	Please **come in**.
come up	arise	That new idea **came up** during the meeting last week.
eat out	eat in a restaurant	Every Sunday they **eat out** at a different restaurant.
grow up	become adult	They **grew up** in the country.
show up	appear	We were surprised when they **showed up** two hours early.
sit down	sit	We **sat down** and had a serious talk about our future.
stand up	stand	After he played the piano, he **stood up** and bowed.

14 | Direct and Indirect Objects

Group One								
Subject	Verb	Direct Object	*To*	Indirect Object	Subject	Verb	Indirect Object	Direct Object
She	sent	a gift it	to	us.	She	sent	us	a gift.

Group Two								
Subject	Verb	Direct Object	*For*	Indirect Object	Subject	Verb	Indirect Object	Direct Object
They	found	a towel it	for	him.	They	found	him	a towel.

Group Three				
Subject	Verb	Direct Object	*To*	Indirect Object
He	repeated	the question	to	the class.

Group Four				
Subject	Verb	Direct Object	*For*	Indirect Object
He	fixed	the shelves	for	me.

Group One Verbs (*to*)		Group Two Verbs (*for*)	Group Three Verbs (*to*)	Group Four Verbs (*for*)
e-mail	sell	buy	explain	cash
give	send	build	prove	close
hand	show	find	repeat	fix
lend	teach	get	say	pronounce
owe	tell	make	whisper	translate
pass	throw			
read	write			

(continued)

RULES FOR DIRECT AND INDIRECT OBECTS

1. With **Group One** and **Group Two verbs**, there are **two** possible **sentence patterns** if the **direct object** is a **noun**.	direct · *to/for* · indirect object · object I gave the **money to him**. = indirect · direct object · object I gave **him the money**. direct · *to/for* · indirect object · object We bought **the book for him**. = indirect · direct object · object We bought **him the book**.
If the **direct object** is a **pronoun**, it always comes **before the indirect object**.	direct · *to/for* · indirect object · object I gave **it to him**. Please get **them for me**. NOT: I gave ~~him it~~. NOT: Please get ~~me them~~.
2. With **Group Three** and **Group Four verbs**, the **direct object** always comes **before the indirect object**.	direct · *to/for* · indirect object · object Explain **the sentence to John**. She translated **the letter for us**. NOT: Explain ~~John the sentence~~. NOT: She translated ~~us the letter~~.

15 | The Present Progressive: Spelling Rules

1. Add **-ing** to the base form of the verb.	drink see eat	drink**ing** see**ing** eat**ing**
2. If a verb ends in a silent *e*, drop the final *e* and add **-ing**.	smil**e**	smil**ing**
3. If a one-syllable verb ends in a consonant, a vowel, and a consonant (**CVC**), double the last consonant before adding **-ing**.	**CVC** sit run	si**tting** run**ning**
However, do not double the last consonant if it is a *w*, *x*, or *y*.	sew play mix	sew**ing** play**ing** mix**ing**
4. In words with two or more syllables that end in a consonant, a vowel, and a consonant (**CVC**), double the last consonant only if the last syllable is stressed.	admít whísper	admi**tting** (*stressed*) whispe**ring** (*not stressed*)

SPELLING RULES FOR THE THIRD-PERSON SINGULAR AFFIRMATIVE

1. Add **-s** to form the third-person singular of most verbs.	Pete works. I work too. Doug wears sweatshirts. I wear shirts.
Add **-es** to words that end in **ch, s, sh, x,** or **z**.	Norma teach**es** Spanish. I teach English. Lulu wash**es** her clothes on Tuesday. Elenore and Pete wash their clothes on Sunday.
2. When a base-form verb ends in a **consonant + y**, change the **y** to **i** and add **-es**.	I study at home. Carol stud**ies** at the library.
Do not change the **y** when the base form ends in a **vowel + y**. Add **-s**.	Dan play**s** tennis. I play tennis, too.
3. *Have, do,* and *go* have **irregular forms** for the third-person singular.	I have. He **has**. I do. She **does**. I go. It **goes**.

∩ PRONUNCIATION RULES FOR THE THIRD-PERSON SINGULAR AFFIRMATIVE

1. The **final sound** for the third-person singular form of the simple present tense is pronounced / **s** / , / **z** / , or / ɪz / . The final sounds of the third-person singular are the same as the final sounds of plural nouns. See Appendix 9 on pages A-10 and A-11.	/ **s** / / **z** / / ɪz / talk**s** love**s** danc**es**
2. *Do* and *say* have a change in vowel sound.	I say. / seɪ / He say**s**. / sɛz / I do. / du / He do**es**. / dʌz /

SPELLING RULES

1. If the verb **ends in an** *e*, add **-d**.	arrive arrive**d** like like**d**
2. If the verb **ends in a consonant**, add **-ed**.	rain rain**ed** help help**ed**
3. If a **one-syllable verb** ends in a consonant, a vowel, and a consonant **(CVC)**, double the last consonant and add **-ed**. However, do not double the last consonant if it is a *w*, *x*, or *y*.	**CVC** hug hu**gged** rub ru**bbed** bow bo**wed** mix mi**xed** play play**ed**
4. If a **two-syllable verb** ends in a consonant, a vowel, and a consonant **(CVC)**, double the last consonant only if the last syllable is stressed.	refér refe**rred** *(stressed)* énter enter**ed** *(not stressed)*
5. If the verb ends in a **consonant + y**, change the *y* to *i* and add **-ed**.	worry worr**ied** carry carr**ied**
6. If the verb ends in a **vowel + y**, do not change the *y* to *i*. Add **-ed**. There are **exceptions** to this rule.	play play**ed** annoy anno**yed** pay **paid** lay **laid** say **said**

∩ PRONUNCIATION RULES

1. The **final sounds** for regular verbs in the past are / t /, / d /, and / ɪd /.			
2. The final sound is pronounced / t / after the **voiceless sounds** / f /, / k /, / p /, / s /, / ʧ /, and / ʃ /.	laug**hed** lic**ked**	si**pped** mi**ssed**	wat**ched** wis**hed**
3. The final sound is pronounced / d / **after** the **voiced sounds** / b /, / g /, / ʤ /, / l /, / m /, / n /, / r /, / ŋ /, / ð /, / ʒ /, / v /, and / z /.	ru**bbed** hu**gged** ju**dged** pu**lled**	hu**mmed** ba**nned** occu**rred** ba**nged**	ba**thed** massa**ged** li**ved** surpri**sed**
4. The final sound is pronounced / d / **after vowel sounds**.	play**ed** ski**ed**	**tied** sno**wed**	arg**ued**
5. The final sound is pronounced / ɪd / after / t / and / d /. / ɪd / adds a syllable.	want instruct rest attend	wan**ted** instruc**ted** res**ted** atten**ded**	

Comparative Form (used to compare two people, places, or things)				
Sally	is	**older** **busier** **more industrious**	**than**	her sister.

Superlative Form (used to compare three or more people, places, or things)			
Sally	is	**the**	**busiest** **most industrious**	of the three.

Equative Form (used to show that two people, places, or things are the same)				
Sally	is	**as**	**tall** **busy** **industrious**	**as**	Bob.

SPELLING RULES FOR COMPARATIVE AND SUPERLATIVE ADJECTIVES

1. When a one-syllable adjective ends in a **consonant**, **vowel**, and **consonant (CVC)**, double the last consonant and add *-er* or *-est (hot–hotter–hottest)*.

   Summers in Miami are **hotter** than summers in San Francisco.
   July is the **hottest** month of the year.

2. When a two-syllable adjective ends in *-y*, change the *y* to *i* and add *-er* or *-est (heavy–heavier–heaviest; easy–easier–easiest)*.

   Traffic is **heavier** at eight o'clock than it is at noon.
   Traffic is **the heaviest** on Fridays.

FUNCTION	MODALS	EXAMPLES
to make polite requests	**Would you (please)** **Could you (please)** **Can you (please)**	**Would you** please lend me your pen? **Could you** please help me? **Can you** please take our picture?
to ask for or give permission	**may** **can**	**May** I use your computer? You **can** return to work on Monday.
to express desire	**would like**	I**'d like** to buy a car. We**'d like** to see you again.
to express possibility (present or future)	**may** **might**	Take an umbrella. It **may** rain. He **might** have a cold.
to express future possibility	**can** **could**	How **can** I get to the library tomorrow? You **could** go by bus or by train.
to talk about the future	**will**	He **will** be three years old next week.
to express present ability	**can**	I **can** type 50 words a minute.
to express past ability	**could**	I **could** run very fast 10 years ago.
to express necessity in the present or future	**must** **have to**	You **must** pay the rent by the first of the month. She **has to** work today.
to express past necessity	**had to**	We **had to** read two new chapters.
to express advisability	**should** **ought to** **had better**	He **should** see a doctor. He doesn't sound very good. We **ought to** study today. They**'d better** return my money.
to promise or assure	**will**	I**'ll be** there at 10:00.
to express strong prohibition	**mustn't**	You **mustn't** smoke near the chemical factory.
to indicate that something is not a requirement	**don't / doesn't have to**	You **don't have to** type your composition. She **doesn't have to** wear a suit at her office.

These are the pronunciation symbols used in this text. Listen to the pronunciation of the key words.

VOWELS		CONSONANTS			
Symbol	Key Word	Symbol	Key Word	Symbol	Key Word
i	beat, feed	p	pack, happy	ʃ	ship, machine, station, special, discussion
ɪ	bit, did	b	back, rubber		
eɪ	date, paid	t	tie	ʒ	measure, vision
ɛ	bet, bed	d	die	h	hot, who
æ	bat, bad	k	came, key, quick	m	men
ɑ	box, odd, father	g	game, guest	n	sun, know, pneumonia
ɔ	bought, dog	ʧ	church, nature, watch	ŋ	sung, ringing
oʊ	boat, road	ʤ	judge, general, major	w	wet, white
ʊ	book, good	f	fan, photograph	l	light, long
u	boot, food, student	v	van	r	right, wrong
ʌ	but, mud, mother	θ	thing, breath	y	yes, use, music
ə	banana, among	ð	then, breathe		
ɚ	shirt, murder	s	sip, city, psychology		
aɪ	bite, cry, buy, eye	z	zip, please, goes		
aʊ	about, how				
ɔɪ	voice, boy				
ɪr	deer				
ɛr	bare				
ɑr	bar				
ɔr	door				
ʊr	tour				

GLOSSARY OF GRAMMAR TERMS

action verb   A verb that describes an action. It can be used in the progressive.

- *Sachiko **is planning** a big party.*

adjective   A word that describes (or modifies) a noun or pronoun.

- *That's a **great** idea.*

adverb   A word that describes (or modifies) an action verb, an adverb, an adjective, or a sentence.

- *She drives **slowly**.*

adverb of frequency   A word that tells the frequency of something.

- *We **usually** eat lunch at noon.*

adverb of manner   A word that describes a verb. It usually answers the question *how*.

- *She speaks **clearly**.*

affirmative statement   A sentence that does not use a negative verb form *(not)*.

- ***I have a car.***

apostrophe   A punctuation mark used to show possession and to write a short form (contraction).

- *He's in my father's car.*

base form   The simple form of the verb without any ending such as *-ing*, *-ed*, or *-s*. It is the same as the infinitive without *to*.

- *Arnold will **come** at 8:00. We should **eat** then.*

be going to future   A verb form used to make predictions, express general facts in the future, or talk about definite plans that were made before now.

- *Mei-Ling says it **'s going to be** cold, so she **'s going to take** a coat.*

capital letter   The big form of a letter of the alphabet. Sentences start with a capital letter.

- ***A, B, C**, etc.*

comma   Punctuation used to separate single things in a list or parts of a sentence.

- *We went to a restaurant**,** and we ate chicken**,** potatoes**,** and broccoli.*

common noun   A noun for a person, place, or thing. It is not capitalized.

- *The **man** got a **book** at the **library**.*

comparative form   An adjective or adverb ending in *-er* or following *more*. It is used in comparing two things.

- *My sister is **older** and **more intelligent** than my brother.*
- *But he studies **harder** and **more carefully**.*

consonant   The letters *b, c, d, f, g, h, j, k, l, m, n, p, q, r, s, t, v, w, x, y, z*.

contraction   A short form of two words. An apostrophe (') replaces the missing letter.

- ***It is** late and **I am** tired. I **should not** stay up so late.*
- ***It's** late and **I'm** tired. I **shouldn't** stay up so late.*

count noun   A noun you can count. It usually has a singular and a plural form.

- *In the **park**, there was a **man** with two **children** and a **dog**.*

definite article   *The;* It makes a noun specific.

- *We saw a movie. **The** movie starred Sean Penn.*

demonstrative adjective   An adjective used to identify the noun that follows.

- ***This** man is resting, but **those** men are busy.*

demonstrative pronoun   A pronoun used in place of a demonstrative adjective and the noun that follows.

- ***This** is our classroom, and **these** are my students.*

direct object   A noun or pronoun used to receive the action of a verb.

- *She sold a **car**. He bought **it**.*

exclamation point   A punctuation mark (!) used at the end of a statement. It shows strong emotion.

- *Help**!** Call the police**!***

formal language Language we usually use in business settings, and academic settings and with people we don't know.

- *Good morning, ladies and gentlemen. May we begin?*

gerund The *-ing* form of a verb. It is used as a noun.

- *Skiing is fun, but we also enjoy swimming.*

imperative A sentence used to give an instruction, a direction, a command, or a suggestion. It uses the base form of the verb. The subject (you) is not a part of the sentence.

- *Turn right at the corner. Drive to the end of the street. Stop!*

indefinite article *A* and *an*; used before singular, nonspecific non-count nouns.

- *Jaime brought a sandwich and an apple for lunch.*

infinitive *To* + the base form of a verb.

- *To travel is my dream. I want to see the world.*

informal language The language we usually use with family and friends, in e-mail messages, and in other informal settings.

- *Hey, Doug, what's up?*

inseparable phrasal verb A phrasal verb that cannot have an object between the verb and the particle.

- *She ran into John.*

irregular verb A verb that does not form the simple past by adding *-d* or *-ed*.

- *They ate a fancy meal last night. The boss came to dinner.*

modal A word that comes before the main verb. Modals can express ability, possibility, obligation, and necessity.

- *You can come early, but you mustn't be late, and you should wear a tie.*

negative statement A statement with a negative verb form.

- *He didn't study. He wasn't ready for the test.*

non-action verb A verb that does not describe an action. It can describe an emotion, a state, a sense, or a mental thought. We usually don't use non-action verbs in the progressive.

- *I like that actor. He is very famous, and I believe he won an Oscar.*

non-count noun A noun we usually do not count. We don't put *a*, *an*, or a number before a non-count noun.

- *All you'll need is rice, water, salt, and butter.*

noun A word that refers to a person, animal, place, thing, or idea.

- *Paula has a friend at the library. She gave me a book about birds.*

noun phrase A phrase formed by a noun and words that describe (modify) it.

- *It was a dark brown leather jacket.*

object A noun or pronoun following an action verb. It receives the action of the verb.

- *I sent a letter. He read it.*

object pronoun A pronoun following a verb or a preposition.

- *We asked him to show the photos to them.*

period A punctuation mark (.) used at the end of a statement.

- *I'd like you to call on Saturday. We need to talk.*

phrasal verb A two-part (or three-part) verb that combines a verb and a particle. The meaning of the parts together is often different from the meaning of the verb alone.

- *We put on our gloves and picked up our umbrellas.*

phrase A group of words that can form a grammatical unit.

- *She lost a red hat. He found it under the table.*

plural The form that means more than one.

- *We sat in our chairs reading our books.*

possessive An adjective, noun, or pronoun that shows possession.

- *Her book is in John's car. Mine is at the office.*

preposition A small word that goes before a noun or pronoun object. A preposition often shows time or place.

- *Maria saw it on the table at two o'clock.*

prepositional phrase A phrase that consists of a preposition followed by a noun or a noun phrase.

- *Chong-Dae saw it under the black wooden table.*

present progressive A verb form that shows an action happening now or planned for the future.

- *I'm working hard now, but I'm taking a vacation soon.*

pronoun   A word that replaces a noun or a noun phrase. There are subject pronouns, object pronouns, possessive pronouns, and demonstrative pronouns.

- *He is a friend—I know **him** well. **This** is his coat; **mine** is black.*

proper noun   The actual name of a person, place, or thing. A proper noun begins with a capital letter.

- ***Tom** is living in **New York**. He is studying **Russian** at **Columbia University**.*

quantifier   A word or phrase that comes before a noun and expresses an amount of that noun.

- *Jeannette used **a little** sugar, **some** flour, **four** eggs, and **a liter of** milk.*

question mark   A punctuation mark (?) used at the end of a question.

- *Where are you going**?** When will you be back**?***

quotation marks   Punctuation marks (". . .") used before and after the actual words a person says.

- *I said, **"**Where are you going?**"** and **"**When will you be back?**"***

regular verb   A verb that forms the simple past by adding -d or -ed.

- *We **lived** in France. My mother **visited** us there.*

sentence   A group of words with a subject and a verb.

- *We opened the window.*
- *Did they paint the house?*

separable phrasal verb   A phrasal verb that can have an object between the verb and the particle.

- *She **put on** her coat. She **put** it **on** before he **put** his coat **on**.*

simple past   A verb form used to show a completed action or idea in the past.

- *The plane **landed** at 9:00. We **caught** a bus to the hotel.*

simple present   A verb form used to show habitual actions or states, general facts, or conditions that are true now.

- *Kemal **loves** to ski, and it **snows** a lot in his area, so he**'s** very happy.*

singular   The form that means only one.

- *I put on **my hat** and **coat** and closed the **door**.*

small letter   The small form of a letter of the alphabet. We use small letters for most words except for proper nouns and the word that starts a sentence.

- ***a, b, c***, etc.

subject   The person, place, or thing that a sentence is about.

- ***The children** ate at the mall.*

subject pronoun   A pronoun used to replace a subject noun.

- *Irene works hard. **She** loves her work.*

superlative form   An adjective or adverb ending in -est or following most. It is used in comparing three or more things.

- *We climbed the **highest** mountain by the **most dangerous** route.*
- *She drives the **fastest** and the **most carelessly** of all the drivers.*

syllable   A group of letters with one vowel sound. Words are made up of one or more syllables.

- *One syllable—**win***
- *Two syllables—**ta ble***
- *Three syllables—**im por tant***

verb   A word used to describe an action, a fact, or a state.

- *He **drives** to work now. He **has** a new car, and he **is** a careful driver.*

wh- question   A question that asks for information. It begins with what, when, where, why, which, who, whose, or how.

- ***What**'s your name?*
- ***Where** are you from?*
- ***How** do you feel?*

will future   A verb form used to make predictions, to talk about facts in the future, to make promises, to offer something, or to state a decision to do something at the time of speaking.

- *It **will** probably rain, so I**'ll take** an umbrella. I**'ll give** you my extra one.*

yes/no question   A question that has a yes or a no answer.

- *Did you arrive on time? Yes, I did.*
- *Are you from Uruguay? No, I'm not.*
- *Can you swim well? Yes, I can.*

REVIEW TESTS ANSWER KEY

Note: In this answer key, where the contracted verb form is given, it is the preferred form, though the full form is also acceptable. Where the full verb form is given, it is the preferred form, though the contracted form is also acceptable.

PART I

I (Units 1–3)
1. B
2. A
3. D
4. C
5. A

II (Units 1–3)
1. D
2. A
3. C
4. A
5. D
6. B

III (Unit 2)
1. Was it cloudy yesterday?
2. Is it cloudy now?
3. Were you in school last week?

IV (Units 1, 3)

It ~~be~~ *is* cold and rainy. But yesterday *was* beautiful. It *was* sunny all day.

PART II

I (Units 5–7)
1. D
2. B
3. A
4. A
5. D
6. B

II (Units 4–6)
1. B
2. B
3. C
4. D
5. C

III (Unit 4)
1. a, a, a
2. an, a
3. Ø, Ø
4. an
5. a
6. an, an
7. an, a, Ø

IV (Unit 7)
1. Where
2. Who
3. Why
4. What

V (Unit 6)
2. is between the Book Nook and QB Bank.
3. is next to Nina's Hair Salon. OR is next to the post office. OR is next to Fogtown post office
4. is on the corner of Maple Street and Second Avenue. OR is on the corner of Maple and Second.
5. is on Maple Street.

PART III

I (Units 8–10)
1. C
2. B
3. C
4. C
5. C
6. A
7. C

II (Units 8–10)
1. Do, need
2. washes
3. has
4. isn't
5. fixes
6. goes
7. does
8. Does, speak
9. Do, wear
10. don't eat
11. worries
12. lives
13. makes
14. does, come
15. do, keep

III (Unit 8)
1. have
2. needs
3. don't need
4. isn't
5. don't eat
6. live
7. don't play
8. speaks
9. doesn't cook
10. wears

IV (Unit 9)

1. **a.** Do you like
   b. I do
2. **a.** Does he need
   b. he doesn't
3. **a.** Do they speak
   b. they don't
4. **a.** Do I know
   b. you do
5. **a.** Do you remember
   b. I don't
6. **a.** Does it rain
   b. it does
7. **a.** Does your brother live
   b. he doesn't

V (Units 9, 10)

2. **a.** Who always wears a hat?
   b. What does Sachiko always wear?
3. **a.** Does Jasmine get up at nine o'clock?
   b. What time/When does Jasmine get up?
   c. Who gets up at nine o'clock?
4. **a.** Does your friend work at a restaurant?
   b. Who works at a restaurant?
   c. Where does your friend work?
   d. What does your friend do?
5. **a.** Who usually goes to bed after midnight?
   b. What time/When does Bob usually go to bed?

VI (Units 8–10)

1. Dan ^doesn't~~like~~ soccer.
2. She isn't ^need~~write~~ to me often.
3. Does your friend ^want~~needs~~ an umbrella?
4. Do they ~~wants~~want any help?
5. My aunt ~~is~~ teaches Spanish.
6. Who does cooks in ~~your~~ family?
7. They don't work or ~~don't~~ live near the train station.
8. What ^does that word mean~~means that word?~~
9. How ^do you spell your name?
10. When ~~do~~does you get up?
11. Why ^do they shop there?
12. How ^does he feel~~feels he?~~

PART IV

I (Units 11–14)

1. C   4. C
2. D   5. D
3. D

II (Unit 11)

1. second   3. seventy-five
2. first   4. eleventh

III (Unit 13)

1. This   4. Those
2. Those   5. these
3. that

IV (Unit 14)

1. ones   4. It
2. It   5. It
3. one   6. ones

V (Unit 11)

1. What
2. Whose; Nuray's
3. Where; at
4. When; on
5. What; at
6. Whose; Fiore's

VI (Units 11, 12)

1. When is Uncle Mike's birthday?
2. Where is Scott?
3. What is his aunt's last name?
4. Who is in the living room?
5. Whose car is in the garage?

VII (Unit 12)

1. Her   4. Its
2. Their   5. Their
3. His

PART V

I (Units 15–19)

1. A   5. C
2. C   6. C
3. D   7. D
4. D

II (Units 16–19)

1. a   5. a
2. a   6. a
3. b   7. b
4. a

III (Unit 17)

2. **a.** Read the directions.
   b. Don't start before 10:00.
3. **a.** Use the side streets.
   b. Don't take the highway.
4. **a.** Wear your jacket.
   b. Don't forget your scarf.

IV (Unit 15)

1. are not/aren't/'re not studying
2. is/'s writing
3. is/'s looking
4. are not/aren't/'re not reading
5. are/'re relaxing
6. are/'re taking

V (Units 16–19)

1. **A:** Is ~~it's~~ *it* raining outside?
2. **A:** Are they ~~play~~ *playing* soccer?
3. **B:** He speaks well now, but last year
   he ~~can't~~ *couldn't* speak at all.
4. **A:** Why don't we ~~to~~ take a walk?
5. **A:** Please ~~you are~~ *be* quiet.

PART VI

I (Units 20–22)

1. B	4. B
2. B	5. B
3. C	6. C

II (Unit 22)

1. a	5. b
2. c	6. b
3. a	7. a
4. c	8. b

III (Units 20, 21)

1. lived	11. went
2. had	12. didn't play
3. loved	13. didn't eat
4. got	14. chopped
5. decided	15. decided
6. went	16. walked
7. chopped	17. did
8. saw	18. chopped
9. felt	19. said
10. walked	

IV (Units 20–22)

1. **a.** did arrive
   b. forgot
2. **a.** ate
   b. didn't eat
   c. don't like
3. **a.** got
   b. sent
4. **a.** does say
   b. missed
5. **a.** studied
   b. did do
   c. played
6. **a.** 's playing (is playing)
   b. 's doing (is doing)
   c. did
7. **a.** hid
   b. did hide
   c. 'm trying (am trying)
   d. want

V (Unit 20)

1. Every Monday
2. this morning
3. ago
4. last

PART VII

I (Units 23–25)

1. C	4. D
2. B	5. C
3. D	

II (Unit 23)

1. Are there; there are
2. Are there; there aren't
3. Is she; she is
4. Are they; they aren't
5. Is there; there isn't

III (Unit 25)

1. an; an
2. a, a; the, the
3. the; the
4. the
5. a
6. an

IV (Unit 25)

1. any	5. a
2. a few	6. a
3. much	7. much
4. some	8. many

V (Unit 24)

1. b   4. b
2. a   5. a
3. b

PART VIII

I (Units 26–29)

1. D   3. B
2. D   4. D

II (Units 26–29)

1. C   3. B
2. C   4. A

III (Unit 26)

1. b   5. a
2. h   6. d
3. g   7. f
4. e   8. c

IV (Unit 26)

1. Every week they go to the bank. OR They go to the bank every week.
2. She rarely wears jeans.
3. They always watch TV at night.
4. Several times a year we go to rock concerts. OR We go to rock concerts several times a year.
5. He is often late. OR Often he is late. OR He is late often.

V (Unit 26)

1. How often does Ellen call her parents?
2. How often do we get a free lunch?

VI (Units 26, 27)

1. tastes
2. a. are wearing
   b. want
3. Do, remember
4. a. Is, eating
   b. likes
5. do, spell

VII (Units 26–28)

1. are
2. says
3. love
4. living
5. meeting
6. have
7. 're/are reading
8. to go
9. to take
10. 'm/am doing
11. to take
12. want
13. go
14. don't study
15. take
16. talk
17. to introduce
18. love
19. 'm/am wearing
20. feel

VIII (Unit 29)

2. When was he born
3. When did he die
4. Where was he born
5. When did he write the Declaration of Independence
6. How long was he president OR For how many years was he president
7. What was

PART IX

I (Units 30–32)

1. C   3. A
2. D   4. B

II (Units 30–32)

1. c   3. c
2. b   4. b

III (Units 31, 32)

1. may
2. 'll
3. 'll
4. a. may
   b. won't
5. 'll
6. 'll
7. might

IV (Units 30, 31)

1. a. rained
   b. 's raining
   c. 's going to rain
2. a. 'm going to help
   b. 'm getting
3. a. Did, hear
   b. won
   c. think
   d. is, going to do
   e. 's going to visit
   f. 's going to take
4. a. did, return
   b. 'll return
   c. closes
   d. won't

V (Units 30, 31)

1. 'm going to go OR 'm going
2. 'll be back OR 're going to be back
3. may, may OR might, might
4. 'm meeting them (on), OR 'm going to meet them

VI **(Units 30–32)**

1. ~~They're~~ going to ~~tomorrow~~ start the job. *Tomorrow they're*
   OR They're going to ~~tomorrow~~ start the job. *tomorrow* ∧

2. He's going to ~~sees~~ the art exhibit this afternoon. *see*

3. How ~~you will~~ travel? *will you*

4. She won't ~~is~~ home this evening. *be*

5. I think they might ~~to~~ buy a car.

6. ~~We maybe~~ will go to the early show. *Maybe we*
   OR We ~~maybe will~~ go to the early show. *may*
   OR We ~~maybe will~~ go to the early show. *might*

PART X

I **(Units 33–35)**

1. B	3. A
2. B	4. B

II **(Unit 33)**

1. How many
2. How many
3. How much
4. How much

III **(Unit 33)**

1. a. a few	6. a. How many
b. friends	b. bottles
c. some	7. enough cooks
2. a. any	8. enough
b. ice	9. a. How many
3. a. some	b. days
b. stamps	10. too many
4. a. a little	11. too
b. time	12. too few
5. a. How much	
b. mail	

IV **(Unit 33)**

1. carton
2. bowl
3. cup
4. jar
5. pound
6. piece

V **(Unit 35)**

1. a. you	4. a. Its
b. yours	b. It
c. your	5. a. they
2. a. mine	b. them
b. me	c. their
c. my	
d. I	
3. a. we	
b. Our	
c. us	
d. Ours	

VI **(Units 33–35)**

1. We didn't buy ~~some~~ bread. *any*

2. They need a ~~little~~ more days to finish. *few*

3. We don't have ~~chairs enough~~ for everyone. *enough chairs*

4. He has too ~~many~~ homework. He can't go out. *much*

5. We can't see that movie today. It's ~~very~~ too late. OR It's ~~very~~ late. *much* / *too*

6. This isn't my jacket. Mine ~~jacket~~ is in the closet. OR ~~Mine~~ jacket is in the closet. It's probably hers. *My*

PART XI

I **(Units 36–39)**

1. C	4. B
2. A	5. A
3. A	6. C

II **(Units 36–39)**

1. to	4. to
2. to	8. to

III **(Units 38–39)**

1. don't have to
2. should
3. mustn't
4. has to
5. had better ('d better)
6. ought to
7. should
8. had better not ('d better not)
9. don't have to
10. can't

IV (Units 36–39)

1. have to
2. don't have to
3. have
4. can
5. can't
6. can't

V (Unit 37)

1. I'd be glad to.
2. No, thanks. I'm full.
3. I'm sorry. I can't right now.
4. Yes, thanks.
5. Sure.

VI (Units 36–39)

1. What should we ~~doing~~ *do* about the missing book?

2. She ought to ~~finds~~ *find* a better job.

3. May I ~~to~~ help you?

4. You mustn't ~~talked~~ *talk* about that in front of him.

5. Yesterday we ~~have~~ *had* to work late.

6. Would ~~please~~ you *please*^ help me?

7. When do we have *to*^ be there?

PART XII

I (Units 40–43)

1. A
2. B
3. C
4. B
5. B
6. A
7. B
8. C
9. A
10. C
11. B

II (Units 41–42)

1. carefully
2. slowly
3. beautiful
4. beautifully
5. well
6. very
7. too
8. good

III (Units 40, 42)

1. than
2. as
3. from
4. as
5. than
6. as

IV (Units 40, 43)

1. the worst
2. worse than
3. the fastest
4. the most interesting
5. funnier than
6. the funniest
7. the best
8. the most industrious
9. older than

V (Units 40–43)

1. He is one of the best ~~student~~ *students* in the school.

2. Who's the ~~most~~ tallest one in their family?

3. The next level is a lot ~~more~~ harder than this one.

4. We're busier in December ~~as~~ *than* we are in January.

5. The workbook isn't as expensive *as*^ the CD.

6. He works ~~hardly~~ *hard*.

7. Taxes are ~~highest~~ *higher* than last year.

8. It tastes ~~deliciously~~ *delicious*.

INDEX

This Index is for the full and split editions. All entries are in the full book. Entries for Volume A of the split edition are in black. Entries for Volume B are in color.